THE SECULAR MIND

THE SECULAR MIND

Transformations of Faith in Modern Europe

Essays presented to Franklin L. Baumer,
Randolph W. Townsend Professor of History,
Yale University

EDITED BY W. WARREN WAGAR

HOLMES & MEIER
Publishers, Inc.
New York   •   London

First published in the United States of America 1982 by
Holmes & Meier Publishers, Inc.
30 Irving Place
New York, N.Y. 10003

Great Britain:
Holmes & Meier Publishers, Ltd.
131 Trafalgar Road
Greenwich, London SE10 9TX

Copyright © 1982 by Holmes & Meier Publishers, Inc.

Book design by Rose Jacobowitz

Library of Congress Cataloging in Publication Data
Main entry under title:

The Secular mind.

Includes index.
Contents: Introduction / W. Warren Wagar—Isaac Newton's *Theologiae gentilis origines philosophicae* / Richard S. Westfall—Secularization in British thought, 1730–1789 / David Spadafora—[etc.]
1. Secularism—Addresses, essays, lectures.
I. Wagar, W. Warren.
BL2747.8.S33   211'.6   81-20019
ISBN 0-8419-0766-8   AACR2

Manufactured in the United States of America

TO

FRANKLIN LE VAN BAUMER

RANDOLPH W. TOWNSEND
PROFESSOR OF HISTORY,
YALE UNIVERSITY

FROM
HIS FORMER GRADUATE STUDENTS
WITH RESPECT, GRATITUDE,
AND LOVE

Contents

Acknowledgments

I wish to thank my colleagues for their loyal cooperation in making this book possible: the former students of Franklin L. Baumer of Yale University. We offer it as our tribute to his lifetime of inspired teaching and scholarship.

Some of Mr. Baumer's protégés were unable, for a variety of reasons, to contribute chapters, but did lend their support and assistance at strategic points. We are especially grateful to Dean Martin Griffin of Yale College, Professor Isabel F. Knight of Pennsylvania State University, and Professor Peter Vinten-Johansen of Michigan State University. Warm thanks are also owed to Mr. Douglas O. McClure, Headmaster of the Princeton Day School; Mr. Norman P. Ross of Dallas, Texas; Dr. William J. Tate III of Princeton, New Jersey, all former students of Mr. Baumer; and to Mr. John R. Hubbard, President Emeritus of the University of Southern California.

I would like to add my deep appreciation, and that of my colleagues, to Jaroslav Pelikan, Sterling Professor of History at Yale University, who honored us by writing the foreword for this volume.

Material from *The Complete Poems and Plays 1909–1950* of T. S. Eliot, copyright 1962 by Harcourt Brace Jovanovich, Inc., is reprinted in chapter X with the permission of the publisher. Further acknowledgment is made to the Regents Press of Kansas, which granted Douglas K. Wood permission to reprint portions of his forthcoming Regents Press book, *Men Against Time*, in the same chapter, and to the National Endowment for the Humanities, which awarded the Senior Fellowship that enabled me to complete much of the research for chapter XII.

W. Warren Wagar
August 1981

Foreword

JAROSLAV PELIKAN

When I think of my friend and colleague Franklin Baumer, the word that comes to my mind is *gravitas*, as used (and exhibited) by Cicero and Saint Augustine: intellectual clarity, moral earnestness, and unimpeachable integrity. In him, though not alas in some others who manifest it, gravitas is rescued from becoming ponderous by a lively wit and an unfailing kindness. During almost twenty years of association with him, both in the Yale History Department and at Pierson College, I have had manifold opportunities to watch this strong and complicated man in action. He comes at issues, whether academic or social, with balance and objectivity, and does not allow friendship or prejudice to overwhelm his judgment. As a colleague and a university citizen, Frank Baumer can be counted on to consider a matter thoughtfully and to weigh the alternatives before he forms an opinion. He can also be relied upon for counsel that is wise and straightforward. In short, to use the current phrase, Frank does not have a hidden agenda.

But in this volume, and in this foreword, it is chiefly Franklin Baumer the scholar whom we are recognizing. And that is eminently appropriate, for it is his lifelong research and writing that have put all of us in his debt—the authors of these chapters in a unique sense, as those whom his example and direction have shaped into scholars, but the rest of us also, as colleagues whose understanding of the history of modern thought would have been quite different if it had not been for his work. As his students could testify with anecdotes and quotations and as his fellow historians have come to know, he has always been able to distinguish between personal regard and scholarly assessment, and has therefore been able to be tough in his criticism of other people's research without impairing his deeper ties with them, principally, of course, because he has been much tougher on himself. This book is in the first instance a fond tribute to him by his students; but the chapters are a tribute in an even more profound manner, for they apply to their various themes the historical methods and the intellectual standards for which he himself has striven. Each of the topics is one on which he might have written (or, for that matter, on which he has written). Yet each of the authors combines gratitude to Baumer as mentor with independence from

Baumer as oracle. And that is especially fitting because it has been the decline in the authority of traditional oracles that has engaged him in his studies.

That decline is part of the phenomenon of secularization, with which, in one way or another, so much of his historical investigation has dealt. After more than forty years, the insights of his *Early Tudor Theory of Kingship* into the process by which the prerogatives and even the titles of sacral power were transferred to the head of state remain incisive for the interpretation of the Reformation, not only in England but on the Continent and even in those lands that remained with the old faith. Already in that monograph he called attention to the ambiguity at work in secularization. For while its outcome has indeed been the undermining of church structure—first the monasteries, then the episcopate, then the sacraments and saints, then revelation itself—its deepest roots are in considerable measure to be sought within the tradition of biblical faith itself. The prophets of Israel, the reformers of the church in all ages, and (lest we forget) the Jesus of the Gospels were all unsparing in their denunciations of priestly claims. It is also part of the tradition of biblical faith to affirm the goodness of the temporal and of the natural order, even though the defenders of biblical faith may not always have recognized this. Therefore what has been called "the sacredness of the secular" is in part a legitimate child of the very heritage against whose established forms the apostles of secularity have protested. But that suggests, in turn, that such apostles of secularity may in fact have been more dependent than they or their ecclesiastical adversaries recognized and admitted upon the intellectual and spiritual resources they all had in common.

To document this ambiguity, it has been necessary to study the way secularization has worked itself out in various fields of modern Western thought. Baumer's *Religion and the Rise of Scepticism* is a treasure of primary historical analysis, tracing the paths, psychological as well as intellectual, by which modern thinkers have traveled in their reconsiderations and eventual rejections of the absolute claims of Christianity. Many of these paths are part of the history of science, and both in the monograph on scepticism and in his histories of modern thought Franklin Baumer has evidenced a powerful grasp of the intricate connections between the development of science and the realm of belief. He helps us to relive the inner struggles and public controversies attendant on the surrender of supernatural and authoritarian faith, as, one by one, the props on which that faith had rested were swept away. Miracles once were represented as a proof for religious doctrine, but eventually miracles became dependent on religious doctrine for whatever plausibility they retained. So it has been with the argument from design, with the notion of divine providence, and with theodicy. Into the vacuum have moved systems of thought and belief that rested on their own props, not all of them as rational as their spokesmen supposed. Thus, in an inversion of Emerson's familiar dictum, when the gods go, the half-gods arrive.

The moral implications of this development are complex and troubling. Several of the chapters in this book have, in one way or another, raised again Ivan Karamazov's question: If God does not exist, is everything permitted? Although the simplistic answers to this question characteristic of many latter-day apologists on both sides are probably not deserving of serious attention, the force of the question itself is unavoidable. And that, in turn, brings us back to the matter of gravitas. For gravitas is the conviction that life is not a game: the intellectual conclusions of one generation may become the moral presuppositions of the next, and it behooves us to consider the potential consequences of what we say and think and do. Because Franklin Baumer knows, with a historical vision that has not been granted to many of us, how dangerous it has been for the well-meaning to put obstacles in the way of critical and disturbing ideas, he has given us his narrative of the evolution of modern ideas with a deep sense of commitment to free and untrammeled research, regardless of the conventional wisdom. But he has combined with this a deep sense of pathos, for it is not obvious that the gains have always outweighed the losses. Here the man, the scholar, and the teacher are one: Franklin Baumer embodies within himself the historical struggles that he has described, and he has taught us all to understand them (and hence ourselves) with greater honesty and depth. In thanking him for this precious gift, the authors of this book have spoken on behalf of us all.

Introduction

W. WARREN WAGAR

Sacred and Profane: The Logic of Secularization

In *Religion and the Rise of Scepticism*, Franklin L. Baumer takes as his point of departure Goethe's dictum that "the deepest, the only theme of human history . . . is the conflict of scepticism with faith."[1] Baumer draws back from unqualified endorsement of so radical a view. But his sympathies with it are obvious. The transition from a sacred to a profane society and world outlook, if indeed such a transition has occurred, is (or would be) an event of incalculable seriousness for the future of humankind and the meaning of all past experience. The evidence for such seriousness is in part sociological, stemming from modern knowledge of the functions of religion in culture, and in part personal. To have lived through the modern conflict between faith and scepticism—by empathetic reenactment in the Diltheyan mode of historiography practiced faithfully by Baumer—is to have some power of gauging the significance of that conflict on one's own authority.

All this assumes, of course, that the axial themes of religious and antireligious thought relate somehow to fundamental human needs. In Baumer's kind of intellectual history, they do. Ideas matter. Beliefs matter. Ideas and beliefs bore down to the center of life, distinguishing human behavior from animal, and making civilization possible.

Yet ideas and beliefs are not everything, nor can hard and fast lines be drawn between events within and outside consciousness. In the same book that proclaims the huge significance of the war of ideas between faith and scepticism, Baumer writes of the "Great Secularization," a process "of which scepticism was but one facet," which has sought to remove Christianity, thread by thread, from the whole fabric of European life and thought. "The history of the Great Secularization is still to be written," he adds, "and in any case is too vast a subject to treat here in detail."[2] But the struggle of faith with scepticism can be understood only in the larger historical context that it supplies.

In effect most of Baumer's scholarly work, and much of the work of his students, reduces to an investigation of the interplay of the religious heritage of

1

Western man and the emergence of "modern" or "secular" civilization. The present volume, consisting of original essays by several of those students, offers glimpses into the tension between the sacred and the profane at various selected moments in modern history. Sometimes, we are discussing "secularization." Then again, the subject at hand is perhaps better described as "desecularization." Or both together. As in Baumer's *Religion and the Rise of Scepticism*, the relation between faith and its secular antitheses and alternatives is more often dialectical than straightforwardly oppositional. Like Owen Chadwick, "We keep running, suddenly and in unexpected by-ways, into the idea that secularization is a religious process."[3]

Some of the confusion inheres in the word itself. To secularize is to make secular, to bring into the *saeculum,* or "world." By convention this means to repugn or ignore religious considerations and substitute for them the values of "this" world. It can also, and just as logically, signify the bringing of religion itself into the world. In Peter Berger's analysis, such was the genius (or curse) of the Reformation.[4] The Reformers in their zeal to revive the Gospel sacrificed otherworldliness for a holy secularity that sought to translate Christian faith into earthly action: typically, the establishment of God's kingdom here and now within time. But immanentization of the Christian message is a two-edged sword. On the one hand, it can transform the world by the heat of faith into a godly place. On the other, it can transform faith by the power of worldliness into a tool of human greed.

In the real universe of history, needless to say, matters are muddier. Secularization occurs in various ways, affecting different nations and classes differently, now opposing and now absorbing elements of religious tradition, and all without benefit of consensus among scholars. Scarcely anyone would contest Basil Willey's discovery of a "secular drift" in modern history.[5] But this is not to say much. What secularization consists of, when it began, when it "triumphed," if it has, and why or why not: each of these questions remains open.

The problem of definition is especially critical.[6] Chadwick notes, in *The Secularization of the European Mind in the Nineteenth Century*, that secularization "is supposed to mean . . . a growing tendency in mankind to do without religion." He fails to associate himself fully with even this much of a definition, and then dismisses the further problem of how to define "religion" as being essentially ahistorical.[7] The difficulty of defining anything, as Nietzsche long ago lamented, is that nothing ever stands still. But words do stand still on the printed page, for the duration of the paper. They also have one or more public meanings at any given time, at least one of which is intended by the person who wrote them. A working definition of "religion" is clearly essential to a working definition of what is "secular," or of what "secularization" consists. Does Chadwick mean doing without religion in an institutional sense or in the sense of belief-structures? Does he mean doing without Christianity, and, if so, who has the privilege of deciding what Christianity is, or at what point it is fatally compromised by the admission of contaminating influences from the *saeculum?* What about the so-called secular religions, such as humanism, or the positivism of Comte, or nationalism? After refusing to commit himself, Chadwick goes ahead and defines his subject matter in terms of certain questions that, taken together, almost constitute a definition.[8] But the whole procedure is cumbersome and pointlessly evasive.

It also dodges the issue of the secularization of religion itself. How can religion do without religion? Chadwick's procedure thereby misses a matter of special interest, the residue of religious faith and practice in the faiths and practices of a secularized world.

Arnold E. Loen illustrates the pitfalls of definition in a quite different way. Writing from a conservative Christian point of view, he offers two definitions of secularization, a "superficial" one and a "Christian" one, designed between them to confound his enemies and, in particular, to give the lie to the secular theology of Dietrich Bonhoeffer and others. The first definition, rejected because of the secularist bias of its presuppositions, follows Nietzsche in treating secularization as "the historical process by which the world is de-divinized (as far as the human consciousness is concerned)." The correct (that is, Christian) definition asserts that "secularization is being conformed to this world, the world which rebels against the fact that 'from him and through him and in him are all things'."[9] Not many scholars outside the world of Christian theology, and conservative theology at that, will want to adopt Loen's second definition, or perhaps even his first. But both have the merit of not avoiding the issue of what the secularization process sets aside. Unfortunately, they do avoid the issue of what it émbraces.

There are other definitions. Martin E. Marty prefers to speak of the "Modern Schism," a time between 1830 and 1870 when the Western nations went over the hump of transition to a secular way of life and belief that demanded not "the disappearance of religion so much as its relocation."[10] Marty refers to the displacement of traditional Christian or Jewish faith by systems of belief grounded in the values of this world—for example, nationalism. His choice of the term "schism" is deliberate, suggesting that what has occurred is yet another wave of rebellion from within, rupturing the unity of Christendom, not unlike the Reformation or the medieval quarrel between Rome and Constantinople.

Pleading the case for a secular theology, Harvey Cox takes the argument a step further. Secularization, he writes, is the passage to a society characterized by the anonymity and mobility of urban living, by pluralism, tolerance, pragmatism, and profanity—the last defined as the disappearance from consciousness of any supramundane reality, the viewing of the world in its own terms, rather than in those of some other. But the rebellion of secularism is ultimately, for Cox, a good thing, and absolutely compatible with the essence of Christian faith. In fact, a secular society is truer to Christianity—properly understood—than the social orders of the past.[11] For all practical purposes, his apologia for the "secular city" rehashes Max Weber's definition of secularization as *Entzauberung*, the disappearance of "magic" or the belief in the power and presence of the supernatural from a progressively more rational and rationalized world. The critical difference is that Cox's version of *Entzauberung* is value-laden, whereas the Weberian original was value-free.

We need not concern ourselves with the issue of what constitutes "true" Christianity, but if there is any merit at all in Cox's definition of secularization, it makes Chadwick's all the more questionable. So, too, does Bonhoeffer's program for a "religionless Christianity" in a world that has "come of age," and the program of yet another German theologian, Rudolf Bultmann, for the *Entmythologisierung* or "demythologizing" of the Christian gospel. What Cox, Bonhoeffer, and Bultmann are all saying, each in his own way, is that secularization means the atrophy of belief in a magical or supernatural realm of being, and of institutions and practices grounded in such belief, but not necessarily the atrophy of religious faith in some reconceived but still authentic form. Without Christian advocacy, twentieth-century sociologists and anthropologists of religion have said much the same thing. Man can live without this or that particular variety of religious belief and practice, they contend, but not without religion of any kind. In this case, secularization would mean not doing without religion but rather transforming religion, transferring the center of ultimate concern (to use Paul Tillich's phrase) from the mythical world of supernature to the "real" world of empirically observable nature, history, and man. In such a real world, it goes without saying, there might still be worship, redemption, holiness, faith, consecration, forgiveness, even divinity.

Curiously, a number of students of secularization who have no theological axes to grind cannot accept such a thesis. Baumer himself has trouble with it, preferring a hard-nosed definition of religion as metaphysical awareness, by which he means a concern for that which lies beyond the "visible natural order." Calvin and Goethe were both religious men, by this criterion; but Marx and Sir Leslie Stephen were not. Similarly, what Baumer calls the "humanistic faith" of the Enlightenment and its heirs, the "ersatz-religions" of the nineteenth century such as nationalism and scientism, were mere substitutes, which failed for good reason to perform the creative tasks once performed by religion.[12]

Baumer's hard-nosedness appears as well in the sociologist David Martin's *A General Theory of Secularization*. "By 'religious,'" writes Martin, "I mean an acceptance of a level of reality beyond the observable world known to science, to which are ascribed meanings and purposes completing and transcending those of the purely human realm." Secularization is nothing less than the decline of religious beliefs and institutions, given this definition of "religious."[13] A philosopher, Vernon Pratt, comes to the same conclusion. In his *Religion and Secularization,* Pratt agrees with T. S. Eliot and the mainstream of Christian thought that the hallmark of the Christian mind is its supernaturalism. Secularization is the process by which the supernatural has been lost, an irrecoverable loss despite all the sophistries of so-called secular theologians, but one that man can learn to accept and even turn to his advantage, as Camus does in his postreligious masterpiece *The Myth of Sisyphus.*[14] Baumer would hardly join Pratt in his celebration of man's self-sufficiency, but both scholars, and Martin, share a conviction that secularization involves fundamental change and traumatic loss. Modern civilization is not simply a new edition of its Christian predecessor, but something profoundly different. All this brings to mind the battles—as it happens, the not irrelevant battles—between those who see the rationalism of the Enlightenment or the idea of progress as essentially "modern" and those who see them as reworkings of medieval beliefs, rooted in the Christian world view.[15]

Because *The Secular Mind* presents the research of several scholars, whose points of view on secularization differ, it is hardly possible to suggest a resolution of the issues addressed above that all of us could accept, or that would work for each of the chapters of this book. Our subtitle, *Transformations of Faith in Modern Europe,* may seem to hint at a less radical idea of secularization than is held by our mentor. But the subtitle was chosen chiefly to underscore the point made earlier, that the interaction in modern Western history between religion (however defined) and secularity (however defined) cannot be reduced to a struggle between sharply opposed and clearly distinguishable forces. The degree of interpenetration is astonishing, and in the process both "sides" have undergone astonishing transformations. Religious faith has both influenced, and been influenced by, the growth of secular belief-systems and institutions. One is tempted to take refuge in Hermann Lübbe's elastic definition of secularization as "the historical relationship in which modern civilization stands to its indelibly Christian past."[16] Too elastic, perhaps; but it brings us closer to the truth than the melodrama of a war to the death between implacable foes.

The Rational City: Sources of Secularization

Another way to get a purchase on the meaning of secularization is to ask how and why it has taken place in the experience of modern Western man, and with what variations from one national society and from one class to another. In some readings of history, secularization occurred as long ago as the sixteenth century, and throughout Western civilization, as the result of deep structural

changes in society, economics, and government. In other readings, secularization was an inevitable by-product of the Scientific Revolution and the Enlightenment. In still others, it did not happen until the middle or last decades of the
nineteenth century, and even so early as that only in a few advanced industrial
countries.

Much of the debate centers on whether the prime impetus for secularization
was furnished by transforming events in the society at large, or in the world of
ideas.[17] Since man is a thinking reed, both "thinking" and "reed" at the same
time, this is always a difficult, and not necessarily a fruitful, question. But the
social and intellectual origins of the secularization process can be distinguished
for purposes of discussion, even if, in history as it actually happened, *wie es
eigentlich gewesen*, they may appear hopelessly tangled.

Studies of the socioeconomic contexts of secularization suggest another
sort of entanglement. Pursued far enough, secularization is simply one face of
modernization. The movement away from traditional faith and ecclesiastical
power is intertwined at every stage with all the other "modernizing" tendencies
in Western history, and has become, like all of them, a subject for interminable
squabbles among scholars. Speaking just for myself, I see modernization (for all
its long time a-coming) as something that did not actually take place until the
nineteenth century. That is to say, not until the nineteenth century did the
majority of the peoples of the Western world begin to live "modern" lives.
Before then, most of them were countryfolk tied to a traditional rural economy,
the ruling class consisted chiefly of landowners, most of the non-Western world
had not yet been Westernized, and nearly everyone in Christendom was a
practicing and believing Christian, in a society where churches (usually state
churches) had at their disposal immense economic, political, and educational
power.

By contrast, in a modern society most people live in towns and cities. The
economy is predominantly industrial and commercial, the system of "social
relations of production" is capitalism or state capitalism, the ruling classes are
the masters of capital and their allies throughout the society, the national state
with its quasi-democratic institutions of government has replaced the feudal-
monarchical polities of the past, and the non-Western peoples have been fully
incorporated into the Western world economy and state system. The majority of
citizens are not practicing or believing Christians. The links between church
and state have been mostly or entirely severed, as churches experience steady
decline in all the categories of their traditional power. Modernization is a
thoroughly organic process by which the way of life of traditional Europe has
evolved into a radically new way of life that serves as a model for all mankind,
and still has some distance to travel before it can be described as "complete."
Such phenomena as urbanization, industrialization, capitalism, and the emer-

gence of a secular society and a secular mind are not intelligible except in terms of one another.

The best strategy for demonstrating the organicity of the modernizing process is to apply to the evidence an overarching theory of historical change such as Marxism. Even without the aid of theory, the evidence for interconnectedness is all but irresistible. As people move to the cities, live in national-democratic states, participate in the industrial-commercial economy of capitalism, and help plant the modern Western way of life in other parts of the world, there is a corresponding diminution of Christian practice and belief that could hardly be coincidental, above all since the unaffiliated and the unbelieving tend to belong to the most advanced segments of the population of each country. By all accounts, the city-dwelling bourgeois or worker is everywhere the most secularized citizen of a modern state; and the least secularized are the people who remain tied to the land, especially small farmers and peasants in areas least affected by modernizing forces in agriculture itself.

Only one major country, the United States, appears not to conform to the pattern established in modern Europe. Urban Americans are more secularized than their country cousins, but the sharp decline in practice and belief for the population as a whole that is so striking in Europe has not occurred in North America. Churches have lost far less political and economic ground; attendance and profession of belief have remained relatively high. Nevertheless, as several students of secularization contend, the American experience is unique only in the way that secularization has occurred, and not in the thing itself. By and large, religion in America has survived the challenge of secularization by joining, rather than opposing, secular trends. "In the United States," David Martin observes, "religion is the matrix and dominant frame of political utopia and it provides the mirrors in which each emerging group envisages its new social self." The ecclesiastical pluralism built into American life since colonial times has made available an almost infinite number of "masks for the newly emerging social faces to wear."[18] Thus, blacks can use religion as a way of promoting black awareness, and whites can use it as a defense of racism. Imperialism, entrepreneurial capitalism, ethnic identity among immigrant populations, and many other causes are readily served by churches with little consciousness of the lethal distortions and contradictions involved.[19]

Comparative European and Near Eastern evidence comes to the aid of this view of American religiosity. It is no accident that where practice and belief have remained most ardent throughout whole populations in modern Europe, the usual reason is the harnessing of religion to serve the secular purposes of an oppressed minority or an endangered nation in its struggles with oppressors and enemies. Examples are Catholicism in Ireland and Poland, Orthodoxy in Cyprus and the Ukraine, and Judaism in Israel. A Pole whose Roman Catholic faith is strong because his native country is sandwiched between two powerful non-Catholic nations may retain his faith when he becomes a Polish-American because his church has been successful in preserving Polish cultural identity from assimilation into the Anglo-Saxon mainstream and in helping Polish-Americans win political power and economic security.

In any event, the turning of the balance from premodern to modern occurred for the Western world as a whole during the nineteenth century. Although some of the authors of this volume might disagree with me, I share Martin Marty's reckoning that the critical decades were 1830 to 1870, for Americans as well as for Europeans. But I do not see, nor does Marty, that the argument for the lateness of modernization gives anyone license to ignore earlier centuries. Each of the processes referred to above, which together constitute the modernizing of Western civilization, can be followed back at least to the sixteenth century, and often to the eleventh and twelfth centuries. Capitalism did not spring out of nowhere in 1870 or 1830 or even 1760, but was already flourishing handsomely in many parts of Europe during the Renaissance. The revival of the cities began in early medieval times. The Reformation was important in dividing Christendom against itself and thereby playing into the hands of secular princes and landowners. The feudal-monarchical state, as it grew more monarchical and less feudal, adopted modernizing policies that challenged and diminished the power of ecclesiastical establishments. By the late eighteenth century, secularism had become a leading force in the revolutionary movements of workers, peasants, and especially bourgeois against church-supported *anciens régimes* on the European mainland. Without these earlier developments, integral to the socioeconomic and political history of the West, the transition to modernity that occurred in the nineteenth century would clearly have been impossible, and Western civilization would still be Christian.

All that has been said about the social sources of secularization applies, more or less, to the intellectual sources. The view, popular among nineteenth-century champions of secularism in the history of ideas, that secularization was simply a process of the liberation of reason from the chains of medieval ignorance and superstition, does not stand up to serious scrutiny. Nevertheless, what Cox dubs the secular city is also a rational city. Ideas had a part to play in its construction. As with the great transformations in socioeconomic life, the crossover to modernity did not occur (in my view) until the middle of the nineteenth century. By the same token, the beginnings of the secularization of consciousness can be followed back to the Renaissance, and even before. Heretical philosophies endorsing classical authority at the expense of Christian teaching were already a familiar part of the landscape of European thought in the thirteenth century. Theological controversy, wars of religion, and voyages of discovery engendered profound scepticism in the sixteenth century, and a studied indifference to Christian politics and ethics in favor of secular values was cultivated by many thinkers from Machiavelli onward. We have also taken note of Berger's argument that the Protestant rebellion helped to discredit, for millions of Europeans, the greater part of traditional Christian otherworldliness, and helped to encourage vigorous involvement in secular vocations.

Most important of all, as Vernon Pratt and others have stressed, the progress of the natural sciences in the seventeenth and eighteenth centuries gave rise to a self-sufficiently secular world view equipped with mind-sets and methods of cognition that promised to solve all problems without resort to supernaturalism.[20] Such a world view would not have triumphed except in a rapidly modernizing social order, but some of its origins must be looked for in the internal history of philosophy and science. By the middle decades of the eighteenth century in the most advanced Western countries, and in particular France, there were men and women alive who had passed completely beyond the boundaries of Christian faith. Their beliefs—moral, metaphysical, political, and otherwise—were explicitly post-Christian. Their religion, if they had one, was a religion of this-worldly values and perspectives only. They did not constitute a majority of the intelligentsia, much less a majority of the population of Europe or America, but they were harbingers.

The avalanche of unbelief that followed in the nineteenth century need not be recapitulated here. The outlines are familiar.[21] Almost all the great movements of nineteenth-century thought were secularizing movements in one way or another: liberalism, positivism, Marxism, Darwinism, historicism and relativism in the emergent social sciences, the nineteenth-century cult of progress, modernism in Catholic France, social Christianity in Protestant Germany. The twentieth century has contributed Freud, Lenin, Russell, Sartre, Camus. Most of the best minds in Christendom have learned to manage quite well without the Christian faith.

Of course de-Christianization is far from absolute, nor is it necessarily the same thing as doing without religion. Christianity continues to permeate Western high culture, through direct evangelism, through the secular uses of biblical myths and symbols, through the persistence of traditional moral values, and much more. Some of us reach out to non-Western religions, or adapt secular ideologies (or philosophies or even vocations) to the service of religious needs. Others, in what Baumer calls our "Age of Longing," follow Kafka and Beckett in taking metaphysical questions seriously.[22] The absence of God in a Kafka novel or a Beckett play is an absence so conspicuous and overwhelming, indeed so God-shaped, that it can do more to awaken religious consciousness than whole libraries of theology.

Nevertheless, most of us are fully aware of where we live, on the far side of the great divide that separates ancestral faith from modern speculation, improvisation, doubt, and raw unbelief. Easily or uneasily, with or without benefit of substitutes for the old gods, we are citizens of the secular city. No yearning for past simplicities, which are mostly imaginary in any case, can call more than a few of us back to the sacred village of our fathers and mothers. We can be bombed out of our city, and perhaps we shall be. We can learn to build a better one, and perhaps we shall learn. But the city is our home.

Case Studies

The chapters that follow offer a series of case studies illuminating the process of secularization in modern European thought from the 1680s to the 1970s. The starting point in these explorations of the secular mind is Isaac Newton, the thinker most responsible for providing the West with a world view capable of supplanting its Jewish-Christian and Platonic-Aristotelian heritage. Newton was a philosopher, a scientist, a mathematician—and something of a theologian. In the same decade that saw the publication of his *Principia mathematica*, he composed a major treatise on theology which he kept to himself. The treatise, *Theologiae gentilis origines philosophicae* (The Philosophical Origins of Gentile Theology), remained unread and unknown until a few years ago. The first chapter, by Richard S. Westfall, traces the history of that manuscript and examines its contents, as well as other theological writings by Newton, for evidence of secular influences on religious belief.

Like so many scientists of his age, Newton was a devout Christian. But the burgeoning rationalism of the seventeenth century, to which he contributed so much himself, deflected him from orthodoxy. Westfall shows that several years before the unfolding of the deist movement of the 1690s, Newton had arrived independently and privately at a position much like deism. John Toland and his fellow deists did not have access to the *Theologiae gentilis*, of course, but they belonged to the same thought-world as the illustrious scientist. For many of the same reasons as he, they set forth views destructive of Christian claims to uniqueness, views that also foreshadowed and helped to make possible the humanistic belief-systems of later generations.

Not that Newton himself was a humanist. Chapters II and III carry us from the unsettling implications of seventeenth-century science and scientific method to the beginnings of unbelief itself. David Spadafora follows the course of secularization in representative British thinkers of the "high" eighteenth century, the period from 1730 to 1789. He finds a slow but inexorable decline in the central position of theology, the emergence of a secular history of religion, the spread of environmentalist theories of human nature, and growing reluctance to believe in the reality or necessity of miracles. Perhaps because of the more rapid pace of economic change north of the Tweed River during the eighteenth century, secularization occurred even faster in Scotland than in England.

John Frederick Logan's chapter on the *philosophe* Gabriel Bonnot de Mably shows yet another face of secularization. Better known as an early protagonist of socialism, Mably also gave attention in his abundant writings to the social uses of religion. Despite a radical secularity of mind typical of the French Enlightenment, he saw the utility of institutional religion for the maintenance of public order and the promotion of public welfare. His formula for a state church anticipates not only the actual function of religion in most of Europe and America in the nineteenth century, and the caustic analysis of that function by Karl Marx, but also—in a curious way—the totalitarian secular ideologies of the twentieth century.

The advent of the romantic consciousness brought with it a powerful criticism of the coldness of the philosophes to religious experience. Currents of evangelistic revival stirred Christians everywhere in the early nineteenth century, and idealist systems incorporating Christian inspirations contested the hegemony of empiricism and materialism in Western philosophy. But the pace of secularization was not slowed significantly. The revivals soon lost momentum and the idealist systems, by radically immanentizing the Christian message, betrayed its kerygmatic essence.

In this context, the fate of the religious philosophy of the poet Samuel Taylor Coleridge, discussed by John T. Miller, Jr., in chapter IV, is altogether typical. Coleridge's faith, like that of Newton, was anything but lukewarm. Yet his insistence on the primacy of subjective religious experience, and his abandonment of a theology of evidences, undermined his own program for Christian reunification, and gave unintended aid and comfort to the secularizing process. The same irony pervades the history of the Victorian ethics of belief, analyzed in *The Secular Mind* by Frank M. Turner and Jeffrey von Arx in chapter V. Theological controversy fueled by evangelical passions, together with liberal fears of an alliance between a resurgent clericalism and the new democracy of mid-century Britain, aided secularization both directly and indirectly. The fragmentation of the Christian community from within was spurred, and its secular enemies were armed with new weapons.

We turn next to examples of overtly secular thought in the second half of the nineteenth century and the first half of the twentieth. In chapter VI Phyllis H. Stock explores the attempt of the great anarchist philosopher Pierre-Joseph Proudhon to lay the foundations of a morality independent of religious sanction. Proudhon's writings inspired important movements in French Freemasonry and French socialism in the 1860s, which, as Stock shows, had a quasi-religious flavor, suggestive of Auguste Comte's scheme for a religion of humanity crowned by a positive science of morality. The secularism of the Third Republic owed much to Proudhonian influence; as filtered through the minds of Charles Renouvier and Emile Durkheim, Proudhonian ethics informed the programs of the Radical politicians who carried through the disestablishment of the French Church in the 1900s.

In chapter VII David Pace considers the interpretative problems posed by the twentieth century's most formidable opponent of religious belief, Sigmund Freud. Although Freud represented his views as the findings of science, Pace argues that his assault on religion was more a strategy for defending his school of psychoanalysis against its Jungian and Christian rivals, as well as a veiled counterattack on the virulent anti-Semitism of Catholic Europe. Pace analyzes the rhetoric of *The Future of an Illusion,* showing how it manipulated the stock ideas of nineteenth-century secularism to serve Freud's professional, ethnic, and class interests.

Two further essays explore secularism in early twentieth-century English thought. Joyce A. Berkman studies in chapter VIII the new secularist pacifism that arose in England during the interwar years, a pacifism rooted not in traditional Christian values, but in a variety of humanistic and mystical belief-systems, from the stridently anti-Christian philosophy of Bertrand Russell to the ever-changing mélange of ideas associated with the pacifism of John Middleton Murry. In chapter IX on George Orwell, James Connors looks at the novelist's life-long campaign against Christianity, and at his project for a secular faith centered on the very English concept of "decency." Orwell's personal credo, and for that matter secular pacifism, Freudian psychoanalysis, and the *morale indépendante* of Proudhon are all, quite clearly, surrogates for the Western religious heritage, would-be agents of social redemption and the rebuilding of the human community on this-worldly foundations. They retain much of the form and feeling, if not the ideational content, of traditional religion.

Chapter X, by Douglas K. Wood, takes note of a major twentieth-century reaction against secularization, and, perhaps more importantly, against the dominant values of modern Western culture. His theme is the "revolt against time" in the thought of such diverse minds as the Russian Orthodox philosopher Nicolas Berdyaev, the British poet T. S. Eliot, the British novelist Aldous Huxley, and the Swiss psychologist Carl Gustav Jung. All four, and many others as well, share a zeal for scouring premodern cultures in search of world views that devalue temporality in favor of a fundamentally mystical approach to life. All four were converts, men who started out as exponents of secularism in one form or another, but who became sickened by the obsession of modern civilization with time, history, and progress. Their leap to traditional religious faith, or a medley of faiths, testifies to the acute anxiety and spiritual homesickness of modern Western man, but also to the triumph of secularization. In the eyes of Wood's rebels against time, the modern Western culture that they repudiate is inevitably and disastrously a secular culture, absorbed in this-worldly destinies, and thereby doomed to self-destruction.

Not every "rebel against time" finds himself ready to make the leap to faith. Indeed, the representative critics of modernity in the Europe of the first post-1945 generation are thinkers in whom the will to believe has been deliberately suspended. They may agree with their earlier comrades-in-rebellion, such as Berdyaev and Eliot, on the subject of the shortcomings of time-obsessed secular civilization, but they want no part of a ready-made formula for private or mass salvation. In chapter XI Michael W. Messmer examines the phenomenon of the suspension of belief in the career of the Rumanian expatriate philosopher E. M. Cioran. Like Samuel Beckett, the man of letters whose consciousness most closely resembles his own, Cioran has made France his adopted home and French his adopted tongue. Messmer delineates Cioran as a master rhetorician who rigorously avoids all commitments but one: a passionate affirmation of the power of language.

In the last chapter I survey the secular uses of Jewish and Christian eschatology in imaginative literature. From romantic novelists like Mary Shelley to the present day, the theme of the end of the world has cropped up many times in such literature, both to meet the psychological needs of writers and readers, and to give expression to a sense of the decadence of modern civilization. Sometimes the terminal vision is literally terminal, leaving no hope of better things, but more often, following in the tradition of biblical prophecies of last things, the end is also the beginning. The survivors of the old order become the first citizens of the new, and the world is redeemed. Secular visions of the world's end furnish a good example of how the premodern mythological consciousness is transformed, but not annihilated, by secularization.

These studies are dedicated, with love and respect, to Franklin L. Baumer. In many ways they are his work. In all ways they are tributes to the genius of his teaching, the stimulus of his scholarly contributions to intellectual history, and the depth of his concern—in the words of Karl Jaspers—for *die geistige Situation der Zeit*.

Notes

1. Goethe, *Wisdom and Experience*, cited in Franklin L. Baumer, *Religion and the Rise of Scepticism* (New York: Harcourt, Brace, 1960), p. 3.

2. Baumer, *Religion and Scepticism*, p. 112.

3. Owen Chadwick, *The Secularization of the European Mind in the Nineteenth Century* (Cambridge: Cambridge Univ. Press, 1975), p. 156.

4. See Peter Berger, *The Sacred Canopy: Elements of a Sociological Theory of Religion* (Garden City, N.Y.: Doubleday, 1967).

5. Basil Willey, *Christianity Past and Present* (Cambridge: Cambridge Univ. Press, 1952), p. 7.

6. A good introduction to the history of the concept, especially for German thought, is Hermann Lübbe, *Säkularisierung: Geschichte eines ideenpolitischen Begriffs* (Freiburg/München: Karl Alber, 1965).

7. Chadwick, *Secularization*, p. 17.

8. Ibid., pp. 17–18.

9. Arnold E. Loen, *Secularization: Science Without God?*, trans. Margaret Kohl (Philadelphia: Westminister, 1967), p. 208.

10. Martin E. Marty, *The Modern Schism: Three Paths to the Secular* (New York: Harper & Row, 1969), p. 11.

11. See Harvey Cox, *The Secular City: Secularization and Urbanization in Theological Perspective*, rev. ed. (New York: Macmillan, 1966).

12. Baumer, *Religion and Scepticism*, pp. 29–30. On the religiosity of the Enlightenment, see especially pp. 57–77; on the "ersatz-religions," see especially pp. 162–184.

13. David Martin, *A General Theory of Secularization* (New York: Harper & Row, 1978), p. 12.

14. Vernon Pratt, *Religion and Secularization* (London: Macmillan, 1970), pp. 5–9 and 76–77.

15. See W. Warren Wagar, "Modern Views of the Origins of the Idea of Progress," *Journal of the History of Ideas* 28 (January–March 1967): 55–70.

16. Lübbe, *Säkularisierung*, p. 86; cf. Chadwick, *Secularization*, p. 264.

17. See, for example, Pratt, *Religion and Secularization*, pp. 5–11.

18. Martin, *General Theory*, pp. 62–63.

19. "Our Government makes no sense unless it is founded on a deeply held religious faith, and I don't care what it is." Dwight D. Eisenhower, quoted in Alasdair MacIntyre, *Secularization and Moral Change* (London: Oxford Univ. Press, 1967), p. 33. The tragedy of Nietzsche's announcement of the death of God yields to the farce of attendance at the church (or synagogue or mosque or pagoda) of your choice!

20. See Pratt, *Religion and Secularization*, pp. 11–20.

21. See J. M. Robertson, *A History of Freethought in the Nineteenth Century* (New York: Putnam, 1930). A conveniently brief synopsis and analysis is available in Baumer, *Religion and Scepticism*, chap. 3, "The Death of God." For a more recent interpretation, consult Chadwick, *Secularization*.

22. See Baumer, *Religion and Scepticism*, chap. 4, "The Age of Longing."

I

Isaac Newton's *Theologiae Gentilis Origines Philosophicae*

RICHARD S. WESTFALL

It was the most ancient opinion of those who applied themselves to Philosophy, that the fixed stars stood immovable in the highest parts of the world; that under them the planets revolved about the sun, that the earth, as one of the planets, described an annual course about the sun . . . This was the philosophy taught of old by Philolaus, Aristarchus of Samos, Plato in his riper years, and the whole sect of the Pythagoreans; and this was the judgment of Anaximander, more ancient still; and that wisest king of the Romans, Numa Pompilius. As a symbol of the figure of the round orb with the solar fire in the center, Numa erected a round temple in honor of Vesta, and ordained a perpetual fire to be kept in the middle of it. The Egyptians were the earliest observers of the heavens, and from them, probably, this philosophy was spread abroad. From them it was, and from the nations about them, that the Greeks, a people more addicted to the study of philology than of Nature, derived their first, as well as their soundest, notions of philosophy; and in the Vestal ceremonies we can recognize the spirit of the Egyptians who concealed mysteries that were above the capacity of the common herd under the veil of religious rites and hieroglyphic symbols.[1]

Thus, writing about 1685, Isaac Newton chose initially to introduce the concluding book of the work destined to be his masterpiece. In the early 1690s, revisions of Book III that he never finally included referred to the "mystic philosophers" of the ancient world who had held opinions about the world substantially like those in his own philosophy.[2] A decade later, when he composed what we now know as Query 31, the most important statement of his philosophy of nature, he concluded with a consideration of the relation of moral philosophy to natural philosophy.

15

And if natural Philosophy in all its Parts, by pursuing this Method [of analysis and composition], shall at length be perfected, the Bounds of Moral Philosophy will be also enlarged. For so far as we can know by Natural Philosophy what is the first Cause, what Power he has over us, and what Benefits we receive from him, so far our Duty towards him, as well as that towards one another, will appear to us by the Light of Nature. And no doubt, if the Worship of false Gods had not blinded the Heathen, their moral Philosophy would have gone farther than to the four Cardinal Virtues; and instead of teaching the Transmigration of Souls, and to worship the Sun and Moon, and dead Heroes, they would have taught us to worship our true Author and Benefactor, as their Ancestors did under the Government of *Noah* and his sons before they corrupted themselves.[3]

Nearly another decade later, in the General Scholium that he added to the second edition of the *Principia*, Newton included two footnotes, one about the etymology of the word *Deus* that mentioned that the heathens had called the souls of dead princes "gods," the other about ancient conceptions of the nature of God that mentioned the worship of heavenly bodies by idolaters.[1]

   In all four instances, Newton drew his material directly from a theological treatise that he called *Theologiae gentilis origines philosophicae* (The Philosophical Origins of Gentile Theology). It is manifest, from his choice to insert references to it, however veiled, into his major works on natural philosophy, that Newton attached great significance to the treatise. It was indeed the most important theological work he ever produced, and theology furnished one of his abiding intellectual occupations from the time when he turned to it seriously in the early 1670s, at about the age of thirty, until his death fifty-five years later. In his old age he used the treatise for a short statement called *Irenicum*, which he told Conduitt could do as much to remove the mischief from revealed religion as his other works had done for philosophy.[5] The *Origines* also transformed itself into his *Chronology of Ancient Kingdoms Amended*, a sanitized rendition which Newton deemed suitable for public consumption and on which he was working when he died. Until the great bulk of his theological manuscripts became available about a decade ago, the very existence of the work that occupied so central a position in his lifetime's endeavor was unknown.

   Like everything on which Newton worked seriously, the *Origines* exists in multiple amended versions, partly in English but mostly in Latin. As far as I have been able to determine, he never imposed a definitive order on the various themes that compose it, and the treatise exists today only as a chaos of notes and drafts. The basic manuscript, on which alone the title *Theologiae gentilis origines philosophicae* appears, belongs to the period soon after late 1683, when a young man named Humphrey Newton (not related to Isaac Newton) came to live in Newton's chamber in Trinity College and to function as his amanuensis.[6] Much of the manuscript is in Humphrey's hand, with numerous addenda and emendations in Newton's. On one sheet, which began with a few lines in

Humphrey's hand, Newton took over the pen in the middle of a paragraph and completed the page.[7] Four and five separate drafts of single passages copied out by Humphrey testify to the intensity of effort that Newton devoted to it, an intensity characteristic of every major undertaking and familiar in the manuscript remains it left behind to every student of Newton. There are also reading notes, apparently from the early or mid-1680s, that are closely related to the *Origines*. With references to works of Eusebius, Josephus, Diodorus, Plutarch, Plato, Ovid, Herodotus, Origen, Strabo, and many other ancients, plus a number of modern authors, they indicate the breadth of study on which the *Origines* rested—another characteristic of Newton's theological papers.[8] Some of the manuscripts associated with the *Origines* belonged to later periods. Newton worked on it in the early 1690s, when one chapter bore the title, "The original of religions." Among these papers is one sheet of notes on the back of a letter addressed to him in Parliament, another with notes from Bentley's 1691 edition on Malalas, and a third on the draft of a letter to Fatio that seems to connect with known correspondence in January 1693.[9] A note about his work as warden of the royal mint on one sheet indicates that at least he was leafing through the papers after the move to London.[10] A later batch, the hand of which seems to belong around 1715, starts with chapter 1, "The original of Monarchies." The presence of a copy in the hand of an amanuensis suggests the possibility that this version was produced to meet Princess Caroline's request in 1716 to see Newton's principles of chronology, before he decided instead on the Short Chronicle.[11] "The original of Monarchies" had already progressed far along the path that led the *Origines* to its final emasculated embodiment in the *Chronology*, and it no longer resembled its own original very closely.

When Newton first began work on the treatise, in the mid-1680s, he had already been engaged in intense theological study for more than a decade.[12] Almost from the beginning, he had entertained doubts about the doctrine of the Trinity, and before he had read very far, he had embraced Arianism as the true statement of Christianity. Undoubtedly his heterodox persuasion had stood behind his refusal to accept ordination in 1675, a decision that had nearly led to his ejection from his fellowship in Trinity College, for which ordination within seven years of incepting M.A. was a requirement.[13] Only a royal dispensation at the last minute had saved his fellowship. If Newton had ever been inclined to make his views public, that incident would have served to convince him of the necessity of silence on issues so delicate. By the mid-1670s, his theology had spilled over into an interpretation of the prophecies that centered on Arianism. The central message of the Book of Revelation was the prophecy of the Great Apostasy of the fourth century, when the archfiend Athanasius and the deceitful Roman church had conspired to impose the doctrine of the Trinity on Christianity. In Newton's interpretation, the barbarian invasions of the Roman empire, foretold in the trumpets and vials of wrath of the Book of Revelation, were God's punishment on a stiff-necked people who had gone whoring after false Gods.[14] The effort to show an exact correlation between prophecy and later events had led Newton into historical study as intensive as his theological study. In the early 1680s, the interpretation of the prophecies also suggested the study of Judaism, the rites and ceremonies of which he saw as prophetic types, and of the Jewish temple, to the exact plan of which he devoted a great deal of attention. All of these theological concerns contributed to the *Origines*. It extended both his Arianism and his historical study. It involved the plan of the Jewish temple. Its attempt to probe the meaning of ancient myths made use of the methodology he had employed on the prophecies. Thus he argued at one point that ancient mythology preserved a record of the wars of the sons of Ham. The rebellion of the Giants against heaven and Typho's seizure of the kingdom of Jupiter referred to Phut's uprising against Ham in Egypt. "For heaven," Newton asserted, "is usually employed by the mystics and Prophets for Throne and dominion." The lightning with which Jupiter struck Typho meant war, for so the prophets employed lightning and fire.[15] Not least, the secrecy in which Newton held the *Origines* drew upon his experience of the consequences that public heterodoxy would entail.

The period that witnessed Newton's plunge into theology also saw his immersion in alchemy,[16] and alchemy too had a connection with the *Origines*. The same mythological figures with whom the treatise dealt furnished the names and in some sense the types of the materials that alchemy, including explicitly Newton's alchemy, manipulated. Among the manuscripts associated with the *Origines* is one paper filled with notes on the myths of Jupiter's rebellion against Saturn, Neptune with his trident, Mars and Venus trapped in the net, Cadmus and his companions and the dragon impaled against an oak, Jason and the Golden Fleece—all of the imagery that appears most prominently in his alchemical papers.[17] Another sheet, which lists the twelve major gods with their various names, assigns to each an alchemical material and symbol.[18] If the connections between the *Origines* and alchemy extended more deeply than the superficial identity of mythological symbols, however, the liaison has eluded me.

On the surface, the message of the *Origines* was straightforward and seemed to be only a new rendition, such as a natural philosopher might give, of themes well established in the learned community of the day. The title of chapter 1 summarized the theme especially related to natural philosophy.

> That Gentile Theology was Philosophical and referred primarily to the Astronomical and Physical Science of the world system: and that the twelve Gods of the ancient Peoples were the seven Planets with the four elements and the quintessence of the Earth.[19]

The ancients cultivated a dual philosophy, sacred and vulgar, Newton stated, the sacred handed down to the initiated through types and figures, the vulgar proclaimed openly. The sacred philosophy, which flourished first and most in Egypt, was founded on the science of the stars, as the annual procession of the priests demonstrated. By joining the science of the stars and of the physical world with theology and by setting science first in the procession, the Egyptians indicated that their theology referred to the stars. Their gods were the planets and the elements, and the Egyptians spread these gods throughout the ancient world.[20]

A second theme, which Newton never integrated completely with the first, argued that the gods were also the deified forefathers of the ancient peoples. To be specific—and Newton was specific—the twelve gods were Noah, his children, his grandchildren, and his great grandchildren. "That the memory of the first Men after the Deluge was worshipped in the stars and elements," the title of chapter 2 proclaimed, "and that those men lived in the first three ages and the beginning of the fourth."[21] Immediately after the Flood, during the Golden Age, mankind lived together in Babylon under the rule of Noah. Noah was the original of Saturn, a god depicted as an old and morose man and worshipped (under a variety of names) by all the ancient peoples. Noah had three sons, the originals of the three sons of Saturn. The Silver Age began with Noah's division of the world among his sons, and especially with the establishment of Ham in Egypt. Ham, the outcast of the Judeo-Christian tradition, was the hero of Newton's account of early human history. In Greek theology he was Jupiter; in Egyptian, Jupiter Hammon, a mighty ruler whose dominion over the gods reflected his original dominion over men.[22] Ham in turn had four sons among whom he divided his lands. "Therefore, when Mercury and Apollo, who were under the empire of Osiris, are omitted, Hercules, Osiris, Antaeus and Busiris will correspond entirely to Cush, Mizraim, Phut and Canaan, the sons of Ham, Gen. 10, and Hercules will be Cush, Osiris Mizraim, Anateus Phut, and Busiris Canaan."[23] The Bronze Age corresponded to this generation, Noah's grandchildren. Mizraim/Osiris had three children, including a bastard son Thoth (his Egyptian name), the first Mercury.[24] To this generation belonged the beginning of the Iron Age.

Thoth or Mercury was also responsible for the instigation of gentile theology.

> The worship of Gods and Gentile Theology do in fact seem to have begun in this way. We have recently seen that Galileo named the stars about Jupiter the Medician stars in honor and memory of his benefactors and that the names of the most illustrious men were given by others to the moon. We also note that the memory of certain men is preserved in the constellations. In the way that more recent Astronomers have done this, so the most ancient applied the names of their forebears to the stars and elements.[25]

A short time after the death of his father Osiris, Thoth ruled over Egypt with
Isis. He instituted funeral rites to be celebrated annually in honor of Osiris. At
the same time he bestowed on the planets the names of his parents and of other
relatives still alive, arranging the names with the eldest most distant from the
sun, and combining astronomical learning with religious rites, he taught his
followers both to celebrate and to conceal these matters in hieroglyphs that he
invented. Thus it happened that religious tradition held the gods were related
and placed them all in the same age. Later the Egyptians claimed that the souls
of these men and women inhabited the planets, and they attributed the qualities
of the souls to the planets. Ultimately they imagined that the soul of Osiris had
transmigrated into a bull and that other souls were present in other animals and
plants and stones and eventually statues. "And so Astrology and gentile Theology were introduced by astute priests to promote the study of the Stars and to
increase the power of the priesthood."[26] Newton regarded the Egyptians with
ambivalence. On the one hand, they were the source of learning; on the other
hand, they were equally the source of error. Not least among their errors was the
religion of twelve primary gods, "which, propagated by the Egyptians to other
people, gave the origin to Idolatry."[27]

When Newton referred to the ancient peoples, he meant primarily three—
the Egyptians, the Chaldeans, and the Assyrians. Crucial to the latter two was
Ham's son Cush, who received the eastern sector of his father's inheritance and,
two hundred years after the Flood, led an expedition beyond Arabia, conquered
the offspring of Shem, and established an empire in Babylon. Cush was a
mighty warrior, the original of Hercules and Mars.[28] Cush had a son Nimrod
(Ninus to the Assyrians), who led an expedition from Babylon that established
Nineveh and the Assyrian empire. The heart of the riddle of gentile theology lay
in the three founders of the three great empires—Ham, Cush, and Nimrod.
Every nation deified their own kings and applied the name of Jupiter to the one
they held most in honor. "For all the ancient people especially celebrated and
venerated the founders of their kingdoms and fathers of the people."[29] To the
Chaldeans, Nimrod (or Ninus) was Hercules and Cush was Jupiter. The Assyrians worshipped Ninus as Jupiter Belus, and hence his father Cush as Saturn.

> The same man who to one people is Hercules is therefore Jupiter to another. For
> Ninus whom the Chaldeans called Hercules was Jupiter to the Assyrians. There-
> fore the Chaldeans, who took Ninus for Hercules, understood Cush, the father of
> Ninus, as Jupiter, and Ham, the grandfather of Ninus, as Saturn, and therefore, in
> order that Noah not be left out, they gave a father, Heaven [Caelus], and a mother,
> Earth, to Saturn, who was the first of the Egyptian gods. Hence it happened that in
> the East, where Chaldean philosophy prevailed, Caelus took the place of Noah
> and Saturn the place of Ham. Among the Assyrians, indeed, where Belus was
> Jupiter, Cush was Saturn and Ham Caelus, but Noah was Hypsuranius.[30]

Thus, Newton concluded, "all began with Noah; for no one recognized a God older than Hypsuranius."[31]

Although he frequently applied the Greek and Roman names to the gods, Newton regarded their theologies as wholly derivative. He believed that Greece was colonized by Egyptians (sometimes he made it Phoenicians, the offspring of Ham's son Canaan), and he claimed that the Greeks simply imported Egyptian theology. With the theology came the names of the Egyptian gods, "but under these names they worshipped their own dead men, it being usual to consecrate the dead by new names, as by giving the name of Bacchus to the son of Semele . . . [a considerable list of the men and women to whom the names were applied] . . . And this confusion of names & persons has very much clouded the history of the ages of the Gods."[32] The concept of the deification of ancestors assumed a different shape here, since the Noachids did not appear. In the case of the Romans, it is true, he argued that Janus was Noah, who fled to Italy after the rebellion of his sons.[33]

As there were many Jupiters and Saturns among the ancient peoples, so the same gods could also be known by different names. Different names applied to the same gods sometimes led to differentiation of the gods as well. Since every nation tried to refer their gods to the sun and moon, the bodies most admired in the heavens, very diverse gods could be taken as the same. "Every nation stud[y]ing to honour their own ancestors they were not content to worship them themselves but sometimes pretended them to be the Gods of other nations also . . ."[34] Thus Egyptians pretended that Dionysius, Bacchus, Adonis, and Pan were their Osiris. "From all this," Newton concluded, "arose the greatest confusion in the names, genealogies, and histories of the gods, though most of it can be cleared up by distinguishing between the Egyptian, Chaldean, Assyrian, and Greek theologies."[35]

None of the arguments above, which provided the framework of Newton's treatise, was original to him. The identification of world history with the multiplication and dispersion of the offspring of Noah, the central role of Egypt, the divinization of heroes, the ascription of basic inventions necessary to settled life to the same divinized heroes (an idea present in Newton's work), the use of etymological arguments based on the assumption that all languages developed from the same common tongue (a form of "demonstration" which Newton employed)—seventeenth-century learning had explored them all extensively. Even the argument that sounds most typically Newtonian, the connection of pagan religion with natural philosophy, had been pursued by others, though not to my knowledge in the systematized form that identified the twelve gods with specific aspects of nature. Certainly the three seventeenth-century authors whom Newton studied intensely and cited frequently—Samuel Bochart, *Geographia sacra*; Sir John Marsham, *Chronicus canon aegyptiacus, ebraicus, & graecus*; Gerard Vossius, *De theologia gentili*—had emphasized these themes. Indeed most of the arguments had been familiar items of intellectual commerce already in the ancient world.[36]

Nevertheless, what Newton composed from familiar materials would have appeared to seventeenth-century readers, had they seen it, not only unfamiliar but dangerous. The authorities on which he drew had proclaimed the Christian ends of their works. Vossius, a bottomless sink of miscellaneous erudition, inserted his purpose in his full title, *De theologia gentili, et physiologia christiana, sive de origine ac progressu idolatriae . . . liber I, et II* (manifestly the source of Newton's title), and whenever he drew back from his fascination with the details of pagan religions, Vossius insisted that his work served to emphasize by contrast the truth of Christianity—to be exact, Protestant Christianity.[37] Bochart devoted his *Geographia sacra* to demonstrating that most place-names in the ancient world derived from Hebrew and that all languages were corruptions of Hebrew, spread primarily by the Phoenicians, who spoke a dialect which hardly differed from the mother tongue.[38] Sir John Marsham's *Chronicus canon* found its ultimate criterion of human history in the scriptural chronology and insisted on reducing the annals of Egypt and Greece to the Hebrew pattern. Even so, Marsham's work had caused some eyebrows to rise, for it had set out frankly to vindicate Egyptian records and in doing so had seemed to ascribe to them a validity resembling the Bible's.[39] Indeed this was a problem endemic in the whole genre of literature on which Newton drew. Even Archbishop Ussher's famous *Annals*, a work of unquestionable orthodoxy which established the exact hour of the creation (6:00 P.M.) on 22 October 4004 B.C. by counting days and years recorded in the Bible and which divided world history into periods based on Christian history, used pagan sources to fill out the biblical account. Bochart had sensed the criticism this procedure might arouse and had tried to allay it. The Scriptures are perfect, he agreed, and nothing in the testimony of pagan writers can add to their certainty. They require explication, however, and pagan authorities can help us to understand their references. Moreover, the demonstration that ancient writers agreed with the scriptural account can strengthen the faith of infirm men and refute the pretensions of atheists.[40] Newton's *Origines* carried the tendency inherent in all of these works another step toward its logical conclusion. He offered no justification similar to Bochart's. The content of his work indicates that for him pagan sources had acquired authority equal to the Bible's. Rather in his eyes the historical books of the Bible had lost their privileged position and the Jewish myths (the only part of the Bible that entered into consideration here) were only one tradition among others. Thus he found a number of pagan accounts of the Flood, the event with which world history began anew.

> From all of which it is manifest that a certain general tradition was conserved for a very long time among the Peoples about those things which were passed down

most distinctly from Noah and the first men to Abraham and from Abraham to Moses. And hence we can also hope that a history of the times which followed immediately after the flood can be deduced with some degree of truth from the traditions of the Peoples.[41]

Years later, near the end of his life, Newton indicated that he did regard the historical books of the Bible, though not the prophecies, merely as the record of the Jewish people.[42] There is every reason to think that he arrived at this conclusion as he composed the *Origines*.

What is one to make of Newton's unequivocal identification of the twelve gods with Noah and the Noachids? When Bochart equated Saturn with Noah, he meant literally that "Noah" (in the Hebrew form of course) was the true name of the common father of mankind. In Newton's case, there is every indication that "Noah," "Ham," "Cush," and the rest were simply the names most familiar to his (hypothetical) English audience. Noah's son was no more Ham than he was Ammon. Perhaps he was less so, since Newton considered Egyptian rather than Hebrew to have been the source from which the other languages of the East derived.[43] He passed readily from the Hebrew to the Egyptian names, using them indiscriminately in the same sentence. All twelve gods, he asserted at one point, belonged to the first four generations, "Thoth, Orus, & Bubaste the great grandchildren of Noah being the last of them."[44]

In a similar manner, he found Moses' account of the early ages seriously inadequate. Manifestly, the expedition of Cush, which led to the Chaldean and Assyrian empires, was a major event in the history of mankind. Moses seemed to refer to it, Newton stated, in his story of the Tower of Babel and his comments on Nimrod. "However, since Moses passes by the first migrations and seats of Peoples in silence and only describes the origin of the kingdom of the Assyrians at the time when it flourished, he barely mentions those things which the founder of this kingdom, Nimrod or Ninus, accomplished."[45] Nimrod/Ninus was one of seven children fathered by Cush. Moses named only six of them, but Sanchuniathon gave the seventh.[46] Newton also filled a sheet with references to pagan sources that confirmed Moses' account of the exodus from Egypt.[47]

Sanchuniathon was a Phoenician chronicler on whom Newton frequently relied for information about the times soon after the Flood. He was, Newton said, "much the oldest writer and a curious investigator of historical origins."[48] Another authority for these times was Berossus, a Babylonian who assembled information from the oldest archives and monuments. Berossus gave an account of the period between the Creation and the Flood which agreed both in its extent of time and in the succession of ten kings or patriarchs with the account in Moses. Berossus also wrote about the Flood, the ark, its landing on a mountain, and the offspring of Noah just as Moses did.[49] Newton did not discover Sanchuniathon and Berossus. References to them abound in Vossius, Bochart, and

Marsham; Eusebius and Josephus furnished his primary sources about them. Nevertheless, his use of them differed. In the *Origines* they appeared as independent authorities on the period after the Flood, authorities as reliable as Moses and frequently more useful.

Whatever the name he gave to the treatise, a description of the origins of gentile theology was not Newton's goal. Rather it was the means to a further end, and in that end lay the ultimate heterodoxy both of the treatise and of its author. One must not believe, he continued, that religion began with the doctrine of the transmigration of souls.

> For there was another religion more ancient than all of these in which a fire for offering sacrifices burned perpetually in the middle of a sacred place. For the Vestal cult was the most ancient of all.

Numa Pompilius established such a religion among the Romans before they received the worship of images. It was the religion of the Etruscans, the original inhabitants of Italy. All of the oldest Greek cities had similar sacred places with perpetual fires, "prytanea" as Newton called them. The Persians had such a religion in the most ancient times. Even the Egyptians did. The perpetual fire that burned before the altar in the Tabernacle and the Temple of the Jews was a form of vestal fire.[50] Indeed Newton found evidence of early vestal worship all over Europe. Prytanea furnished the model from which temples were later copied in all nations. This religion with the sacred fire he insisted,

> seems to have been as well the most universal as ye most ancient of all religions & to have spread into all nations before other religions took place. There are many instances of nations receiving other religions after this but none (that I know) of any nation's receiving this after any other. Nor did ever any other religion wch sprang up later become so general as this.

Newton therefore concluded what the evidence seemed to demand, that the religion based on prytanea was the religion of Noah and his sons which spread with them in the initial peopling of the earth. It was, he argued, "the true religion till ye nations corrupted it."[51]

The prytaneum with the fire in the center was a symbol of the universe.

> The whole heavens they recconed to be ye true & real temple of God & therefore that a Prytaneum might deserve the name of his Temple they framed it so as in the fittest manner to represent the whole systeme of the heavens. A point of religion then wch nothing can be more rational.[52]

The fire represented the sun, of course, and the universe symbolized by the prytaneum was heliocentric. Newton regarded the Jewish temple as an enlarged model of the prytaneum. "In the Apocalypse," he asserted, "the world natural is represented by the Temple of Jerusalem & the parts of this world by the analogous parts of the Temple."[53] When the priests approached the altar, they always circled the fire and lighted seven lamps which represented the planets circling the sun (a numerical problem with a Copernican universe which Newton did not pause to explicate).[54] One purpose of the true religion, he decided, was to propose to mankind, through the structure of the temple, the study of nature "as the true Temple of ye great God they worshipped."

> So then the first religion was the most rational of all others till the nations corrupted it. For there is no way (wthout revelation) to come to ye knowledge of a Deity but by the frame of nature.[55]

He inserted the parenthetical phrase, "wthout revelation," above the line as an afterthought.

Newton had several related accounts of the corruption of true religion. In one, men were led by degrees to venerate the symbols, in the prytanea, of the heavenly bodies. Thus the worshiping of heavenly bodies was the first corruption of the true religion. The "grossest corruption" was the worship of dead men and statues. The Egyptians were its author.

> The first ages studying to honour their ancestors imposed their names upon ye Stars & Elements & countries & Cities & rivers & Mountains & represented them by various hie[ro]glyphical figures wth wings like angels to denote ye motions of ye stars, & by this means their names being preserved grew into more & more veneration. At length they feigned their souls or spirits to be translated into ye stars y^t by these spirits or intelligences ye stars were animated & shone & moved in their courses & understood all things below. . . . And to make this hypothesis the more plausible they feigned that ye stars by vertue of these souls were endued wth ye qualities of ye men & according to these qualities governed the world. . . . And by means of these fictions the souls of ye dead grew into veneration wth ye stars & by as many as received this kind of theology were taken for ye Gods wch governed ye world.

Because the "nature of mankind is prone to superstition," men began to pay respect to these gods together with the true God and eventually in place of the true God. "Thus was ye world soon filled with Gods."[56]

Other superstitions came after the worship of the stars.

> For they believed that the souls of the dead transmigrated not only to the stars and the elements, but also into cows, oxen and other lower animals, and into plants and unformed stones, and finally into statues and sculptures of all kinds Whence the veneration of sacred animals and plants and the worship of gems and columns and statues and various prophetic and magic and necromantic incantations and

arts by which the souls of the dead were feigned to be induced into statues and evoked from them and were ordered at will to be present or absent and to carry out orders & reveal future things.[57]

A corruption of philosophy followed the corruption of religion. The vestal fire was taken for some fire in the center of the earth; hence the earth was placed in the center of a new order of planets. Men began to believe that the heavens were solid orbs moved by intelligences, that is, by souls of the dead that they worshipped as gods.[58] Thus was born the geocentric system fully elaborated by a later Egyptian, Ptolemy.

Writing in the early 1690s, immediately after the Glorious Revolution, Newton inclined to treat the corruption of religion as the deliberate policy of kings to increase their authority. To promote the veneration of their ancestors, kings "called ye stars & elements by their names & caused them to be honoured with such solemnities & pompous ceremonies as soon created in the people a superstition towards them as Gods & by consequence a veneration of ye whole race of kings as descended from these Deities."[59]

> And which I pray is more likely [he asked in a later manuscript] that ye Court should promote ye honour of Kings among ye people or ye people find out these refined ways of doing it & introduce them into Courts? Was it ye interest of ye people to cheat themselves into slavery by such kinds of state policy or was it not rather the business of ye court to do it?[60]

The policy of kings was not necessarily opposed to the interest of priests, and Newton did not hesitate to assign an equal measure of blame for the corruption of religion to the trickery of the priesthood.[61]

For Newton, the Jewish religion was the religion of Noah freed from the superstitions of gentile theology. Moses promulgated the law to purge the true religion of such corruptions. Nothing is more revealing of Newton's outlook than his handling of Abraham. To the Christian scholars Newton cited, Abraham was a critical personage. His selection by God and the promise that in his seed would mankind be blest established the old covenant with the Jewish people and prefigured the new one delivered to all mankind by a Messiah sprung from the seed of Abraham. In Archbishop Ussher's periodization of world history, God's choice of Abraham concluded the second age and inaugurated the third. To Newton, in contrast, Abraham was a peripheral figure mentioned only to illustrate the early prevalence of the religion of Noah. The fire that Abraham carried with him was the vestal fire found in prytanea everywhere.[62] It would have been more correct, in Newton's view, to say that the house of Israel chose God than that God chose the house of Israel. That is, the Jews restored for a time the original true religion that was the common heritage of all mankind.

Newton seemed even to say that, having fallen away, Israel rediscovered the true religion in Egypt, for there was little in Mosaic religion that was not in use among the Egyptians. Hence the religion of the Egyptians was also the true religion though corrupted by the worship of false gods; "& by consequence ye religion of ye Jews was no other then that of Noah propagated down in Egypt till ye age of Moses."[63] When they fell away anew, later prophets recalled them. Jesus was another prophet cast in the same mold, one who came, not to institute a new religion, but to restore the original true one, a prophet not solely to the Jews, however, but to all mankind.

About the content of the religion of Noah beyond the worship of the one true God in prytanea that represented his creation, Newton said little in the *Origines*. More than thirty years later, during the final decade of his life, he did elaborate its meaning in a short essay that he named *Irenicum*.

> All nations were originally of one religion [he still asserted] & this religion consisted in the Precepts of the sons of Noah . . .

The precepts were two in number—love of God and love of neighbor. This religion descended to Abraham, Isaac, and Jacob (who were barely more prominent in this account than Abraham was in the *Origines*). Moses taught it to Israel again. Pythagoras learned it in Egypt and carried it back to the West. "This religion," Newton concluded, "may be therefore called the Moral Law of all nations."[64] He repeated the same theme in the opening sentences of his history of the early church, which stemmed from the same period.

> The true religion was propagated by Noah to his posterity, & when they revolted to the worship of their dead Kings & Heroes & thereby denyed their God & ceased to be his people, it continued in Abraham & his posterity who revolted not. And when they began to worship the Gods of Egypt & Syria, Moses & the Prophets reclaimed them from time to time till they rejected the Messiah from being their Lord, & he rejected them from being his people & called the Gentiles, & thenceforward the believers both Jews & Gentiles became his people.[65]

The Gospels added a third precept to the two basic ones of Noachian religion—to believe that Jesus was the Christ foretold in prophecy. Phrased in Newton's peculiar manner, which repeated the special role that prophecy held in his view of Christianity, the third precept said nothing of salvation through the redemptive sacrifice of the God-man. Newton the Arian never emphasized such doctrines. Rather the third precept, in calling for belief in the dominion of God over the course of history, which the prophecies demonstrated, merely elaborated on the first precept—to love God. When the risen Christ (exalted because of his obedience to sit at the right hand of God) commanded his disciples to preach repentance and remission of sins in his name, Newton argued in *Irenicum*, he referred to transgressions against the two precepts—such as idolatry, a failure to love God; and covetousness, a failure to love one's neighbor.[66] When asked what the great commandment of the law was, Jesus replied that it was to love God, and he added to it the second commandment—to love one's neighbor. "This was the religion of the sons of Noah established by Moses & Christ & still in force."[67]

The two basic commandments, Newton repeated, "always have & always will be the duty of all nations & The coming of Jesus Christ has made no alteration in them." Mankind has repeatedly turned from them; as often God has sent a prophet to restore them—Noah, Abraham, Moses, the Jewish prophets, Jesus. "And in all the reformations of religion hitherto made the religion in respect of God & our neighbour is one and the same religion (barring ceremonies & forms of government wch are of a changeable nature) so that this is the oldest religion in the world . . ."[68] "These are the laws of nature," another paper from this period added, "the essential part of religion wch ever was & ever will be binding to all nations, being of an immutable eternal nature because grounded upon immutable reason."[69] On a scrap of paper that has survived, Newton attempted to work out the best formulation of the relation in which Christianity stood to the religion of Noah.

> The law was ancienter then the days of Moses being given to Noah & all his posterity, & therefore w^n the Apostles & Elders in the Council at Jerusalem declared that the Gentiles were not obliged to be circumcised & observe the law of Moses, they excepted this law as being imposed on all nations not as the sons of Araham [*sic*] but as the sons of Noah not by circumcision but by an earlier law of God not by conversion to the Christian religion but even before they were Christians. And of the same kind is the law of absteining from meats offered to Idols. & from fornication.
>
> not as Christians but as Gentiles
>
> —as being imposed on all nations not by the law of Moses but by an earlier law of God, not as sons of Abraham but as sons of Noah, not as Christians but even as Gentiles. And of the same kind is the law of absteining from meats offered to Idols & from fornication.[70]

In yet another paper, which he titled "A short schem of the true Religion," Newton asserted that Socrates, Cicero, Confucius, and other philosophers had taught the heathen the duties that fill out the commandment to love one's neighbor and that Moses taught them to the Israelites and Jesus to the Christians. "Thus you see there is but one law for all nations the law of righteousness & charity dictated to the Christians by Christ to the Jews by Moses & to all mankind by the light of reason & by this law all men are to be judged at the last day."[71]

Newton had embraced Arianism in the early 1670s, and in his interpretation of the prophecies he had explored the process in which scheming and evil men had corrupted the purity of the Christian faith by the introduction of idolatry and superstition. In his *Theologiae gentilis origines philosophicae,* he generalized the experience of the fourth century and converted the coming of Christ from the climactic event of human history into one repetition of a cyclical pattern. During the Golden Age of Noah mankind worshipped the one true God and practiced the one true religion. Scheming men pursuing their selfish ends had corrupted it with idolatry and superstition, and, as often as prophets restored it, the schemers corrupted it anew. Jesus of Nazareth was another in the long line of prophets who preached the pure religion of Noah. In the fourth century Athanasius, another product of Egypt, the fertile source of idolatry, renewed the pattern of corruption once more. The doctrine of the Trinity, which inculcated the worship of a dead man as god, repeated the basic tenet of all idolatry.

Newton made it abundantly clear that the Church of England was, in his opinion, involved in the same corruption and that a new reformation was needed. He may even, in his innermost heart, have dreamed of himself as a prophet called to restore the true religion. Certainly in his early interpretation of the prophecies he placed himself among the tiny remnant in whom the true church was preserved,[72] and in 1675 he prepared to lay down his fellowship rather than accept "the mark of the Beast" in ordination. Even then, however, he quailed at the prospect of open confrontation, and he readily accepted the compromise offered by the royal dispensation whereby, at the price of silence, he could stay on in Trinity. When his role in resisting the tyranny of James cast him into prominence in Cambridge and soon thereafter offered rich patronage in London, he never again seriously entertained the notion of leading a new reformation.

To the end of his life Newton continued to compose Arian statements on the nature of Christ.[73] Nevertheless, the *Origines* appears to be incompatible with Arianism, to go beyond its recognition of the special status of Christ, who was more than a man even if he was not wholly divine, and to verge on a frankly deistic position. It is instructive to compare Newton with deists such as Toland and Tindal. He shared their hatred of superstition and mystery and their conviction that evil men had introduced false doctrines into religion to promote their selfish interests. He shared their concept of an immutable God who would not conceal necessary truths through thousands of years in order arbitrarily to reveal them later to a small minority of mankind. Newton's religion of Noah was identical to Tindal's Christianity, as old as the Creation.[74] Both insisted on the two basic precepts to love God and to love one's neighbor, and both argued that Christ came, not to deliver a new religion, but to restore the original pure one. It is also instructive to compare Newton's *Origines* with the *Discourse Concerning*

the Unchangeable Obligations of Natural Religion by his friend and disciple
Samuel Clarke. Clarke's title included a second part: *and the Truth and Certainty of the Christian Revelation*. Clarke supported the implications of that title
by arguing for the necessity of a revelation beyond natural religion to guide man
in his fallen state. Thus Clarke's treatise repeated the standard Protestant
position that divine grace is necessary to restore fallen nature to its original
status, both enlightening clouded understanding and quickening degenerate
will.

> Indeed in the original uncorrupted State of Humane Nature, before the Mind of
> Man was depraved with prejudicate Opinions, corrupt Affections, and vicious
> Inclinations, Customs, and Habits; right Reason may justly be supposed to have
> been a sufficient Guide, and a principle powerful enough to preserve Men in the
> constant Practice of their Duty. . . . To remedy all these Disorders, and to conquer
> all these Corruptions; there was plainly wanting some extraordinary and super-
> natural *Assistance;* which was above the reach of bare Reason and Philosophy to
> procure . . .[75]

Though Newton certainly believed that the biblical prophecies were divine
revelation, the whole thrust of the *Origines* ruled out the sort of revelation, of
truths unto life eternal, for which Clarke contended, and the concept of the true
Noachian religion implicitly denied the Fall. Clarke was scarcely an orthodox
Christian theologian. An Arian like Newton, perhaps an Arian because of
Newton, he was notorious in his age and barely escaped being defrocked by
Convocation. Newton's *Origines*, with its assertion that the necessary truths had
been learned from nature in the age of Noah and its effective denial that Christ
revealed any truth, clearly went beyond Clarke—indeed well beyond.
    In the 1680s, when the *Origines* proper was composed, it still only hinted
at its own implications. To fill out the content of the religion of Noah as Newton
understood it, I have had to call upon manuscripts from the final decade of his
life. If the early *Origines* seemed to imply such a position, it did not explicitly
state it. At one point, it came close to doing so. On the verso side of one sheet,
Newton jotted down the titles of six projected chapters. The last of the six was
chapter 11.

> What the true religion of the children of Noah was before it began to be corrupted
> by the worship of false Gods. And that the Christian religion was not more true
> and did not become less corrupted.[76]

He squeezed the title onto the very bottom of the page, almost as though he
feared to write the words and be forced to examine the full implications of his
own treatise. As far as I know, he did not at the time venture to compose the
chapter itself, and he only returned to the thought the title expressed after thirty

years had passed, and then very privately. By that time the deist tide had burst across England, a decade after Newton composed the *Origines*. There is no evidence that men like Toland and Tindal had ever heard of the treatise; rather they responded independently to stimuli like those that had animated Newton. In important respects, however, Newton differed from the deists. Their essentially negative spirit did not belong to Newton. His hatred of the corruptions of religion flowed directly from a profound adoration of the living God that suffused his entire life. One looks in vain for a similar sense of worship among the deists. Nevertheless, for all the difference in ultimate outlook, Newton arrived at conclusions remarkably similar to theirs.

In December 1692, probably within a month of the time when he wrote passages for the *Origines* allied to the one jotted over the draft of a letter to Fatio, Newton sent a famous letter to Richard Bentley.

> When I wrote my treatise about our Systeme [he began] I had an eye upon such Principles as might work wth considering men for the beleife of a Deity . . .[77]

The passage is well known and has been much quoted as evidence of Newton's piety, as no doubt it is. Against the background of the *Origines*, however, the statement reveals new levels of meaning, not hitherto understood, that color his words with a heterodoxy not usually linked to piety.

Notes

1. Cambridge University Library, *Add. MS. 3990*, f. 1. Newton almost certainly composed this version of the final book, which he originally intended to be Book II, in 1685. After his death it was published separately, in the original Latin, as *De mundi systemate*, and in an English translation as *A Treatise of the System of the World*. This translation is republished at the end of *The Mathematical Principles of Natural Philosophy*, trans. Andrew Motte, rev. Florian Cajori (Berkeley, 1934). The passage I quote is found on p. 549. I have altered the translation minimally. Newton eliminated the passage completely from Book III, which completed the published *Principia*.

2. The principal body of the manuscripts in question are in *Gregory MS. 247* at the Royal Society. They are in Newton's hand. For extensive quotations and a full discussion, see J. E. McGuire and P. M. Rattansi, "Newton and the 'Pipes of Pan'," *Notes and Records of the Royal Society*, 21 (1966): 108–143.

3. *Opticks*, based on 4th ed. (New York, 1952), pp. 405–406. The Query first appeared in 1706 in the Latin *Optice*. In that version, the passage I quote did not contain the final clause beginning "as their Ancestors did . . ." (*Optice*, p. 384.)

4. *Principia*, pp. 544–545.

5. *Keynes MS. 130.6*, Book 3 (King's College, Cambridge). Multiple, much-revised versions of this short essay are found in *Keynes MS. 3* and scattered through *Yahuda MS. 15* (The Jewish National and University Library, Jerusalem). Herbert McLachlan published a badly mutilated version of *Irenicum*, a composite put together from several papers in *Keynes MS. 3*, which fails to capture the central thrust of the piece. Isaac Newton, *Theological Manuscripts*, ed. Herbert McLachlan, (Liverpool, 1950), pp. 28–35.

6. *Yahuda MS. 16.2*. The rest of *MS. 16* also concerns itself with the *Origines*. *Yahuda MS. 17* contains rougher material connected with it.

7. *Yahuda MS. 16.2*, f. 58.

8. *Yahuda MS. 13.3*, ff. 1–20; the Newtonian manuscript in the American Philosophical Society Library.

9. *Yahuda MSS. 41; 17.1*, ff. 13 and 5ᵛ; *New College MS. 361.3*, f. 34 (Bodleian Library, Oxford). In connection with the last of these, cf. Newton to Fatio, 24 January 1693; *The Correspondence of Isaac Newton*, ed. H. W. Turnbull, et al., 7 vols. (Cambridge, 1959–1977), *3*; 241.

10. *Yahuda MS. 16.2*, f. 20ᵛ.

11. *Keynes MS. 146; Yahuda MSS. 7.1a*, f. 1; *25.2*, ff. 26–31, 34–58; *New College MS. 361.3*, passim. The copy (incomplete) in the hand of an amanuensis is in *Yahuda MS. 25.2*, ff. 34–43.

12. While there are indications of religious concerns from earlier periods, notes from intensive theological reading date back only to the early 1670s. It is true that dating of the notes relies almost entirely on one's assessment of the hand. Nevertheless, the hand of the early 1670s had some distinct characteristics such that I am reasonably confident in my dating. A notebook, *Keynes MS. 2*, contains what I take to be the earliest theological notes.

13. See his letter to Oldenburg, late January 1675; *Correspondence, 7*, 387.

14. What appears to me to have been the earliest sketch of his interpretation is found in *Yahuda MS. 10.3*, ff. 14–29. *Yahuda MS. 1* contains the early full-scale treatise in multiple drafts.

15. *Yahuda MS. 16.2*, f. 62.

16. See especially, B. J. T. Dobbs, *The Foundations of Newton's Alchemy. The Hunting of the Greene Lyon* (Cambridge, 1975).

17. *Yahuda MS. 13.3*, ff. 21–23.

18. *Babson MS. 420*, pp. 1–2.

19. *Yahuda MS. 16.2*, f. 1.

20. *Yahuda MS. 16.2*, ff. 2–3, Cf. f. 8; *Yahuda MSS. 13.3*, f. 5; *17.2*, ff. 5, 6, and 14.

21. *Yahuda MS. 16.2*, f. 7ᵛ.

22. "Chap. 3 That Noah is Saturn and Janus, and that Ham is Jupiter Hammon and that the sons of Ham together with the grandsons are both the remaining Gods and the Giants who lived with the Gods in Egypt during the third age: and how Ham with his family descended into Egypt and divided the region among his sons." *Yahuda MS. 16.2*, f. 53ᵛ.

23. *Yahuda MS. 16.2*, f. 18ᵛ. *Cf. Yahuda MS. 17.2*, f. 10ᵛ.

24. "Chap 5 That Mizraim is Osiris and Serapis and Menaetius & Dis or Pluto and that Pathros the son of Mizraim is Horus or Apollo and that he [Mizraim] had a daughter Bubaste or Diana and a bastard son Thoth or the first Mercury." (*Yahuda MS. 16.2*, f. 68ᵛ.) Cf. ff. 67ᵛ and 73, and *Yahuda MS. 17.2*, f. 10ᵛ.

25. *Yahuda MS. 16.2*, f. 10. Cf. ff. 15 and 17.

26. *Yahuda MS. 17.3*, f. 5ᵛ. Cf. ff. 3–6 (two successive sheets despite their foliation).

27. *Yahuda MS. 17.3*, f. 3.

28. "Chap. 4 That Cush is Hercules, Mars, Moloc, and the first Belus." (*Yahuda MS. 16.2*, f. 65.)

29. *Yahuda MS. 16.1*, f. 6. Cf. *Yahuda MS. 41*, f. 13.

30. *Yahuda MS. 16.2*, ff. 28–29. Cf. ff. 42–43; *Yahuda MSS. 16.1*, ff. 1–1ᵛ, 7, and 9; *17.2*, ff. 2–2ᵛ.

31. *Yahuda MS. 16.2*, f. 67. Cf. f. 69.

32. *New College MS. 361.3*, f. 57. This MS. appears to me to date from the second decade of the eighteenth century; the same theme was present in the first drafts of the *Origines*.

33. *Yahuda MS. 16.2*, f. 12. Cf. *Yahuda MS. 17.2*, f. 11.

34. *Yahuda MS. 16.2*, f. 19ʳ.

35. *Yahuda MS. 17.3*, f. 8. Cf. f. 1 and *Yahuda MS. 16.2*, f. 25.

36. Newton's exhaustive program of study had also brought him into contact with the ancient sources—early Christian chronicles such as Eusebius's works, and Josephus's Jewish counterparts, and a wide variety of ancient discourses on religion and the gods, including that of Euhemerus (as reported by Ennius), whose name became synonymous with the interpretation of ancient mythology that Newton adopted. See his notes in *Yahuda MS. 13.3* and the manuscript in the library of the American Philosophical Society. He cited Euhemerus in *Yahuda MS. 16.2*, ff. 13 and 39. See also the very interesting note, written on the back of a letter addressed to him in Parliament, about nonscriptural sources on the exodus (*Yahuda MS. 17.1*, f. 13ʳ).

37. Gerard Vossius, *De theologia gentili*, 3 vols. (New York, 1976—a reprint of Amsterdam, 1641). See especially chapters 41 and 42 of Book I (*1*, 292–304). Cf. *1*, 606.

38. Samuel Bochart, *Geographia sacra* (Frankfurt, 1681). See especially the prefaces to Books I and II. The whole of Book II concerns itself with the derivation of languages from Hebrew-Phoenician.

39. John Marsham, *Chronicus canon aegyptiacus ebraicus graecus* (London, 1672). The famous argument central to the book—that there were a number of contemporary Egyptian kingdoms, each with its own dynasties, and that therefore the record of Egyptian dynasties did not constitute a single series that stretched back beyond the creation as the Hebrew Scriptures recorded it—was not original with Marsham. Vossius had suggested it thirty years earlier (*De theologia gentili*, *1*, 211). I do not know if he in turn borrowed it from an earlier source.

40. Bochart, *Geographia*, preface to Book I, n.p.

41. *Yahuda MS. 16.2*, f. 48. Cf. f. 51. In a different version of the same argument, Newton ascribed priority over the Greeks to the Egyptian, Chaldean, and Phoenician traditions without even mentioning the Hebrews (f. 49ʳ.)

42. *Observations on the Prophecies of Daniel, and the Apocalypse of St. John* (London, 1733), pp. 4–13. Cf. *The Chronology of Ancient Kingdoms Amended* (London 1728), pp. 357–358; *New College MS. 361.2*, ff. 132–133; Frank Manuel, *Isaac Newton, Historian* (Cambridge, Mass., 1963), pp. 59–60.

43. *Yahuda MS. 16.2*, f. 59.

44. *Yahuda MS. 41*, f. 13.

45. *Yahuda MS. 16.1*, f. 9. Cf. ff. 2, 4 and 6.

46. *Yahuda MS. 41*, f. 24.

47. *Yahuda MS. 17.1*, f. 13ʳ.

48. *Yahuda MS. 16.2*, f. 74.

49. *Yahuda MS. 16.2*, f. 11ʳ; the manuscript is in the library of the American Philosophical Society.

50. *Yahuda MS. 17.3*, ff. 8–10. Cf. *Yahuda MSS. 13.3*, ff. 6–6ʳ and *17.1*, ff. 6ʳ and 8ʳ, two sets of notes from Ovid, Cicero, Dionysius of Halicarnassus, Plutarch, Tacitus, Augustine, and two moderns, Lipsius and Casaubon, on vestal worship. Cf. also *Yahuda MS. 41*, f. 26 and *New College MS. 361.3*, f. 34.

51. *Yahuda MS. 41*, ff. 3–4.

52. *Yahuda MS. 41*, f. 6.

53. *Keynes MS. 5*, f. V. This manuscript on the prophetic language appears to date from the early 1680s.

54. *Yahuda MS. 17.3*, f. 11.

55. *Yahuda MS. 41*, f. 7.

56. *Yahuda MS. 41*, ff. 9–10ᵛ. Cf. *Yahuda MSS. 16.2*, ff. 44, 57, 67, 69; *17.2*, f. 21ᵛ; *17.3*, ff. 14–15.

57. *Yahuda MS. 17.3*, f. 8.

58. *Yahuda MS. 17.3*, f. 12.

59. *Yahuda MS. 41*, f. 11.

60. *New College MS. 361.3*, f. 32. It appears to me that this manuscript dated from the second decade of the eighteenth century.

61. *Yahuda MSS. 17.2*, ff. 20ᵛ, 21; *41*, f. 26.

62. *Yahuda MSS. 17.3*, f. 10; *41*, f. 2ᵛ.

63. *Yahuda MS. 41*, f. 5. Cf. *Yahuda MS. 17.3*, f. 12.

64. *Keynes MS. 3*, p. 27.

65. *Yahuda MS. 15.3*, f. 57.

66. *Keynes MS. 3*, p. 1.

67. *Keynes MS. 3*, pp. 5–7.

68. *Keynes MS. 3*, p. 35.

69. *Yahuda MS. 15.5*, f. 91.

70. *Yahuda MS. 7.2p*, n.f.

71. *Keynes MS. 7*, pp. 2–3 (printed in McLachlan, ed. *Theological Manuscripts*, p. 52). Cf. a sheet with nine "Propositions"; *Keynes MS. 3*, pp. 17–18 (*Theological Manuscripts*, pp. 28–31).

72. *Yahuda MSS. 1.1*, ff. 1–10; *10.3*, f. 27ᵛ.

73. See *Yahuda MS. 15.3*, ff. 45–46 for one particularly full one from the period after 1715. Cf. *Yahuda MSS. 15.3*, ff. 58, 66ᵛ; *15.4*, ff. 67–68; *15.5*, ff. 87, 90ᵛ, 95ᵛ, 96–98; *15.7*, f. 108; *Keynes MSS. 3*, pp. 43–45; *11* (*Theological Manuscripts*, pp. 44–47).

74. Matthew Tindal, *Christianity as Old as the Creation: or the Gospel, a Republication of the Religion of Nature*, (London, 1731—not the first edition, which appeared in 1730). See especially pp. 7–8, 11, 17–18, 322, and 348.

75. Samuel Clarke, *The Works of Samuel Clarke, D.D. Late Rector of St. James Westminister*, 4 vols., (London, 1738), *2*, 666. The *Discourse* occupies pp. 579–733 of vol. 2. In it, see especially in this connection pp. 597–598, 605–607, 652–656, 659–680. For the same conception, see also the following sermons in vols. 1 and 2: XXVI, XXIX, XXX, XXXI, LXXVIII, CXL, CXLI.

76. *Yahuda MS. 16.2*, f. 45ᵛ.

77. Newton to Bentley, 10 December 1692; *Correspondence, 3*, 233.

II

Secularization in British Thought, 1730–1789: Some Landmarks

DAVID SPADAFORA

I t would be natural to expect the history of secularization in eighteenth-century Britain to have received considerable attention. After all, it was then and there that modern industrial society first began to emerge, a type of society that ultimately played a significant role in the increasingly secular orientation of later Europeans. And the historical analysis of secularization was actually invented by students of the eighteenth-century mind, such as Lecky, Bury, and Robertson.[1] Nevertheless, social historians have not begun to do for Georgian Britain what Michel Vovelle, in particular, has done for *ancien régime* France: to examine in detail the degree to which "de-Christianization" manifested itself in the life of the common people.[2] Nor have intellectual historians explored secularizing trends in the world view of educated, literate Englishmen and Scots of the period with nearly so much care as has been devoted to the French philosophes, except insofar as Sir Leslie Stephen and his successors have made repeated forays into the thicket of the deist controversy.[3]

To map the first of these two largely uncharted territories would demand extensive local research on such topics as church attendance patterns, with a view to pursuing the historical background to K. S. Inglis's claim that staying away from church or chapel was already a well-established habit among many urban working-class Britons by the Victorian period.[4] From circumstantial evidence, it does appear likely that anticlericalism ran higher in the eighteenth century than at any time since the Lollards;[5] but whether anticlericalism was a cause—or even a symptom—of de-Christianization remains to be seen.

As for the second unmapped area, the place of secularization in the opinions of Georgian intellectuals and their reading public, several landmarks can be established for the decades from the 1730s through the 1780s. This period—

the high eighteenth century—lay between the Augustan and Romantic eras, between deism (the number of whose adherents has often been exaggerated) and the intellectual reaction produced by the French Revolution (the significance of which should not be underestimated). It was an age permeated in many respects by Lockeanism and Newtonianism, and it coincided with the height of the philosophe movement in France, a movement still appropriately depicted as one in which a "whole complex of ideas and experiences, usually lumped together in the slippery word 'secularization,' came together. . . ."[6]

For the purpose of identifying the intellectual landmarks referred to, this elusive term "secularization" will here be taken to mean the "growing tendency . . . to do without religion, or to try to do without religion," as a mode of understanding life. More specifically, it means the gradual removal of theology and traditional theological explanations from one sphere of knowledge after another; the setting up, within each of these spheres, of a nontheological orientation and autonomous explanatory "laws"; and ultimately the confinement of theology to matters of religious faith alone, excluding even morals. Even more narrowly, the "axiom, *'miracles do not happen,'* comes near the heart" of secularization.[7]

On this basis, secularization may be said to have become a notable though not a dominating feature of the British intellectual landscape by the high eighteenth century. It was more visible in Scotland than in England, less prominent in either than among the French philosophes.

Its degree of prominence can be judged, to begin with, by recognizing the declining but still important role of theology in the British intellectual world as a whole. For centuries, theology had been queen of the sciences, the single focus around which all other spheres of knowledge revolved. This system had undergone significant changes by the early seventeenth century, when a few men like Bacon and Galileo announced that the study of the natural world ought to have an existence independent of the things that are faith's. But Galileo was still willing to concede a "regal preeminence" to revealed theology, in that it "excels in dignity all the subjects which compose the other sciences." And Bacon considered it one of the two fundamental parts of knowledge ("philosophy" being the other), the part that is in fact "the haven and sabbath of all human contemplations." He also argued that "all knowledge is to be limited by religion," and that just "as to seek divinity in philosophy is to seek the living among the dead, so to seek philosophy in divinity is to seek the dead among the living." At the end of the century, the decline of theological centrality was far enough advanced for Locke to reverse Bacon's disclaimers. He found it necessary to insist that of the three categories into which he divided all science, the first—*"natural Philosophy"* or the "Knowledge of Things, as they are in their own proper Beings, their Constitutions, Properties, and Operations"— concerned "not only Matter, and Body, but Spirits also" (such as God himself and angels). For his second and third categories—ethics and logic—he made no attempt to establish a direct theological connection.[8]

By the time of the French Enlightenment, it was possible for d'Alembert— in the scheme of human knowledge he prepared in 1751 for that great philosophe enterprise, the *Encyclopédie*—to subordinate theology to philosophy, in a conscious modification of Bacon's classification. This view, so typical of the French philosophes, was echoed across the Channel in another dictionary that appeared during the same year. The compiler of that work, one John Barrow (fl. 1735–1756), made it clear in his long prefatory remarks that theology was to be included *within* philosophy and metaphysics. The point was underscored by the fact that Barrow's synoptic listing of the major arts and sciences covered in the dictionary contained no mention of theology. Similarly, although the Scottish *Encyclopedia Britannica* (first published 1771) followed Locke's tripartite division of science, none of the three categories was any longer presented as having a direct concern with spiritual beings.[9]

Barrow and the *Britannica* notwithstanding, however, by and large d'Alembert's British contemporaries went less far than he in circumscribing the intellectual role of theology, even though that role did in general hold somewhat less importance for them than it had for their predecessors in the seventeenth century and before. For example, most lexicographers continued to define it as the science—rather than merely the study—of God and the divinely revealed word, but their definitions did not specifically assign it a central place in the realm of knowledge.[10] Then too the ongoing warfare over ancient versus modern preeminence in the arts and sciences focused almost exclusively on attainments in secular knowledge and activities. This had not been the case as recently as the turn of the century, when two leading participants in the controversy, Sir William Temple and William Wotton, took opposite sides on the question of whether early or more recent Christians were superior in theological learning. In those rare instances when theology did become a battleground in this war, the conclusion that the moderns must have greater religious knowledge than the ancients was reached as a mere corollary to a general principle: in modern times, "men's understandings are more refined, and their researches into truth more enlarged, than ever they were before!" Indeed, those who believed in the ongoing progress of religious knowledge tended to support that belief by analogy to advances in secular learning, not the reverse.[11]

The declining fortunes of theology in British intellectual life is visible in yet another way. Throughout the eighteenth century, religious works remained the largest single category of books published, and not surprisingly so in light of the fact that religious subjects continued to occupy many writers, including some of the best minds of the age, both clerical and lay. Religious controversies evoked outpourings of printed words from men as notable as Joseph Butler, William Warburton, and Richard Watson; collections of sermons still sold well;

recondite topics like eschatology never lacked for scholarly as well as popular commentators; and even such an extreme sceptic as David Hume found matters of faith important enough to write about them at length and with considerable circumspection. Nevertheless, the publication of theological and devotional works appears not to have kept pace with the expansion of the market for other types of literature. Works on history, travel, politics, and even science found an ever-wider audience, and so above all did novels and periodic essays. In short, contemporary readers "had increasingly secular tastes,"[12] and there were plenty of contemporary writers willing and able to satisfy those shifting tastes. Just as the expansion of leisure in this period (especially among the middle class) gave rise to an increasing preoccupation with such entertainments as theatergoing, organized horse-racing, and public performances of nonsacred music, so the related demand for new kinds of literature was associated with the emergence of an independent "profession of English letters" whose members specialized in secular works.[13]

The extent to which theology was losing its prestige in England and in Scotland can be measured by the careers and attitudes of two men, Joseph Priestley (1733–1804) and Adam Ferguson (1723–1816). For their era, both were "advanced" thinkers, the former being a Unitarian and political radical and the latter a member of the Scottish Enlightenment. Both taught for some years at highly respected institutions (the dissenting academy in Warrington and Edinburgh University, respectively) and wrote notable books on history and political science, among other subjects. Both were trained to be clergymen. But whereas Ferguson left the ministry for obscure reasons at age thirty-one, Priestley continued to preach and to tend congregations the rest of his life.

Priestley once observed that theology was his "original and proper province," for which he had a "justifiable predilection" because of the "superior dignity and importance of theological studies to any other whatever." Coming as it does at the beginning of one of the major scientific works written by the discoverer of oxygen, this remark serves to illustrate Priestley's priorities. He wrote at greater length on religious subjects than on all others combined, although he admitted that natural philosophy had, "perhaps, but too strong charms" for him, and that during at least one stage of his life he spent most of his waking hours in the laboratory. Still, even his scientific labors were inseparable from the concerns of faith. Like most of the seventeenth-century virtuosi before him, he wanted to be a "man who, from a supreme veneration for the God of nature"—the governor as well as the creator of the world—"takes pleasure in contemplating his *works*. . . ." More than this, he claimed that a proper spiritual attitude was psychologically essential to scientific achievement: "religion and piety," he wrote, "tend to cure the mind of envy, jealousy, conceit, and every other mean passion, which both disgrace the lovers of science, and retard the progress of it, by laying an undue bias upon the mind, and diverting it from the calm pursuit of truth."[14]

So while Priestley intended never to neglect science, he also tried "to keep it in its proper place." This meant not devoting himself so much "to the study of the laws which govern *this* world, as to lose sight of the subservience of this world, and of all things in it, to another and better. . . ." For men must think it "of infinitely more moment to discover whether there be a future, and especially an endless, life after this, and how to secure a happy lot in that future life, than to make the best provision possible for ourselves in this life, which is the ultimate object of all natural philosophy."[15] In Priestley's case, secularization clearly remained circumscribed within rather definite boundaries.

For Ferguson, by contrast, its limits were broader. Although he remained an active communicant in the Scottish church after leaving ecclesiastical life, the volumes he wrote during his later career as a professor almost never touched on theological subjects. They were concerned, instead, with the "science of man" and with history, and none of them relied on traditional Christian doctrines. This was true even in his moral philosophy, where he tended to equate virtue with the most complete development of the rational faculties of man rather than with adherence to a code of judgment formation and behavior laid down by divine ordinance. On the one occasion when he discussed a religious issue—immortality and afterlife—at length, he did so in a way that could hardly be considered orthodox. And that discussion laid down a principle which would have made Priestley wince: "Happiness is to be valued more for the present, than for the future. . . ." As with most of the other Scottish luminaries, Ferguson's intellectual orientation was this-worldly, not otherworldly; anthropocentric, not theocentric. Despite his Calvinist background, theology and Christianity had lost much of their hold over his mature thought.[16] In this he was similar to the philosophes of France. But unlike them he did not take the next step of arguing against revealed religion. Nor did any other leader of the Scottish Enlightenment except Hume.

The difference between English and Scottish patterns of secularization, as reflected by Priestley and Ferguson, reappears in the context of a second landmark—attitudes toward the history of religion. The writing of purely "profane" history (as opposed to "profane" chronicle) can be traced back at least as far as the political narratives of the *quattrocento*. While this type of historiography continued to develop throughout the early modern period, sacred history maintained its fascination for Europeans, so much so that even after Bossuet there were those who, like Claude Fleury, Charles Rollin, and Sir Isaac Newton, tried to make the course of profane events fit into an overarching providential scheme.[17] Yet by the mid-eighteenth century, in the hands of such philosophes as Voltaire the study of secular history broke free of its remaining ties to theology, dispensing with divine causation and taking all peoples for its proper province, regardless of their lack of connection to the Judeo-Christian tradition. Once this independent status was attained, no subject could escape the piercing gaze of critical, secular historians, not even religion itself, which helps to explain the widespread Enlightenment attempt to elucidate the origins of religion on a scientific basis in anticipation of modern anthropology and sociology.[18]

In Britain, the most aggressive and—to many contemporaries—objectionable examples of that effort were Hume's *Natural History of Religion*, the very title of which brought matters of faith down into the realm of the mundane, and Gibbon's even more notorious chapters in the *Decline and Fall of the Roman Empire* on the rise of early Christianity. If Gibbon really believed that "an age of light and liberty would receive without scandal, an enquiry into the *human* causes of the progress and establishment of Christianity,"[19] he seriously misapprehended the commitment still felt to the traditional view that the true religion, at least, had been *divinely* founded. The degree of this commitment is illustrated by his need to write a vindication of the offending chapters, in response to criticism from orthodox circles.

Still, Gibbon's book had good sales, and some men of the time—mostly Scots—applied his kind of human-centered analysis to the evolution of religion in general (if not Christianity in particular) with impunity. Thus, Adam Smith traced the beginnings of religious systems to the primitive mental capacity of savages. Being unable to discover the causal links connecting the "seemingly disjointed appearances of nature," he argued, early men ascribed every event that did not seem completely regular (such as comets and fierce storms) to the superhuman "direction of some invisible and designing power." From this source sprang polytheism, with its "intelligent, though invisible beings, . . . gods, daemons, witches, genii, fairies." Smith's friend, Henry Home, Lord Kames, carried this "conjectural history" of religion further. He divided primitive religion into six stages, from a polytheism in which all deities were malevolent through various polytheisms with both evil and good gods to a monotheism whose supreme being is perfect in every way. To Kames, the gradual transition from stage to stage was the result of two developments: improvements in human mental faculties and knowledge of the natural world, which "lead by sure steps, though slow, to one God"; and the substitution of the "social affections" for barbarous behavior, by means of which benevolence itself becomes known and therefore transferrable to that God. Revelation was not cited as a factor in the emergence of monotheism.[20]

Most educated Englishmen would have rejected this interpretation, just as John Wesley condemned the new kind of historiography that was "excluding the Creator from governing the world." But something of the spirit of Kames's views can be detected even among Anglican clerics. In 1751, James Fortescue (1716–1777), a Northamptonshire rector, published a long poem of which part was devoted to sketching the broad outlines of religious history. There he traced the rise of what he called "Sacred Science," beginning with fable (the "dawning of Science"), proceeding to the Christian gospel (the "completion of Science"), and culminating in the use of reason to examine the "credentials of religion." As he portrayed it, the development of theology manifested a notable trend: the gradual elimination of superstition and ignorance in favor of submission—through intellectual conviction—to the authority of revelation. By harmonizing God's word with man's reason in this regard, Fortescue to some extent anticipated Lessing's notion of a three-step "education of the human race." In a different context, Richard Watson (1737–1816), the very liberal Bishop of Llandaff, exhibited a similar tendency to go halfway toward a secular history of religion. Remarking in 1788 on a proposal to proselytize in India, he contended that Christianity would continue to spread across the globe, but by means of the civilizing extension of Western commerce and, especially, science rather than by the activity of missionaries. To support his opinion, he noted that

> the Romans, the Athenians, the Corinthians and others, were highly civilized, far advanced in the rational use of their intellectual faculties, and they all, at length, exchanged Paganism for Christianity; the same change will take place in other countries, as they become enlightened by the progress of European literature, and become capable of justly estimating the weight of [its] historical evidence. . . .

To Watson, the propagation of the true faith depended as much on the self-enlightenment of mankind as on initial divine illumination, since that faith was "a rational religion."[21]

Watson was no Gibbon, nor even a Kames, because he still preserved a place for revelation. This was the primary distinction between liberal Anglican and Scottish Enlightenment views on religious history, and it becomes quite clear if we compare two prominent clergymen from opposite sides of the Tweed. Edmund Law (1703–1787) was an extreme Latitudinarian who served in ecclesiastical posts in Cumberland before becoming Knightbridge Professor of Moral Philosophy at Cambridge and later bishop of Carlisle. In 1745, he wrote a book entitled *Considerations on the Theory of Religion* (published in seven continually revised editions by 1784), designed to refute one of the potent arguments of some deists that traditional Christianity could be objected to on the grounds of its lack of universality. His thesis was that God had revealed himself gradually over the ages, in a series of increasingly sophisticated "dispensations." From the time of Adam to Christ, each of these was "delivered in its proper *season*, . . . as soon as it became fully necessary," and was "as perfect as it could be

supposed to have been, considering the season in which it was delivered. . . ."
Underlying this manner of proceeding was a plan of accommodating revelation
to the changing circumstances and advancing intellectual abilities of man:

> Without some tolerable degree of learning and civility, men do not seem qualified
> to reap the greatest benefit of the *Christian* institution; and together with these,
> they generally do receive it; the same human means serving to improve their
> notions in religion, which help to enlarge their knowledge in all other subjects;
> and at the same time directing, and in a natural way, enabling them to arrive at,
> the most perfect dispensation of it.

For that reason, Law believed, religious knowledge "held pace in general with
all other knowledge, from the beginning," and would continue to do so in the
future, as human minds become "much farther opened and enlarged, their
reason more freely exercised, in this great *mystery* of divine love."[22]

In essence, Law looked at the development of theological understanding as
following a divine program that was itself conditioned by the human situation.
The whole amounted to the interaction of revelation with mankind's secular
evolution. An almost identical view was adopted in a youthful sermon by William Robertson (1721–1793), then pastor of Gladsmuir in East Lothian and new
leader of the progressive "Moderate" party in the Church of Scotland. When he
came to write his famous histories, however, he no longer spoke of religious
history as a scheme of "temporary and incompleat" dispensations serving "to
introduce that concluding and perfect revelation [Christianity], which would
declare the whole council of God to man." Rather, by then the origin of religion
was for him the result not of a "dark and mysterious" lesson from God but
merely, as Kames and Smith held, of the barbarous proclivity to ascribe the
"extraordinary occurrences in nature to the influence of invisible beings." Instead of attributing the Reformation to the dawning of a more perfect revelation,
he traced it to spreading secular knowledge, an increasingly bold "spirit of
innovation," and a disgust with the haughty and hypocritical clergy.[23] In this
leader of the Scottish Enlightenment and important ecclesiastical official, the
outlook of sacred history had given way before a concern with secular processes,
as it never did in the case of Law.

The pattern that we have seen emerging—some secularization among the
English, more among the Scots—also marks a third landmark, this one concerning the nature of man. During the Middle Ages, the prevailing view of human
nature amounted to a combination of pessimism with a modicum of optimism.
From the Pauline-Augustinian tradition came a strong emphasis on the deprav-
ity of fallen man, his failure to will the good, his inability to attain by himself
the true ends of existence. Tempering to a degree the gloom associated with
original sin was a quasi-Pelagian sacramentalism, focusing on the possibility of
salvation through divine grace. The positive side of this outlook was enhanced

by the reawakened classical humanism of the Renaissance, with its new feeling for the dignity of man; the negative side by the Reformation, which mainly followed the Augustinian line. In the seventeenth century, Pascal's finding of both greatness and wretchedness in man remained characteristic of Western European thought as a whole. By then there were "secular Augustinians" (such as La Rochefoucauld, Hobbes, and Boyle), who could paint man in dark hues with or without direct reference to the Fall, and "Promethean" optimists (Bacon and his followers, in particular), who saw salvation at least partially in science and technology. These were hardly majority views as yet, and for the most part the element of wretchedness in man still seemed stronger than his real or potential greatness. But a more secular, sanguine anthropology had clearly begun to gain strength.[24]

As for eighteenth-century Britain, it has been asserted that the Augustinian perspective on human nature "was that in which Swift, Johnson, and most of their contemporaries were educated and to which they subscribed."[25] This theory has considerable truth in it with regard to the early decades of the century, at least if we concentrate on the Augustan poets and satirists. It generally does not apply, however, to the period beginning in the 1730s. Certainly, clear evidence for it lies in Wesley and the entire Evangelical movement, in Johnson's work and life, and in a number of other figures of note in the British republic of letters. Yet a far larger group of thinkers and writers had reached a more optimistic and more secular position on the question of human nature: a modified environmentalism.

The environmentalists' mentor was Locke, whose sensationalism received a practical application in his *Some Thoughts Concerning Education* (1693). That book contained an admission that, because each child is unique and born with certain natural tendencies in temper, constitution, and ability, its mind "can hardly be totally alter'd, and transform'd into the contrary." Nonetheless, within these limits there is a great deal that nurture can do. In fact, proclaimed Locke, "of all the Men we meet with, Nine Parts of Ten are what they are, Good or Evil, useful or not, by their Education." This being the case, education can instill proper habits in the child and promote virtue—its true goal—"by Custom, made easy and familiar by an *early* Practice." The same Locke who, in the *Essay Concerning Human Understanding*, denied the existence of innate ideas has here made original sin disappear, and with it the need for divine grace. Or rather, he has substituted education for grace, thereby transferring to the human sphere the power (and the responsibility) for making men good.[26]

After about 1730, this change became immensely influential in thinking about the nature of man, and not just in Britain. Most of the French philosophes adopted something like Locke's position, while Helvétius pressed the claims of nurture so far that he believed men to be nothing more than the products of their education. Such an extreme view had few British supporters until William

Godwin's *Political Justice* (1793). Nor did many Britons join Locke and the philosophes in rejecting outright the doctrine of original sin.[27] They were generally content to leave the question of the Fall to one side, and to point out the other ramifications of Locke's brand of environmentalism.

Of those who did so, a substantial number were psychological theorists engaged in propounding the newly popular principle of the association of ideas. Associationism began with the premise that ideas ultimately come from sensations, and it went on to suggest that simple ideas tend to get linked together by repetition, so as to form complex ideas of all types and even the passions. The implications of such a psychology—control sensations and associations and you control mental and moral operations—quickly became clear. Like most Scottish intellectuals of the age, George Turnbull (1698–1748), who taught at Aberdeen University before serving as chaplain to the Prince of Wales, believed in the existence of an innate moral sense. But he also held that the contents of the mind depend very largely on externally received sensations, and that the process of association affects all or nearly all ideas. For these reasons, he could say that mental tempers, abilities, and dispositions "may in a great measure be changed by our own proper care," which "only requires, that we should give due attention to the natural connexions [i.e., associations] on which they depend. . . ." Thereby, even the moral sense "is greatly improveable by instruction and exercise," so that "it is in our power to change any temper we may have contracted, and to form ourselves to any desireable one." Given these considerations, Turnbull announced that men "are made for progress in virtue" through proper utilization of the principle of association, that *"law of improvement to perfection."*[28]

Abraham Tucker (1705–1774), a Surrey squire, reached similar conclusions about the significance of the association—or, as he sometimes called it, "translation"—of ideas in his *Light of Nature Pursued*, a massive treatise on psychology, moral philosophy, and religion that appeared between 1768 and 1778. He argued that associations become habitual over time and give rise to tastes, inclinations, sentiments, the moral sense, and virtues and vices; in fact, he stated flatly that "virtue . . . is a habit." But the mind can be gradually diverted from one customary track to another by controlling associations, can "like a tender twig . . . be brought to grow in any shape by continual bending." So men are able and ought to cultivate good habits and avoid bad ones, producing "progress in virtue" through their own efforts and by exposing themselves to appropriate instruction, exhortation, and examples. The goal of this moral advancement should be "the temporal happiness of our fellow-creatures" and, in the end, the attainment of "the bliss of heaven."[29]

Tucker and Turnbull were only two of the many writers who promulgated associationism, yet their conception of man as a being capable of making himself good without divine aid was representative of them all. And of most commentators on education in the narrower sense: pedagogy too seemed to be a fertile field for the application of environmental conditioning. In some instances, this application was presented as directly related to the principle of association. George Chapman (1723–1806), a Scottish schoolmaster, contended that "the passions receive their direction, in a great measure, from the ideas which we have learned to associate, and the opinions we have formed." Therefore, since "education is known to have a powerful influence in forming the tempers and characters of men," parents and teachers should endeavor not only to strengthen a child's general sense of right and wrong, but also in particular to prevent him from forming "those false associations of ideas which are so destructive of human happiness." For the mind is, by its constitution, "highly susceptible of improvement," and this improvement "is closely connected with the perfection and happiness of mankind." Likewise, David Fordyce (1711–1751), another Aberdeen professor, recognized the importance of "those *early Associations of Ideas*, we form in the first Part of our Life" to the later habits, tempers, and manners of men. "It must, therefore," he wrote, "be an Affair of the utmost Importance in Education, to settle just *Associations* in the Minds of Youth, and to break and disunite wrong ones. The doing this aright, I take to be the grand Art or Engine of *moral Culture*." It could lead, Fordyce believed, to "a sober, manly, virtuous Youth," in confirmation of his thesis that the business of education is, "like a second Creation, to improve Nature" by "*unfolding and exercising those* NATURAL *and* MORAL *Powers with which Man is endued*. . . ."[30]

Not all pedagogical writers of the time placed so great an emphasis on associationist psychology. Still, even among those who did not, education continually appeared in the same light. As the famous dissenter and political radical Richard Price expressed it, "On the bent given to our minds as they open and expand, depends their subsequent fate; and on the general management of education depend the honour and dignity of our species." He added that God has left so much "to depend on the turn given to the mind in early life" that there may remain a secret in education that, when discovered, "will contribute more than any thing to the amendment of mankind. . . ." Conversely, in the words of James Wadham Whitchurch (1749?–1776), a young Anglican clergyman, "most of the Miseries of Human Life are the Effects of a wrong Education."[31] To such educational theorists as these, man seemed to be very much in control of his own destiny, for good or ill.

While the environmentalist stance was adopted by both Englishmen and Scots, the anthropology of the former contained a more substantial religious component than that of the latter. English writers on psychology and education made the possibility of human control over mental and moral processes subservient to a higher—and traditional—end: the achievement of eternal life with God. There is no clearer illustration of this pervasive tendency than David

Hartley's well-known *Observations on Man* (1749). Hartley was a physician and devout Anglican layman who probably did more than anyone else to develop the principle of association, which he called "the general Law, according to which the intellectual World is framed and conducted." His medical learning and interests, along with some hints derived from Newton's *Opticks*, encouraged him to account for the operation of associations on physiological grounds, and the resulting theory of "vibrations" in turn led him to a materialist, mechanistic, and necessitarian view of man. Despite this position, which the philosophes La Mettrie and Holbach would have applauded, Hartley was an essentially religious thinker. To him, the goal of life was "Happiness in being united to God" or "perfect Self-annihilation, and Resting in God as our Centre," which was attainable by transforming sensuality into spirituality through the associative mechanism. "It is of the utmost consequence to Morality and Religion," he wrote,

> that the Affections and Passions should be analysed into their simple compounding Parts, by reversing the Steps of the Associations which concur to form them. For thus we may learn how to cherish and improve good ones, check and root out such as are mischievous and immoral, and how to suit our Manner of Life, in some tolerable Measure, to our Religious Wants. And as this holds, in respect of Persons of all Ages, so it is particularly true, and worthy of Consideration, in respect of Children and Youth.

Education, then, like association itself, can be "the Instrument of Salvation, temporal and eternal, to Multitudes," if it is geared to spiritual concerns so as to focus the passions and affections on "the pure Love of God."[32]

For most of the Scots by contrast, it was temporal "salvation" alone that mattered. In his *Treatise of Human Nature*, the young David Hume agreed with Hartley and others that association was a central law in the mental world, parallel to the law of gravitation in the physical, and he prided himself on having shown its importance. Along with this brand of psychology went acceptance of the basic elements of contemporary environmentalism. By far the "greatest part of our reasonings, with all our actions and passions," he said, "can be deriv'd from nothing but custom and habit," so that habit is really a "powerful means of reforming the mind, and implanting in it good dispositions and inclinations." Considerations such as these prompted Hume to remark on the great uses to which education could be put. Men "are generally contented to acquiesce implicitly in those [social] establishments, however new, into which their early education has thrown them." Hence, "general virtue and good morals in a state, which are so requisite to happiness, . . . must proceed entirely from the virtuous education of youth. . . ." And because the sense of justice "arises artificially, tho' necessarily from education, and human conventions," it can be enlarged only by "private education and instruction" and by public praise and condemnation. Not for nothing do parents "inculcate on their children, from the earliest infancy, the principles of probity, and teach them to regard the observance of those rules, by which society is maintain'd, as worthy and honourable. . . ." As these comments indicate, when Hume noted the "mighty influence" that education, custom, and example have in "turning the mind" toward pursuits productive of human happiness,[33] the happiness that he meant was to be found in private life and social concord, not in eternal bliss. Like Jeremy Bentham later, Hume and the Scottish Enlightenment were concerned solely with the secular effects of environmental conditioning.

We come finally to a fourth landmark, inscribed with the heading "miracles." This word is indeed central to the historical analysis of secularization, demarcating as it does supernaturalism from naturalism, religion from science. In the eighteenth century, it was a fighting word, arousing the passions of Christians, deists, and atheists alike. That it could have become such a focus of contention was due to the meaning invested by the Scientific Revolution in another term: "law of nature." The concept of immutable laws in the operation of the physical world is, at base, antithetical to the concept of miracles, except to the degree that *both* such laws *and* miraculous occurrences are held to originate in the will of an omnipotent being. Seventeenth-century scientists did not ordinarily accept this antithesis, precisely because they still conceived of omnipotence as the chief characteristic of God. Just as the all-powerful deity had imposed certain laws on the universe, thought the virtuosi, so he could have imposed others by an equally autonomous act of will—and so he could override any current law by a "special providence" or miracle, if it suited him.

The physicotheologian Thomas Burnet, for example, did not want to "flie to miracles" to explain physical events that are "otherwise intelligible from second Causes." But, he contended, "the other extream is worse than this," for to deny all miracles is not only to deny revealed religion but also to ignore the fact that along with

> the ordinary Providence of God in the ordinary course of Nature, there is doubtless an extraordinary Providence. . . . This, methinks, besides all other proof from the Effects, is very rational and necessary in it self; for it would be a limitation of the Divine Power and Will so to be bound up to second causes, as never to use, upon occasion, an extraordinary influence or direction. . . .

Similarly, Robert Boyle always preserved a place in his conception of the operation of the universe for miracles and other divine suspensions of the laws of nature. Even Newton, as is well known, suggested that the solar system might occasionally require a renewal by its creator. Defending him against Leibniz on this and other issues, Samuel Clarke in 1715 rejected the analogy of the universe to "a great machine, going on without the interposition of God, as a clock continues to go without the assistance of a clockmaker. . . ." For this notion "tends, (under the pretence of making God a *supra-mundane intelligence*,) to exclude providence and God's government in reality out of the world." Such views were quite normal in the late seventeenth and early eighteenth century, and the recording of special or extraordinary providences remained widespread.[34]

By their very success, however, the scientists helped to put belief in miracles on the defensive. They described a universe that did in fact appear, like an unattended clock, to observe the most regular kinds of laws, thereby making divine interruptions seem unlikely. Moreover, these laws had such inherent perfection, in themselves and in their concatenation (as Newton synthesized them), that their creator began to be assigned more and more the characteristic of wisdom and rationality, instead of omnipotence. God became bound to his own system, because of its perfection. Where this change in outlook occurred, miracles lost their *raison d'être*, as Voltaire made clear:

> A miracle is the violation of mathematical, divine, immutable, eternal laws. By this very statement, a miracle is a contradiction in terms. A law cannot be immutable and violable at the same time. . . . [I]t is impossible for the infinitely wise Being to make laws in order to violate them. They say he might unsettle his machine, but only to make it go better; however, it is clear that, being God, he made this immense machine as best he could: if he had seen some imperfections resulting from the nature of the material, he would have attended to it in the beginning; so he will never change anything in it.
>
> Moreover, God cannot do anything without reason; now what reason could make him temporarily disfigure his own work?

The philosophes' "always implicit and often explicit repudiation of miracles" received perhaps its most revealing expression in this passage, which symbolizes their critical and naturalistic spirit, their penchant for a "disenchanted" universe.[35]

A similar naturalism permeated the Scottish Enlightenment. To the extent that its members believed at all in the divine guidance of the world, that belief was typified by the words of James Dunbar (d. 1798), yet one more Aberdeen academic: "we observe the determinations of heaven to coincide with a regular and established order of second causes." Smith made the same point with the standard watchmaker analogy, arguing that, in the universe, means are "adjusted with the nicest artifice to the ends they are intended to produce," by "the wisdom of God." The famous principle of the "invisible hand" was a conception of general providence without traditional Christian connotations and leaving no room for divine intervention. As Kames asked, "Is it not obvious, that the great

God of heaven and earth governs the world by inflexible laws, from which he never can swerve in any case, because they are the best possible in every case?" Even Robertson, who had stronger connections to established religion than any of the others, referred disparagingly to the "superstition" of those who look for "particular and extraordinary acts of power under the divine administration." And Hume, of course, constructed a more complete and sophisticated philosophical case against the possibility of miracles, which prompted a great furor.[36]

That furor itself testifies that miracles had many proponents in high eighteenth-century Britain. It is erroneous to suggest that an empirically minded, naturalistic outlook on the world grew up among the members of the British social and political elite between 1680 and 1720 only to be largely rejected by them in the second half of the century, meanwhile finding a new home among the lower orders of society, the dissenters, and others outside the "establishment."[37] In fact, the shift in the "search for causation" from the "providential world" of the earlier seventeenth century to the "observable world" associated with the Enlightenment was far from complete in the age of Newton, as we have seen. Nor was supernaturalism later confined to Anglican ecclesiastical circles. It could be found among nonconformist leaders like Philip Doddridge (1702–1751), head of the dissenting academy at Northampton. He observed that "Miracles are possible in general, . . . and possible in any given instance, when the wisdom of God does not require that the course of nature should be preserved. . . ." David Hartley, a good specimen of the contemporary scientific spirit, declared that "If any one should affirm or think, as some Persons seem to do, that a Miracle is impossible, let him consider, that this is denying God's Omnipotence and even maintaining, that Man is the supreme Agent in the Universe." The connection between omnipotence and special providences also surfaced in the thought of Thomas Hartley (1709–1784), a Northamptonshire Anglican rector, who despised "that irreligious kind of philosophy, which teaches men now-a-days to explain away God's warnings and judgments into unmeaning effects from natural causes. . . ." Men should not "give laws to God," for he "is not bound by human prescription, but is pleased at times to vary his proceedings from the ordinary course of things" by giving "notices of his will in nature."[38]

But in spite of such forthright statements, the believers in miracles were retreating somewhat before the forces of naturalism, even in England. For one thing, the work of the scientists began to take its toll. In light of the ongoing progress of natural philosophy, might it not eventually be possible to explain apparent miracles as simply the effects of laws of nature not previously recognized? David Hartley responded to this question cautiously, saying that it amounted to "a mere conjecture": "Since we do not yet know what these true Laws of Matter and Motion are, we cannot presume to say whether all

Phaenomena are reducible to them, or not." It could turn out that supposed divine interpositions "may not be at all contrary to [nature's] Fixedness and Immutability," or that the laws include "the Instrumentality of Beings superior to us."[39] Even to admit the possibility of the first of these outcomes, however, amounted to a hedging of bets, based on scientific advances.

A retreat of an equally significant sort came in reaction to the blows delivered by the deists and Hume to the evidentiary foundation of miracles, both individually and collectively. Faced with these attacks, orthodoxy contracted its perimeters to defend only the essential: the scripture miracles. This was certainly true of the three major replies to Hume, made by two Anglican clergymen, William Adams (1706–1789) and John Douglas (1721–1807), and the Scottish minister George Campbell (1719–1796). To be sure, each took pains to argue for the *possibility* of an extraordinary providence at any time, and the two Englishmen explicitly based this argument on the characteristic of divine all-powerfulness. As Douglas wrote, "Who would not have thought that an Almighty Being could produce every possibility, and consequently depart from *his productions in the usual course of nature?* A person of a plain ordinary understanding would have thought, that the very idea of Omnipotence implied the power of doing this. . . . " But they were all most concerned only with the interruptions of the natural order described in the Bible. Douglas thought he could determine the "period, beyond which we may be certain that miraculous powers did not subsist," that period being the age of the apostles. Along the same lines, Campbell considered it likely that "in the infancy of the world, . . . interpositions should be more frequent and requisite, till nature, attaining a certain maturity, those laws and that constitution should be established which we now experience."[40] In effect, these apologists for Christianity were limiting the existence of the miraculous to times remote from modernity and, therefore, despite their protestations about the potentialities of divine power, were making their own universe seem entirely law-bound in its operation.

This backing away from supernaturalism cannot disguise the fact that English intellectuals generally remained more accepting of miracles than the dominant Scottish thinkers of the day. The divergent attitudes manifested themselves even within the scientific community itself. William Whiston (1667–1752) was a Newtonian and an Arian who, for a time, held the Lucasian Chair of Mathematics at Cambridge. Throughout his life, he had a substantial interest in physicotheology, publishing *A New Theory of the Earth* (1696) in which he contended that God had originally formed the world along the lines of a great machine, so that secondary causes alone could account for the Flood and the Conflagration. This opinion continued to appear in the last edition of his book that he prepared, as did the general comment that God governs the world without disturbances to the "settled Course of Nature." But although Whiston thought that *"Miracles are not ordinarily to be expected,"* he did not deny that they could occur. In fact, in 1749 he wrote, "I verily believe Providence is, in an extraordinary Degree, now interposing in the Affairs of the World, and beginning to set up the *Millennium. . . .*" The next year two earthquakes shook London, and he delivered a public lecture on them. Many of "our *minute Philosophers,*" he said, "(and very *minute Philosophers* they must be who reason thus) pretend that all this is done by the *Air,* or *Water,* or *Earth,* or *Fire;* that all this is no more than the necessary Effects of natural Causes. . . ." To this interpretation he objected strenuously. In his view, "an higher Agent or Agents are concern'd," so that "Our business therefore, is not here with aerial Vapours, with Sulphur, or Nitre, which are the inanimate Instruments on these occasions, &c. but with the rational Instruments themselves employ'd by God. . . ." These were the "*good Angels,* acting according to the Direction of God himself; or else the *evil Angels,* or *wicked Daemons,* acting according to their own evil Inclinations, by God's Permission. . . ."[11] Obviously, there still was room in the world view of Englishmen, even of an English scientist, for divine interpositions and active higher beings, as well as for regular laws.

This was much less the case with Colin Maclaurin (1698–1746), a mathematician and natural philosopher who popularized Newtonianism while teaching at Edinburgh University. He still talked, like Newton himself, about God's general governance of the universe and the possibility of divine renewals of the physical world; but he never mentioned miracles or angelic beings. He continued to make obeisance in the direction of the Deity's omnipotence, which made the planets rotate from west to east "tho' it is evident . . . that he might have made them move from east to west"; but now the emphasis was more on the "consummate *Wisdom*" and "unbounded *Goodness*" of the creator of "so excellent a system." Indeed, Maclaurin objected to those philosophers who, "under the pretence of magnifying the essential power of the supreme cause, make truth and falsehood entirely to depend on his will," a principle that actually "tends to weaken all science and confound its principles." In brief, while he was not inclined to make God an *intelligentia extramundana*, he insisted forcefully on the fact that the "laws of nature are constant and regular." The resolution of this apparently contradictory position appears in the following passage:

> As we cannot but conceive the universe, as depending on the first cause and chief mover, whom it would be absurd, not to say impious, to exclude from acting in it; so we have some hints of the manner in which he operates in nature, from the laws which we find established in it. Tho' he is the source of all efficacy, yet we find that place is left for second causes to act in subordination to him; and mechanism has its share in carrying on the great scheme of nature.[12]

So while the world does not amount only to matter in motion because there is a "supreme cause," that cause acts in it through mechanical laws. Maclaurin has banished the miraculous without ever explicitly denying miracles.

From the fate of supernaturalism, then, as from attitudes toward theology, human nature, and the history of religion, we may reasonably conclude that secularization was making inroads among the intellectual classes of high eighteenth-century Britain, though less deeply into the English than the Scottish mind. Yet we have only established *some* landmarks; others remain to be found, which will help to refine our generalizations: the whole question of what "happiness" meant, for example, or the connection between politics and religion.

A complete mapping must also detail causes. Why were the British, with rare exceptions, less aggressively secular than the French philosophes? It is not enough to answer that they had had their revolution, while in France criticism of the oppressive establishment inevitably expanded to include not only the church (and the state) but also religion itself. For we must still account for such pronounced secularists as Hume and Gibbon, who hardly lived under oppression, as well as for relatively devout dissenters like Priestley and Price, who suffered real discrimination. Why did secularization go forward at all? Part of the answer lies in purely intellectual factors, in the influence of the new science, travel literature, and the philosophes themselves, and in the challenge of the deists to orthodoxy. But part is also to be found in social considerations, especially the economic changes and technological marvels associated with the preparation for and onset of the Industrial Revolution. Before the Romantics arrived, these developments directed attention in the most powerful way to what *man* could accomplish, apart from heaven. Perhaps it is this factor that explains the difference in degree of secularization between Englishmen and Scots. In relative terms, economic change occurred less rapidly south of the Tweed than north, where the seventeenth century had seen a virtually medieval pattern of life. The sudden leap forward in the Lowlands, where the Scottish Enlightenment centered, undoubtedly stimulated the type of anthropocentric, this-worldly outlook necessary to the secular spirit.

But whatever the precise constellation of factors involved, their combined effect—uneven though it may have been—was surely changing the face of British thought in the age of the Enlightenment.

Notes

1. Owen Chadwick, *The Secularization of the European Mind in the Nineteenth Century* (Cambridge, 1975), 5.

2. Michel Vovelle, *Piété baroque et déchristianisation en Provence au XVIIIe siècle: Les attitudes devant la mort d'après les clauses des testaments* ([Paris], 1973).

3. The emphasis on France can be seen, for example, throughout Peter Gay's by-now standard volumes on the Enlightenment, although he does offer some interesting general observations that include liberal Anglicans as well as philosophes: *The Enlightenment: An Interpretation*, 2 vols. (New York, 1966–1969), I, 322–327, 336–347. Neither of the best studies of English deism—Norman Torrey's *Voltaire and the English Deists* (New Haven, 1930) and Roland N. Stromberg's *Religious Liberalism in Eighteenth-Century England* (Oxford, 1954)—actually deals

directly with the question of secularization. At least in the context of the deists, that question is addressed, however, in two more recent and more general works on English thought: Gerald R. Cragg, *Reason and Authority in the Eighteenth Century* (Cambridge, 1964); and John Redwood, *Reason, Ridicule and Religion: The Age of the Enlightenment in England, 1660–1750* (London, 1976).

A notable exception to my generalization is Anand Chitnis's suggestive discussion of secularization in the Scottish universities, in *The Scottish Enlightenment: A Social History* (London, 1976), 155–158.

4. K. S. Inglis, *Churches and the Working Classes in Victorian England* (London, 1963), 4. Although his sources were impressionistic rather than statistically based, Norman Sykes suggested that in the eighteenth century, at least until the effects of the Methodist revival began to be felt in the Church of England, "the proportion of communicants to the adult population of parishes was remarkably high in most parts of the kingdom": "The Church," in A. S. Turberville, ed., *Johnson's England: An Account of the Life and Manners of His Age*, 2 vols. (Oxford, 1933), I, 32.

5. See, for example, [Thomas Secker], *The Charge of Thomas Lord Bishop of Oxford to the Clergy of His Diocese, In His Primary Visitation 1738*, 2nd ed. (London, 1739), [3]–4. Cf. John H. Overton and Frederic Relton, *The English Church from the Accession of George I. to the End of the Eighteenth Century (1714–1800)* (London, 1906), 63. The fact that a number of popular works of fiction, such as Fielding's *Tom Jones*, contained highly unflattering portraits of clergymen further illustrates the prevalence of contemporary anticlericalism.

6. Peter Gay, *The Party of Humanity: Essays in the French Enlightenment* (New York, 1964), 120. On the small number of deists, see Roland N. Stromberg, "Lovejoy's 'Parallel' Reconsidered," *Eighteenth-Century Studies*, I, iv (June 1968), 383–384.

7. Chadwick, *Secularization*. 17; Franklin L. Baumer, *Religion and the Rise of Scepticism* (New York, 1960), 112.

8. Galileo Galilei, "Letter to the Grand Duchess Christina" (1615), in Stillman Drake, trans. and ed., *Discoveries and Opinions of Galileo* (Garden City, N.Y., 1957), 192–193; Francis Bacon, *De Dignitate et Augmentis Scientiarum* (1623), Bk. III, Chap. i, and Bk. IX, Chap. i, in *The Works of Francis Bacon*, ed. James Spedding, R. L. Ellis, and D. D. Heath, new ed., 7 vols. (London, 1870–1872), IV, 336, and V, 117; idem, *Valerius Terminus of the Interpretation of Nature* (1603?), Chap. I, in *Works*, III, 218; John Locke, *An Essay Concerning Human Understanding* (1690), ed. Peter H. Nidditch (Oxford, 1975), 720–721 (Bk. IV, Chap. xxi).

9. Jean le Rond d'Alembert, *Preliminary Discourse to the Encyclopedia of Diderot*, trans. Richard N. Schwab with Walter E. Rex (Indianapolis, 1963), 53–54, 144; [John Barrow], *A New and Universal Dictionary of Arts and Sciences* (London, 1751), 5–6, 33–34; *Encyclopedia Britannica; Or, A Dictionary of Arts, Sciences, &c.* (1771), 2nd ed., 10 vols. (Edinburgh, 1778–1783), IX, 6976:2 (s.v. "Science").

10. See, for instance, s.v. "Theology" or "Divinity": N. Bailey, *Dictionarium Britannicum* (London, 1730); Samuel Johnson, *A Dictionary of the English Language* (1755), 2nd ed., 2 vols. (London, 1755–1756), I; William Rider, *A New Universal English Dictionary* (London, 1759); Thomas Sheridan, *A General Dictionary of the English Language*, 2 vols. (London, 1780), I; John Walker, *A Critical Pronouncing Dictionary and Expositor of the English Language* (London, 1791).

11. Sir William Temple, "Some Thoughts Upon Reviewing the Essay of Ancient and Modern Learning" (first published 1701), in *The Works of Sir William Temple, Bart.*, 2nd ed., 2 vols. (London, 1731), I, 300–301; William Wotton, *Reflections upon Ancient and Modern Learning* (1694), 3rd ed., corr. (London, 1705), 363–376; [John Gordon], *A New Estimate of Manners and Principles: Being a Comparison between Ancient and Modern Times*, 2 vols. (Cambridge, 1760–1761), I, 112–113. On the support provided to the concept of theological progress by the evidence

of secular learning, see, for example, Joseph Butler, *The Analogy of Religion* (1736), in *The Works of Joseph Butler*, ed. W. E. Gladstone, 2 vols. (Oxford, 1896), I, 234–235.

12. Ian Watt, *The Rise of the Novel: Studies on Defoe, Richardson and Fielding* (Berkeley, 1957), 49–50.

13. J. H. Plumb, "The Public, Literature, and the Arts in the Eighteenth Century," in Michael R. Marrus, ed., *The Emergence of Leisure* (New York, 1974), 11–37; J. W. Saunders, *The Profession of English Letters* (London, 1964), 116–145; A. S. Collins, *The Profession of Letters: A Study of the Relation of Author to Patron, Publisher, and Public, 1780–1832* (London, 1928), 17–27.

14. Joseph Priestley, *Experiments and Observations on Different Kinds of Air* (1774–1786), Preface, in *The Theological and Miscellaneous Works of Joseph Priestley*, ed. John Towill Rutt, 25 vols. in 26 ([London, 1817–1832]), XXV, 379, 384, 374; idem, *The History and Present State of Electricity, with Original Experiments* (1767), ed. Robert E. Schofield, 2 vols. (New York, 1966), I, xxv.

15. Priestley, *Experiments and Observations on Air*, in *Works*, XXV, 384, 379.

16. Adam Ferguson, *Principles of Moral and Political Science*, 2 vols. (Edinburgh, 1792), I, 334; David Kettler, *The Social and Political Thought of Adam Ferguson* ([Columbus, Ohio], 1965), 171–174, 131.

17. Gay, *The Enlightenment*, I, 75, and II, 372–373; Frank E. Manuel, *Isaac Newton, Historian* (Cambridge, Mass., 1963), 11–13, 163.

18. For the secularization of history in the Enlightenment, see Hugh Trevor-Roper, "The Historical Philosophy of the Enlightenment," *Studies on Voltaire and the Eighteenth Century*, XXVII (1963), 1669–1670; G. Christie Wasberg, "'Transcendence' and 'immanence' in the philosophy of history from Enlightenment to Romanticism," *SVEC*, LVIII (1967), 1829–1838; Gay, *The Enlightenment*, II, 385–396. On the quest for the origins of religion, see Frank E. Manuel, *The Eighteenth Century Confronts the Gods* (Cambridge, Mass., 1959), which not surprisingly concentrates almost exclusively on continental figures (except for Hume).

19. Edward Gibbon, *Memoirs of My Life*, ed. Georges A. Bonnard (New York, 1969), 157.

20. Adam Smith, "The History of Astronomy" (first published 1795), in *The Works of Adam Smith, LL.D.*, 5 vols. (London, 1811), V, 84–88; idem, *An Inquiry into the Nature and Causes of the Wealth of Nations*, ed. Edwin Cannan, Modern Library ed. (New York, 1937), 723; Henry Home, Lord Kames, *Sketches of the History of Man* (1774), new ed., 3 vols. (Edinburgh, 1813), III, 269–290.

21. *The Journal of John Wesley*, entry for July 6, 1781, in *The Works of the Rev. John Wesley, A.M.*, 14 vols. (London, 1872), IV, 210; [James Fortescue], *Science; A Poem. (In a Religious View)* (Oxford, 1751), iii, 1–7; Richard Watson, Jr., ed., *Anecdotes of the Life of Richard Watson, Bishop of Llandaff* (London, 1817), 196, 198.

22. Edmund Law, *Considerations on the Theory of Religion*, new ed. (London, 1820), 53, 31–32, 256, 204–209.

23. William Robertson, *The Situation of the World at the Time of Christ's Appearance, and its Connexion with the Success of his Religion, considered* (Edinburgh, 1755), 6–8; idem, *The History of America* (1777), Bk. IV, in *The Works of William Robertson, D.D.*, 8 vols. (Oxford, 1825), VI, 353; idem, *The History of Scotland* (1759), Bk. II, in *Works*, I, 108, 114–123.

24. For a survey of seventeenth-century anthropology, see Franklin L. Baumer, *Modern European Thought: Continuity and Change in Ideas, 1600–1950* (New York, 1977), 79–95.

25. Donald Greene, "Augustinianism and Empiricism: A Note on Eighteenth-Century English Intellectual History," *Eighteenth-Century Studies*, I, i (Sept. 1967), 48–49.

26. John Locke, *Some Thoughts Concerning Education*, in *The Educational Writings of John Locke*, ed. James L. Axtell (Cambridge, 1968), 244, 159, 114, 325, 138, 237. See also John Passmore, *The Perfectibility of Man* (New York, 1970), 159–165.

27. An exception was the anonymous author of *A Letter from a Man to his Fellow Creatures* (London, 1745), who—in the course of expressing the environmentalist view—called the doctrine of original sin a "vile and ungodly, . . . inhuman and most odious Notion" (p. 23). This condemnation runs parallel to Voltaire's: "Péché Originel," *Philosophical Dictionary*, trans. Peter Gay, Harvest Book ed. (New York, 1962), 415–417. Although it was couched in more temperate terms, Locke's explicit rejection of original sin (in *The Reasonableness of Christianity* [1695], Sect 3) was immediately attacked: J. A. Passmore, "The Malleability of Man in Eighteenth-Century Thought," in Earl R. Wasserman, ed., *Aspects of the Eighteenth Century* (Baltimore, 1965), 22.

28. George Turnbull, *The Principles of Moral Philosophy* (London, 1740), 39–40, 78–79, 81–96, 139–140, 104, 223, 272.

29. Abraham Tucker, *The Light of Nature Pursued*, 3rd ed., 2 vols. (London, 1834), I, 87–104, 128, 150–153, 215, 218, 254–256, 259; II, 569–570, 680.

30. George Chapman, *A Treatise on Education* (Edinburgh, 1773), 33, 5–6, 2; David Fordyce, *Dialogues Concerning Education* (1745–1748), 3rd ed., 2 vols. (London, 1757), I, 269–270, 344, 117, and II, 97.

31. Richard Price, *The Evidence for a Future Period of Improvement in the State of Mankind* (London, 1787), 34; idem, *Observations on the Importance of the American Revolution* (London, 1785), 50; James Wadham Whitchurch, *An Essay upon Education* (London, 1772), 101 (see also 12–27).

For an interesting, somewhat earlier combination of environmentalism and Augustinianism in the context of education, see Isaac Watts, *A Discourse on the Education of Children and Youth*, ca. 1740, in *The Works of the Reverend and Learned Isaac Watts, D.D.*, 6 vols. (London, 1810), V, 357–360.

32. David Hartley, *Observations on Man, His Frame, His Duties, and His Expectations*, 2 vols. (London, 1749), II, 21, 183, 282, 453–454; I, 81. It should be noted that Hartley believed the Fall had corrupted or "ruined" the world and man: see, for instance, ibid., II, 236.

33. David Hume, *A Treatise of Human Nature* (1739–1740), ed. L. A. Selby-Bigge (Oxford, 1888), 10–13, 60–61, 92–93, 116–118, 483, 500–501; idem, *An Abstract of A Treatise of Human Nature* (1740), ed. J. M. Keynes and P. Sraffa (Cambridge, 1938), 31–32; idem, "The Sceptic" (1742), "Of Parties in General" (1741), and "Of Refinement in the Arts" (1752), *Essays Moral, Political, and Literary*, ed. T. H. Green and T. H. Grose, new impression, 2 vols. (London, 1898), I, 221–223, 127, 300; idem, *The History of England, from the Invasion of Julius Caesar to the Revolution of 1688* (1754–1762), new ed., 8 vols. (London, 1789), IV, 127 (Chap. XXXI).

34. Thomas Burnet, *The Sacred Theory of the Earth* (1684–1690; 2nd ed., 1691), reprint ed. (Carbondale, Ill., 1965), 281, 220–221, 89; Samuel Clarke, "First Reply" (Nov. 26, 1715), in H. G. Alexander, ed., *The Leibniz-Clarke Correspondence* (Manchester, 1956), 14. On Boyle and Newton (who certainly was of two minds on this whole question), see Richard S. Westfall, *Science and Religion in Seventeenth-Century England* (New Haven, 1958), 73–92, 200–206. Some examples of the continued belief in special providences are contained in Keith Thomas, *Religion and the Decline of Magic* (New York, 1971), 89–96, 109.

35. Voltaire, "Miracles," *Philosophical Dictionary*, 392–393; Gay, *Party of Humanity*, 196; idem, *The Enlightenment*, I, 145–150.

36. James Dunbar, *Essays on the History of Mankind in Rude and Cultivated Ages* (London, 1780), 251; Adam Smith, *The Theory of Moral Sentiments* (1759), ed. D. D. Raphael and A. L.

Macfie (Oxford, 1976), 87, 184–185; Kames, *Sketches*, III, 293; William Robertson, "A View of the Progress of Society in Europe, from the Subversion of the Roman Empire to the Beginning of the Sixteenth Century" (preliminary dissertation to *The History of the Reign of the Emperor Charles V* [1769]), in *Works*, III, 46. Hume's essay on miracles, though written in the 1730s, was not published until 1748, and now is included as Sec. X of *An Enquiry concerning Human Understanding*.

37. The theory and terms cited are those of J. H. Plumb, "Reason and Unreason in the Eighteenth Century: the English Experience," in idem, *In the Light of History* (New York, 1972), 3–24.

38. Philip Doddridge, *A Course of Lectures on the Principal Subjects in Pneumatology, Ethics, and Divinity* (written ca. 1750–1751, first published 1763), in *The Miscellaneous Works of Philip Doddridge, D.D.* (London, 1839), 333:1; David Hartley, *Observations on Man*, II, 149; Thomas Hartley, *Paradise Restored: Or A Testimony to the Doctrine of the Blessed Millennium* (London, 1764), 311, 328.

39. David Hartley, *Observations on Man*, II, 143–145. See also George Campbell, *A Dissertation on Miracles* (1762), new ed. (London, 1839), 38n.–39n.

40. John Douglas, *The Criterion; Or Rules by which the True Miracles Recorded in the New Testament Are Distinguished from the Spurious Miracles of Pagans and Papists* (1752), new ed. (London, 1807), 6–8, 21–24, 402–403; Campbell, *Dissertation on Miracles*, 128–129, 80–116 passim. See also William Adams, *An Essay in Answer to Mr. Hume's Essay on Miracles* (1752), 3rd ed. (London, 1767), 19–22, 32, and passim.

41. William Whiston, *A New Theory of the Earth, From its Original to the Consummation of All Things*, 6th ed. (London, 1755), 431–437, 439, 445 (cp. 1st ed. [London, 1696], 357–363, 367, 371); idem, *Memoirs of the Life and Writings of Mr. William Whiston*, 1st ed. (London, 1749), 626; idem, *Memoirs*, 2nd ed., 2 vols. (London, 1753), II, 58–69, 190–195.

On the reaction of the English to the London and Lisbon earthquakes, which more often reflected a supernaturalistic than a naturalistic disposition, see G. S. Rousseau, "The London Earthquakes of 1750," *Cahiers d'histoire mondiale*, XI, iii (1968), 436–451; T. D. Kendrick, *The Lisbon Earthquake* (Philadelphia, [1957]), 11–44, 219–243.

42. Colin Maclaurin, *An Account of Sir Isaac Newton's Philosophical Discoveries* (1748), 2nd ed. (London, 1750), 4, 71, 89, 398–408.

III

Superstition, Impiety, and an Enlightened Legal Order: The Theological Politics of the Abbé Mably

JOHN FREDERICK LOGAN

Superstition provided the *philosophes* of the eighteenth century with a favorite target in their wars against social and intellectual evil. In the *Encyclopédie*, for example, ·Jaucourt described superstition as an excess or abuse of religion and found atheism preferable to superstition:

> Even atheism . . . never destroys natural feelings, never attacks either the laws or customs of a people; but *superstition* is a despotic tyrant which brings all to submit to its chimeras. . . . An atheist values public order out of the love of his own tranquility; but fanatical *superstition* overturns empires.[1]

And Voltaire's *Dictionnaire philosophique* contains a long list of the horrible consequences of superstition, which is defined as "almost anything which goes beyond the adoration of a Supreme Being and the heart's submission to His eternal commands. . . ."[2] Yet superstition, often linked with "fanaticism," remained an elusive target for the philosophes, in large part because such terms took on varying meanings for different writers. The most constant element in the philosophes' uses of these notions appears to lie in the attributes of excessive zeal, in the lack of measure, moderation, and "reason." Even the careful Abbé de Condillac, who tried, in his *Dictionnaire des synonymes*, to give the Prince of Parma clear and useful definitions of important concepts, provided little precision or clarity. He described superstition by referring to the personal qualities of the superstitious person rather than to the characteristics of the thing itself. "Superstition," he wrote, is simply the "religion of a weak soul and of an unenlightened mind." And fanaticism similarly was perceived in reference to those who possess this quality: "fanaticism" is the "enthusiasm of one who substitutes or adds his own visions to the true spirit of religion." Both definitions refer to "religion," which Condillac characterized as the "worship which is rendered to the divinity."[3] In Condillac's *Dictionnaire*, the meaning of fanaticism and superstition thus depended on the meaning of religion, a notion that itself remained vague.

Condillac's imprecision in defining superstition and religion may have resulted from a desire to avoid controversy and even impiety,[1] but it also reflected a dilemma common to those who wished to condemn religious excesses and abuses while still holding to deistic, theistic, or even Christian beliefs.[5] How could a line be drawn between false, irrational religious beliefs and practices and those that are valid and that contribute to the well-being of the individual and of society?

In this respect, the writings of Condillac's older brother, the Abbé Mably, are particularly instructive. A prolific writer whose *Oeuvres complètes* fill some fifteen volumes and touch on a wide variety of topics, Mably (1709–1785) was to influence both the Jacobins and the Babouvists, as well as much of subsequent revolutionary socialism.[6] Although Mably's views on private property have provoked considerable scholarly debate, his confrontation with the pivotal issue of the proper scope and role of religious belief has largely escaped attention. Yet Mably did, in several of his works, come to grips with this issue, most explicitly in his essay entitled "De la superstition."

Ostensibly a dialogue, this essay consists in the detailed response of "Cléante" to the assertion of "Ariste" that

> Nothing degrades man more than those terrors and irrational hopes engendered by superstition. . . . Our philosophers will have rendered a great service to humanity by describing in detail all the evils produced by superstition.[7]

Cléante reacts to this charge in a conciliatory manner: he fully recognizes that unhappiness at times results from superstition. But he also points to a number of reasons why superstition cannot—and, perhaps, should not—be eradicated. Cléante's discourse on superstition may be read as Mably's wide-ranging defense of religion and as a reply to the all-encompassing charges made by philosophes such as Voltaire that superstition is a fundamental evil which must be totally eliminated.

Perhaps the most striking argument of Cléante is that even the philosophers themselves, even those who loudly proclaim that they are materialists, are not immune to religion and superstition; those who reject a belief in God easily fall prey, especially in times of trouble or danger, to a belief in magic, miracles, and fortune-telling. Cléante offers what might today be termed a "psychological" explanation of this phenomenon. "If they [these philosophers] did not feel strangely attracted to superstition," he asserts, "they would not be so very proud of despising it." (XIII, 293) Cléante's defense of superstition goes, however, beyond this argument *ad hominem*. His lengthy and, at times, rambling discourse in fact constitutes a vigorous and comprehensive justification of religious belief and practice. Several recurrent arguments emerge from this discourse.

Religion and superstition often benefit humanity. Ancient deities like Hercules, Castor, and Ceres, Cléante points out, provided worthy models for mankind, models that inspired men to honor, courage, virtue, and prudence.[8] Examples from Roman history reveal that superstition "can be linked with the greatest enlightenment [*lumières*] and the greatest virtues." (XIII, 297)

Since humans are imperfect, superstition is unavoidable and often inoffensive. Philosophers, Cléante suggests, have an overly optimistic view of human nature:

> they do not see how many contradictions to which we are exposed by our unhappy weakness. We are surrounded by errors; there is no one among us without a prejudice which is taken as truth. These errors and prejudices balance and temper one another; and from our very constitution, a little superstition in the world does no harm. [XIII, 299–301]

Cléante offers no systematic explanation of this rather negative view of human nature. But he does, at later points in the dialogue, reiterate this view. He sees mankind as being ruled, inevitably, by two passions: fear and hope. Fear, "which never leaves us," results from our awareness of our weaknesses; and hope comes to reassure and comfort us when we experience fear. "These are the two passions which fight powerfully against philosophy. . . ." (XIII, 314, 305) Mably does acknowledge and accept the theories of Locke and Condillac regarding the origins of human knowledge in the senses. But he perceives in these principles limits that restrict human knowledge and that open the way to religious belief and to superstition.

> I have talked . . . about the weakness of our reason which owes all its knowledge to our senses and for which the nature of things will remain an eternal mystery. I have spoken . . . of our curiosity, our fear, our vanity, and our hope. [XIII, 317]

Man's dependence on his senses becomes a barrier to his amelioration: "We are animals terribly turned to the earth. We obey too much our senses to look often towards God. . . ." (XIII, 337)

Because of the slow progress of knowledge, contemporary philosophers may still not perceive the truth. Cléante asserts that, historically, reason has been very slow to advance and to establish truths, but he goes on to suggest a kind of relativism that in fact questions the entire Enlightenment. In a startling passage he wonders if the philosophes themselves may be guilty of gross error.

We call our century the age of enlightenment [lumières]; [but] perhaps in a hundred years we will be judged very ignorant. Who can assure me that Newton's philosophy will not undergo the same reversal as did that of Descartes? [XIII, 305]

The common man is unprepared to accept the philosophers' view of superstition. Mably's attitude toward the common people is essentially negative. He refers to "that ignorant and gross multitude whose vision and thoughts are directed to the earth." It is this multitude, Cléante claims, "that will rule the world, will be followed and feared. . . ." (XIII, 313) Religion is necessary for such people; wise men would do best to leave them with superstitions that bring individual consolation and social tranquility. (XIII, 314)

Superstition does not necessarily follow from religious beliefs. At a number of places, Mably's arguments mingle superstition and religion and imply that the advantages and disadvantages of one are those of the other. But, near the end of his argument, Cléante faces this distinction directly and asserts that "religion and superstition . . . , although naturally enemies, always seek and work to be joined." (XIII, 325) Cléante defends this paradox by pointing out that theologians—much like philosophers—wish to extend their dominion over all matters and to overcome their adversaries by any means. Superstition thus appears to result from the theologians' efforts to gain power and authority. The question then arises as to precisely what is the proper scope of theology. Cléante responds by reasserting the time-honored proposition that theology or religion teaches men what they cannot learn through the unaided exercise of their own reason. It is inconceivable that God would duplicate His efforts, that He would give us truths by Revelation which we can discover through philosophy. Consequently, there is no possibility of real conflict between philosophy and theology, between reason and Revelation: even theologians recognize that revealed truth, although superior to reason, cannot be contrary to reason. (XIII, 325–326)

For Cléante, superstition has often corrupted men's idea of, and worship of, a God who is infinitely good, wise, and powerful. Cléante professes a belief that might be labeled as theism, accompanied by a highly critical view of certain Roman Catholic practices.[9] Yet this "theism" does not specifically exclude Christianity and, perhaps, even a purified Catholicism. Near the end of his discourse, he accounts for the excesses of Catholic Christianity (which is never mentioned by name) by comparing the virtues of the early Apostles to the ambition and corruption of the Roman priests:

. . . truth is changed as it is carried to peoples whose laws favor differing abuses. In Rome, religion acquired a certain tenor by adopting the ambition which constituted the Roman character. . . . You see the errors leading to ambition nearly becoming dogmas. The morality of the Apostles will become forgotten; and, in order to defend and protect these unjust pretentions, it was necessary to give in to that barbarous superstition which spilled torrents of blood. [XIII, 335]

The general conclusion to which the reader of "De la superstition" appears to be led by these arguments is that religion constitutes an inevitable element in society and that, freed from some of the excesses of superstition, it uplifts the human character, provokes virtuous and honorable actions, and fosters social tranquility and political order.

Cléante's discourse contains many elements of a conventional defense of traditional religion: man is a feeble being easily prey to evil; reason alone is an insufficient and at times misleading guide to truth; religious faith leads men to virtue and happiness; and mankind has an obligation to follow the directives of an all-wise, omniscient, omnipotent deity.[10] But Cléante's "religion" remains remarkably secular. His deity speaks to mankind through reason and nature, not directly through prayer or through saints, teaching authorities, or sacred books. Cléante certainly respects divine Revelation: "Let us have the deepest respect for Revelation." (XIII, 325) But this Revelation has little content beyond general moral principles; it is defined and limited by what human reason reaches without such Revelation. That which is beyond reason is less revealed truth than an "eternal mystery." (XIII, 317) The primary aim of Cléante's religion is neither to ascertain the relationship between the human soul and a transcendent Deity nor to guide mankind to an afterlife or a goal outside the temporal, historical process.[11] The proper scope of theology is quite definitely not set by theologians or by Revelation, but rather by reason. In fact, this religion rejects or ignores transcendentality in favor of public utility and social morality. But how is such a religion to be properly formulated and imposed within a specific political context?

"De la superstition" offers little in the way of practical proposals; it ends on an appeal for a social or political resolution of the problems posed by superstition and fanaticism. "May the government, the politicians, and the scholars seek the means, the rules, the laws, by which they can temper, calm, and direct our passions." (XIII, 341–342) But in other works, and notably in *De la législation ou Principes des lois* (1776), Mably does offer more specific, practical proposals regarding the establishment of religion in society. Like "De la superstition," *De la législation* takes the form of a dialogue in which one character (here, a Swedish philosopher) expounds at length theories that appear to be those of Mably himself; the second speaker, an English aristocrat, does little more than raise brief, general issues that provoke the discourse of the "philosopher."

The recurrent theme of *De la législation*, that "mankind's happiness or misery depends on good or bad legislation," pervades the "Swedish" philosopher's discussion of religion. (IX, 2) The goal of the wise legislator should be "to make men happy in this world"; in pursuit of this goal, he should view religion "as the linking force among citizens and as the guarantor of their uprightness." (IX, 375) The argument that religious faith can reinforce the unity of a nation and can bring about virtuous conduct echoes similar points in "De la superstition." God is, in fact, placed in the role of an omnipresent, omniscient overseer who knows far more about each individual's every action than does any human policeman and who holds rewards and punishments far greater than those of any human magistrate. (IX, 323–324) To this defense of religion as a guarantor of social order, Mably adds justifications of the political necessity of religion, justifications based on history, on the nefarious civil consequences of an atheist government, and on the emotional satisfactions resulting from religious faith.

Referring to history and to voyagers' accounts of primitive peoples, Mably concludes that religion has always been a prerequisite to the government, as well as to the sciences and arts, of developed societies: "Have we ever found men with laws and magistrates but without religious beliefs?" (IX, 333) Mably then constructs a kind of anti-utopia wherein atheists proscribe all belief in God, in Providence, and in spirituality. The results of such a program, he suggests, would be the denial of free will and the unchecked reign of pleasure as the goal of human life. With no firm ideas of justice and virtue, men would pursue their own selfish goals and the social order would collapse. (IX, 333–341) Finally, Mably offers a lengthy, emotional declaration of faith worthy of Rousseau's Savoyard Vicar:[12]

> His [God's] name is clearly inscribed on all parts of the universe; the greatness and the beauty of the product proclaim . . . the power and wisdom of the Maker. . . . This witness, this judge of all our actions and all our thoughts . . . is absolutely necessary to our happiness; this is the most convincing proof that there is a God. It [this proof] is written in both our minds and our hearts. . . . Without Him, we float in eternal uncertainty; without Him we would forever see the decline of the weak edifice of society. My weakness, my strength, my needs, my happiness, my misfortunes, my fears, my uncertainties, my hopes, all the sentiments that I experience, are but many voices calling me to this Supreme Being. . . . If human justice oppresses me, I still have a consoler, and my innocence will keep me happy in the midst of misfortune if I can appeal from the evil or stupidity of men to the tribunal of divine wisdom. [IX, 348–350]

Mably sets out a number of juridical proposals to guide the lawmaker in his actions toward religion. Some of these are principles that appear to be of a fundamental or constitutional character; others fall more within the scope of laws or regulations.[13] Perhaps first among such principles is that the government must not mingle in affairs that properly belong to theologians and priests: "there should be fundamental laws which always keep spiritual matters apart from temporal things." (IX, 377) History proves that a society where politics and religion intertwine quickly falls into fanaticism that, in turn, engenders impiety. (IX, 376)

Yet, on a more immediate level, Mably's legislator exercises a remarkably active and specific control over religion. He protects and fosters religion by preventing atheists and even deists from making their impious attacks on religion; he restrains priests' avarice and ambition by restricting these priests to a simple life and by keeping religious edifices plain and unpretentious; and he prevents theological disputes by limiting dogmas to a set of basic beliefs. (IX, 361–363, 380–382, 387–389) This state-protected religion is, however, not entirely austere. Mably encourages religious ceremonies insofar as they foster virtue and remind citizens of their duties. Moreover, such ceremonies remain under the control of the priests:

> Just as laws would be useless without judges, so religion . . . would become a source of conflict, of hatred and of error without an authorized worship and without priests who would supervise its organization and its ceremonies. [IX, 357]

Near the end of Mably's life, events in the New World provided an occasion for him to apply the general program of *De la législation* to a very specific political situation. In the *Observations sur le gouvernement et les lois des Etats-unis d'Amérique* (1783), a commentary on the new nation's legal system addressed to John Adams, Mably reaffirms his basic principle on the role of religion in the political order:

> Because religion exercises the most absolute power over the mind of men, it doubtlessly would be extremely useful for all the citizens of a State, united by the same worship, to obey the same divine laws, just as they obey the same civil laws; in this way, religion would join forces with the government to make the citizens happy. [VIII, 343]

Evaluating the laws of the new states and, particularly, the constitutions of Pennsylvania and South Carolina, he expresses deep reservations about the extreme degree of religious toleration and about the lack of governmental control of religious teaching and worship.[11] Since the United States have not yet had time to develop a unified national spirit, they are easily subject to the political instability and religious strife that led to so much bloodshed and unhappiness in Europe. The absence of a state-controlled and -protected religion, he reiterates, fosters the development of religious fanaticism, as well as the pernicious growth of deism and atheism: "one cannot take too many precautions against either fanaticism or the indifference which appears to open the way for a multiplicity of religions." (VIII, 350) Mably proposes, as initial corrective measures, firm restrictions on the creation of new sects and on the teaching of established sects and, on a more positive level, the composition of a Continental Catechism incorporating the basic principles of religious faith and worship to be observed by all citizens into a "complete treatise on morality." (VIII, 350–351)

In the context of the Enlightenment's general attitude toward institutional Christianity, Mably's forceful rehabilitation of religion and superstition may seem surprising. He accepts, and even praises, many practices and traditions of French Christianity, including certain "superstitions," priesthoods, and cere-monies, as well as the governmental suppression of deistic and atheistic impi-ety. Yet these practices and institutions do not, for Mably, rest upon any transcendental imperative, but rather upon the realities of the social and polit-ical order.

Mably gives no indication of being aware of the possible conflict between his fundamental principle, enunciated most clearly in *De la législation*, of separation between spiritual and temporal orders and his imposition on the state of regulatory duties toward religion.[15] He merely asserts that religion and the state pursue the same goal—the happiness and virtue of the people—and presumes that religion's criteria of happiness and virtue do not differ from those of the state. The use of the notion of happiness was not, of course, unique to Mably. As Robert Mauzi has suggested, earthly happiness constituted a recur-rent preoccupation throughout the eighteenth century, a kind of common de-nominator in the thought of both the philosophes and many of their adversaries.[16] As a goal and a standard of judgment, happiness was invoked to explain Christian morality as well as atheistic virtue, to further individual as well as political amelioration, and to propose moderate social reform as well as radical political reorganization. In the case of Mably, earthly happiness pro-vided a justification for religious belief and practice and for the political use of religion.

The intellectual antecedents of such a view of religion are numerous and varied.[17] Among the admired ancients, Cicero linked individual morality with civic virtue and stability: nothing, he asserted, pleases the Supreme Being more than the gathering of men in the interests of a just social order. Moreover, like Mably, Cicero saw the fear of divine punishment as an efficient check on the individual's actions and as a deterrent from crime:

> We must persuade our citizens that the gods are lords and rulers of all things, and that what is done, is done by their will and authority; that they are likewise great benefactors of man, observing the character of every individual, what he does, of what wrong he is guilty. . . . For surely minds which are imbued with such ideas will not fail to form true and useful opinions.[18]

A more striking expression of a view of the political utility of religion similar to that of Mably may, however, be found in the works of Plato. That Mably's views on religion might here follow those of Plato is not surprising: Mably is one of the political writers of the Enlightenment who is most consciously indebted to Plato.[19] Mably frequently cites Plato's political theories with approval; in the *Entretiens de Phocion* (1763), for example, the reader is advised to "read his *Republic* and see the watchfulness with which he [Plato] seeks to master passions and the austere standard by which he measures virtue." In particular, Mably admires "how much he [Plato] believes morality [*moeurs*] to be necessary for the preservation of his government." (IX, 67) In formulating his own views on the role of religion in the state, Mably appears to have drawn more on the *Laws* than on the *Republic*.[20] In Book Ten of the *Laws*, religion emerges as the essential basis of individual morality and, consequently, of the social order.[21] Like Mably, Plato envisages a state in which religion, along with education, would be sponsored and supervised by the state. The principal doctrines of Plato's state religion are that the gods do exist, that they are concerned with mankind, and that their judgments of human actions cannot be affected by prayers and sacrifices. The state punishes deviations from these doctrines as impieties harmful to the social order and organizes public festivals and ceremonies that foster individual virtue and social unity.[22]

Even though Mably appears to have followed much of Plato's program, he evidences little concern for the philosophical basis of this program. In the *Laws*, Plato goes to great lengths to establish the priority of soul over matter and the importance of a proper conception of the human soul as the foundation of all morality and thus of both the legislator's and the individual's every action.[23] But Mably, in spite of occasional references to the soul and to Revelation, avoids dwelling on the soul's links to any transcendent being, authority, or standard.

Plato and Mably approach religion from different points of view. For Plato, prior transcendent forces have created morality and virtue and, therefore, dictate the appropriate structuring of the social order in conformity with these forces; for Mably, the needs of the social order dictate what is moral or virtuous and, therefore, what is the proper content and role of religion within this order. In fact, Mably's justification of state control over religion reflects a statesman's appreciation of religion's power more than a philosopher's concern with virtue, goodness, or justice. Mably, it should be noted, did have some direct exposure to practical politics. For several years he served as secretary to the Cardinal de Tencin, a prominent minister under Louis XV; in this capacity, Mably is credited with the negotiation of important treaties and with the composition of numerous reports and dispatches.[24]

The central elements in Mably's theological politics—the rehabilitation of religion and "superstition" as socially beneficial forces, the orientation of religion toward the goal of earthly happiness, and the advocacy of governmental action to establish, foster, and protect a state religion—all continued to find exponents in the nineteenth century. Forms of "utilitarian" religion constituted an essential part of the projects of French utopians like Saint-Simon and Comte. The philanthropic "New Christianity" of Saint-Simon and the "Religion of Humanity" of Comte both envisaged social morality as the basis of religious doctrine, used dogmas and ceremonies as tools for bringing political unity and tranquility, and provided for religious uniformity as an indispensable foundation of civil order.[25] The use of religion to foster political or social goals was also advocated by Catholic thinkers, such as Bishop Frayssinous, the minister of ecclesiastical affairs and of public instruction under Charles X.

The "political theology" expounded in Frayssinous' *Première conférence sur la religion* bears certain similarities to Mably's theological politics.[26] Central to this work is the proposition that religion is necessary to social order and progress. For Frayssinous, religious faith keeps human passions in check and prevents social and political chaos: "there can be no society without laws, no laws without morality, no morality without religion." He further argues that, historically, religion has provided the indispensable basis of civil society:

> religion presided over the formation of human societies; it softened vicious tempers, purified manners, tightened the links of benevolence and fraternity, [thus] cementing the body politic in all its aspects.[27]

Like Mably, Frayssinous advocates state action to establish public ceremonies, to create public religious instruction, and to eliminate deism, atheism, and impiety.

Frayssinous did, of course, relate his political theology to Christian Revelation and to the historical context of post-Revolutionary France. But his affirmation of the social utility of religion is formulated in universal terms and may be applied to non-Christian faiths and societies; implicit in his theory are the assumptions, stated more explicitly by Mably, that true religion brings earthly order and happiness and that civil virtue coincides with religious morality.

As Charles Rihs has pointed out, "it is never easy to classify Mably in the history of ideas and of social doctrines."[28] More specifically, Mably does not appear to fit easily into the usual categories imposed on the Enlightenment's view of religion. Placing a great emphasis on reason, he still points to the inevitability and desirability of the emotional element in religion. Mably passes over the transcendent Revelation taught by an independent Roman Catholic church, just as he avoids the transcendent philosophical doctrine of Plato. But he proposes in their stead a largely intolerant religion created and imposed in the name of political order.

Mably may be more easily classified among the advocates of the temporal order's supremacy and among European statesmen and political theorists, like

Richelieu and Frayssinous, who were keenly aware of the social power of religious belief and who sought to use this power in the service of political ends. Mably's ambivalent attitude toward superstition—his advocacy of beneficial superstitions and rejection of beliefs and practices harmful to the social order—reflects an overriding concern with providing practical proposals for political and social amelioration, proposals that take into account both the emotional component in human nature and the necessity for dealing with this component in constructing a more enlightened legal order. As a realistic reformer, Mably saw impiety as a force more potentially divisive and harmful than ubiquitous superstition.

Notes

1. "Superstition," *Encyclopédie ou Dictionnaire raisonné des sciences, des arts et des métiers,* (Translations, unless otherwise noted, are mine.)

2. Voltaire, "Superstition," *Dictionnaire philosophique*, ed. J. Benda (Paris: Garnier, 1961), p. 394ff.

3. Condillac, *Dictionnaire des synonymes* in *Oeuvres philosophiques*, ed. G. LeRoy (Paris, 1951), III, 274, 485, 524,

4. Condillac's *Dictionnaire* was a part of the program of study specifically designed for the pious Prince of Parma. See J. F. Logan, "Condillac et les lumières," *Revue de l'Université de Bruxelles* (1972–1973), pp. 210–222.

5. For a valuable survey of the Enlightenment's complex relationship to religious faith, see Paul Hazard's classic *European Thought in the Eighteenth Century* (New York, 1963), esp. pp. 44–92.

6. On Mably and his influence, see Brigitte Coste, *Mably: Pour une utopie du bon sens* (Paris, 1975); E. Harpaz, "Mably et la posterité," *Revue des Sciences humaines*, fasc. 73 (1954), pp. 25–40; and Renato Galliani, "Quelques aspects de la fortune de Mably au XXième siècle," *Studies on Voltaire and the Eighteenth Century* LXXXVIII (1972), pp. 549–565.

7. Mably, *Oeuvres complètes* (Lyon, 1796), XIII, 292. Subsequent citations to Mably's works, given in the text, refer to this edition.

8. On the eighteenth-century uses of pagan deities, see Frank E. Manuel, *The Eighteenth Century Confronts the Gods* (Cambridge, 1959), Chap. I, and, more recently, Michel de Certeau, "Writing vs. Time: History and Anthropology in the Works of Lafitau," in *Yale French Studies*, LIX (1980), pp. 37–64 (a special issue entitled "Rethinking History: Time, Myth and Writing").

9. Mably did, on occasion, specifically praise Christianity: In *Le Droit public de l'Europe* (1748), he referred to "Christianity, a religion of peace and charity which, by its very nature, detests persecution and fanaticism." (VI, 39) Cléante's "theism" has certain similarities to that of Diderot's *Pensées philosophiques* (in *Oeuvres philosophiques*, ed. P. Vernière [Paris, 1964] p. 9ff), although Diderot prefers atheism to superstition, while still professing adherence to Roman Catholicism (Pensées XII and LVIII).

10. On the position of French Catholic thinkers in opposition to the philosophes, Robert R. Palmer's *Catholics and Unbelievers in Eighteenth Century France* (Princeton, 1939) remains indispensable.

11. In his *Observations sur le gouvernement et les lois des Etats-unis d'Amérique*, Mably explains more explicitly his neglect of the transcendent or supernatural aspect of religion: "One can

easily be misled regarding the relationship of religion with God because it is wrapped in mystery; but the relationship of religion with society is known in the most evident way. Who can doubt that God wanted to unite men by the link of morality and virtue upon which is founded the happiness of every citizen and of society." (VIII, 351)

12. Like Mably's Cléante, the Savoyard Vicar in Book IV of Rousseau's *Emile* rejects the elaborations of philosophy and theology in favor of an interior light or truth which discloses a wise and benevolent Supreme Being. But Mably places less emphasis on the individual's conscience and gives greater importance to the social and political benefits of religious faith. The similarities between the ideas of Mably and Rousseau have been analyzed most often in the context of political theory: see, for example, Lutz Lehmann, *Mably und Rousseau: Eine Studie über der Grenzen der Emanzipations in Ancien Régime* (Frankfort, 1975).

13. On the perception of fundamental constitutional principles in the history of European legal thought, see Charles Szladits, *European Legal Systems* (Parker School of Foreign and Comparative Law, Columbia University, 1976).

14. Mably in fact may have misjudged the degree of religious toleration obtaining in the new states. See Goldwin French, "Religion and Society in America's Revolutionary Era: Some Preliminary Reflections," in P. Hughes and D. Williams, eds., *The Varied Pattern: Studies in the 18th Century* (Toronto, 1971), pp. 321–331. On Mably's view of the United States, see Werner Stark, *America: Ideal and Reality* (London, 1947), pp. 36–57 (Chap. III: "Mably the Pessimist").

15. The dividing line between theoretical separation of the two orders and practical state supervision or "entanglement" remains, of course, difficult to draw. See Sharon L. Worthing, "'Religion' and 'Religious Institutions' under the First Amendment," *Pepperdine Law Review*, VII (1980), pp. 313–353.

16. Robert Mauzi, *L'Idée du bonheur au XVIIIe siècle* (3rd ed.; Paris, 1967).

17. The identification of antecedents, influences, or sources is elusive and often illusive, especially where the issue under consideration is as broad as the nature of religion and of its relationship to the state. Some guidance, however, may be found in Ira O. Wade, *The Intellectual Origins of the French Enlightenment* (Princeton, 1971), esp. pp. 133–162, 173–206, 418–436, and, of course, Franklin L. Baumer's classic *Religion and the Rise of Scepticism* (New York, 1960).

18. Cicero, *The Laws*, trans. C. W. Keyes (Loeb ed.; Cambridge, Mass., 1961), II, vii, 15–16.

19. The complex relationship of the philosophes to Plato and the other ancient philosophers is discussed in Peter Gay, *The Enlightenment: An Interpretation*, Vol I: *The Rise of Modern Paganism* (New York, 1966), pp. 31–126.

20. Although Mably refers with some frequency to both the *Laws* and the *Republic* throughout his writings, it is difficult and perhaps impossible to ascertain how consciously Mably followed Plato's program or to know whether Mably initially "took" his ideas directly from Plato's works or from others who had themselves adopted some of Plato's principles. And it remains, of course, possible that Mably formulated his ideas independent of any influence of Plato and that Plato served merely to confirm or lend authority to Mably's views.

21. Plato, *The Laws*, trans. T. J. Saunders (Penguin ed.; Harmondsworth, England, 1975), X, p. 408ff.

22. The state religions envisioned by both Plato and Mably would merit an extensive comparison with the civil religion set forth in the controversial Chapter VIII of Book IV of Rousseau's *Social Contract*. See Rousseau, *Oeuvres complètes* (Pléiade ed.; Paris, 1964), III, 460–469, and the editorial notes, 1498–1507.

23. Plato, *The Laws*, pp. 420–427.

24. On Mably's political career, see the Abbé Brizard's "Eloge historique de l'Abbé de Mably" in Mably's *Oeuvres complètes*, I, 93–95, and Ernest A. Whitfield, *Gabriel Bonnot de Mably* (London, 1930), pp. 6–7.

25. A useful survey of the nineteenth-century utopians may be found in Frank E. Manuel and Fritzie P. Manuel, *Utopian Thought in the Western World* (Cambridge, Mass., 1979), pp. 581–693.

26. See Roland Mortier, "Une théologie politique sous la Restauration," in G. Cambier, ed., *Christianisme d'hier et d'aujourd'hui: Hommages à Jean Préaux* (Brussels, 1979), pp. 93–107.

27. Quoted in ibid., pp. 96, 100.

28. Charles Rihs, *Les Philosophes utopistes: Le Mythe de la cité communautaire en France au XVIIème siècle* (Paris, 1970), p. 83.

IV

Private Faith and Public Religion: S. T. Coleridge's Confrontation with Secularism

JOHN T. MILLER, JR.

The "secularization of modern consciousness" is a theme that pervades the works of Samuel Taylor Coleridge, although he never spoke of it in just those words. Coleridge, who wrote social commentary and lay theology as well as poetry, was among the first to speak systematically of the social—one might even say the sociological—consequences and implications of secularization. He was a first-hand observer of the syndrome of social and economic transformations generally refered to as the "Industrial Revolution." And he was an early articulator of the connections between secularization, on the one hand, and the movements of industrialization and urbanization, on the other, associations that have become commonplaces of modern thought, both popular and scholarly.

Coleridge viewed secularization from the standpoint of religious advocacy, and he regarded it as an unqualified tragedy. But it will be one of the arguments of this essay that his theological views actually contributed to the sustenance and promotion of the secularizing process. Secularization is a process, as Harvey Cox has stated, by which religion is "privatized."[1] And Coleridge espoused a radically private approach to Christian faith and apologetics, although at the same time he was pressing for the revival of the Church of England as a public, and indeed a political, institution. Our examination of Coleridge's theological ideas will suggest that secularization arises, at least in part, from the inner dynamic of modern theology itself.

The word "secularization," as it is commonly used, refers to at least two distinguishable movements: to the actual decline of belief and to the diminution of religion's role and influence in state and society. This distinction is not always recognized, and the two processes are often regarded as virtually identical.[2] But the recent history of religion in the West seems to indicate that the

70

personal and social trends can and do proceed independently of each other. In the United States, particularly, the state is and always has been constitutionally secular, but the persistence of avowed religious faith is seemingly unflagging.[3]

This is not a turn of events that Coleridge anticipated—although we will have subsequent occasion to argue that his thought can help to explain it.[4] Coleridge regarded the personal and social trends of secularization as integrally related and he believed that, in his day, they were discernibly proceeding in parallel directions. Of the two, he regarded the decline of personal faith as the primary, causal force. Scepticism, that is to say, was the driving impetus of secularization in its social aspects. The withdrawal of human attention from holy things and spiritual concerns removed an essential "counterpoise" to human greed and thereby facilitated the ascendancy in social relations of materialism and worldly impulses. The result was the rise of what Coleridge called "commercialism," the epitome of social secularization.

—Coleridge's remedy for the malady of secularism was twofold. First, he sought to attack the root-cause of spreading disbelief. This he identified in the prevalent Anglican fashion for rational theology and an apologetic relying too heavily upon arguments of biblical evidence. He sought to establish, instead, an emphasis upon inner religious experience and the yearning for salvation. Second, Coleridge proposed to annul the social consequences of secularism with a renovation of the national church as an integral part of the state. There is a tension, if not a contradiction, in this dual prescription of inner faith and political religion. We will explore it further after a more complete exposition of Coleridge's views.

Coleridge, as is well known, was not an invariable champion of established religion. In his younger days he was a Unitarian and very nearly took a position as a Unitarian minister. William Hazlitt heard him preach on one occasion in 1798 and recalled that he spoke "upon church and state—not their alliance, but their separation."[5] As a Unitarian, the young Coleridge founded his faith upon the very bases of evidence and logic that he subsequently came to despise. He abhorred "enthusiasm" and affected a stoic impassivity in the face of life's trials (in keeping with Priestley's religious necessitarianism).

Coleridge eventually found, however, that such attitudes did not comport with his temperament or with the difficulties he faced during much of his life: artistic insecurity, occupational uncertainty, marital discord, opium addiction, and a long parade of real and imagined physical ailments. His early letters reflect a growing conviction that emotional sustenance was among the principal functions of religion and that mere rational deduction could not support that function. Religion was his "Joy in sorrow," he wrote in 1796, never to be bartered "for a few subtleties from the school of the cold-blooded Sophist!" In 1798 he praised a friend as "one in whom Christianity is an habit of feeling in a still greater degree than a conviction of the understanding."[6]

Ultimately, as this last statement implies, Coleridge became convinced that faith might be founded upon feeling, indeed that feeling might engender ✓ conviction even in the absence of decisive evidence. He wrote, shortly after the death of one of his children, that he found it "wise and human to believe, even on slight evidence, opinions, the contrary of which cannot be proved, & which promote our happiness without hampering our Intellect."[7]

By 1799 Coleridge was prepared to recognize the incompatibility of his own doctrines of internal faith with the tenets of Unitarianism. But his approach to full Trinitarian orthodoxy was a gradual one. And he seems, interestingly, to have approached religious orthodoxy by way of political orthodoxy—that is to say, he acknowledged the constitutional legitimacy of the Church of England as an establishment before he was prepared to embrace all of its teachings. It was Bonaparte's concordat with the Papacy, Coleridge wrote to his brother in 1802, that "first occasioned me to think accurately & with consecutive Logic on the force & meaning of the word *Established* Church and the result of my reflections was very greatly in favor of the Church of England." The "wretched" concordat, he concluded, had produced a church entirely dependent for sustenance and legitimacy upon the will of a "transient legislature" and a military dictator. The Church of England, on the other hand, was an independent *"Estate* of the Realm,"* an "elementary part of our constitution" whose claim to its property and status was "truly antecedent to any form of Government in England. . . ."

Coleridge was not yet prepared to endorse all of the "peculiar Doctrines" of the Church of England, even though he regarded it as a legitimate and salutary national institution. His reading of Scripture had convinced him that the Unitarian view was untenable, but he had not yet embraced the Trinity. The "Nature of the Being of Christ is left in obscurity," he told his brother. But he now accepted Original Sin and the Atonement. And here again he grounded his faith upon feeling and need rather than upon a rational persuasion: "This I believe—not because I *understand* it; but because I *feel*, that it is not only suitable to, but needful for, my nature and because I find it clearly revealed."[8]

Coleridge's residual doubts were ultimately overcome, and by about 1805 his *fides quaerens intellectum* had reached a final Trinitarian resolution.[9] He recounted his crisis of faith as follows in a letter of October 1806 to his brother-in-law George Fricker:

> I was for many years a Socinian; and at times almost a Naturalist, but sorrow, and ill health, and disappointment of the only deep wish I ever cherished, forced me to look into myself; I read the New Testament again, and I became fully convinced, that Socinianism was not only not the doctrine of the New Testament, but that it scarcely deserved the name of a religion in any sense.[10]

He conceded that the testimony of scriptural accounts, relied upon by the orthodox as well as the Socinians, was impeachable. Indeed, excessive reliance for the "evidence of Christianity upon miracles, to the exclusion of grace and inward faith" had "increased the number of infidels;—never could [that number] have been so great, if thinking men had been habitually led to look into their own souls, instead of always looking out, both of themselves and of their nature." But the doctrines of Christianity remained "binding," Coleridge affirmed, even in the absence of external evidence. These truths were their own verification. He counseled the sceptic: "with the grace of the spirit consult your own heart, in quietness and humility," and "they will furnish you with proofs, that surpass all understanding."[11]

Coleridge habitually spoke of "heart" and "head" as complementary and coordinate faculties. The problem of interplay between thought and emotion was a staple of his philosophic musings. He once planned a treatise upon "the affinities of the Feelings with Words & Ideas" that would "supercede all the Books of Metaphysics hitherto written/and all the Books of Morals too."[12] "I feel strongly and I think strongly," he wrote in 1796, "but I seldom feel without thinking, or think without feeling." A letter of 1801 gave this sentiment a general application: "My opinion is this—that deep Thinking is attainable only by a man of deep Feeling, and that all Truth is a species of Revelation."[13]

In The Friend (1818) and The Statesman's Manual (1816) Coleridge systematized this doctrine into a conception of Reason that amalgamated feeling with "thought" in the cerebral sense of the word. "Reason" in this context was contrasted, through an adaptation of Kantian terminology, with "Understanding." The latter was a merely empirical faculty, capable only of apprehending the realm of sense impressions. But Reason was an "inward sense" or "mind's eye"—an "organ of the Supersensuous." It possessed the "power of acquainting itself with invisible realities or spiritual objects."[14] It was the means whereby men beheld directly and immediately the truth of spiritual things and recognized the validity of religious revelation. "Reason," Coleridge wrote in Aids to Reflection in 1825, "is a direct aspect of Truth, an inward Beholding." It differed from religion "only as the two-fold application of the same power."[15]

Coleridge's espousal of this doctrine of inward faith was correlative with his vehement rejection of the predominant Anglican theology of his time. The prevalent view, articulated by the influential writings of William Paley (1743–1805) and established as Anglican orthodoxy by the Latitudinarians of the seventeenth century, held that faith in Christianity was founded upon the rational—or more precisely the empirical—grounds of Apostolic testimony to Christ's life and miraculous works, as passed down by the Scriptures. Coleridge deplored the contemporary emphasis upon arguments from evidence as a "judicial, law-cant" sort of Christianity. Such a theology was, he insisted, at best irrelevant and at worst inimical to genuine Christian faith.

Evidences of Christianity! I am weary of the word. Make a man feel the *want* of it; rouse him, if you can, to the self-knowledge of his *need* of it; and you may safely trust it to its own Evidences. . . .[16]

The evidentiary conception of faith, Coleridge maintained, had never been stressed in Christian thinking before the time of Hugo Grotius (1583–1645), the Dutch jurist and Arminian apologist. Coleridge branded Grotius the "greatest Enemy" of the Christian religion for introducing a preoccupation with evidences into theological currency.[17] The "broken reed of outward Evidence," Coleridge warned, would never sustain the faith in the face of historical criticism of biblical accounts or logical assaults upon the theory of miracles, such as those of David Hume. And, more importantly, the "Bustle about evidences" was directly and actively corrosive of genuine belief. Too frantic an effort to sell the faith by empirical inducements to those not prepared by inward grace to receive it would devalue the article and distract its possessors from its true basis in the believer's inner "self-knowledge." Coleridge, for his own part, preferred to bear the "character of a mystic" rather than indulge the "passion of proselytism."[18]

This devaluation of personal faith, Coleridge believed, contributed mightily to the dilution of Christian influence within society at large, i.e., to social secularization. And secularization contributed, in turn, to a variety of societal misfortunes that Coleridge enumerated under the rubric of the "over-balance of the commercial spirit." It was in 1817, in the aftermath of Waterloo, that Coleridge published his most complete exposition upon these sociomoral issues. His commentary was entitled *A Lay Sermon, Addressed to the Higher and Middle Classes on the Existing Distresses and Discontents*. It sought to explain the economic depression and popular unrest that marked the era of Spa Fields and Peterloo. Why had peace not brought general contentment and "the advantages expected from Peace."[19]

The current Discontents, Coleridge concluded, were partially attributable to "factious demagogues." But unrest was substantially explained, if not justified, by the very real economic Distresses that the nation was currently enduring. And the present depression was but one instance of a recurring phenomenon, Coleridge warned. Periodic "Revolutions of Credit" had occurred at intervals of about twelve or thirteen years over the "last sixty years," he argued, and such alternations of prosperity and dearth were likely to continue unless British society undertook fundamental reforms.[20]

The reforms that Coleridge had in mind were moral and, ultimately, religious. For he was convinced that the economic instability besetting his society had its origins in certain endemic moral failings and that only moral and religious renewal would dampen the vicious cycle of boom and bust. The predicament was created, he argued, by the prevalence of business practices that resembled the "wicked lunacies of the Gaming Table." "Impatience and

Incaution" combined with "Want of principle and Confederacies of false credit" to render "movements of Trade . . . yearly gayer and gidier" until the onset of the inevitable "Crash."

And while the periodic depressions of trade brought material want, the occasional spates of exaggerated prosperity revealed a moral disequilibrium that was equally to be deplored. Unwonted opulence, impermanent by its very nature, disarmed the sturdy husbandman of his habitual frugality and temperance and insured that his suffering would be all the worse when an economic reversal inevitably arrived. The "remorseless mania of Speculation" in good times, "the frequency of Failures with all the disgraceful secrets of Fraud and Folly" in bad, and withal the "drunken stupor of usurious Selfishness" did "serious injury to the Moral Sense."[21]

These excesses were attributable, Coleridge argued, to an "OVERBALANCE OF THE COMMERCIAL SPIRIT IN CONSEQUENCE OF THE ABSENSE OR WEAKNESS OF THE COUNTER-WEIGHTS." He hastened to insist that he did not think "hostilely" of commerce itself and that he did not blame commerce alone for the nation's ills. But he believed that certain countervailing influences, which had once held the spirit of trade in proper balance, were now either diminished or extinct. Among these "natural counterforces" Coleridge numbered the influence of religious faith, along with the "ancient feeling of rank and ancestry" and the spirit of philosophy in the pure, contemplative sense of the word. These counterweights, he contended, had the function of diverting the mind from immediate, material gain in favor of higher pursuits and concerns. They consequently had the effect of curbing the "Spirit of Barter," which was ultimately founded upon selfish instincts and was therefore potentially inimical to the public weal as well as to private morality.

Coleridge believed that the overbalance of the commercial spirit had ill effects in all spheres of British society. But the greatest damage was done by the "extension of the commercial spirit into our agricultural system." The spirit of commerce was native to the world of merchants and manufacturers, and an acquisitive mentality (properly tempered) had a valid role to play in that realm. But the world of agriculture, the sphere of the landed proprietor, was properly distinct from that of commerce and industry. "Agriculture," Coleridge argued, required "principles essentially different from those of Trade." A "gentleman," he insisted, "ought not to regard his estate as a merchant his cargo, or a shopkeeper his stock."

The landed proprietor had a responsibility to attend directly and deliberately to the common good, and most immediately to the good of his tenants and dependents. The unit of agricultural production was more than an economic enterprise. It was also, and essentially, an institution of governance. Landed property possessed an "official" character.[22] The landed gentleman or nobleman must regard the "*marketable* produce" of his lands as a "subordinate consideration to the living and moral growth that is to remain on the land"—"I mean a healthful, callous-handed but high-and-warm-hearted Tenantry."[23]

Coleridge warned that the seduction of the landed class by the spirit of commerce and the consequent neglect of the tenantry presaged enduring damage to the social structure. For instance, small tenants and proprietors were displaced in the movement toward larger and more efficient farming units, and thereby "some of the intermediate rounds in the social ladder have been broken and not replaced." The "peasantry" were "sinking into pauperism, step for step with the rise of the farmer's profits and indulgencies." And, most disturbing of all, this elimination of the "most important rounds in the social ladder" contributed to the migration of the rural population to the manufacturing towns. Here, Coleridge concluded, lay the "ultimate cause of our liability to distresses like the present." Society had reached "a state of things so remote from the simplicity of nature, that we have almost deprived Heaven itself of the power of blessing us." And the heart of the predicament was to be found in *the vast and disproportionate number of men who are to be fed from the produce of the fields, on which they do not labor.*"[24]

It will be evident from this outline of Coleridge's social philosophy that he stood near the head of that long and prolific tradition of social commentary which has associated the decline of religious influence, either as cause or consequence, with industrialization, urbanization, growing social and geographic mobility and, in general, the passing of *Gemeinschaft* in the face of advancing *Gesellschaft*.[25] He was among the first, in short, to treat secularization as part of a more general pathology of modernity.

But Coleridge's perspective and hence his emphases differed in certain interesting, and perhaps significant, ways from those of later exponents of similar ideas. Coleridge placed less emphasis upon the imposing machinery of industrialization and more upon the interpersonal give-and-take of commerce. And he viewed secularization as a cause of social and economic change rather than strictly a result. He found the ultimate source of commercialization (and industrialization, urbanization, and so forth) in the contemporary climate of opinion and specifically in the ascendancy of the empiricist philosophy of Locke and Newton et al. The empirical "understanding" had triumphed over its rightful superior, the spiritual "reason." The spirituality of personal faith had been vitiated by a preoccupation with outward evidence at the expense of inward reflection. And the resulting decline of attention to otherworldly matters had permitted an "over-balance" of commercialism, the embodiment and fruition of empiricism and materialism. "We live . . . under the dynasty of the understanding," Coleridge lamented, "and this is its golden age."[26]

Coleridge regarded social change as something that man did to himself, through his own ideas and attitudes, rather than something that was imposed upon him by vast and impersonal and hence uncontrollable forces. It is a perspective worth pondering, and perhaps recapturing, in the writing of the history of "industrial society."

Coleridge's prescription for the national malady that he diagnosed in the *Lay Sermon* of 1817 did not emerge with any clarity in that particular tract. The sermon contented itself with a declamatory plea for moral revival: "Let us become a better people, and the reform of all public (real or supposed) grievances, which we use as pegs whereon to hang our errors and defects, will follow of itself."[27] It was not until 1829 that Coleridge spelled out, in his final political work, the actual instrumentality by which the British might expect to "become a better people." That treatise was *On the Constitution of the Church and State,* prompted by the Catholic emancipation controversy. The instrument of reform was to be the Church of England, or, as Coleridge called it, the National Church or "clerisy." "Religion, true or false," Coleridge argued, "is and ever has been the centre of gravity in a realm, to which all other things must and will accommodate themselves." Theology "comprised all the main aids, instruments, and materials of NATIONAL EDUCATION," because "to divinity belong those fundamental truths, which are the common ground-work of our civil and religious duties. . . ."

It was the principal role of the church (in its civil capacity as an institution of the state) to promote, by means of a cradle-to-grave, theologically based program of education, a "character of general civilization" conducive to national strength and social stability. A strong and influential national church would ensure that civilization encompassed, not merely material advancement, but a comprehensive and "harmonious development of those qualities which characterized our *humanity*." By that means alone would the nation be endowed with a "Will in harmony with the Reason, and a consequent subordination of the appetites and passions to the ultimate ends of our Being."[28]

Needless to say, the actuality of the Church of England in Coleridge's day did not live up to the ideal or "idea" of the national church as he conceived it. The established church was properly an integral and constitutional element of the state whose prerogatives and property were held by an inalienable tenure. But contemporary opinion seemed bent upon reducing the Anglican establishment "to *a* religion," i.e., one among many, without special duties of public tutelage or special rights to public property. If this attitude were carried to its logical conclusion the national church would be, at best, reduced to the dependent status of the Gallican church under Napoleon or, at worst, entirely despoiled of its property and civic responsibilities.[29] Only the reversal of this trend and the restoration of the church to its proper status and prominence would provide for the maintenance of a proper respect for religion, a proper curbing of materialistic impulses and the redressing of the "over-balance of the commercial spirit."

Coleridge evidently intended his theology of inner faith and his proposals

for establishmentarian revival to be mutually reinforcing elements of a program
for national reform and personal fulfillment. But the course of Western religious
and social history since Coleridge's time has seen one of these components
flourish while the other has faded from effective existence. And there is a
tension, perhaps a contradiction, between them that made such a "trade-off" all
but inevitable. Personal faith based upon inner experience and need, to wit, has
become a dominant motif in modern theology, while established religion has
retreated in the face of secularization.

Basil Willey, for one, argues that the ascendancy of inward faith is a
crucial development for the viability of Christianity, and he argues that Coleridge contributed significantly to this course of theological events. Coleridge,
Willey says, abandoned the "pseudo-foundations" for the faith "in historical,
prophetic, natural or miraculous 'evidences'" and adopted instead "a firmer
foundation in the specific religious experience, in man's need for a God who
comes to meet and redeem him." Consequently, the "debt of modern theology to
Coleridge is very considerable," for he thereby helped to establish the position
from which Christianity subsequently "held its ground" against the attacks of
"biblical criticism and scientific agnosticism."[30] And Willey is certainly correct
that a course very much like Coleridge's is the one that much of "modern
theology" has adopted amidst the rocks and shoals of subsequent controversy.[31]

But, while this approach may justify all that has been said for it as an
advance in the understanding of genuine Christianity, it represents a setback for
the public establishment of religion. Indeed, the reliance of post-Restoration
Anglicanism upon Evidences arose precisely from a concern for the sustenance
of the national church. In abandoning that ground Coleridge was in fact abandoning the last best hope for an enduring partnership of church and state. More
generally, the prevalence of a radically private conception of faith may well be
one major cause of the "privatization" of religion that is the obverse of secularization.

The motivation for the "trumpeting of outward Evidences" among post-
Reformation theologians is frequently misunderstood. According to James
Boulger, for instance, "Evidence-writing" arose from the Enlightenment
penchant for application of "Locke's premises" to theological matters. And, he
says, "Coleridge urged that such demonstrations are the product of scientific
rather than religious enthusiasms. . . ."[32] But Coleridge urged no such thing.
Rather, he attributed the theology of Evidences to the paternity of Grotius, not
Locke. And he correctly discerned its motivation, not in an enthusiasm for
science, but in the "passion for proselytism."[33]

Grotius was not a scientist, and neither was William Chillingworth (1602–
1644), his principal Anglican disciple. And they did not pursue an apologetic of
Evidences out of any desire to ape the new science (which in their pre-
Newtonian day was hardly the imposing force it would later become).[34] Instead,

their overriding concern was with achieving some basis for the restoration of Christian unity amidst the chaos of schism and bloodshed which was the aftermath of the Reformation. The theology of Evidences took its fundamental impetus not from Newtonian empiricism but from Erasmian irenicism.

Chillingworth argued that an appeal to the empirical evidence of Biblical testimony—an appeal to what he called "reason"—was the only basis upon which an amicable national consensus could be established and the national church maintained. "Reason being a public and certain thing," he wrote, it was "exposed to all men's trial and examination" and provided the means by which all reasonable men might come to agreement. Appeals to the "private spirit," on the other hand, bred only idiosyncrasy of doctrine and divisiveness of sectarian allegiance.[35] Chillingworth's successors as champions of this "Grotian" philosophy within the Anglican clergy were the Latitudinarians of the later seventeenth century, whose anxiety to curb sectarian strife was powerfully reinforced by the experience of the civil wars (1641–1660). It was they, i.e., John Wilkins, John Tillotson, and others of like mind, who were brought into the principal sees of the church by William III at the Revolution of 1688 and who established empirical theology and ecclesiastical Whiggery as the Anglican orthodoxy of the eighteenth century.[36] They established, that is, the theological system that Coleridge attacked in his writings of a century and a half later. Their motivation in continuing to stress an apologetic of Evidences, let it be emphasized once again, was the conviction that denominational peace was best ensured by the comprehensive appeal of the established national church.

Coleridge was correct, of course, about the legalistic—"judicial, law-cant"—quality of such a theology. But the legalism was there because the national church was a ward, if not a creature, of the law. Its survival as the representative of the religious majority depended, the "Grotians" knew, upon its ability to make its case persuasively at the bar of public opinion. And in rejecting the legalism of Grotian theology, Coleridge failed to come to terms with the apologetic problem that that theology had been designed to meet. Coleridge may well have been correct that a constantly combative proselytory stance was destructive of the repose of inner faith. But the Grotians realized that a national church was, for better or for worse, a political animal that must possess the capacity, in an age of spreading education and mounting scepticism, to convince the nation of the truth of its teachings as well as the utility of its services.

Coleridge, it is true, was equally enamored of the ideal of Christian unity within the national church. In 1834, for instance, he spoke of hopes of achieving "a large comprehension" of Protestant sects under "four or five articles of faith."[37] But his theology provided no language or logic by which Dissenting denominations could conceivably have been persuaded to renounce their differences. Reason, for Chillingworth, was "a public and certain thing." But Cole-

ridge's "Reason" appealed entirely to the "private spirit," to the Inner Light and
the "mind's eye," which was precisely the basis for Dissent and dissension
among English Christians.

Coleridge conceived of the national church as the molder of national
civilization and the guarantor of social health. It was to accomplish this formidable mission by means of national education based upon Christian theology. But
Coleridge's theology was not suited to the task. When religious apologetic
withdraws from public discourse into private "self-knowledge," it qualifies, or
renounces, its efficacy as a tool of social engineering. One of Coleridge's
notebook entries seems almost to acknowledge this disparity between his personal credo and his theology of social action. Questions of "inward Religion,"
he wrote, are solely the concern of the "inwardly religious"—"what have the
PUBLIC to do with this?"[38]

It is apparent that the privatization of religion and hence the secularization
of society draw impetus not merely from "worldly" forces but also from the very
forms of modern religion. Religion, by following the course that Coleridge
helped to chart, has privatized itself.

It was the aim of the Latitudinarians to promote the universality of religion
by couching apologetic theology in the common language of the world. They saw
no other way of preserving the national church as a public and political entity.
But theologians of the nineteenth century found this brand of rational theology
inadequate to the communication of the Christian message and ineffective in the
conversion of sceptics. They turned to inner reflection and the "specific religious experience" as the only means of preserving the Christian faith. In so
doing they founded religion upon a language and an epistemology wholly dispa-
rate from the empiricism of ordinary life.

There may be some explanation here for the apparent paradox, touched
upon above, of the persistence of faith in a secularized world.[39] Religion that is
privatized is also immunized, as Cox suggests, from social persecution or even
criticism.[40] When religion and society speak different languages, there is little
basis for argument. But if the Coleridgean theology of inner reflection has
permitted the coexistence of prevalent faith with inexorable secularization, it
has at the same time doomed the sort of religious society and ecclesiastical
polity that Coleridge urged as the only basis for genuine civilization.

Notes

1. Harvey Cox, *The Secular City* (New York, 1965), p. 2.

2. See, e.g., Andrew M. Greeley, *Unsecular Man: The Persistence of Religion* (New York,
1972). Cf. Cox, *Secular City*, who argues, correctly I think, that man can be both secular and
religious at once.

3. According to a recent Gallup poll, 94 percent of Americans believe in God or a "universal

spirit" and substantial majorities adhere to more specific Judeo-Christian tenets. *Washington Star*, Dec. 15, 1979, p. A–7.

4. See my discussion below, p. 80.

5. Quoted by John Colmer, "Editor's Introduction" to Coleridge's *On the Constitution of the Church and State* (Princeton, 1976), p. xl.

6. E. L. Griggs, ed., *Collected Letters of Samuel Taylor Coleridge*, I, 235, 409.

7. Ibid., p. 479.

8. *Collected Letters*, II, 803, 806–807. Cf. *The Notebooks of Samuel Taylor Coleridge*, Kathleen Coburn, ed. (New York, 1957) I, entry 1123 of February–March 1802: "The strongest argument for Xstianity the weak Argument that do yet persuade so many to believe—i.e. it fits the human heart—." See also entry 989.

9. See *Notebooks*, II, 2444 & n.

10. Coleridge does not specify his "only deep wish," but it was probably the plan for emigration to America conceived with Robert Southey in 1794; see *Notebooks* II, 2398. See also ibid., 2437 on personal tribulations and "weakness" as the basis of faith.

11. *Collected Letters*, II, 1189–1190.

12. Letter of Feb. 3, 1801, to Sir Humphrey Davy, ibid., p. 671.

13. *Collected Letters*, I, 279; II, 709.

14. *The Friend*, Barbara Rooke, ed. (Princeton, 1969) I, 156–157; *The Lay Sermons*, R. J. White, ed. (Princeton, 1972), p. 61.

15. *Aids to Reflection and Confession of an Inquiring Spirit* (London, 1913), p. 148; *Lay Sermons*, p. 59.

16. *Aids*, p. 272.

17. *Collected Letters*, II, 861.

18. *Notebooks*, III, 3966, 3754; II, 2196.

19. *Lay Sermons*, pp. 140–142.

20. Ibid., pp. 202–203.

21. Ibid., pp. 203–208.

22. *Specimens of the Table Talk of the Late Samuel Taylor Coleridge*, Henry Nelson Coleridge, ed. (New York, 1835) II, entry for Mar. 31, 1833, p. 70.

23. *Lay Sermons*, pp. 216–223.

24. Ibid., pp. 212, 227–228.

25. On these associations see Cox, *Secular City* and, in a more general vein, Robert A. Nisbet, *The Sociological Tradition* (New York, 1966). I have developed this theme further in my "Ideology and Enlightenment; The Political and Social Thought of Samuel Taylor Coleridge" (Ph.D. diss., Yale University, 1977; University Microfilms, 1978).

26. *On the Constitution*, p. 59.

27. *Lay Sermons*, pp. 226–230.

28. *On the Constitution*, pp. 69–70, 44, 42–43, 87.

29. Ibid., chapter VII, "Regrets and Apprehensions."

30. Basil Willey, *Nineteenth Century Studies, Coleridge to Matthew Arnold* (New York, 1966), pp. 31–32.

31. On this theological trend and Coleridge's relation to it, see Claude Welch, *Protestant Thought in the Nineteenth Century* (New Haven, 1972), esp. pp. 112, 126, and 306ff. On Cole-

ridge's influence in nineteenth-century religious thought, see: Charles R. Sanders, *Coleridge and the Broad Church Movement* (Durham, N.C., 1942); John Coulmer, *Newman and the Common Tradition: A Study in the Language of Church and Society* (Oxford, 1970); Stephen Prickett, *Romanticism and Religion, the Tradition of Coleridge and Wordsworth in the Victorian Church* (Cambridge, 1976).

32. James D. Boulger, *Coleridge as Religious Thinker* (New Haven, 1961), pp. 24–26, 10. No citation is provided for the latter statement.

33. See my discussion above, p. 74.

34. In fact, their thought had a considerable influence upon the development of science, rather than vice versa. See Henry G. Van Leeuwen, *The Problem of Certainty in English Thought, 1630–1690* (The Hague, 1963).

35. Chillingworth quoted in Robert Orr, *Reason and Authority: The Thought of William Chillingworth* (Oxford, 1967), p. 93.

36. See Martin I. J. Griffin, "Latitudinarianism in the Seventeenth-Century Church of England" (Ph.D. diss., Yale University, 1962) for an account of their thought.

37. *Table Talk*, II, 146.

38. *Notebooks*, III, 3948.

39. See my discussion above, pp. 70–71.

40. Cox, *Secular City*, p. 2.

V

Victorian Ethics of Belief:
A Reconsideration

FRANK M. TURNER and JEFFREY VON ARX

For one of his most successful assignments to undergraduates in his course on British and European intellectual history, Franklin Baumer in the late 1960s asked his students to compose a letter purportedly written in the 1870s by an English university student explaining to his father why he could not take Holy Orders. The twentieth-century students at first encountered some difficulty in comprehending why anyone should think twice about, let alone redirect his life over, the matter of the Virgin Birth unless the question were likely to appear on the entrance examination for medical school. However, the assignment produced exceedingly thoughtful papers. For, once their initial inhibitions had been overcome, the undergraduates realized that for most of those young Victorians the problem of religious belief was one of conscience. And the American undergraduate of the late 1960s, fully aware of the moral dimension of the great national debates of that decade, discovered a certain kinship of conscience with those troubled English students and scholars of a century ago.

Yet, we are by no means certain that today or a decade from now the epistolary assignment that Franklin Baumer employed with such success would continue to elicit good essays. It may be that the brotherhood of conscience between the young of our time and those of Britain's intellectual elite of a century ago may have diminished or vanished. We suspect that the students of the early 1980s may react to those troubled mid-Victorian consciences or the character of Robert Elsmere as John Maynard Keynes and his friends reacted to the demise of religious faith recounted in the biography of Henry Sidgwick when it appeared in 1906. Sidgwick had wrestled with the questions of what doctrines he could believe in good conscience throughout the 1860s. In 1869 he resigned his fellowship at Cambridge not because it required him to take Holy Orders but rather because its occupation presupposed acceptance of the Apos-

tle's Creed. Reading about the early life of his one-time teacher, Keynes wrote
to B. W. Swithinbank in March 1906:

> Have you read Sidgwick's Life? . . . He never did anything but wonder whether
> Christianity was true and prove that it wasn't and hope that it was. He even learnt
> Arabic [sic] in order to read Genesis in the original, not trusting the authorized
> translators, which does seem a little sceptical . . . I wonder what he would have
> thought of us; and I wonder what we think of him. And then his conscience—
> incredible. There is no doubt about his moral goodness. And yet it is all so
> dreadfully depressing—no intimacy, no clear-cut crisp boldness. Oh, I suppose
> he was intimate but he didn't seem to have anything to be intimate about except
> his religious doubts. And he really ought to have got over that a little sooner;
> because he knew that the thing wasn't true perfectly well from the beginning.[1]

Perceptions as well as opinions do change. The pursuit of the dictates of
conscience may be a necessary part of our humanity, but that pursuit does not
necessarily manifest itself in the same way at all times or in all places. In the
years separating Sidgwick's spiritual crisis and Keynes's letter a profound
change had occurred among British intellectuals. Put quite simply, they had
become more secular in their outlook. By the close of the century religious
questions, concerns, and institutions troubled the inner lives of such people far
less than they had in the 1860s. The debate over the ethics of belief, of which
Sidgwick's doubts were a part, was a key engine of transition in that movement
from religious to more nearly secular preoccupations among the British intellectual classes.

The issue of the ethics of belief arose in Britain during the late 1830s.
Earlier in the century it had been assumed that to be an *honest Christian* was a
problem of character and not one of intellect. That assumption received several
challenges. First, the question arose of what it meant to be an honest Christian
clergyman, and at a later point doubts were expressed as to whether one could
be both an intellectually honest person and a Christian. The issue grew out of
the Oxford movement and initially took the form of asking what did it mean on
the part of a clergyman to indicate intellectual and religious acceptance of the
Thirty-nine Articles of the Church of England? Did he interpret them in a
Catholic manner as suggested by Newman's Tract 90 or in a more nearly
Protestant manner? Was it morally right to accept them in the former fashion
without so indicating publicly? By the late 1850s and 1860s the issue had
largely redefined itself into a question of what meaning one ascribed to the
Articles, the Creed, and the Bible? Could a clergyman or a layman who by
virtue of his profession was presumed to accept those documents do so in a
nonliteral manner or could he actually disbelieve a particular clause or portion
of one of those documents? Again there arose the question of whether those

reservations must be made public? Toward the end of the 1860s and throughout the 1870s, as the clergy quarreled among themselves, agnostics, including T. H. Huxley, John Morley, and W. K. Clifford entered the fray. They raised the question of the morality of accepting or asserting the truth of any religious or philosophical statement on nonempirical evidence. Consequently, by the closing years of the century, when Keynes and his generation were coming of age, the problem of the truth of the interpretation of the Articles and the Bible seemed a much less significant issue than that of the perhaps fundamental incompatibility of maintaining both intellectual integrity and religious faith.

The question we wish to explore is what were some of the particular circumstances that caused or more properly allowed this debate over the ethics of belief to occur and that sustained it for so many years. Let us immediately caution that we are not contending that conscience itself was not a primary factor in the actions that men and women pursued in working through the ethics of belief for themselves and in making personal sacrifices, such as separation from their families and vocations. We believe, in other words, that they were sincere. However, we also believe that certain social, political, and ecclesiastical circumstances existed without which the debate either would not have occurred or would have taken a different direction.

Some of these circumstances were directly intellectual and related to books published and read or in vogue at a particular time. Religious and intellectual historians have been quite alert to these intellectual factors, such as the impact of Tract 90 upon the meaning of accepting the Thirty-nine Articles and the dissolvent influence upon religious faith of the works of Mill, Darwin, Spencer, and the higher critics of the Bible. However, in future studies we believe scholars of Victorian theology and religion must also address themselves to nonintellectual factors and must pose new, more skeptical questions to familiar documents. They must seek to understand the larger social and religious framework of ideas and institutions that both conditioned and channeled the personal responses to the dissolvent scientific and theological literature of the third quarter of the century. Both clergymen and laymen had experienced various modes of religious doubt and philosophic skepticism before this period, but only during these years did the experience take so collective a form and give rise to broad discussions and debate in essays, sermons, poetry, and novels.

In the remainder of this essay we will consider three conditions that made possible, though did not in and of themselves bring about, the Victorian manifestation of conscience in regard to the ethics of belief. They are *(a)* the religious revival of the first half of the century, *(b)* the passage of the Clerical Disabilities Act of 1870, and *(c)* the political and social implications of different positions on the ethics of belief.

The Religious Revival

It must never be forgotten that the immediate background and context for the years of theological doubt and scepticism was a period of ecclesiastical and devotional revival. The emergence of the problem of the ethics of belief was one by-product of the religious renewal within the Church of England. The leaven of Evangelicalism still touched the lives of young men and women coming of age in the 1840s and 1850s. The Tractarian influence continued to work its way even after the departures of Newman, Manning, and others to Rome. Moreover, the Broad Church party was stressing both a learned ministry and a heightened sense of social responsibility on the part of the Establishment. All of these developments meant that those people who were religious tended to regard both doctrine and devotion more seriously than in the first quarter of the century and that the ministry itself had come to be considered a more distinctly religious vocation. The problem of defining the ethics of belief was almost always closely related to the problem of vocation. And at the center of the crisis over the ethics of belief were young men about to enter the Anglican priesthood or recently ordained. The sense of the ministry as a religious vocation rather than one of social status was one result of the religious revival that had marked the Church of England in the first half of the century.

A letter written in 1816 by a young clergyman explaining the conditions of his acceptance of a particular curacy may serve to illustrate the contrast between Victorian clerical life and that which preceded it.

The necessity of residing at Waterperry, did, I confess, at first make me hesitate from religious scruples, whether I ought to take the Curacy of it, that is, whether the kind of residence I meant was perfectly compatible with the full discharge of my pastoral duties in such a Parish. This led me to make enquiries, the results of which I am happy to say is satisfactory to me, principally on these two grounds;— first that the Parish is not so large as to require the constant residence of a Minister on the spot—and second, upon enquiring into the state of the Parish, I find such a system of education adopted under the liberal auspices of the Family presiding over it, as to render my daily attendance unnecessary, though I shall make it a point of duty to give it whenever I am in the parish.—These two considerations have chiefly prevailed with me to accept your offer, and have contributed materially, and I think, justly, to remove the scruples before mentioned. If I be asked what motives have induced me to divide my time between two places—I reply that it is certainly not done to unite the pecuniary advantages of both:—by sacrificing, as I shall do, those which I already possess by a constant residence here, I become a loser on point of income. My real and sole motive then, is this, to make myself as useful as I am able to my Ministerial office, without giving up the advantages I derive from hence in point of Society. And now

I think in the case under consideration that I may be permitted to unite the advantages without prejudice to either, lawfully and conscientiously.[2]

Even as they were written, these sentiments and the view of the ministry they implied were encountering grave difficulties. By 1816 the success of the Methodists, the growing vigor of the Nonconformists, and the ever-growing presence of rationalism, secularism, and Owenism stirred the Church of England from without as the efforts of the Evangelicals and later the Tractarians did from within. The Low Church stressed the preaching ministry, the High Church the sacramental ministry, and the Broad Church the socially responsible ministry. Each of the major ecclesiastical parties for its own particular reasons was reinterpreting the ministerial vocation from one of political and social patronage into one of devotional duty. All would have criticized the new curate of Waterperry.

The revival of the first half of the century stirred a new understanding of the Church of England as a corporate religious body and its priesthood as a devotional vocation actively supporting defined doctrine. The ethics of belief could become problematical only for clergymen or potential clergymen who had learned to take seriously and earnestly the life of the church and its theological foundations. Such was the state of mind of a significant number of vocal clergymen by the third quarter of the century. The Oxford movement had initially called forth a new religiosity and devotion on the part of the Anglican ministry. The theological extremes to which for better or worse some of its leaders carried their convictions elicited a reaction that sought to delineate more strictly and dogmatically the parameters of Anglican doctrine. As a result of this new awareness of devotion, doctrine, and religious duty, those people who grew up in either Evangelical or Tractarian homes during the 1840s and 1850s always viewed the Church of England primarily as a religious institution and its ministry as a body of men called to devotional service and theological loyalty. It was for such people, who became the articulate spokesmen of the 1860s, that the ethics of belief became problematical. It was for this reason that to the end of his life Sidgwick, himself an unbeliever, argued that the Anglican clergy must genuinely believe the doctrines of the Articles and the Creed. Unlike Matthew Arnold, the heir of the latitudinarian tradition, Sidgwick and others like him even in their unbelief could not regard the church merely as an institution of national culture.

This new sense of the church as a distinct corporate body clearly defined by devotion, doctrine, and ministry also had the effect of exacerbating and hardening the differences between churchmen and doubters. When one group came increasingly to understand itself in terms of an exclusive clerical identity, for a person even to begin to doubt was to place himself beyond that charmed

circle, and even over against it. When, for example, in 1862, the Reverend
Leslie Stephen of Trinity Hall, Cambridge, began to entertain doubts about the
literal truth of Noah's flood, he immediately concluded that he could no longer
conduct the services in the college chapel that fell to him.[3] This decision in its
turn precipitated a request from college authorities that he resign the position of
tutor to undergraduates, which he held in virtue of being a fellow in orders.
Soon thereafter, Stephen left Cambridge for London to embark on a career in
journalism, never to return again in an academic capacity. Where once Stephen
had been a liberal churchman, working from within the Anglican university
system for moderate reforms, such as the admission of Dissenters to degrees, he
very rapidly found himself thrust outside it. That he became a bitter opponent of
any privileged place for the English Church in education was due in no small
measure to this peculiar dialectic affecting doubt in a period of clerical resurgence: even to begin to question the accepted beliefs of the group had the
ineluctable effect of excluding one from the fold.

Moreover, this same period witnessed both a new emphasis on the authority of the Bible and the Articles and a widespread disagreement over their
interpretation. The more seriously the doctrines and documents of the faith were
taken from the Tracts onward, the less agreement there existed over their
meaning. The answer of the state to this impasse was to relieve the ecclesiastical authorities of their power of enforcing conformity and to impose theological
pluralism through the major ecclesiastical judicial decisions and legislation of
the 1850s and 1860s. This solution addressed the problem from an erastian
point of view, but skirted the theological issues by failing to consider the
Church of England as part of the Holy Catholic Church. And it was as part of the
latter, whether in an Evangelical or Tractarian sense, that a large number of
clergymen considered themselves ministers.

This heightened religiosity of the clergy meant that judicial decisions
outlining legal conformity could not define the ethics of belief as Rowland
Williams, one of the contributors to *Essays and Reviews*, once explained to the
consternation of Fitzjames Stephens, his counsel.[4] Consequently in a legally
latitudinarian state church, the genuinely faithful and self-examining clergyman
was thrown back upon no other support or authority for his theological integrity
than his own conscience. As a nameless minister wrote the *Times* in 1862,

> Who at this day shall say what really is the doctrine, or where is to be found the
> defined discipline of the Church? People travel a good deal in the summer
> months, and it for ever happens that you find in one church different ceremonial,
> different preached doctrine from what you found in the place you last left. . . . We
> are at sea with compasses unadjusted, with no true chart, no real pilots . . . What
> is next to heresy in one diocese is unorthodox in another; what is laid down in one
> parish as vital truth in the next is denounced as most opposed to it.[5]

Theological pluralism imposed by the state on an ecclesiastical body served by a clergy with a new distinctly religious and doctrinal conception of their vocation resulting from the years of devotional and ecclesiastical revival was the fundamental condition that made wholly problematical the ethics of belief.

The Clerical Disabilities Act (1870)

In 1862 criticizing the authors of *Essays and Reviews*, Bishop Samuel Wilberforce contended that men holding such liberal theological views "cannot, consistently with moral honesty, maintain their posts as clergymen of the Established Church."[6] It was all very well for Wilberforce to make this statement and for other people to entertain similar sentiments in silence. However, at the time when the bishop wrote, there existed no legal means whereby an Anglican clergyman might renounce his calling without encountering considerable social, legal, and financial obstacles. An Anglican priest could resign his offices and livings, but under Canon 76 he could not relinquish his vows and legally become a layman. Nor could a clergyman who had resigned his benefice enter any of the other learned professions, sit in the House of Commons, or serve as a member of a municipal corporation. Moreover, he could not without danger of prosecution in ecclesiastical courts become a Protestant Nonconformist minister. As a writer in the *Quarterly Review* of 1850 explained the situation, clergymen might conceal their disagreement with Anglican doctrine (in this context as that disagreement related to Nonconformity) or forego the exercise of their priestly functions,

> but if their own inward persuasion urges them to active and public exertion—nay, as it would seem, even if they become private or lay members of any religious sect—they are liable not only to censures properly ecclesiastical, as consisting in the deprivation of ecclesiastical privileges, but to monitions respecting their personal conduct, the disregard of which may entail the penalty of imprisonment.[7]

Paradoxically, the only calling that a resigned Anglican clergyman could undertake without danger of legal difficulties of any kind was the Roman Catholic priesthood, which the law protected from prosecution.

The Clerical Disabilities Act of 1870 removed these various prohibitions that had meant that only an Anglican clergyman with substantial private means could follow the dictates of conscience if he disagreed with doctrine. Yet the story of its passage illustrates how far the concerned members of Parliament stood from any real perception or understanding of the problem of the ethics of belief.

The matter originated in the mid-1840s in the diocese of Bishop Philpotts of Exeter when an Anglican priest by the name of Shore, being possessed of what seventeenth-century writers called a "tender conscience," wished to leave the ministry of the established church to serve a Nonconformist chapel in the same neighborhood. Mr. Shore began his new ministry, but soon found himself in the Bishop's Court accused and then convicted of a violation of canon law. He was duly deprived of his offices and privileges. The bishop said that he had followed this course of action so that Mr. Shore might properly move to his new congregation. The only meaningful penalty imposed on Mr. Shore was court costs, which he refused to pay. For that refusal he was promptly imprisoned. Though Mr. Shore was ultimately released, the upshot of his case was a formal decision by the Court of Queen's Bench that a clergyman of the Church of England could not relinquish his calling.[8]

The second result of the Shore case was a more than twenty-year sporadic effort to modify the laws binding the Anglican clergy to their occupation. A measure to this end first came before the House of Commons in 1848 but was only fully debated in 1849. On February 22, 1849, Edward Bouverie submitted a private bill that would have permitted an Anglican clergyman to declare his dissent from the Church of England and then be permitted to enter the Nonconformist ministry. None of the debate on this measure touched directly on the ethics of belief. The first question posed to Bouverie was whether the resigned clergyman would be eligible to sit in the House of Commons. Bouverie replied in the affirmative. In the debate of March 14, 1849, a speaker voiced fear that there might be some clergy "who would be induced to leave the Church, solely because they saw some good opportunity of holding a secular employment of profit and advantage either by death, or some other changes in their own families."[9] Here the issue was that of younger sons who because of the death of an elder brother might inherit an estate and with it the possibility of a political career. Bouverie himself saw the chief problem as clergymen being compelled to preach insincerely or to face ecclesiastical penalties for preaching to a Nonconformist congregation. Throughout the debate the question was considered exclusively in terms of the relationship between the Establishment and Nonconformity. At no time did anyone raise the possibility that an Anglican clergyman might not simply dissent from the Articles but actually disbelieve them in a substantial theological rather than liturgical manner. The bill passed the Commons, but reached the Lords too late in the session for action before Parliament was prorogued.

Bouverie revived his effort in 1862. There was no clear reason for the long delay, but as before he seemed to have been responding as a private member to outside pressure. This time he emphasized that the new measure would aid both those clergymen who wished to become Nonconformists and those who for one reason or another wished to renounce the clerical vocation but still remain in the Church of England. He stressed that there were men of goodwill and genuine honesty who had quite simply changed their minds about their vocation since as young students they had taken Holy Orders. *In passing,* he also noted that men such as the authors of *Essays and Reviews* could not presently leave the church. He did not suggest whether or not they wished to leave or should leave.[10]

Opponents of the measure continued to avoid the matter of fundamental theological convictions. For example, William Heathcote suggested there were really very few people who would benefit from the measure. He raised the matter of membership in the House of Commons and also insisted that a distinction be drawn between those who wished to leave the ministry for sound reasons and

> others who might be tempted to enter the Church for the purpose of trying whether they should draw prizes or blanks, and who, if they should draw blanks would not hesitate to leave it to try their hand in some mercantile or legal occupation, or perhaps, to obtain seats in that House.[11]

Another opponent feared clergymen might take the opportunity of leaving the ministry to avoid prosecution in an ecclesiatical court for some grave moral offense. However, in the final debate Bouverie declared that "unless some measure of the kind were passed, the clergy of the Church of England would remain the only people in the kingdom who were deprived of all liberty of conscience."[12] Again the bill failed when its third reading was postponed past the date of the recess. There seems to have been no concerted effort to stop the measure, but as a private bill it simply became lost in the legislative shuffle. The need for passage did not yet seem acute.

During the rest of the 1860s even without the benefit of a clerical disabilities measure numerous clergymen or potential clergymen abandoned their vocation. Certain developments made this act of conscience (and in some cases an act of prudence) somewhat easier and in very meaningful ways reduced both the financial and social cost of the action. The growth of a liberal, industrial, secular state and society created new vocational opportunities for educated men and presented a constant panorama of change. During the 1860s it became possible from the standpoint of the Bar for an Anglican clergyman to enter the legal profession if he promised he would no longer pursue his clerical duties. The same decade also witnessed the expansion of the publishing industry with several new journals appearing in London. It will be recalled that earlier the editorship of *Fraser's* had provided employment for James Anthony Froude after he decided against the clerical vocation. Various journals in the 1860s did the same for Leslie Stephen. And, of course, the passage of the Education Act of 1870 opened new vocational opportunities in the teaching profession. Moreover, there must also have been academic figures or potential academic figures who realized that it would be only a matter of time until religious tests were removed from the universities as they finally were with certain exceptions in 1871. Yet the Anglican ministry remained a profession without the possibility of legal exit.

The Clerical Disabilities Act was enacted in 1870. The act originated again from a private bill, but one that enjoyed Gladstone's public blessing.[13] It permitted an Anglican clergyman to leave the ministry by registering a deed of relinquishment with the Chancery. After the passage of six months he again became a layman in the eyes of the law, possessing all the normal rights of a layman. The measure that had originally passed the Commons had also permitted the former clergyman to return to the ministry. This clause was removed in the Lords. There the bishop of London voiced anxiety that the two doors would allow a man who had failed in a secular career to return to the security of the church. Only the bishop of Llandaff supported the idea of re-entry, because he believed that certain men who entertained serious theological or vocational doubts would be able to return to their clerical calling after they had come to peace with themselves. The other bishops and lords were not so persuaded.[14] The Commons agreed to the change in order to save the bill from another parliamentary demise. On August 9, 1870, the Clerical Disabilities Act became law.

Only when such unhampered departure from the ministry became both legally and practically feasible was much of the discussion about the proper ethical behavior of the clergy in regard to the ethics of belief, such as Sidgwick's *Ethics of Subscription* of 1870, functionally valid. Only with this law on the books could one discuss whether a liberal clergyman should fight for his convictions within or without the Church of England. To depart over matters of conscientious theological disagreement was no longer tantamount to signing one's economic death warrant. This act in conjunction with new vocational opportunities for educated men allowed the Anglican clergy to afford to be conscientious. Moreover, the law also meant that the decision to stay within the church to fight for the liberalization of theology now became a decision that could stem from conscience rather than from economic or legal necessity. Finally, the knowledge on the part of church authorities that departure of clergy was freely possible may well have played a role in the gradual but steady liberalization of creedal requirements for the clergy. In effect, the act permitted conscience to be more liberally exercized and ultimately required that conscientious differences be recognized and tolerated.

Concrete Implications of Intuitive and Empiricist Epistemology

From the appearance of Tract 90 until the late 1860s the debate over the ethical implications of belief remained primarily an intrachurch matter. But from the close of the 1860s until the early 1880s the ethics of belief became discussed in a wide public arena where questions and considerations other than those applying to the church and clergy were raised. The public discussion was largely the result of the existence of the Metaphysical Society and the work of enterprising editors who saw that many of the papers read before the society and issues debated there appeared in the new journals.[15] But both the activity of the society over more than a decade and the public interest in these ethical and epistemological debates as manifested in the success of the *Contemporary Review*, the *Fortnightly Review*, and the *Nineteenth Century* suggest that in the 1870s the participants and observers saw immediate matters of social, educational, and political policy, as well as existential issues of determining right and wrong, involved in these discussions. It is this public interest in these debates that differentiates them from the later discussions of the Aristotelian Society, where similar philosophical issues were aired.

There were at least three major national questions about which the epistemological issues debated at the Metaphysical Society carried immediate implications. The first of these was the direction of the Church of England and of those institutions that it controlled or influenced. It is often assumed that the controversy over the direction of the Church of England in the period under consideration continued to be principally an affair among factions within the church—of Ritualists, Broad Churchmen, and Evangelicals struggling for control of doctrine, discipline, and worship. Certainly it was true, as the career of someone like Archbishop Tait illustrates, that party conflict was the most pressing of all the issues confronting Anglican leadership in these decades.[16] If, for example, the parties of orthodoxy prevailed, whether of the Ritualist or the Evangelical variety, the intellectual life of the church as a national institution would be very different than if a moderate freedom of thought accommodating the church to science, criticism, and historical method won out. If the Church of England through its bishops, leading spokesmen, and clergy wrapped itself in the cloak of intuition, that institution would become a major roadblock to intellectual and educational progress and enlightenment. From the standpoint of liberal churchmen, such as A. P. Stanley or J. R. Seeley, who wanted the Anglican Establishment to survive as a sensible and moderately progressive institution, adherence to intuitive epistemology on the part of the clergy meant the church would cut itself off from the nation and ultimately from the future.

But what is less clearly perceived is the degree to which events within the church occupied the attention and set the terms for broader discourse about social issues among thinkers who viewed the church from without. The attitudes of these outsiders—who had left the church but who related to it from a stance of doubt—toward the question of belief was inevitably colored by their perception of what the social effects of ecclesiastical developments might be. One receives a striking impression of how large religious and ecclesiastical affairs could loom for a typical freethinker by looking at the journalistic output of Leslie Stephen

between 1866 and 1873. During these years Stephen, who had for some time
ceased to consider himself a Christian, published articles under the following
titles: "Ritualism," "Dr. Pusey and Dr. Temple," "The Broad Church," "The
Religious Difficulty," "Matthew Arnold and the Church of England," "Mr.
Voysey and Mr. Purchas" (in the matter of two clergymen, one a theological
liberal, the other a Ritualist, both threatened with legal action), "Religion as
Fine Art," "Darwinism and Divinity," and "Are We Christians?"[17] At the same
time, he contributed a fortnightly column on English affairs to the American
magazine the *Nation*. These columns provided a continuous and detailed narrative of events and controversies affecting the church: the trials and tribulations
of Ritualist clergymen, the latest heterodox publication by a theological liberal,
the prospects of disestablishment. From a certain perspective, it is not surprising that an opponent of the church like Stephen should be concerned to follow
so closely its fortunes. If indeed the progress of society depended on the
liberation of the intellect from the constraints of theological doctrine, it was well
to know the movements of the enemy. But this perspective on Stephen's interest
in ecclesiastical affairs does not do justice to the way in which this preoccupation affected his outlook on many other things besides.

It is often assumed that, in the late 1860s and 1870s, the epistemology of
religious belief was under serious attack, and that as a consequence the church
was on the retreat on the social front as well. If men like Stephen took the time
to write against the church, so this interpretation runs, it was to deliver telling
blows against a staggering foe on behalf of a new world view that was scientific,
secular, and progressive. However, if one looks closely at the theological and
ecclesiastical writings of Stephen for this period, an interpretation that views
them as the initiatives of aggressive freethought must be revised. Almost without exception, the articles cited above were written in reaction to some threat
posed by one or another party in the church. In "Ritualism," for example,
Stephen perceived two grave dangers. First, the exaltation of the priesthood as a
caste, which Stephen calls sacerdotalism, exploited the need of uneducated or
unintelligent people—he notes the appeal of Ritualism to women and to the
poor—for leaders in whom they could place their trust. Second, the use of
gorgeous ceremonial responded to a widespread desire for "embodiments in
image of the spiritual aspirations of mankind." Though he believed sacerdotalism and religious ceremonial were profoundly retrograde in their social tendency, he could not help wondering whether the upsurge of Ritualism
represented "the resuscitation of faiths which have suffered a temporary eclipse."[18] Similarly, developments within the Broad Church party or liberal wing
of the church filled Stephen with foreboding. The reinterpretation of dogmas on
terms more acceptable to the modern mind by men like Matthew Arnold undercut efforts of freethinkers like Stephen to construct a new post-Christian intellectual synthesis. Moreover, the attempts of Broad Churchmen to achieve

religious comprehension by these measures of theological accommodation threatened one of the strongest points in the secularist critique of the church: that Christianity inevitably tended toward sectarian exclusivism, and therefore could never serve as a firm basis for national unity.[19]

Finally, not only the terms, but even the structure, of discourse about the social implications of belief in this period were strongly influenced by events within the church. For Stephen as for other freethinkers like John Morley and Frederic Harrison, disestablishment became the key to a new direction in the development of society. Stephen conceived this new direction from a progressive point of view that owed much to Auguste Comte's law of the three stages. The goal of intellectual development, according to Comte's law, was a stage in which all phenomena, including social phenomena, could be understood according to scientific law. But in order for this positive stage to be reached, it was necessary first for the restrictions that supported an older, theological point of view to collapse. For this reason, Stephen scanned the signs of the times, looking for indications of the demise of the established church that would presage the emergence of a new, positive age. He followed with great interest the growing consensus among Ritualists that the freedom and autonomy of the church required the severance of its links with the state. When Evangelicals, upset by the reluctance of the courts to move against heterodoxy and ritualistic excesses, began agitating for disestablishment as well, Stephen took this as a sign that the demise of the church had begun, and the new age was at hand.[20]

What Stephen did not realize was that these signs both permitted and received just the opposite interpretation. The agitation of Ritualists and Evangelicals for disestablishment, and the initiatives of Broad Churchmen could signify just as well an intensification of the sense of mission by groups within the church. Stephen borrowed from church parties, especially from the Ritualists, the conviction that new departures in the church's self-understanding were closely connected with the advent of a new age. Where churchmen viewed the connection eschatologically—a new age required new forms of witness—Stephen chose to see it from the perspectives of a developmental theory that equated progress with the decline of the church. From this perspective, the growing sense of clerical corporate identity and mission that led churchmen to reexamine—whether critically or positively—the link with the state, seemed to Stephen a symptom of collapse. Which perception of the significance of controversy within the church was accurate is not relevant to the purpose of this essay. More important is to recognize that for Stephen, social progress was a matter that depended on what he perceived to be the direction of the Church of England.

The second public issue on which epistemological questions had broad implications was education. From the mid-1860s through the mid-1870s (and really well beyond) the questions of the relationship of public education to church-supported schools and religious teaching was one of the most bitterly disputed of political topics.

One need only consider the controversies surrounding the Education Act of 1870 to see how the debate about belief carried over into the public arena. The Education Act, drawn up by W. E. Forster, vice-president of the Council Board on Education in Gladstone's first ministry, had been designed to meet one of the most pressing needs of an industrial democracy: an effective system of universal elementary education. However, in framing the act, Forster had to contend wth two conflicting interests. On the one hand, the majority of already existing schools in the kingdom were controlled by the Church of England, which was not likely to surrender them to state control. On the other hand, the strongest advocates of universal compulsory education were Protestant Nonconformists, who demanded that any national system, especially one supported through the rates, be nonsectarian. To compromise these interests, Forster proposed what amounted to a mixed system. Voluntary schools that already existed, or that would be established in a certain period of time, would receive outright grants from Parliament. But wherever they were needed, local school boards could be set up to run nonsectarian schools financed through the rates. Additionally, if parents wished to send their children to denominational schools, and could not afford the fees, these local boards might pay the fees from the rates.

This solution, though acceptable to Anglicans and Roman Catholics, met with strong opposition from Protestant Nonconformists and freethinkers. For not only did it leave an extensive system of religious education in place, but it even encouraged the Church of England to set up new schools, and provided them with new sources of revenue. A campaign to rescind or modify the act was undertaken by Joseph Chamberlain's Nonconformist National Education League. But this campaign was also the occasion for Nonconformists and freethinkers to unite against a common foe. After consultation with Chamberlain, John Morley, the editor of the *Fortnightly Review*, published a series on "The Struggle for National Education," probably the most effective piece of anti-Act propaganda.[21] Morley's series reveals some of the reasons freethinkers had for fearing the impact on public affairs of a religious motivation, especially within the established church. According to Morley, the church had decided to take advantage of the national consensus on the importance of education to extend its own influence. The National Society, the educational arm of the church, had been quite direct in announcing its intention to use the provisions of the new act to "imbue . . . the two-thirds of the voters of England under her direct teaching . . . with her principles, and secure their allegiance to her cause."[22] Morley saw the threat of clerical control over education as a Europewide phenomenon, and explicitly identified the cause of English secularists with that of Bismarck, then in the midst of the *Kulturkampf*. In 1873 he wrote,

The expediency of entrusting the [Anglican] clergy and the Catholic priests—with the control of national instruction turns upon the same set of general considerations with reference to progress, enlightenment and the common weal as those which determine the expediency of allowing Jesuits and others to corrupt public spirit and weaken national life in Germany. This is really a true account of the matter, and it brings us to the root of the present dispute.[23]

The education controversy was therefore, from the perspective of a freethinker like Morley, only one aspect of a much broader and more serious problem that faced those countries where an expanded franchise was altering the condition of politics. This was the threat of political and religious reaction associated with the resurgence of clerical forces, and it is the third aspect from which many who had abandoned organized religion in the late 1860s and 1870s viewed its claims. It is a temptation for the modern reader to discount the fear so often voiced in the 1870s by thinkers like Morley and Stephen that the entrance of new classes into political life brought with it the danger of increased clerical domination. After all, these men had themselves favored a more democratic constitution as a way to break clerical and aristocratic power, and they had supported an expanded franchise in 1867. In addition, our subsequent convictions about unchurched masses and the inseparable link between the Church of England and the upper classes make talk about the alliance of church and democracy seem exaggerated. Against this impression it is important to recognize that in the 1870s, English freethinkers had before them what they believed were two striking examples of the very alliance they feared. On the one hand, Louis Napoleon had combined plebiscitary democracy with clerical support to create what English radicals considered one of the most oppressive regimes in Europe.[24] Closer to home, the militant Catholicism growing in Ireland in the late 1860s and 1870s appeared to have found political expression in Fenianism and in the growth of a Home Rule party. Even so experienced an observer of the Irish scene as the Anglo-Irish historian W. E. H. Lecky missed the bitter opposition of the Catholic hierarchy to Fenian agitators, and their refusal to endorse the goals of Isaac Butt's moderate Home Rule party. According to Lecky, the "diseased state of public opinion in Ireland" was due to the joint action of ambitious clergy, who "subordinated all . . . questions to ecclesiastical interests," and political demagogues, who felt "only indifference to . . . constitutional means," and who were motivated by "a blind persistent hatred of England."[25]

Lecky's association of clerical ambition with political opportunism as the moving forces in Irish public life sounds a theme that recurs more than once in the political reflection of those who had come to question revealed religion. Several reasons help to illustrate and explain why the fear of clerical reaction in this decade should be linked to distaste for popular political movements. The

Education Act itself was an instance of how a clerical interest group had been able to mobilize public support and exploit the weakness of the party system to achieve its own ends. It was particularly galling to radicals like Morley, Stephen, and Harrison that the act had been passed, not by Tories, but by a Liberal ministry under a leader from whom they had expected great things. Morley especially took the passage of the Education Act as a lesson in the inherent tendency of party government to compromise and temporize, to solve political problems by trying to gratify conflicting interests, in short, to act out of expediency rather than on principle.[26] While Gladstone's government wasted time and energy on an unacceptable Education Act, thinkers like Stephen and Morley became increasingly pessimistic about the ability of party government to frame progressive policies, or even to deal with national issues of pressing importance.[27] They attributed these failures to the ability of obstructive and reactionary forces—especially the clergy—to use the techniques of managing public opinion and manipulating party government for their own sectarian purposes.[28] After the fall of Gladstone's government, both men agreed that in view of this debacle, if reform were to have any future, it would be necessary to accomplish two things. First, the power of the church in national politics would have to be broken by ending its established status; second, party government must be replaced with a system of government by men of education and ability.[29]

The connection between the political ambitions of religious denominations and the evils of the party system became even clearer in the minds of English freethinkers with the emergence of a united Irish Nationalist party in the late 1870s. At first, Parnell and his followers were able, through their disruptive tactics, to thwart or delay legislation proposed by the ministry and desired by the English majority. As the party grew in strength through the early 1880s, its support or defection could make or break English governments. When Gladstone finally decided to introduce a bill for home rule, his action was viewed by many English agnostics as surrendering the government of Ireland to priests, and he was suspected of having done so in exchange for the political support of the Irish Nationalist party.[30] Once again, observers in England assumed uncritically that the Catholic church and the Nationalist party were in close alliance. Lecky, for example, described the home rule bill as a plan "to entrust the government of Ireland . . . to the tender mercies of priests and Fenians and agitators."[31]

Finally, it is impossible not to recognize that home rule encountered such widespread opposition among English freethinkers not just because it was home rule for the Irish, but because it was home rule for Irish Roman Catholics. Certainly in mid-Victorian Britain, one did not have to be agnostic to be anti-Catholic. However, almost all freethinkers who opposed home rule associated their opposition with vehement hatred of Catholicism.[32] This fear and hatred of

Roman Catholicism was often inspired by the disturbing role of that church in the politics of other European countries: recall John Morley's approval of the *Kulturkampf*; and one can find similar concern over the conduct of the church in France, Belgium, Italy, and Austria in the writings of other English freethinkers. But it is also important to recognize how much the anti-Catholicism of English freethinkers was a reaction to the inroads made by Rome on English life in general, but especially on the Church of England. These inroads were not only the growth of the Roman church in England, nor the dramatic conversions, nor even the more extreme manifestations of Catholic revival among the Ritualists: the mass, auricular confession, religious orders. Of even greater concern to freethinkers were the more pervasive clericalizing tendencies mentioned earlier in this essay, which they discovered in every party in the church. The growth of clerical caste-consciousness—manifested, for example, in the prevalence of clerical dress among all groups of the clergy—the reassertion of the authority of ecclesiastical institutions, especially schools, over the minds of individuals; the new aggressiveness of the church in the political arena: all these developments were redolent to English agnostics of the theory and practice of Rome. If English freethinkers spent as much time as they did worrying and writing about the threat from Rome, it was because developments within the Church of England made this threat of clerical repression seem very real.

These and other concrete issues made the problem of belief much more than a problem of epistemology and infused such passion into debates and controversy on the subject. The theological and ethical arguments about belief carried on in books and periodicals had, not only for their authors, but also for those who read them, immediate ramifications for the way people lived and the authorities by which they guided their lives.

Conclusion

We hope that consideration of these three disconnected issues will illustrate how religious, legal, and political conditions, as well as the more familiar dissolvent literature, helped to foster the debate over the ethics of belief and led to the emergence of a secular frame of mind among British intellectuals. The ironic element in this situation was the role played by religion and by the religious revival itself, first in making the character of belief both more intense and problematical, and then by so strengthening the political and educational influence of religion so as to call forth a strongly secular response. The religious revival led to the deep divisions within the Church of England that prevented a uniform interpretation of the Articles and the Bible and that ultimately required the secular state to enforce theological pluralism. The novel mid-century rigor of definition of the clerical vocation eventually called forth passage of the

Clerical Disabilities Act that sustained the debate over the ethics of belief by making departure from the ministry possible and reasonably simple. Finally, the role of ecclesiastical institutions in education and politics throughout the British Isles made the issues of the honesty of religious belief a powerful weapon for intellectual and political polemic. And it was a weapon that the religious community had given its enemies through its own internal quarrels. Once the discussion of what one could truthfully and honestly believe passed from religious circles to the intellectual nation at large it became a way of breaking the hold of the church and of religion over the culture as a whole.

Notes

1. Quoted in R. F. Harrod, *The Life of John Maynard Keynes* (London: Penguin Books, 1972), p. 135.

2. Quoted in D. McClatchey, *Oxfordshire Clergy, 1777–1869: A Study of the Established Church and of the Role of Its Clergy in Local Society* (Oxford: 1960), pp. 35–36.

3. See Stephen's account of his loss of faith in "Some Early Impressions," *Nation* 42 (October 1903), 70ff.; also in the "Mausoleum Book," an unpublished memoir Stephen wrote for his children, now in the British Library, BM AddMss 57920, especially p. 4.

4. Rowland Williams, *Hints to My Counsel in the Court of Arches* (London: 1861–1862). Williams was concerned to separate a legalistic manner of avoiding conflict over the affirmation of the Thirty-nine Articles and a genuinely theological consideration of what such affirmation implied.

5. *Times* (London), June 25, 1862, p. 9.

6. Quoted in James C. Livingston, *The Ethics of Belief: An Essay on the Victorian Religious Conscience* (Tallahassee, Fla., 1974), p. 4. The authors are much indebted to this excellent monograph.

7. *Quarterly Review*, American ed., 87 (1850): 25.

8. For further details of the Shore case, consult *Quarterly Review*, American ed., 87 (1850): 22–43.

9. *Hansard*, 3rd ser., 103 (1849): 697.

10. Ibid., 166 (1862): 718, 722–724.

11. Ibid., p. 728.

12. Ibid., 168 (1862): 92.

13. *Times* (London), Feb. 9, 1870, p. 12.

14. *Hansard*, 3rd ser., 203 (1970): 928, 1065–1068.

15. See Alan Brown, *The Metaphysical Society: Victorian Minds in Conflict, 1869–1880* (London, 1947).

16. See P. T. Marsh, *The Victorian Church in Decline: Archbishop Tait and the Church of England 1868–1882* (London, 1969).

17. "Ritualism," *Macmillan's Magazine* 17 (1868), 479–494: "Dr. Pusey and Dr. Temple," *Fraser's Magazine* 80 (1869), 722–737; "The Broad Church," *Fraser's* NS 1 (1870), 311–325; "The Religious Difficulty," *Fraser's* 1 (1870), 623–634; "Matthew Arnold and the Church of England," *Fraser's* 2 (1870), 414–431; "Mr. Voysey and Mr. Purchas," *Fraser's* 3 (1871), 457–468; "Religion

as Fine Art," *Fraser's* 4 (1872), 156–168; "Darwinism and Divinity," *Fraser's* 5 (1872), 409–421; "Are We Christians?" *Fortnightly Review* 19 (1873) 281–303.

18. See "Ritualism," 492, 480; also "Religion as Fine Art," 160, 162.

19. See the articles "The Broad Church," especially 318; and "Matthew Arnold and the Church of England," especially 427.

20. See Stephen's columns in *Nation* (New York) for October 3, 1867; Jan. 23, 1868; July 2, 1868; Feb. 11, 1869; Dec. 23, 1869; July 14, 1870; Apr. 11, 1872; Nov. 21, 1872.

21. Morley to Chamberlain, July 4, 1873, Chamberlain Papers, Birmingham University Library.

22. John Morley, quoting from the *Monthly Paper* of the National Society in *The Struggle for National Education* (London, 1873), 42–43.

23. Ibid., 47–48.

24. See, for example, Morley's two articles in the *Fortnightly Review*, "France and Germany," 45 (September 1870), and "England and the War," 46 (October 1870).

25. W. E. H. Lecky, *The Leaders of Public Opinion in Ireland* (London, 1871), x.

26. For his next political sally after *The Struggle for National Education*, Morley told Chamberlain he wished to write a manifesto against expediency in politics, "as forceful and intrepid" as he could make it, castigating Liberal party leadership for "deserting our principles" and making Liberalism into "a catchword for parliamentary intrigues" (Morley to Chamberlain, March 12, 1874, Chamberlain Papers). In fact, Morley's *On Compromise* (London, 1874), published serially in the *Fortnightly* later that year was an effort to define the place of principles in politics, and the limits of compromise.

27. For Morley on the failure of Gladstone's government to discern progressive forces, see *The Struggle for National Education*, 71; for Stephen's strictures on the inefficiency of party government see *Nation* (Sept. 28, 1871), 208.

28. *On Compromise*, 33; Stephen, "The Religious Difficulty," 623–624.

29. These were the two facets of a political program of action planned by Morley and Chamberlain in 1873–1874. See their correspondence from July 19, 1873, to March 12, 1874. For Stephen's awareness of the same two needs, see "Matthew Arnold and the Church of England," 426; also "Social Macadamization," *Fraser's Magazine* 6 (1872), 161–162.

30. For reaction of English intellectuals to home rule, see Lewis P. Curtis, Jr., *Anglo-Saxons and Celts* (Bridgeport, Conn., 1968), 98–107. Goldwin Smith accused Gladstone of having "flung himself into the arms of . . . public plunder and treason" in order to maintain his parliamentary majority. See G. Smith, "The Moral of the Late Crisis," *Nineteenth Century* 20 (September 1886), 307.

31. W. E. H. Lecky, letter to the *Times*, June 7, 1886.

32. John Morley was an exception to the general opposition of English intellectuals to home rule. However, his reasons for supporting home rule were not unrelated to those of other thinkers for opposing it. He hoped by granting the Irish control over their own affairs to end the disturbing influence they had on English parties. Removing the temptation to play for partisan advantage on the religious passions aroused wherever Ireland was concerned might, Morley expected, purify English politics and open the way for disinterested statesmen to develop a truly national political consensus. See D. A. Hamer, *John Morley, Liberal Intellectual in Politics* (Oxford, 1968), pp. 183–194.

VI

Proudhon and *Morale Indépendante:* A Variation of French Secular Morality

PHYLLIS H. STOCK

O ne of the characteristics of modernity in the Western world has been a
progressive secularization in virtually every area of life. Nowhere has this
process been more self-conscious than in France, where it received its first
expression in the writings of the *philosophes,* and where peculiar conditions
created more than a century of debate on the subject.

The crucial French circumstance was the modern version of the struggle
between church and state. Opposed to the Revolution, the church became a
symbol of the Old Regime living on in postrevolutionary France. It resisted
every step in the liberalization of French political life throughout the nineteenth
century. Thus it became anathema to progressive thinkers in every stage of
political development. After mid-century, the Republic began to seem an impossible dream as long as the church remained the predominant influence in the
society.

For the most part, Frenchmen, although anticlerical, were not prepared to
give up the social order assumed to be guaranteed by religious morality. Particularly after such periods of disorder as June 1848, even such liberals as
Adolphe Thiers were willing to pay the price of a Falloux law restoring church
influence in education. However, over the nineteenth century in general, following the Enlightenment pattern, advanced thinkers moved from anticlerical to
antireligious solutions. That is, early nineteenth-century secular moralists, following Victor Cousin's spiritualism, claimed to be purely philosophical while
retaining belief in God and the immortal soul; or, following Auguste Comte's
religion of humanity, they claimed to be social, while incorporating transcendental concepts by deifying society.[1] In both cases, discussion was confined to the educated bourgeoisie. But during the period of the Second Empire,

liberals, frustrated by the hegemony of Louis-Napoléon in politics and the church in society, began to discuss the possibility of a truly nonreligious morality. Drawing on both the practical reason of Immanuel Kant and on Comte's law of the three stages, such a morality was elaborated by an unusual and undisciplined thinker, Pierre-Joseph Proudhon. Under the rubric *morale indépendante* it spread in the circles of the Masonic order and of a portion of the organized working class.

Proudhon's morale indépendante was in the tradition of the Enlightenment, like that of the Utopian socialists. But at mid-century he was the only leading French socialist who could claim working-class origins. Son of a cooper and a cook, he was forced to leave his formal education before completing secondary school and to work for a printer, reading proofs to help support his family. Beside the Bible and the classics he had read in school, he read in proof the works of Fourier, books of theology and linguistics. He even wrote an *Essai de grammaire générale* on his own, to accompany a book on linguistics by Abbé Bergier. For a time, believing himself to be suited to the role of Christian apologist, he also began to read antireligious works, only to find that they sorely tried his faith. After long years of poverty, Proudhon at age twenty-five found himself without a position when the printinghouse with which he was associated failed. He was persuaded by a friend to apply for the Suard pension offered by the Besançon Academy to a needy scholar.

In his application Proudhon elaborated a project that would establish the truths of the Christian religion by means of linguistics. He believed that he could discover that "primitive philosophy or religion" of which the Christian religion was an expression, by a comparative study of religious systems and the formation of languages, "independent of any other revelation." His purpose, he stated, was to work for "the moral and intellectual amelioration of those whom I like to call my brothers and my companions," and to spread among them "the seeds of a doctrine which I regard as the law of the moral world."[2] In a sense that was unpredictable by him at that time, this was what Proudhon was to do for the rest of his life.

The academy responded favorably to his application, and Proudhon moved to Paris to study. Soon leaving linguistics behind, he became immersed in the study of economics, where he sought the explanation of the social misery he knew firsthand. When, in November of 1838, the academy announced a competition on the subject of the celebration of the Sabbath, Proudhon entered it with his first work of social commentary. At the time he referred to it as his "program."[3] In this work one can perceive the outline of his later thought; it established him as a moralist above all.

Proudhon based his essay on the ancient Hebrews, and on Moses as the wise lawgiver whose purpose in ordering the Sabbath was to create a unity among his people stronger than one of material interests. "He wanted, in a word, not an agglomeration of individuals, but a truly fraternal society." Noting that the Hebrews were a people of the book, he claimed that the Sabbath was the day for instruction of the people—in religion, politics, and morality. It was not, he emphasized, a day when the people could make their own laws, for laws were a matter of science. Thus any law, to be holy, had to be endowed with the character of necessity; all jurisprudence consisted in a simple exposition of principles. "Justice and legality are two things as independent of our assent as mathematical truth; to be obligatory, it suffices that they be known." Moses spoke to the people in the name of God, that is, in the name of truth. Proudhon bewailed the fact that, although religion might still have an emotional influence, it had not for a long time appealed to the intellect. Why, he asked, when the preacher spoke of morality, did he not speak of the conditions of the social order, of the equality that should reign among citizens, of the duties of government, of the independence of reason? Why had religion become divorced from politics?[4]

Examining the fourth commandment, he noted that it prescribed leisure, not only for the householder, but for the servants within the household. On that day servants regained their dignity as human beings and were on the same level with their masters. The Sabbath was the celebration of human dignity, and of the recognition that that dignity was too great to allow the degradation of social ranks. Proudhon also claimed that the Hebraic law was an attempt to keep anyone from becoming too rich or too poor. Moses was aiming at a society of fraternal solidarity, in which each would have the right to gain his living by work, and to be considered equal in the apportioning of property and privileges. Property could not be considered absolute; its enjoyment was to be regulated by law, since one always received more from the society than he could return to it. "All inequality of birth, of age, of force or capacity is nullified before the right to produce one's subsistence, which is expressed by the equality of conditions and of goods . . . the differences of aptitude or facility in the worker, of quality or quantity in the execution, disappear in the social product, when all members have done what they could, because they have done their duty . . . in a word, the disproportion of power in individuals is neutralized by the general effort."[5]

The social problem, to Proudhon, was "to find a state of social equality which is neither communism, nor despotism, nor division, nor anarchy, but liberty in order and independence in unity."[6] There should exist, he declared, a science of society, based on human nature and human relationships, a science that did not have to be invented, only discovered. The aim of such a science would be social action. The discovery and definition of economic laws would make possible the equality of social circumstances, because the right to live and develop one's self completely was equal for all, and the inequality of conditions was an obstacle to the exercise of that right.[7]

Thus the principles of social science were objective; its use was normative. In political life also, the principles were objective: "The authority of the majority over the minority, of some over all, even of all over one, is nothing, without the authority of the law, which must conform to reason." The law should be neither the expression of a single will nor of the majority will; "it is the natural relationship of things, discovered and applied by reason." In ancient times, Proudhon pointed out, civil law and sacred law were one. Religion was both politics and science. But the priest became dogmatic and intolerant; the judge, violent and despotic; the philosopher, contemptuous of both, persecuted. Thus arose the contradiction between conscience and law.[8]

In this first work Proudhon gave the Sabbath a social interpretation, as an institution that implied human liberty, equality and fraternity. Here are the germs of his later "program" for the moral life of society: human dignity and equality as the bases for morality; the right of fulfillment for the individual and the duty of society to make this possible; the negation of absolute property rights, which prevent equal opportunity; the right of the individual to acquiesce in those arrangements that concern his well-being; the objectivity of moral law, independent of individual interests; and the importance to humanity of education as the revelation of truth—religious, political and moral. Although he had clearly equated the law and truth with God, the clergy at Besançon prevented the sale of the published work,[9] a move also prophetic for the future. They undoubtedly sensed that Proudhon was more of a deist than a good Catholic. In fact, he believed that both Moses and Jesus had professed "pure deism."[10]

The role that Proudhon had given to religion in *Dimanche* was completely negated in *La Création de l'ordre dans l'humanité* of 1843. Here he agreed with Comte that it belonged to a past stage of human development and was at this stage antithetic to human progress. Philosophy, the stage that followed, had now reached the level of eclecticism, which was preparatory to the elaboration of metaphysics—a term that corresponded somewhat to Comte's stage of positivism.[11] In the following year he noted that the people were moving further from religion. "The people conceive of a virtue without the assistance of religion. Think where that will lead," he wrote to a friend.[12]

By the time he wrote *Contradictions économiques* (1846) Proudhon had developed his thoughts on God. The idea of God was not an individual concept but "an act of faith in the collective mind." Whereas an individual felt he moved in a self-determined way, society tended to move by a kind of inner spontaneity, which it then deified. Thus, as Feuerbach had claimed, the God that man adored was himself, in ideal projection. However, believing this critique of theism correct, Proudhon nevertheless denied any implication that the collective, Humanity, was to be worshipped, as Comte had concluded. The question was whether the nature that humans had given the Deity was compatible with human nature. Proudhon's answer was a resounding No. For humans to exist and perfect themselves, they must deny God—not that God existed, for one could not know that. But "God, if there is a God, resembles not at all the effigies that philosophers and preachers have made of him . . . intelligence, freedom, personality in God are constituted in another way than in us." The uniqueness of nature, Proudhon insisted, "makes of God a being essentially anti-civilizing, anti-liberal, anti-human." Since God represented the principle of the authoritarian, the arbitrary, he was synonymous with the state in politics and with property in economics, which was why he must be opposed in science, in labor, in political life. In positing God, we deny ourselves, impose upon ourselves an ideal that negates our own essence. Thus Proudhon's famous statement, ranking with his "Property is theft": "God is evil."[13]

During the 1848 Revolution, Proudhon expressed some of the same ideas in his newspaper *Le Peuple*.[14] In its successor, *Voix du peuple*, he concluded, "Thus morality, justice, order, laws are not things revealed from on high, imposed on our free will by a so-called creator, unknown and unintelligible; they are things which are as proper and essential to us as our body and blood. In two words, Religion and Society are synonymous terms: Humankind is sacred to itself as if it were God." Not that man was God, he added, at least not the God of the philosophers—immutable, infinite, eternal and absolute. Humans were perfectible, progressive and changing. Therefore their progress was not served by identifying humanity with God.[15]

The only absolute in human life, he insisted, was the objective moral law within him. When Jesus said, "Blessed are the pure in heart, for they shall see God," he meant that the pure in heart were conscious of their own virtue. "Thus morality has no sanction but itself; it would derogate its dignity, it would be immoral, if it took its cause and its end from elsewhere."[16] Proudhon compared it with the truths of mathematics: that two and two made four was true independent of God. What was true of mathematics was true also of all science and of human society.[17] Thus Proudhon preferred to view the moral law as an ideal rather than an idea, because of its origin in human beings. In *Contradictions* he wrote that the human race was on the verge of recognizing and affirming something that would be for it the equivalent of the old divinity.[18] In 1858 he decided to examine whether it was not possible to follow the moral law without any religion at all; to this task he devoted a long work, *La Justice dans la Révolution et dans l'Eglise*.

Throughout his works Proudhon had been developing a view of human nature. In *Création de l'ordre* he had emphasized human equality, insisting that intelligence was the same in all; it was modified in each by his particular aptitudes, but all aptitudes were equally estimable. The apparent inequalities between men were the result of abnormalities—improper education of the intelligence, physical abnormalities, the mutilation of aptitudes by poverty.[19] In

Contradictions he took up the question of man's original moral nature. Opposing both the concept of original sin and the modern assertion that human nature was basically good, Proudhon insisted that human beings were conglomerates, oscillating between vice and virtue. One was morally inconsistent because one was free. And this moral vacillation meant that the inevitability of moral progress could not be assumed.[20]

Proudhon's explanation of human freedom was a curious blend of acceptance of materialism and insistence upon one's ability to surmount it. The essential condition of all human existence, he said, was the antinomy of necessity and freedom.[21] Although all the elements of human beings were determined, each person, as a collectivity of those elements, was free.[22] In essence, human liberty was simply an indeterminate faculty to act or not. Its positive character was the result of the development of reason. The more one's freedom and one's reason were in accord, the more happiness one could attain: "The progress of humanity can be defined as the education of the reason and of human liberty by necessity." However, endowed with activity and intelligence, humans had the power to disturb the order of the world in which they were part. Thus the presence of disorder in the human world was to Proudhon a proof of human freedom. Reason, if one followed it, set the limits to freedom.[23]

Human beings were also social creatures. At first, Proudhon tended to attribute all morality to man's basic sociability. In its primary form, sociability was merely human sympathy. However, the addition of reflection to this simple instinct resulted in a second level of sociability, "the recognition in the other of a personality equal to our own," which Proudhon called justice. The addition of an aesthetic, ideal element created a third level of sociability, called equity, which included friendship and devotion. In his early work, Proudhon tended to base rights and duties on needs (eating, sleeping, working, family life, appreciation) to whose fulfillment each person had a right, and which others had a duty to make possible. In *Qu'est-ce que la propriété?* he defined justice as "the end of privilege, the abolition of slavery, equality of rights, the rule of law," while noting that justice was not the result of law, but that law was the application of the just.[24]

In this early stage, Proudhon viewed the presence of morality in the individual as a product of society, as the revelation that the society, the collectivity, made to man, the individual.[25] Conscience was to him "the social Essence, the collective being that contains us and penetrates us."[26] In the introduction to *Philosophie du progrès* he described the society as an organism perfecting itself bit by bit, changing form perpetually.[27] However, by the time he wrote *Justice* he was insisting that the society did not transcend human beings, but existed as a result of the reciprocal action and common energy of individuals, of which it was the expression and synthesis. He denied any solution of the social problem that would subordinate the individual to society, as well as any solution of unlimited liberty that presumed the harmony of divergent interests.[28]

Justice dans la Révolution et dans l'Eglise was organized as an opposition between the principles of the church and those that Proudhon believed were replacing them, those of the Revolution of 1789. The church represented the principles of authority, transcendence and the absolute. The Revolution represented human freedom, immanence, and the progressive. To the first belonged all systems that derived justice from revelation, from the society itself, or even from Kant's "great human Being." The system of the Revolution declared the immanence of justice in human consciousness. Proudhon's demonstration of this was psychological: What does a person feel when faced by another person? His own dignity and the dignity of the other. "To feel and affirm human dignity, first in all that pertains to us, then in the person of the next man," that was right *(droit)*. "To be ready in all circumstances to undertake the defense of that divinity with energy, and if need be against one's self," that was justice. What all people had in common was this individual dignity and their desire that it be respected. From this fact moral rights and duties might be deduced. Each person's right was to demand from others the respect of human dignity in his person; each person's duty was to respect that dignity in the person of others. Basically the two were identical. Since all men were the same in reason and in dignity, justice also implied equality.[29]

One's dignity was individual, a part of him; the justice by which he conducted his relations with other men was social. A person in society under the law of justice was not the same as he was in a state of isolation. As he subordinated his own interest to what was just, he developed a social ego, a second nature that was social. Therefore each individual was aware of himself at the same time as person and as species. An injustice was resented at the same time by the injured, by the onlooker, and even by the offender himself. Thus, although justice was a characteristic of human beings in society, Proudhon no longer felt that it derived from society, for the species could not have in common anything that was not already in the individual. Nor could justice come from religion, whose authoritarian nature negated the human dignity that was both the basis and the object of justice. "Justice is human, all human, nothing but human. . . . The theory of Practical Reason subsists by itself; it neither supposes nor requires the existence of God and the immortality of the soul." For Proudhon, justice did not transcend human beings, but was immanent in them.[30]

As a human faculty, justice was also not immutable, but susceptible to development; "it is this development which constitutes the education of humanity." Moral science was therefore progressive, growing by the experience of reciprocal human relationships. It supposed a constant readjustment as human contacts grew and developed. "We will never know the end of Right, because we will never cease creating among ourselves new relationships. We are born perfectible, we will never be perfect." Justice operated in society, according to Proudhon, by means of free contracts between individuals, extending gradually throughout the whole society. Because we are free, we may turn our backs on justice, but it always survives. The very fact that all invoked it, even when they violated it, proved to Proudhon that progress was possible. To support people in the accomplishment of justice the church had provided Grace; he instead found this support in another purely human faculty, creation of the ideal. Human beings were artists, who, by virtue of their freedom, were able to construct their ideal, which then operated in their conscience. "The task of freedom is the idealization of the human being and his domain. It aims at universal fraternity, at the unity of humanity, at the general harmony of humankind and the forces of the earth."[31] The ideal in *Justice* seems to be a development out of Proudhon's third, aesthetic stage of sociability in *Propriété*.

Although he agreed that the just act might vary in different times, he insisted that the principle did not depend upon temperament, climate or other external factors, but always upon the reciprocity of respect among persons. Thus he emphasized the second part of the categorical imperative, treating persons as ends rather than means, instead of the first, which would make moral rules universal. By his criterion, although the determination of what the just act was might be in error, justice itself was infallible. Like Kant, Proudhon insisted that if one possessed the notion of the good, it was automatic to follow and practice it as something that was properly one's own. The faculty of man whose content was justice was *conscience* (here, it would seem, in the sense of both consciousness and conscience). The perception of justice was, then, identical to justice itself; the sanction of justice was an inner sanction. Public sanctions were external developments of inward convictions.

However, Proudhon did not approve of punishment as such. A wrongdoer should make restitution for his act, thereby reestablishing the equilibrium demanded by justice. By instructing the criminal concerning his duties, by insisting upon reparation of his wrongdoing, society could bring him back within the boundaries of the common conscience. But reparation must be reciprocal. Not only must the individual make amends; the society must revise the institutions that made injustice seem natural to the criminal. Proudhon named as one cause of immorality in the society "the lack of equilibrium which exists between forces, services and products."[32]

Like Victor Cousin, Proudhon made the distinction between acts of precept (justice) and acts of counsel (charity). It was "de précepte" to abstain from stealing from a person, "de conseil" to assist him in his poverty. However, unlike Cousin, Proudhon insisted that charity was only the compensation by the generous for the injustice of the current system. Where true justice reigned, all moral acts were acts of precept, relating to recognized rights. In economic life, justice required a system of "reciprocity of services." This implied that the salary of a worker would equal the value of what he produced; that there would be equivalency in all exchange of products; and that credit would be extended without interest.[33]

Proudhon always expressed the manifestations of justice in terms like "equilibrium," "reciprocity," "equivalency," "equality," depending upon the application. He conceived of the laws of justice as universal laws, like the laws of nature. If justice had never been fully accomplished in the human world, it was because its cultivation had been neglected, so that it had not developed at the same rate as intelligence. This was the result of viewing justice as an idea in the mind, rather than as a force in human life. Proudhon admitted that religion had attempted to repair the faults in justice as practiced by men; but any society where justice was dominated by another principle, such as religion, would eventually be annulled and society would perish.[34]

What was necessary was education—by the society, not the church. This would be the methodical development of the physical, intellectual, and moral faculties of the child. Proudhon's theory of education was based on labor. He saw human beings primarily as workers, analyzing the instruments and operations of their labor after the fact, not conceiving an operation and then employing it. The education of the intelligence would be training in a series of industrial operations, graduated in complexity, with subsequent analysis of the basic concepts on which each one rested—"a simultaneous education of the intelligence and the organs." The young worker would serve an apprenticeship in every special operation of an industry; he would also be given an overall view of the work done by all industries. This would not only give him a sense of the contribution each job made to the whole, it would also serve to pay his "labor debt," teaching him that he owed his developed capabilities to the society of which he was part. Later on, in association with his fellow worker, he would participate in the direction and the benefits of his particular workshop.[35]

Proudhon linked this concept of education with the degrees of the Masonic order. He chided the Masons for not developing the philosophical sense of their symbols, and for retaining in their constitution belief in God and the immortal soul. Recalling his own initiation into the order in 1847, he explained his acceptance of the Grand Architect of the Universe as "anti-conceptual." God to him was the personification of universal equilibrium and, in the moral order, of justice.[36]

By the time *Justice* was issued in a second edition in 1868, a group of Masons had founded a review to support Proudhon's idea of a morality independent of religion. He himself was feeling a sense of urgency about the necessity for a "popular philosophy": "When religions are dying . . . when the republic, everywhere the order of the day, seeks its formulation . . . the time has come to attempt, through a new propagation, the social restoration." Justice, he insisted again, did not belong to a transcendental world; it was the point of transition between the real and the ideal. In morality, it was the reciprocity of rights and duties; in logic, the principle of equality; in art and imagination, the ideal; in nature, equilibrium. Thus science and conscience were fundamentally identical. Adored under many names—God, the Absolute, Pure and Practical Reason, the Rights of Man and Citizen—justice was immediately accessible to all persons equally, Proudhon insisted, as what was most primitively human. In this sense, "the people, by their native intuition and their respect for right are more advanced than their superiors; they are only lacking . . . the word. It is the word that we wish to give to the people . . . in presenting ourselves simply as missionaries of right we need not make use of any authority, divine or human, nor pose as geniuses or martyrs or saints . . . the verities we bear are not ours . . . [they] belong to everyone; they are written in every soul." Therefore, according to Proudhon, society needed "no authority, no priesthood, no churches."[37]

During his lifetime Proudhon exerted little influence on the French Establishment. Elected to the Assembly in 1848, he shocked that body by proposing economic measures that threatened property. Even most Socialists refused to follow him; only one man, the worker Jean-Louis Greppo, voted for the bill. During the Second Empire, Proudhon spent a good deal of time in jail or exile for attacking the authorities. However, his influence was to extend into the Third Republic—not only in workers' movements, but even into the Establishment, through a group known as *Morale indépendante*. And many Proudhonian themes emerged later in the social theories of Emile Durkheim.

There was one organized group that was ripe for a moral philosophy like that of Proudhon, because of its growing adversary relationship with the church: French Freemasonry. After a period of government persecution early in the Empire, the order was again growing by 1862—at the very time when French Masonry was definitively splitting with Catholicism.[38] In that year the Paris lodge *France maçonnique* was preparing to counter church influence by founding schools and libraries to extend the moral and intellectual ideas of Freemasonry. In October a school for working-class women was founded at the Rue de la Perle by Mme Charles Lemonnier and other women.[39]

Nevertheless, at the death in 1865 of Maréchal Magnan, Grand Master of the Grand Orient, Archbishop Darboy was still willing to bless the coffin, emblazoned with Masonic symbols. This ceremony proved to be the end of any formal relationship between the French clergy and the Masonic order. Pope Leo IX took the occasion to make another denunciation of Freemasonry, the third since 1830. The result was a further falling-off of Catholic membership and a relative increase of Protestant and freethinking members.[40] The Masons were

left with a philosophy of deism, since a profession of faith had always been
required of initiates into the Masonic order. This profession had been modified
by none other than Proudhon himself, at his initiation on January 8, 1847.
When asked the traditional question, What does man owe to God? he had
answered: War. Invited to explain this response, he had argued that antitheism
was not necessarily atheism. Later he explained his position in writing:

> The God of the Masons is neither Substance, nor Soul, nor Monad, nor Creator,
> nor Father, nor the Word, nor Love, nor Paraclete, nor Redemptor, nor Satan, nor
> anything which corresponds to a transcendental concept: here all metaphysics is
> eliminated. He is the personification of the universal Equilibrium: God is Ar-
> chitect; he holds the compass, the level, the square, the hammer, all the instru-
> ments of labor and of measure. In the moral order he is Justice. That is all the
> Masonic theology.[41]

In June 1865, less than a year after Proudhon's death, the Grand Orient decided
not to demand any profession of faith from its initiates. Nevertheless, while
refusing to bar anyone on the basis of his beliefs, it maintained as principles of
the Masonic order the existence of God, the immortality of the soul, and human
solidarity.[42] The Grand Orient had by that year 230 French lodges, plus chapters and consistories. Another 70 lodges followed the Scottish rite. There was
continual growth in Masonic membership into the Third Republic.[43]

Throughout the period of the "liberal Empire" Masons explored their position on the popular issue of morality. Already in 1863 a discussion had begun in
the pages of *Monde maçonnique* on whether Masonry was a universal religion.
This had been provoked by a speech of Marie-Alexandre Massol at the Renaissance lodge.[44] A disciple of Proudhon, Massol called for moral renewal, claim-
ing that ethics was weakened by being cut off from its roots. He posed the
question: Has morality a principle of its own, or is it deduced from a superior
principle? The editor of the journal, Jules Favre, answered that morality had
essentially human origins, and did not derive from any absolute. He agreed on
the necessity to investigate the human bases of morality, which would not, he
added, be an atheistic or materialistic project. "We leave to God what is God's,
and we try to define the narrow domain where the human will operates." From
this time on, discussions of *morale* filled the Masonic journal, with Massol the
leading figure in the debates. In September of that year (1863) he called upon
the members of the Isis-Montyn lodge to work for an organizing principle to
replace those of raison d'état and revelation. Masonry would have accomplished
its task, he declared, when the moral idea, respect for the human person,
should unite all in human fraternity.[45]

In April 1864, Massol outlined his theory at the Renaissance lodge. Although many said there was no morality without religion, Masonry itself was, in
a sense, a pure morality. Certainly it was necessary to free ethics from theology

as all other areas of life had been gradually freed. What Masonry represented, he claimed, was "the idea of a *morale indépendante*, pure from all outside elements." This idea was based on the fact that a human being was a person, conscious and free; therefore he treated other persons as such. "He *respects* himself, therefore he demands *respect* of his person from his peers. But the *respect* which he demands for himself he feels strongly *demandable* by others, *owed* to others. In other words, he affirms the inviolability, the dignity of the *human person* in *himself* and in *others*; he affirms *rights* and *duties* . . . . That *reciprocity of respect*, and the *peace* or the *discomfort* which accompanies it, constitute *conscience* . . . . Such is, in its simplicity, the *moral law* . . . a law which is not at all, as one can see, the commandment of an exterior will, nor a mysterious impression from an outside power, nor a participation in a universal reason, but really the expression of our nature; consequently, a law which is one, identical, and equal in all men.

"From this it follows that the person carries in himself the moral world; that he is the seat of it, that he is the source of right and justice; that he finds in himself the rule of his behavior." Massol went on to outline how conscience, thus described, could become an active force in love and devotion, in spreading justice, in creating a society where the liberty and inviolability of the human person would be the principle, end and means of every institution. In rendering itself independent of religion, morality would become human.[46]

This was Massol's first complete expression of the concept of morale indépendante; it was clearly derived from Proudhon. After a discussion at the Rose of the Perfect Silence lodge later that year, he printed and distributed one thousand copies of a letter restating his moral theory. He maintained that good and evil could be clearly defined by it: "*Good* is all that favors, preserves and increases respect of the human person. *Evil* is all that tends to destroy or decrease this same respect. *Obligation, duty* is the impossibility of the mind or reason to deny that this same respect (which one demands for oneself) is demandable by others, owed to others . . . . Human dignity, elevated to its ideal state, completes the moral order." By November the Masons of Paris had begun to argue over the necessity of the term "Grand Architect of the Universe" in the preamble to their constitution; many lodges accepted the project of rewriting to remove God and the immortal soul and to substitute the principle of "the inviolability of the human person." It was argued that this would leave the supernatural to the realm of individual belief and would concentrate Masonic research on what was demonstrable and human.[47]

That Freemasons should become interested in a morality that did not require Catholic dogma is not surprising, considering their relationship to the church. They were not, however, quite ready to dispense with God and the immortal soul. The attempt to remove these concepts from the constitution was not successful during the Second Empire.[48] Despite this fact, interest in morale indépendante continued and was intensified by the civil funeral of Proudhon in December 1864. Three thousand persons followed his casket to the burial in Passy, for which a collection had been taken. Massol, one of the three speakers at the graveside, described Proudhon as "one of those who have worked hardest at the building of the major work of this century, the founding of a morality exclusive of all superstition." No one, Massol insisted, had a greater feeling for the dignity of man than he, no one proclaimed more than he the respect of the human person. Massol and others who were promulgating morale indépendante made it clear that they considered themselves disciples of Proudhon.[49]

However, as Masons wishing to substitute their new moral theory for the Grand Architect of the Universe, they soon realized that they were in the minority. The July 1865 convention of the Grand Orient was not moved to provide Massol with a majority, despite his eloquence.[50] Supporters from Paris and the provinces caucused at a banquet, and decided to publish a journal devoted to their cause. Of the fifty present, almost all subscribed immediately.[51] Having failed to take over Freemasonry, the new movement began the effort to convince the general public of their ideas, while continuing the campaign in the lodges. The five years of the journal's existence were to make morale indépendante a respected and influential term.

The first issue of *Morale indépendante* appeared on August 6, 1865, with Lazare Caubet as director and Massol as editor. It included articles by Henri Brisson, Frédéric Morin, Charles Renouvier, Louis Redon, Amédée Guillemin. A letter from the philosopher Etienne Vacherot promised his aid in the "great work" of making morality a matter of science rather than of faith. After outlining his definition of ethics (essentially as given above), Massol described the purpose of the journal:

> To disengage the moral idea from all which could denature it, to set it in a clear light, to show what it actually is, one, identical, equal to itself in all human beings, constituent of all humanity; to work in this way so that it becomes the sovereign of our wills, the guarantee of our judgment and our supreme ideal;
>
> By this emancipation from all which could alter its purity and compromise its power, to liberate the mind entirely; to thus forcibly bring about the convergence of minds by the homogeneity of methods, the convergence of hearts, the synergy of efforts and the identity of aim.[52]

Thus the journal aligned itself with the forces seeking renewal and unity of French society, the forces preparing for the Republic.

An article by Renouvier, who was to be the philosopher of the early Third Republic, declared that all religions taught the same morality, which made it possible to speak of *the* moral law. But the imposition by an outside force prevented people from feeling the moral law as a link with their fellow human beings. Therefore religious morality failed to contribute to the solution of the problem of human relationships. He attributed the concept of a morality based on the person to Kant.[53] Renouvier later regretted his enthusiastic endorsement of *Morale indépendante*, and again used its pages to clear up any misunderstandings. Although he had said that immortal life was not an absolute necessity for ethics, he personally believed in it; the presence of the moral law within, a law impossible to fulfill in this life, added credence to a future life. In this second article he wondered if, in its efforts to separate morality from history as well, morale indépendante had not ignored the law of moral solidarity.[54] Two years later his own publication, *L'Année philosophique*, was to link morale indépendante with Proudhon, rather than with Kant, and to criticize it for starting from the feeling of respect, rather than from a sense of duty.[55]

There was a real difference between the spiritualist Kantians and the Proudhonians in ethical thought. Both emphasized the reciprocity of rights and duties. (My right is your duty, and vice versa.) Both claimed *conscience* as the seat of morality. But whereas the Kantians stressed the primacy of duty in the moral equation, Proudhonians stressed the primacy of rights. Thus they stressed the consciousness aspect of *conscience;* each person was aware that as a free human being he had rights. One demanded the respect of these rights by others. But reason also leads one to acknowledge that other persons have the same rights, which one therefore has the duty to respect to the same extent.

In a review of Renouvier's *Essai de critique générale* in the journal, Clarisse Coignet criticized Renouvier's use of love as the basis for the moral law. As Proudhon had pointed out, love did not lead to justice, because it was a passion. The foundation of justice and the moral law was reason.[56] Morin elaborated on the relationship of morale indépendante to Kant: "We are with Kant when, pursuing the practical analysis of our duties, he subordinates them all to the active respect of personal dignity, that is, to freedom; we are no longer with him when, by an excessive idealism, he tries to define duty, or the categorical imperative, without setting foot on the living and concrete fact, and when he wants to remain in the absolute domain of abstraction."[57] Massol also maintained that Kant had never really freed himself from dependence on theological concepts.[58]

The writings of the main proponents of morale indépendante show a range of opinion that makes it difficult to define the doctrine too precisely. Massol himself tended to be simplistic and repetitive, and leaned toward an empirical definition, starting with the fact of the consciousness of personal dignity. Coignet leaned toward a more Kantian interpretation, while differing from other French Kantians on the meaning of the master. Morin fell in between, insisting that the moral conscience was a "primitive irreducible faculty of the mind, not derivable from any metaphysical or theological conceptions. He traced the concept of an independent morality back to Cicero and Aristotle.[59]

Coignet's book, *La Morale indépendante*, written in 1869, is worthy of note because she was to write textbooks on morale for the schools of the Third Republic.[60] She began with the rights of the person, based upon the fact of human freedom. This fact was accessible to each, by reason and consciousness, in his own experience. "It is freedom which rules itself by virtue of a law which it provides itself and which it alone can accomplish; freedom which in establishing the individual on rights and obligations, establishes society on the equality of rights and the reciprocity of obligations, and makes of the human being the origin, the end and the creator of morality." Morality was not the condition of human rights, but the consequence of them, since human rights were anterior to society, were absolute and unconditional. Once this was recognized, the rights of man gave birth to justice in society. Thus, by an extension of the rights of individuals and their duties to observe each other's rights, one attained to collective freedom and justice.[61]

Human beings were born unequal in physical characteristics and in social and economic position, Coignet agreed. But they were equal in rights. Therefore the moral person attempted to alter society in such a way as to reduce distinctions between people. This involved the suppression of class privilege and monopoly, among other things that tended to inequality of rights. The implication was that those endowed with natural and social benefits had a greater duty toward those who had not. (However, unlike the later solidarity theories, this duty was deduced, not from the idea of social debt, but from the equality of individual rights.) In this way strict equity, or justice, could become that devotion or moral heroism which had previously been associated with the supernatural.[62]

While calling the study of morality a science, Coignet stressed the psychological approach, used by Proudhon and typical of nineteenth-century French moralists. As did many supporters of independent morality, she compared the "primitive fact" of individual freedom to the axioms of geometry. Just as the basic principles of mathematics were abstract concepts, so the basic principle of ethics was a living fact of the inner experience. Thus it differed from the positive sciences. But, in order to raise individual morality to the level of social justice, the positive sciences were necessary—to regulate physical phenomena for the general well-being, to free people from manual labor, to achieve economic justice. "Morality determines the aim of human life, and the natural sciences contribute to its realization."[63]

The collective form of morality was politics. Coignet referred to the Revolution as the time when human rights had been recognized as replacing the rights of God. The mistake had been, however, to replace the old state religion with either deism or materialism. The true solution to the revolutionary problem was the separation of metaphysics and life, of religion and morality, of church and state. But this was only possible with the recognition that morality was truly independent of metaphysics, of religion, of the church. Such a recognition would not in any way prevent individual devotion to religious ideas, as long as these did not enter into the collective life. She gave as an example the United States.[64]

The periodical *Morale indépendante* was greeted enthusiastically by much of the Paris and provincial press. Louis Jourdan in *Le Siècle*, Charles de Rémusat in the *Revue des deux mondes*, Emile Déschanel in the *Journal des débats* agreed on the importance of the topic, with *La Presse* commenting, "The journal which we announce responds to a preoccupation which has become almost general today in the current movement of ideas." Readers suggested that the editors provide a small treatise to guide ordinary people in the development of moral truths. The periodical did conduct a contest for a moral catechism for children, with a 500-franc prize offered by the editor of *Annuaire philosophique*, which was won by a mother.[65]

In December 1865, Père Hyacinthe began a series of six Advent sermons at Notre Dame in Paris on the subject of morale indépendante, which he declared a topic worthy of discussion because it was, not just a child of Freemasonry or democratic journals, but the echo of a broad stratum of thought and feeling. In the first sermon he indicated his willingness to extend the hand of friendship to all Christians, even all deists. But he accused the partisans of the new morality of being disciples of Proudhon, and of trying to be independent, not only of particular religions, but even of the natural religion that was the basis of all religions. By the third week his attacks on morale indépendante and the increasing orthodoxy of his statements led to suspicion that even this first sermon had had repercussions in the church hierarchy. At the last sermon, Monseigneur Darboy thanked Père Hyacinthe, summed up the series, and ended with a warning to mothers to guard their children against the doctrine.[66]

In the autumn of 1867 three courses on morale indépendante were being offered at the Sorbonne—by Emile Caro, Charles Lemonnier, and Emile Beaussire.[67] Meanwhile, discussions had been taking place in Masonic lodges about the importance of teaching an independent morality in the schools. Masons were exhorted to organize public opinion to that end; although it was impossible to organize for this purpose under the laws of the empire, Masons should propagandize for it as individuals. A Society for the Encouragement of Public Education was formed nevertheless. Masonic lodges began to open schools for both sexes, as at Marseilles and Lyon.[68] Speeches at the distribution of prizes in such schools were invariably on the subject of moral training as a preparation for democracy and the independence of morality from religious concepts.[69] The general assembly of the Grand Orient in 1869 discussed the problem of education. It was decided that Masons should concern themselves with educational affairs and should patronize the secular schools.[70] Many Masons patronized Jean Macé's *Ligue de l'enseignement*, founded in 1866.[71]

Another section of the population close to Proudhon in its ways of thinking was at this time developing ideas on morality separate from religion. Sharing the anticlericalism of the bourgeois intellectuals, but viewing the unification of French society from a socialist viewpoint, conscious members of the working class began gradually to demand universal and secular education for their children. The two groups mingled occasionally in Masonic lodges and in the Ligue de l'enseignement. But it was in the socialist milieu that the term *solidarité* was first used in France. Jean-Louis Greppo, a Mason and the one man who voted for Proudhon's economic project in the Assembly, wrote a *Catéchisme sociale, ou espose succint de la doctrine de la solidarité*, depicting solidarity, as opposed to competition, as the natural rule of society. It should be the base of all human relations. The society should concern itself primarily with its children, Greppo insisted—lodging, nourishing, and clothing them and instructing them in public schools—to the end that they would become socially useful. This would involve, not religious training, for that was a personal matter, but moral training, which would be provided in the society as a whole.[72]

During the short-lived Second Republic a group of socialist educators published a program stressing the need for moral reform, including an entire outline of moral education for children from the cradle to age eighteen. There would be no catechism or dogmatic religion taught; but the history of religion might be offered, as well as the rights and duties of persons in society, from a very young age, the committee decided. "In the absence of a unitary and complete dogma, we can give our children, not a religion, but religion. . . . It is from ethics and from history understood philosophically that all our religious teaching will emerge." At the age of fifteen, each student would be instructed on how to fulfill his duties as a person, a member of a family, a citizen. Politics, economics, philosophy of history, even art and music would be presented more in a moral than in a didactic form. Politics, they stated, could only be ethics. From the age of six, students would begin their active contribution to society through part-time work in fields and workshops. By the age of twelve, one-third of the school hours would be devoted to real work, either industrial or agricultural.[73]

It has been said that Proudhon was the only leading writer of the period who expressed the thoughts of the working man, and that many workers were Proudhonians before they found their ideas expressed in his works.[74] This program of education, published before *Justice*, verifies that statement. Nevertheless, the socialists of mid-century were still bound to religious concepts, or at least to a vague religiosity. Even the Proudhonian Henri-Charles Leneveux still defined religious training as one aspect of education in 1861, although he maintained it had no place in the schools. "One could say," he wrote, "that in France the civil society is more surely and more truly Christian than the religious society. . . . That new road of Christian philosophy was opened by the authors of our great Revolution."[75]

Another Proudhonian, Auguste Vermorel, criticized the republicans of 1848 for seeking liberty through political formulas, "when it resides in the sovereignty of individual conscience." The work of democracy was to proclaim the moral and social equality of all persons, leading to liberty in justice. The indispensable condition of justice was the abolition of ignorance and misery. In the manifesto of his journal, *Courrier français*, in 1866, Vermorel maintained that any politics that did not have as its direct and immediate aim the moral education and the amelioration of the lot of the people (in that order) was necessarily sterile and unsuited to a democracy.[76]

Reviewing Jules Simon's *L'Ouvrière*, Vermorel called the education of the people a matter of capital importance. "What is necessary is not a religion, but a moral law," he wrote. Religion might be an excellent adjunct to morality in the beginning of a society; but as human beings learned to think for themselves, they rejected its depotism. "It is then that the moral law must be made precise, determined in its absolute existence, shown to be sufficient unto itself." In place of the absent religion there should be individual responsibility; there was no need for a new religion, as Fourier and the Saint-Simonians had thought.[77]

In the 1860s a few workers' groups moved away from religious concepts as a base for ethics. They insisted upon a rational education for all children, in order to improve public morality. At the 1867 Exposition the metalworkers stated that education should inspire the sentiments of justice, which were the best social guarantee; the tanners, one of the few groups to reject religious morality altogether, advocated a moral training based on the biographies of the benefactors of humanity. Many of the Proudhonian workers' groups opposed a state-run educational system in favor of one run by the local commune. All tended to stress the moral value of manual labor. The workers interested in educational matters were not those in big factories, but those in workshops— artisans, construction workers, typographers, and metalworkers; this may have shaped their ideas on education and morality to the Proudhonian model.[78]

The teaching of morality was also on the agenda at the International Socialist Congress of September 1867, in Lausanne. Henri-Louis Tolain spoke against seeking the bases of morality in any *a priori* conception outside of humanity. André Murat, a mechanic and follower of Massol, spoke for morale indépendante, inviting the International to become collaborators of the movement.[79] In Marseilles the Ligue de l'enseignement, backed by the Masonic lodges, did become linked with a section of the International. The Masonic lodges in Paris, particularly those of the Scottish rite, had sections of working men who discussed social and political questions.[80]

Freemasonry and the Ligue were both active in helping to systematize the views of the working class on education. By the end of the Second Empire the workers in large cities were overtly hostile to religious education, on the grounds that it was unscientific and created divisions in society. The laboring class elite were almost all Freemasons.[81] Macé, founder of the Ligue, had both Masonic and working-class ties. A direct tie to morale indépendante was Massol himself, whose years as a traveling metalworker, as well as his stint on Proudhon's *Voix du peuple*, had developed his ability to relate to the needs and thinking of working men.[82] Charles Sauvestre, another Freemason, had a wide working-class readership for his articles in *La Presse*; Leneveux published articles on secular education in *Le National*. The works of François-Vincent Raspail, close to Proudhon on matters of education, were widely read by the workers.[83]

In 1869 a Société d'enseignement was founded in Paris to offer an education for both sexes that would foster moral and intellectual self-discipline "outside any dogmatic conceptions."[84] Freemasons, including Massol, served on the committee along with some socialist leaders like Lefrançais. M.-L. Boutteville, who had lost his position as professor of philosophy for his writings, was to be in charge of the school. More than one hundred members of the society raised a tenth of the necessary capital, then sought official registration. No notary in Paris would handle the matter; the society was illegal because no religious instruction was provided and because the administrative council included three women. The committee returned the money in a public meeting.[85]

Workers were also involved in free-thinking associations of students during the late empire. One such organization, called Agis comme tu penses, insisted in its constitution that it was "necessary to separate progressive and scientific morality from the superannuated dogmas which reason condemns and which feelings should censure," that "conscience repels doctrines which direct man through fear and most unworthy motivations," that "these doctrines have disunited man by falsifying ethics and by corrupting the notion of right. . . ." Therefore they swore to receive no sacrament of religion, and to form an association with "science as its law, solidarity as its condition, justice as its aim." The young Georges Clemenceau was one of the members who recruited workers for the association.[86] Students also associated with workers in the more militant Masonic lodges, and at public lectures. (A law permitting public meetings was passed in 1868.) Although most were held for bourgeois audiences, there were also working-class lectures on social issues.

At these lectures spiritualist speakers were often booed by the workers; the predominant attitude of those attending was antireligious.[87] Prolonged applause followed the demand of a speaker at Menilmontant on November 28, 1868, that the catechism be replaced by a philosophic history of humanity and the New Testament by the civil code. Education, he said, should produce citizens, not slaves. A member of the International, speaking against religious training, propounded Proudhonian and mutualist theories of education.[88] Thus by the end of the empire the conscious portion of the working class was exposed to and beginning to accept, not only the end of religious education, but a moral education independent of religious concepts.

Under the Commune, only one member of the Council, Marie Vaillant, worked at secularization of the schools. But there was a popular movement to this end. On April 2, 1871, the Commune received a delegation from a Société d'éducation nouvelle, demanding that all religious or dogmatic instruction be left to families and be immediately eliminated from the schools, along with religious objects.[89] Six days later, in the seventeenth arrondissement, it was ordered that the teaching of *morale* be disengaged from any religious or dogmatic principle. Teachers who could not stand this situation should resign.[90] Thus morale indépendante found a foothold in the Commune, insuring that it would be anathema to the bourgeois society, which hated and feared what the. Commune represented to them.

Only a stage in the nineteenth-century development of French secular morality, morale indépendante was more radical in its elimination of religious concepts than the secular ethics of the Third Republic that followed. Nevertheless, since beside it the *morale laïque* of the Republic seemed to the majority at worst "neutral" to religion, and at best, "the grand old morality of our fathers," as Jules Ferry put it,[91] the more radical theory paved the way for at least some kind of civic morality to support a republic opposed by the church. Further, by promulgating a purely social basis for ethics, it led to the theory of *solidarité*, explicated first by Renouvier on a philosophical level, then by Emile Durkheim on a sociological level. This doctrine provided, at the turn of the century, the inspiration for Radical party politics, which successfully separated church and state and captured a large portion of the bourgeoisie. But the Radicals failed to attract the working class, whose interests they did not represent. At this time the ideas of Proudhon, an authentic voice of the French proletariat, lost out to those of his old opponent, Karl Marx.

Notes

1. D. G. Charlton, *Secular Religions in France, 1815–1870* (London, 1963), p. 65.

2. Pierre-Joseph Proudhon, *Lettre de candidature à la pension Suard* (Paris, 1926), pp. 11–12, 15, 16.

3. Lettre à Pauthier, *Correspondance*, 14 vols. (Geneva, 1975), I, 162.

4. Pierre-Joseph Proudhon, *De la célébration du dimanche* (Paris, 1926), pp. 41, 42, 45, 46, 47.

5. Ibid., pp. 50–51, 53–57, 58.

6. Ibid., p. 61. Note the comparison with Rousseau's *Contrat social*.

7. Ibid., pp. 89, 90. Proudhon considered the eighth commandment a proscription, not only of stealing, but of "any kind of gain obtained of others without their full acquiescence" (Ibid., p. 59).

8. Ibid., pp. 90–91, 93–94.

9. Lettre à Bergmann, *Correspondance*, I, 172.

10. Lettre à Muiron, *Correspondance*, I, 14.

11. Pierre-Joseph Proudhon, *De la création de l'ordre dans l'humanité*, pp. 37, 44, 121–122.

12. Lettre á Bergmann, *Correspondance*, II, 169.

13. Pierre-Joseph Proudhon, *Contradictions économiques*, 2 vols. (Paris, 1923), I, 34–37, 41, 385, 389.

14. *Le Peuple*, Sept. 2, Oct 17, 1848; May 6, 1849.

15. *Voix du peuple*, Nov. 4, 1849.

16. Pierre-Joseph Proudhon, *Philosophie du progrès* (Paris, 1946), p. 83.

17. Pierre-Joseph Proudhon, *Ecrits sur la religion* (Paris, 1959), pp. 270–271.

18. *Contradictions*, I, 44.

19. *Création*, pp. 246–249.

20. *Contradictions*, I, 367.

21. Pierre-Joseph Proudhon, *De la Justice dans la Révolution et dans l'Eglise*, 4 vols. (Paris, 1930), III, 432. Proudhon was familiar with Kant from reading his works in Tissot's translations during the early 1840s, a reading he admitted was only superficial. But he was impressed by Kant enough to dedicate a portion of *Création* to Tissot, and he used Kantian terms in this book as well as in correspondence.

22. *Justice*, III, 501.

23. *Contradictions*, I, 178, 387–388.

24. Pierre-Joseph Proudhon, *Qu'est-ce que la propriété?* (Paris, 1926), pp. 303–306, 311–312, 134, 144.

25. *Contradictions*, I, 34.

26. Lettre à Bergmann, *Correspondance*, VII, 370. An early suggestion of Durkheim's collective consciousness.

27. *Progrès*, p. 13.

28. *Justice*, I, 304, 269–300.

29. Ibid., I, 316–316, 323, 413–415, 422–424.

30. Ibid., I, 410–21, 415, 416, 324.

31. Ibid., I, 426, 328; III, 513, 517–18, 520–26, 542.

32. Ibid., III, 346, 363; IV, 363–75, 382, 393.

33. Ibid., III, 360–62; II, 76–78, 149–51.

34. Ibid., IV, 433; I, 314, 415, 434.

35. Ibid., II, 332; III, 83–85, 92–93.

36. Ibid., III, 122ff, 63ff.

37. Ibid., I, 226, 217, 221, 223–224, 227–228.

38. J.-A. Faucher and A. Ricker, *Histoire de la Franc-maçonnerie en France* (Paris, 1967), pp. 302–304, 307, 310–13, 315, 283, 293.

39. *Monde maçonnique*, V, 164, 321ff.

40. Msgr. Darboy, a Gallican, excused himself to the Pope by saying that he had not noticed the Masonic emblems on the casket; he also claimed not to have known of the previous papal encyclicals against Freemasonry (1832 and 1846) because they were not published in France. Faucher and Ricker, *Histoire*, p. 316.

41. *Justice*, III, 63ff.

42. Faucher and Ricker, *Histoire*, pp. 315–316.

43. *Monde maçonnique*, VIII, 270ff.

44. Massol had been a teacher at Marseilles during the Restoration. In Paris during the July Monarchy, he became a Saint-Simonian, although repelled by their theocratic doctrines. As a missionary of social reform he traveled France as a manual laborer; later he followed Père Enfantin to Egypt to found schools. After the dispersal of the group he went to England and started *L'Observateur français*. In 1848 he returned to Paris, where he was connected with *La Réforme* and then with Proudhon's *Voix du peuple*. He was the tutor of Proudhon's children and one of the executors of his will. Gustave Vapereau, *Dictionnaire universel des contemporains* (Paris, 1858), p. 1226; I. Tchernoff, *Le Parti républicain au coup d'état et sous le second empire* (Paris, 1906), p. 316.

45. *Monde maçonnique*, V, 722, 261–262, 267, 271–272.

46. *Monde maçonnique*, VI, 706–721.

47. *Monde maçonnique*, VII, 162–172, 181.

48. It was to take place finally in 1876. Faucher and Ricker, *Histoire*, p. 358.

49. *Monde maçonnique*, VII, 561–65.

50. The vote was 120–80. *Annuaire philosophique*, II, 327.

51. *Monde maçonnique*, VIII, 147–157.

52. *Morale indépendante*, Aug. 6, 1865.

53. Ibid.

54. *Morale indépendante*, Oct. 8, 1865. Renouvier was to provide in this period a philosophical basis for the theory of *solidarité*.

55. François Pillon, "La Morale indépendante," *L'Année philosophique* vol. 1867–1868, pp. 261ff., 362ff.

56. *Morale indépendante*, Oct. 29, 1865. Madame Coignet, née Gauthier, was active in women's education, and may have taught in Mme Lemonnier's school for working women. Her first book on public education came out in 1856. She was active in educational reform in the Third Republic, writing books on education and *morale*. She also published a work on Kantian philosophy, *De Kant à Bergson*. *Dictionnaire de biographie française* (Paris, 1961).

57. *Morale indépendante*, March 31, 1867. Morin, a pupil of Ravaisson at the Ecole normale supérieure, was a teacher of philosophy who refused to take the oath to Napoleon III, and was teaching in private schools. He had been a liberal Catholic, writing for *L'Avenir*. Tchernoff, *Le Parti républicain*, pp. 308–309.

58. *Morale indépendante*, Sept. 17, 1865.

59. Frédéric Morin, *Politique et philosophie* (Paris, 1876), pp. 173–174.

60. *Cours de morale à l'usage des écoles laïques* (Paris, 1874); *De l'éducation dans la démocratie* (Paris, 1881); *La Morale dans l'éducation* (Paris, 1883).

61. Clarisse Coignet, *La Morale indépendante* (Paris, 1869), pp. 6, 8, 29, 62.

62. Ibid., pp. 97–98, 102–103. The Proudhonian influence is clear here.

63. Ibid., pp. 118–122, 123–149, 151–154, 155.

64. Ibid., pp. 170–173, 177–178.

65. *Morale indépendante*, Aug. 20, Aug. 27, Oct. 29, 1865; Dec. 23, 1866. F.-V. Raspail donated 5,000 francs to the Société contemporaine de l'enseignement libre to found a school at Lyon without religion, on the condition that *morale*, that is, rights and duties, be taught daily. *Morale indépendante*, Apr. 24, 1870.

66. It was noted that the theologically radical aspects of his first sermon had been omitted from reports in the Catholic press. *Monde maçonnique*, VIII, 470–478; *Morale indépendante*, Dec. 17, 24, 31, 1865.

67. *Annuaire philosophique*, IV.

68. *Monde maçonnique*, IV. Oct. 1866, p. 406; Feb. 1867, p. 625 ff.; May 1869, p. 19ff.; *Morale indépendante*, Apr. 24, 1870.

69. *Action maçonnique*, Nov. 1, 1869, p. 357ff.

70. *Monde maçonnique*, July 1869, pp. 148–149.

71. Jean Macé had been a teacher of history in lycées until the coup of Napoleon III, after which he, as a republican, left Paris. He became involved in founding popular libraries in the provinces, and founded the Ligue de l'enseignement to boost popular education in preparation for the republic. A. Dessoye, *Jean Macé et la fondation de la Ligue de l'enseignement* (Paris, 1882).

72. J.-L. Greppo, *Catéchisme sociale* (Paris, n.d.), pp. 5–6, 15–16. Greppo was a silk-weaver of Lyon, who organized mutual societies there and participated in the revolts of 1831 and 1834. He later belonged to Blanqui's Society of Families, participated in the 1848 revolution in Lyon, and was elected to the National Assembly. Jean Maitron, ed., *Dictionnaire biographique du mouvement ouvrier français*, 9 vols. (Paris, 1965), II, 1, 300. Maitron does not agree with the theory that Greppo was not educated enough to produce this book, and that the author was Constantine Pecqueur.

73. Gustave Lefrançais, et al., *Programme d'éducation, association fraternelle des instituteurs, institutrices et professeurs socialistes* (Paris, 1849), pp. 7–8, 9, 11. Lefrançais was arrested after publication of the program and spent three months in prison. Once a Freemason, he left the order because he found it too religious. After 1871 he joined the International. Maitron, *Dictionnaire biographique*, V, 475–476.

74. Georges Duveau, *La Pensée ouvrière sur l'éducation pendant la deuxième république et le second empire* (Paris, 1948), p. 147.

75. H.-C. Leneveux, *La Propagande de l'instruction* (Paris, 1861), pp. 95, 104, 105. Leneveux, a typographer, had been one of the founders of Buchez's *L'Atelier*, but had turned against Catholicism. In 1859 he launched a project for popular education, La Bibliothèque des connaissances utiles. Toward the end of the empire he collaborated on *Le Siècle*. He opposed centralized socialism and favored cooperatives.

76. Vermorel was a collaborator on *La Presse*. At the end of the empire he tried to revive *La Réforme* with Prosper-Olivier Lissagaray as editor. He was later a member of the Commune. Maitron, *Dictionnaire biographique*, IX, 300.

77. *La Jeune France*, XII, 89.

78. Duveau, *La Pensée ouvrière*, pp. 184–187, 194–195, 321, 311. However, in 1869, *La Démocratie* published a program by socialist workers which demanded "complete secular education, obligatory for all and at the expense of the nation" (Ibid., p. 42).

79. Ibid., p. 115. Tolain was one of the signers of the Manifesto of the Sixty during the 1864 election campaign, arguing that the workers should put up their own candidates rather than rely on the bourgeois opposition to the empire. Proudhon highly approved. Although a member of the International, he was one of the group of mayors who tried to cooperate with Versailles during the

Commune, and was therefore expelled from the organization later. Frank Jellinek, *The Paris Commune of 1871* (New York, 1965), pp. 37, 38, 157, 413.

80. Tchernoff, *Le Parti républicain*, pp. 318, 323.

81. Duveau, *La Pensée ouvrière*, pp. 163–165, 187.

82. Tchernoff, *Le Parti républicain*, pp. 308–309.

83. Duveau, *La Pensée ouvrière*, pp. 314–315.

84. *Action maçonnique*, Oct. 15, 1868, p. 18.

85. *Monde maçonnique*, April 1869, p. 759ff. Gustave Lefrançais, *Souvenirs d'un révolutionnaire* (Brussels, 1902), pp. 334–335.

86. During the empire young *normaliens* were reading Proudhon. Maxime Leroy, *Histoire des idées sociales en France*, 3 vols. (Paris, 1950), II, 187, and Georges Weill, *Histoire de l'idée laïque au xixe siècle* (Paris, 1925), pp. 192–193.

87. Tchernoff, *Le Parti republicain*, p. 495. Duveau, *La Pensée ouvrière*, p. 314.

88. Auguste Vitu, *Les Réunions publiques à Paris, 1868–1869* (Paris, 1869), pp. 18, 85.

89. *Journal officiel de la Commune* (Paris, 1879), p. 129.

90. Duveau, *La Pensée ouvrière*, p. 45.

91. Jules Ferry, *Discours et opinions*, 4 vols. (Paris, 1893–1896), IV, 30, 127, 135–136, 142, 158.

VII

Freud contra Ecclesiam: Rhetorical Structures in *The Future of an Illusion*

DAVID PACE

I t is, perhaps, not entirely without justice that the highest honor received by Freud during his lifetime was not a Nobel Prize for Science, but rather a Goethe Prize, granted in recognition of his accomplishments as a man of letters. Despite his self-image as a scientist, Freud did not treat language positivistically. He did not create a transparent prose in which his own interests and tastes were obliterated so that only naked facts were left exposed. Instead, he operated like the novelist or poet, playing with or manipulating the forms of language itself.

This literary aspect of Freud's work is nowhere more evident than in his writings on religion. In these works Freud developed a complex rhetorical system in which he employed the semantic structures of his time in order to sway his audience. In books such as *The Future of an Illusion* the power of Freud's argument rests, not upon his appeal to the scientific evidence—for there is scarcely any—but rather upon his manipulation of the semantic conventions of his day. Like any great rhetorician, Freud's impact resides in his control over a form of discourse, not in his references to a world of facts outside that discourse.

This rhetorical aspect of Freud's writings on religion has, however, frequently been ignored or minimized. In part this is due to the low esteem in which rhetoric is held in our era. In an age of mass propaganda we are apt to equate all rhetoric with the crass manipulations of a Goebbels and to forget the rich rhetorical tradition that stretches back to ancient Greece. Socrates seems at last to have won in his battle against the Sophists, for today, more than a century after Nietzsche proclaimed the glory of the Greek agon, we still demand that our great ones be emotionless and uninvolved seekers after truth, not passionate defenders of the interests of their community.

This is particularly true in the case of Freud because we have tended to accept his self-image as a pure seeker after scientific truth. Through the efforts of Ernest Jones and other sympathetic biographers, Freud's life has been cast as a heroic quest, and under the influence of this myth we have been desensitized to the fact that Freud may have been pursuing very concrete personal ends through his writings on topics such as religion.

Fortunately, in the last decade there have been impressive efforts to de-mythologize Freud. To mention two of the most important contributions to this process, Frank J. Sulloway in his recent *Freud, The Biologist of Mind* has systematically undercut the mythical archetypes that have structured our notion of Freud's life,[1] and Paul Roazen in *Freud and His Followers* has begun to unravel the internal and external politics of psychoanalysis.[2] From such studies a new image of Freud is emerging, one in which he is seen as the politically astute leader of a faction, striving for hegemony in the field of mental health.

From this perspective Freud's writings on religion take on a new significance. We must view his works, not simply as expressions of his evolving concepts of the human psyche, but also as political acts that must be assessed in the context of the problems facing the psychoanalytic movement. As Roazen has written, "It is generally a good principle in intellectual history, and even more so with Freud, to keep in mind a writer's opponents."[3] Such an approach does not lessen the greatness of Freud, unless we are to believe that Pericles was of lesser stature because he defended Athens or Augustine lacked greatness because he used his rhetorical skills to further the cause of Christianity. But it does force us to be very sensitive to the manipulative aspects of Freud's writing.

The image of Freud as a debater aggressively seeking support for his community fits well with the information we have about his early life. By his own account Freud was a somewhat pugnacious youth, ready to defend the interests and the honor of the Jewish community. At the age of ten or twelve he learned that his father had once passively submitted to anti-Semitic insults, and he seems to have compensated by identifying with heroes such as the Semitic Hannibal and the Napoleonic General Masséna, whom he erroneously believed to be Jewish.[4] In a letter written to his fiancée in 1883 when he was twenty-seven, Freud told of how he had turned on an anti-Semitic antagonist in a train car and demanded that he come forward to fight. The anti-Semite did not respond to the challenge, but Freud cheerfully informed his future wife that he had been "quite prepared to kill him"[5] This aggressive defense of his ethnic honor was also in evidence when Freud enthusiastically supported his colleague Karl Koller after the latter responded to an anti-Semitic insult first with a fistfight in a hospital emergency room and then with a duel.[6]

As Freud matured he abandoned such threats of physical violence, verbal insults, and support of duels, but there is ample evidence that he continued to stand up for the group with which he most strongly identified. There is evidence, however, that Freud's identification shifted from the larger Jewish community to the psychoanalytic movement of which he was the absolute leader. In the process his will to combat found a new form of expression. To use Nietzschean terminology, his agon was spiritualized; his field of combat shifted from face-to-face interactions to the printed page.[7]

Freud's will to struggle and desire to defend his own was given its greatest expression in *The Future of an Illusion*. This is the most polemical of all his writings, and the one in which his manipulation of rhetorical forms is most evident. And yet many serious commentators have treated the work as an objective expression of Freud's ideas about religion, civilization, and science. Henri Ellenberger wrote, for example, that "religiously minded psychoanalysts objected that Freud had overstepped the boundaries of psychoanalysis [in *The Future of an Illusion*] and was expressing his personal philosophical opinion; but Freud no doubt believed that psychoanalysis could unmask religion as it could any neurotic symptom."[8] Richard Wollheim treated the work without even considering whether or not Freud had a personal or professional interest in discrediting religion. And even Paul Roazen, who has made a major contribution to our reevaluation of Freud, wrote in *Freud: Political and Social Thought* that *"The Future of an Illusion* can best be understood as a passionate restatement of the Enlightenment ideals of reason and progress."[9]

This tendency to treat *The Future of an Illusion* as a lively but disinterested study of religion was encouraged by Freud himself. He drew about himself the cloak of invisibility treasured by all scientists and wrote in ego-less prose of the objective scientist. Unlike such introspective works as *The Interpretation of Dreams, The Future of an Illusion* will tolerate no true "I"; the words seem to emerge, not from the experiences and prejudices of one individual, but rather from reality itself. Moreover, Freud seemed to lean over backward to assure the supporters of religion that he was not their enemy. In an often quoted letter to the Swiss Protestant clergyman and psychoanalyst Oskar Pfister, he insisted that it was not necessary for other members of the movement to share his opinions on religion:

> Let us be quite clear on the point that the views expressed in my book [*The Future of an Illusion*] form no part of analytic theory. They are my own personal views, which coincide with those of many non-analysts and pre-analysts, but there are certainly many analysts who do not share them. If I draw on analysis for certain arguments—in reality only one argument—that need deter no one from using the non-partisan method of analysis for arguing the opposite view.[10]

These words create the impression that Freud was an unbeliever himself but that he was not interested in imposing his views upon others. This image is reinforced by other passages in his writings, when he appears to be very willing to concede the virtues of religion. In "The Future Prospects of Psycho-analytic Therapy" (1910) he spoke of "the extraordinary increase in neuroses since the enfeeblement of religion,"[11] and in one of his case histories he described a patient whom religion had protected from the worst consequences of his childhood situation:

> . . . in the present case religion achieved all the aims for the sake of which it is included in the education of the individual. It put a restraint on his sexual impulsions by affording them a sublimation and a safe mooring; it lowered the importance of his family relationships, and thus protected him from the threat of isolation of mankind. The untamed and fear-ridden child became social, well-behaved and amenable to education . . . religion did its work for the hard pressed. child—by the combination which it afforded to the believer of satisfaction, of sublimation, of diversion from sensual processes to purely spiritual ones, and of access to social relationships.[12]

But other texts from Freud's works reveal a much less tolerant attitude toward religion. In other letters to Pfister, for example, he referred to "my completely negative attitude towards religion, in any form and however attenuated . . . ,"[13] and he asked "how the devil do you reconcile all we experience with your assumption of a moral world order?"[14]

Such comments do not, however, capture the depth of Freud's negative reaction to religion. It is clear at least by the late 1920s that Freud viewed Catholicism as a dangerous rival to his own movement. Religion was not just an untenable intellectual and moral position; it was a negative force in Freud's world, which had to be countered. In his *New Introductory Lectures on Psychoanalysis*, published in 1933 just six years after *The Future of an Illusion*, Freud abandoned the pretense of toleration and attacked religion directly:

> It is not acceptable to say that science is one province of human mental activity and that religion and philosophy are others at least its equal, that science should not disturb the other two, that they all have similar claims to truth, and that each man is free to choose where he wishes to place his belief and locate his faith. Such a way of thinking is considered particularly noble, tolerant, broad, and free of narrow-minded prejudice. Unfortunately it is not tenable; it shares all the destructiveness of a totally unscientific *Weltanschauung* and in practical terms amounts to the same thing. It is simply a fact that truth cannot be tolerant, can permit no compromise or restriction, that scientific research examines all areas of human activity as its own and must become relentlessly critical when another power wishes to seize a bit of it.[15]

There is reason to believe that even in passages such as this Freud was moderating his position on religion for basically strategical reasons. A little more than a decade after the appearance of *The Future of an Illusion* Freud admitted that he had temporarily suppressed his own study of *Moses and Monotheism* because he felt that it would anger the Catholic church at a point when he needed its protection from the National Socialists. It must be stressed that political events may have changed Freud's perspective in the interval between 1927 and 1938, but nonetheless worth considering are his final comments on Catholic Christianity:

> Nevertheless, it appears that today the conservative democracies have become the guardians of cultural progress and that strangely enough the very institution of the Catholic Church places a powerful force in opposition to this spreading danger to culture [National Socialism]—the church which has hitherto been the relentless enemy of the freedom of thought and of progress towards the knowledge of truth.
>
> We live in a Catholic country under the protection of the Church, uncertain as to how long this will last. But so long as it endures, we are naturally reluctant to do anything which would arouse the hostility of the Church. It is not cowardice, but rather prudence. The new enemy, whom we will guard against serving, is more dangerous than the old, which we have already learned how to endure. The psychoanalytic research, which we cultivate, is moreover, the object of suspicious attention on the part of Catholicism. We do not maintain that this suspicion is unjust. . . . It is likely to come to pass that the practice of psychoanalysis will be forbidden to us. Such violent methods of suppression are, indeed, in no way alien to the Church; it perceives it rather as an invasion of its privileges, when others help themselves to such methods.[16]

Such an aggressive attitude toward religion is not surprising from someone who had long suffered from the anti-Jewish prejudice of the Austrian Empire. As Philip Rieff has written, "Aiming at religion in general, Freud's critique hits Christianity most accurately; and by Christianity he had in mind mainly the Roman Catholic Church, as he saw it in the fiercely anti-Semitic Vienna of his day."[17] Thus in part, Freud's attacks on Christianity may be seen as an extension of the defense of Jewish honor, which was so important to him in his youth.

But such an explanation ignores the fact that for almost half of his life Freud's primary identification was with the psychoanalytic movement. His ego was inseparably intertwined with psychoanalysis, and its success was overwhelmingly important to him. And from this perspective his attacks on religion take on the appearance of an attempt to eliminate a dangerous rival in a territorial dispute.

Throughout the Western world in the late nineteenth and twentieth century there was a great redivision of intellectual territory as traditional groups vied with new professions and academic disciplines for the right to dominate certain social functions. Psychoanalysis was, of course, in competition with neural physiology, the medical profession, and other schools of psychotherapy for the right to establish a monopoly on the scientific treatment of psychological problems. But many of these problems could also be defined as spiritual and, thus, could be assigned to the care of the church.[18]

As the passage from the *New Introductory Lectures* quoted above indicates, Freud was very concerned with establishing the priority of scientific method over religious belief, and it is easy to see how this position was crucial to the territorial claims of psychoanalysis. In one of Freud's letters to Pfister he explicitly referred to "our predecessor in psychoanalysis, the Catholic fathers,"[19] and in another he outlined his conception of the institutional position of his movement:

> I do not know if you have detected the secret link between the [*Question of*] *Lay Analysis* and the [*Future of an*] *Illusion*. In the former I wish to protect analysis from the doctors and in the latter from the priests. I should like to hand it over to a profession of *lay* curers of souls who need not be doctors and should not be priests.[20]

As this passage indicates, in his correspondence Freud was willing to admit that *The Future of an Illusion* had a clear polemical purpose. But it is also clear that this purpose could not be made too explicit. To assume the role of the defender of a faction would have required Freud to drop the mantle of the scientist which was so important to him. And it might have subjected psychoanalysis to even stronger attacks from outside.

Thus, Freud had to use the tools of rhetoric carefully and indirectly to lead his readers toward the conclusion that science, as represented by psychoanalysis, was superior to religion. To do this he constructed a rhetorical maze, through which readers might wander at random but from which they could ultimately exit only by following a path preordained by Freud.

It is impossible to determine to what extent Freud was aware of this manipulation of his audience. A conscious knowledge of all the stratagems being employed in an argument is as unnecessary for the skilled rhetorician as a conscious knowledge of all the rules of grammar is for a native speaker. But in the analysis that follows I will accept the psychoanalytic dictum that the result suggests the motivation, and I will use the language of intentionality to describe Freud's rhetorical strategies, whether or not they were actually conscious.

But how was Freud to construct his rhetorical maze? Two devices were available to him: the careful use of conceptual dichotomies and the implicit appeal to commonly accepted beliefs. The use of dichotomies is perhaps the most striking aspect of the work. As Stanley Hyman has noted in his study of Freud as a creative writer, "Everything in *The Future of an Illusion* is dualistic and shaped by antitheses."[21] But these oppositions are not simply literary flourishes. As we shall see, they serve implicitly to organize the universe of the reader, to exclude certain approaches to the questions at hand, and to make others seem quite natural.

To support and to exploit further these conceptual dichotomies, Freud drew upon a vast and often contradictory reservoir of folk beliefs, scientific facts, truisms, and implicit proverbs. These beliefs generally functioned at a subliminal level, and no specific justification for them was provided. They functioned, not as assumptions underlying a logical argument, but rather as conceptual barricades that discouraged the reader from pursuing a line of thought inimical to Freud's purposes.

The role of such common beliefs in creating conviction was recognized at the turn of the century by the French writer Alfred Jarry, who proclaimed that "Clichés are the armature of the absolute." But a more systematic treatment of the role of the truism in the formation of a text may be found in Roland Barthes' *S/Z*, an exhaustive analysis of a short story by Balzac. Barthes believed that literary works made use of "cultural" or "reference" codes that united them with a larger body of knowledge outside the text itself. The information brought into the text by means of these codes could, for example, be physical, physiological, medical, psychological, literary, or historical,[22] but within the literary text this knowledge functioned, not as a provable, scientific statement, but rather as a proverb.

> The utterances of the cultural code [Barthes wrote] are implicit proverbs: they are written in that obligatory mode by which a discourse states a general will, the law of a society, making the proposition concerned ineluctable or indelible.[23]

Since *The Future of an Illusion* functions largely as a rhetorical, and hence a literary work, it is filled with cultural codes that carry popular wisdom into the text in the form of implicit proverbs. An analysis of these cultural codes not only sheds light on Freud's thought, but also makes explicit the basis of credibility in Freud's milieu. The pages that follow will present a systematic analysis of some of the cultural codes and the structural oppositions that helped make *The Future of an Illusion* a powerful rhetorical weapon. The focus throughout will be upon the structure of the argument, not its logic, and upon its implicit content, not its explicit dictums. And, finally, Freud's text will be treated, not positively, as a series of reasons leading the reader to accept a certain position, but rather negatively as a set of constraints that serve to hinder the reader from exploring avenues antithetical to Freud's goal.

Freud began *The Future of an Illusion* with one of the oldest of rhetorical devices, a brief apology for undertaking such a difficult task as speculating upon the future of civilization. But even in this standard apologia there are appeals to cultural codes that serve Freud's purposes. He reminds the reader that "there are only a few people who can comprehend human activity in its full expanse" and that "the less one knows what is past and what is present the more dubious one's judgments of the future will turn out to be."[24] The first of these truisms helps legitimate Freud's project (he is not invading the domain of another profession), and the second calls for the historicization of the question of civilization, a demand we will later see to be highly advantageous to his argument.

But, ironically, Freud began the main body of his argument with a totally ahistorical definition of civilization:

> Human culture [*Kultur*]—by which I mean everything which has raised human existence above the conditions of animals and which has differentiated it from the life of the beasts—and I disdain the separation of culture [*Kultur*] and civilization [*Zivilisation*]—reveals, as we all know, two sides to the observer. It includes, on the one hand, all the knowledge and skill which men have acquired in order to master the powers of Nature and to win over its resources for the satisfaction of human needs, and, on the other hand, all the arrangements which are necessary in order to regulate the relationships of humans to one another and in particular the distribution of available wealth.[25]

It would be too time-consuming to list all the culture codes that are embedded in this definition of culture. But for our present purposes it is important to note what qualities have been united by Freud. Culture has been associated with humanness, with all knowledge and capacity to control nature, and with all regulation of social interactions. Freud's refusal to accept the common distinction between *Kultur* and *Zivilisation* prevented any ambiguity from creeping into his definition. He left no room to oppose the artistic qualities of Kultur to the social regulation and technology of Zivilisation, and all the positive aspects of human life remained associated with the idea of culture.

But every definition serves to exclude as well as include. The instant Freud created this definition of civilization he also created a corresponding image of anticivilization. He has created a linguistic niche that he filled with negative qualities. Anticivilization was to be automatically associated with ignorance, poverty, powerlessness in the face of nature, and a *bellum omnium contra omnes*. By connecting this negative definition with some other specific idea, Freud could create a powerful conceptual dichotomy, with great ideological power.

Therefore, it is of great importance to observe the fashion in which Freud drew other concepts into association with this anticulture. On this point it is worth quoting *The Future of an Illusion* at length:

. . . every individual is virtually an enemy of culture, even though it should be a universal human interest. . . . Culture must, therefore, be defended against the individual, and its organisation, institutions, and laws all serve to further this task; they aim not only at establishing a particular division of wealth but also at maintaining it; indeed they must protect against the hostile impulses of men everything which serves the mastery of nature and the production of goods. . . .

It appears rather that each culture must build itself upon force and the renunci-ation of the instincts. . . . One must, I believe, reckon with the fact that there are present in all men destructive, anti-social, and anti-cultural tendencies and that in a large number of people these are strong enough to determine their behaviour in human society.[26]

Juxtaposed to Freud's initial definition of culture, this passage creates a Manichean view of the world. On the one hand, there are the forces of order and plenty, represented by culture and association with scientific knowledge, eco-nomic power, and social harmony. Opposed to this is the instinctual individual, who automatically stands against all that is good in the human universe. There is no choice as to which side is to be favored, since all the qualities associated with culture are unambiguously good, whereas those in the opposite camp are all bad.

In these passages and in the pages immediately following them, Freud produced a complex matrix of qualities that served to organize the mental space of his readers. At the risk of oversimplification, the matrix may be presented as follows:

CULTURE	vs.	*INDIVIDUAL*
Higher		Lower
Culture		Nature
Artificial		Natural
Human		Animal
Learned behavior		Instinct
Knowledge		Ignorance
Control over nature		Powerlessness before a hostile nature
Wealth		Poverty
Regulations and institutions		Chaos and formal freedom
Social harmony		Social strife
Reason		Passion
Maintains particular distribution of wealth		No fixed distribution of wealth
Elites		Masses
Hard work		Laziness
Creativity		Destructiveness

In dealing with such a conceptual matrix it is extremely important to recognize that Freud created a structure of discourse, not a description of reality. Culture and the instinctual individual are not empirical realities. They draw their meaning, not from their correspondence to actual experiential entities, but rather from their role in a Wittgensteinian language game. There is no inherent reason why the qualities associated with the two extremes of Freud's dichotomy should adhere to one another in this particular manner. For example, given the social nature of our species and of our ancestors for many millions of years, there is no external reason why instinct should be associated solely with the individual and automatically opposed to the collectivity. Nor is it obvious outside Freud's system why social harmony should be identified with the competitive world of modern capitalism, and why strife is linked with small, decentralized communities. But in each case, there were cultural codes that made Freud's way of organizing the material convincing to his audience.

Once this rhetorical structure was established, however, Freud could use it for all sorts of polemical purposes. For example, two different groups on the same side of the matrix may be equated with one another. In Freud's system the small group of individuals who are able to control their emotions are opposed to the majority, which lacks such control, and the economic elite is contrasted to the vast masses of suffering humanity. Freud offered no empirical evidence whatsoever to prove that these two divisions coincided with one another, and, yet, once his matrix was established, he could write convincingly that "just as it is impossible to dispense with the compulsion to cultural work, so it is impossible to give up the rule of the minority over the masses because the masses are lazy and lacking in judgment, they do not love the renunciation of the instincts, they are not convinced by argument of its necessity, and each one of them encourages the others to indulge their impetuosity."[27]

The power of Freud's system was demonstrated at the end of the first chapter of The Future of an Illusion when Freud dealt briefly with the question of the Soviet Union. We know from a letter written in 1928 that Freud considered Lenin a despot of the same stripe as Mussolini,[28] and there is no reason to believe that he was more kindly disposed toward the Bolsheviks when he wrote The Future of an Illusion the previous year. Yet, Freud assumed the role of an objective scientist and referred to the Soviet Union as a social experiment in process that it would be premature to judge. He was free to be so generous because no one who had accepted the conceptual framework laid out by Freud could possibly see the Soviet Union as anything but a threat to the cultural forms that stand between ourselves and chaos.

However, religion, not the Soviet Union, was Freud's primary target in this work. Yet, in the first chapter Freud has presented little that the orthodox Christian could not accept. To be sure, his approach is rather materialistic and this-worldly, but his division of human experience into two warring tendencies and his characterization of individual instincts as harmful would be very familiar to the Christian. In fact, with a few changes in terminology and emphasis Freud's argument might almost be taken for a passage from de Maistre or any of the other conservative Christian critics of the Enlightenment. It was just this image of destructive human nature that had been used by Christian apologists since the French Revolution to prove that religion was necessary to maintain the social order.

Thus, in the first chapter of *The Future of an Illusion* Freud seems to have conceded many of the basic arguments of the conservative apologists of religion. He seems to have given them a position from which they can identify the defense of Christianity with the defense of property and equate atheism with anarchy. But, as will become apparent, these concessions were the bait of a trap. Having created such a radical dichotomy between culture and the instinctual individual, Freud began to create a mental structure in which it would appear that religion was detrimental to the effort to protect culture from the animalistic impulses of the biological individual.

Freud began the second chapter with a statement that seems even more in keeping with traditional religious arguments:

> With the knowledge that each culture rests upon the compulsion to work and the renunciation of the drives and that inevitably an opposition is created by the confusion of these demands, it becomes clear that wealth itself, the means of obtaining it and the regulation of its distribution can not be the essence or the single definition of culture. For these are threatened through the resistance and will to destruction of those who take part in culture. Alongside the wealth there exists the means to defend culture, the means of force and other techniques through which men are reconciled to culture and are compensated for their sacrifices. These last can be described as the spiritual [*seelische*] possessions of culture.[29]

With these words Freud seemed to have set the stage for a defense of religion, for we are accustomed to thinking of religious beliefs as the great spiritual possessions of culture. But at this point Freud shifts the context of the discussion. It is not religion, but the super-ego that fulfills this role for culture. "This strengthening of the super-ego," Freud wrote, "is a cultural possession of the greatest value. Individuals, in whom this has been accomplished, are changed from opponents of culture to bearers of culture."[30] Thus, it is the psychological entity "super-ego" that fills this role for culture, not the spiritual entity "conscience" or the social entity "Church."

With the substitution of the super-ego for religion Freud began a process of "familialization" of reality that was to continue throughout *The Future of an Illusion*. The term "super-ego" is embedded in the discourse of the family; it carries us away from the theological, the political, and the economic and returns us to the sexual constellation of the family. The "real" for Freud ultimately resides in this constellation, and other realms of being are ultimately projections of the family. It is possible to reduce all other languages to the language of the family, but this last language—primal in two senses—can be reduced to no other. By making the super-ego the crucial bulwark against the onslaught of the instincts, Freud implicitly made psychoanalysis the privileged instrument of social control, for it was the psychoanalyst, not the priest, physician, or professor, who could decipher the hieroglyphics of the family.

But this statement of his territorial claim was not sufficient. Freud had to discredit the claims of religion. He did this by appealing to a series of cultural codes that served to identify religion with the very instinctual forces it had traditionally claimed to oppose. The first step in this identification was contained in a seemingly innocent description of the evolution of the super-ego:

> It is not true that the human mind [Seele] has undergone no development since the earliest ages and is in contrast to science and technology still today as it was at the beginning of history. In the course of our development the external compulsions gradually became internalized, as a particular mental faculty, the super-ego, took them under its command. Every child relives for us the occurrence of such a transformation, becoming by means of it moral and social.[31]

In this passage Freud appealed specifically to the set of cultural codes that were given explicit expression in nineteenth-century cultural evolutionism. These codes included the belief that human history consisted of a series of stages, that these stages were cumulative, that a particular society generally stood at the same stage of development in all spheres of its culture (technological, political, familial, emotional, and so forth), and that the culture of contemporary "backward" societies resembled that possessed at earlier stages by societies that are now "advanced." Without these cultural codes the passage quoted above would hang meaninglessly in a conceptual vacuum; but with these beliefs firmly established in the minds of his audience, it opened the way to a whole universe of underconnected notions about the nature of culture.

By the time Freud wrote *The Future of an Illusion* this set of cultural codes had been subjected to a devastating critique by a group of American anthropologists centering around Franz Boas and such disciples as Robert Lowie. There is no evidence that Freud had any knowledge of their arguments that the ethnographical evidence did not support the theory of evolutionary stages or the notion that "primitive" cultures were survivals of our own distant past. But this movement among professional anthropologists was irrelevant to Freud's discourse in any case. He was not operating on the level of empirical ethnography, but rather on the level of popular discourse. His arguments were convincing, not because they were backed up by specific evidence, but rather because they followed the basic contours of the European imagination.

In order to employ these cultural codes, however, Freud had to establish a bridge between the technologically centered evolutionism popular in the late nineteenth century and the emotionally centered evolutionism that favored psychoanalysis. Such a bridge already existed in the form of two metaphors that were among the most powerful of all modern cultural codes: the primitive as insane and the primitive as child.

The connection between the insane and the "primitive" was implicit in the very language used to describe non-Western cultures. The words "savage" in English and "sauvage" in French capture a widespread association of the "primitive" with the kind of emotional chaos believed to be present in the insane. To pick examples from two of the most famous evolutionists, Edward Tylor wrote that a "savage" turned loose on the streets of London would quickly be locked up because he would not be able to live up to the high ethical standards of European conduct,[32] and Herbert Spencer described "primitives" as "governed by despotic emotions," and subject to "explosive, chaotic, incalculable behaviour."[33]

As the master theoretician of "incalculable behaviour," Freud could use the cultural code and draw the prehistory of culture within his psychoanalytic sphere. But the identification of the child with the primitive was even more useful to him. Freud accepted the recapitulationist theory of cultural evolution, which held that the development of each individual repeated the evolution of the species. And, since psychoanalysts were the experts on the emotional development of the individual, they automatically assumed the role of expertise in the evolution of the passions.

But, Freud did more than simply reuse these common cultural codes; he fused them into a new unity that extended their life in the culture at the very moment when they were under the greatest attack from the professional anthropologists. Before Freud these two metaphors, the primitive as insane and the primitive as child, were used interchangeably, but they could not be united. Within a Victorian framework, it was difficult to complete the triangle and see the child as insane. But, Freud shattered the notion of childhood innocence and created a new image of the neurotic or schizophrenic as one who had become trapped in a childhood stage of emotional-sexual development. When this theory was added to his notion that the psychology of the primitive was like that of the Western child, he had completed the missing link and had provided a seemingly firm scientific basis for the triple equation of the primitive, the child, and the mentally disturbed.

Thus, Freud created a new unity to the European cultural codes about human development. He created a mental space in which all human activity could be situated along three parallel axes that stretched, respectively, from the child to the adult, from the primitive to the modern European, and from the mentally disturbed to the sane. In each case the primary criterion for establishing the position of a particular individual upon the spectrum was the degree of self-control he or she exerted over the natural instincts. And, in each case the continuum was a temporal one: earlier always meant more chaotic.

In the process of formulating these cultural codes Freud created a second conceptual matrix that closely paralleled the first but that added new elements. This pattern can be roughly expressed as follows:

Control of Instincts	vs.	No Control over Instincts
Later		Earlier
Adult		Child
Modern		Prehistoric
Technologically advanced		Technologically primitive
Sane		Neurotic or schizophrenic

The ideological potential of these two interlocking matrices is enormous. They may be used as a justification for suppressing social revolution by simply identifying the revolutionaries and their demands with the primitive, the child, the insane, and the destructive instincts. Similarly, they may be used to support imperialism, since through these metaphors it becomes as unreasonable to leave colonial peoples to their own devices as to abandon infants or to let the insane out of their asylums. But in the context of the polemic of *The Future of an Illusion*, what is the rhetorical role of this conceptual pattern?

The answer to this is quickly provided when one attempts to situate religion within the mental universe created by Freud. Religion is not a new phenomenon. Unlike science, its origins are in the earliest times of our species. Again, unlike science, it appeals to children as well as to adults, the masses as well as the educated elite, and it rests upon the emotions at least as much as on reason. It is a cultural phenomenon, but it claims to have its roots in man's deepest nature.

In short, within the mental universe created by Freud, religion must be assigned the role of a mediator between extremes. It bridges the gap between oldest and most basic urges and our most civilized concepts of behavior. In another system this might be a highly valuable role. But Freud had loaded the system from the very beginning. In his Manichean system all the value lies on one side of the balance sheet. There is nothing to be gained by getting in touch with the more natural and primitive side of human nature. Religion becomes childish, neurotic, unreasonable, a useless survival of the past.

In the latter chapters of *The Future of an Illusion* Freud develops a more complex argument to defend his position on religion. He borrows the entire historical schema of Auguste Comte, and treats religion as the most important tool in raising man above savagery and yet as a tool that must now be discarded.

But from a rhetorical point of view these arguments are almost irrelevant. Freud's trap was laid in the first ten pages of the work.

It is interesting to note how much Freud fought this battle on the church's own turf. Although he is supposed to be one of the most revolutionary thinkers of our century, Freud constructed his argument out of the clichés of his childhood. And, by so doing he brought into the twentieth century much of the cultural baggage of an earlier time. One has only to compare *The Future of an Illusion* with a truly twentieth-century document, such as André Breton's 1924 *Surrealist Manifesto* to realize that Freud was fighting nineteenth-century battles with nineteenth-century weapons. But, his obsession with social control, his ethnocentrism, his terror of spontaneous expression of the emotions, and his desire to protect the existing distribution of wealth suggest that he was not nearly so far as he might have imagined from the reactionary forces he deplored.

Notes

1. Frank J. Sulloway, *Freud, Biologist of the Mind: Beyond the Psychoanalytic Legend* (New York, 1979).

2. Paul Roazen, *Freud and His Followers* (New York, 1976).

3. Paul Roazen, *Freud: Political and Social Thought* (New York, 1970).

4. Sigmund Freud, *Gesammelte Werke* (London, 1942), vols. 2 and 3, pp. 202–203.

5. Ernest L. Freud, *Letters of Sigmund Freud* (New York, 1960), p. 78.

6. Hortense Koller Becker, "Carl Koller and Cocaine," *Psychoanalytic Quarterly*, vol. 32 (1963), p. 346.

7. In his provocative study of nineteenth- and twentieth-century Jewish intellectuals, John Murray Cuddihy has suggested that much of the work of these figures must be seen as an attempt to deal with the kind of face-to-face contact between ethnic groups described above. See Cuddihy, *The Ordeal of Civility: Freud, Marx, Lévi-Strauss, and the Jewish Struggle with Modernity* (New York, 1974).

8. Henri Ellenberger, *The Discovery of the Unconscious: The History and Evolution of Dynamic Psychiatry* (New York, 1970), p. 525.

9. Richard Wollheim, *Sigmund Freud* (New York, 1971), pp. 252–273; Roazen, *Freud: Political and Social Thought*, p. 160. It should be noted that elsewhere in this volume Roazen does suggest that Freud's attacks on religion should be seen in the context of his hostility to Jung. Roazen, *Freud: Political and Social Thought*, pp. 161–162.

10. Heinrich Meng and Ernest L. Freud, eds., *Psychoanalysis and Faith: The Letters of Signmund Freud and Oskar Pfister* (New York, 1963), p. 117.

11. Sigmund Freud, *Gesammelte Werke*, vol. 13, p. 109. A similar idea is expressed in Freud's study of Leonardo. See ibid., p. 195.

12. Sigmund Freud, *The Standard Edition of the Complete Psychological Works* (London, 1955), vol. 17, pp. 114–115.

13. Meng and Freud, *Psychoanalysis and Faith*, p. 110.

14. Ibid., p. 123.

15. Sigmund Freud, *Gesammelte Werke*, vol. 15, pp. 172–173.

16. Sigmund Freud, *Gesammelte Werke*, vol. 16, pp. 157–158.

17. Philip Rieff, *Freud: The Mind of the Moralist* (New York, 1961), p. 282.

18. For an interesting discussion of the triangle between physician, priest, and therapist in France, see Jacques Donzelot, *The Policing of Families* (New York, 1979), pp. 171–198.

19. Meng and Freud, *Psychoanalysis and Faith*, p. 21.

20. Ibid., p. 126.

21. Stanley Edgar Hyman, *The Tangled Bank: Darwin, Marx, Frazer, and Freud as Imaginative Writers* (New York, 1962), p. 405.

22. Roland Barthes, *S/Z* (New York, 1974), p. 20.

23. Ibid., p. 100.

24. Freud, *Gesammelte Werke*, vol. 14, p. 325.

25. Ibid., p. 326.

26. Ibid., pp. 326–328.

27. Ibid., p. 328.

28. Ernest Freud, *Letters of Sigmund Freud*, p. 381.

29. Sigmund Freud, *Gesammelte Werke*, vol. 14, p. 331.

30. Ibid., p. 332.

31. Ibid.

32. Edward Tylor, *Primitive Culture: Researches into the Development of Mythology, Philosophy, Language, Art, and Custom* (New York, 1874), vol. 1, pp. 30–31.

33. Herbert Spencer, *The Principles of Sociology* (New York, 1910), vol. 1, pp. 71–73.

VIII

Transformations in Pacifist Consciousness in England, 1914–1939

JOYCE A. BERKMAN

> In reality, there is nothing strong enough to fight the spirit of war except the spirit of religion. . . . Ethical idealism is not enough: humanitarianism is not enough: sentimental internationalism is emphatically not enough: nothing is strong enough to fight the spirit of war except a living personal faith in a God who has demonstrated to all time that He is Himself a Pacifist.
>
> John S. Hoyland

It is most improbable that John Hoyland, a Quaker leader writing the above in 1926, would have made these remarks a decade earlier.[1] Between 1914 and 1937 British conscientious objection to war underwent a dramatic transformation. Pacifism was historically, up to 1914, the expression of the religious convictions of certain small Protestant sects. By 1939, it had become the creed as well of secular thinkers and groups. Indeed, the majority of pacifists between World War I and World War II based their opposition to war on secular premises, no longer relying upon religious arguments either for their own ethical nonconformity or for their appeal to others for support. Even those pacifists inspired by religious motivations increasingly turned to secular reasoning.[2] This evolution in British pacifism, which has its parallels elsewhere in Europe and America, reflects a far broader phenomenon, the secularization of modern consciousness and the search for new authorities for moral actions.

During World War I, conscientious objection to war challenged the fundamental moral tenets of its advocates in a way perhaps more agonizing than the decision to enter the trenches. Most Britons were psychologically and morally armed with conveniently packaged church and state justifications for the slaughter of Germans. The bravery of wartime soldiers evoked popular understanding and enthusiastic support. By contrast, only a small minority of individuals dared to defy long-conditioned patriotic reflexes. Their choice required such moral stamina that only a profound conviction of rightness could sustain it. Social authorities, ordinary folk, and even pacifists' own friends constantly demanded that they explain and justify their refusal to join the war effort. A number of conscientious objectors lost their lives and suffered permanent debilitating illness from the hardship of consecutive prison terms, no mean test of their moral hardiness. It was essential that they be impregnable to hostile examination and political coercion and root their conviction on solid compelling theory.

With the end of World War I and the growth, between then and World War II, of a peace and pacifist movement, veteran pacifists were joined by many others who claimed similar tenacity and depth of conviction. Aware that the pacifism of many of these new adherents was not anchored in transcendental belief, Hoyland, as shown in the statement quoted above, doubted their capacity for pacifist sturdiness. With the onset of World War II, the pacifist recantations of over half the members of the Peace Pledge Union (PPU), the largest nonsectarian and secular pacifist organization of the 1930s, lent credence to Hoyland's apprehension. Furthermore, those leaders of the PPU who abandoned pacifism were, strikingly, among the principal proponents of interwar secular pacifism—Bertrand Russell, C. E. M. Joad, Rose Macaulay, A. A. Milne. Their defections might have been logically predictable had their pacifism been situational, i.e., had they espoused the right to refuse to fight in a particular international war. Such was not the case; they regarded all twentieth-century international warfare as morally indefensible. By contrast, most of the prominent religion-based pacifists, affiliated or not with a religious denomination, generally held fast to their opposition to war throughout the World War II.

It would be gross error to contend secular pacifism was inherently unstable because its champions lacked resolve or, conversely, to claim religious pacifism was vindicated because its proponents proved stauncher. The question of secular pacifist resolve easily has less to do with inherent weaknesses of pacifist logic than with pacifists' personality structures, thoroughness of integration of their pacifist tenets, and confusion over pacifist strategy. The focus, therefore, of this essay is not on the behavioral advantages of a religious as opposed to secular pacifist philosophy but on the unprecedented effort of interwar British pacifists to establish an enduring pacifist commitment within a society in which for many people the traditional Judeo-Christian God, or indeed God in any form, was dead.

This interwar effort to restructure pacifist philosophy was not the work of a small band of marginal intellectuals and clergy. Unique to the history of Western pacifism, the interwar pacifist movement in England embraced a highly diverse constituency, representing the entire range of socioeconomic classes, political parties, and religious denominations. *The Peace Year Book* of 1938, an annual publication of the British National Peace Council, lists 68 national peace organizations and 25 pacifist groups. Local pacifists groups were, of course, more numerous. At its height in 1938 the Peace Pledge Union had recruited almost 150,000 pledges and coordinated 1,150 local affiliates. In 1937 the Council of Christian Pacifist Groups listed pacifist associations from 11 Christian denominations while the British Fellowship of Reconciliation boasted 4,600 local branches. Originating in 1936, a Parliamentary Pacifist Group, composed of 12 members of Parliament, added further to the national prominence of pacifism. From the various pacifist quarters poured forth newsletters, periodicals, pamphlets, and books. Along with these: regional, national, and international conferences, demonstrations and public parades, workshops, theater productions, and summer camps. Despite the wide divergence of religious, philosophical, and political persuasions among pacifist groups, they frequently collaborated. Though never commanding the allegiance of the majority of interwar Britons, pacifists could, for the first time, take comfort in their status as a substantial and respected national minority.

The remarkable flowering of interwar pacifism was due less to unique forms of pacifist argumentation than to a series of historical experiences that imparted credibility and appeal to pacifist thinking. The number of adherents to pacifism would have been far fewer, of course, had pacifists not presented their reasoning in a manner suited to the times. A brief overview of relevant interwar historical events will clarify this point.

Pacifism in the 1920s grew as one dimension of a more sweeping peace movement, epitomized by the League of Nations Union, committed to peaceful resolution of international differences, military disarmament, and collective security within the framework of the League. During the 1920s, pacifism in the public mind did not constitute a position distinct from a general peace advocacy. Antiwar and antimilitaristic writing, campaigns and educational reforms involved both pacifist and nonpacifist peace crusaders. All varieties of peace advocates benefited from the deluge between 1928 and 1933 of fictional and nonfictional literature exposing the hideous realities of World War I. Pacifists in 1933, however, remained an insignificant, if growing, minority within the larger peace movement.

What sparked the rapid expansion of pacifism and placed pacifists at the forefront of the peace movement was a sequence of disillusioning experiences with existing approaches to peace, simultaneous with an increasing awareness of the predicted nature of a second world war and accompanying fear of that prospect. Authoritative reports from military and political experts documented England's vulnerability to devastating aerial bombardment. With radar yet to be developed, England could not successfully be defended. As Britons assessed strategies to prevent their own annihilation, they steadily discovered the ineffectiveness of each. Advocates of collective security through the League, for instance, lost heart in face of the League's failure to stem the Italian invasion of Abyssinia and Japanese aggression in Manchuria. At the same time collective security outside the League framework, with national rearmament, its corollary, was equally doomed, especially given recent exposés about armament firms pressuring governments into war, the historic futility of arms races, and the proven incompetency even of the Labour government to offer (1) fresh economic approaches to the Depression and (2) creative diplomatic measures to ease international tensions. In this context, pacifism with its specific proposals for averting war and its active peace advocacy appeared to many former nonpacifist peace proponents as the only alternative to a regression to international anarchy.

The appeal of pacifism involved as well its ability to serve as a surrogate creed in an era when many Britons were adrift from traditional religious moorings. The interwar articulation of pacifist belief entailed far more than the renunciation of war. Most pacifists insisted that opposition to war was but the cutting edge of a comprehensive program of constructive social and ethical reform. Proponents maintained that pacifism offered a throughgoing approach to the solution of many social ills and to the realization of a genuinely democratic and humane society.

The affirmative and embracing character of pacifism was heightened by the strong sense of community among many pacifist associations. Both the small group-training sessions promoted by Richard Gregg (a disciple of Gandhi) and his followers, as well as more conventional gatherings of like-minded pacifists, instilled among participants a sense of belonging to a heroic enterprise, one that was indeed a "moral equivalent for war."

As a final dimension to its serving as a surrogate creed, pacifism, like most religions, stressed the reciprocity between personal (private) and public relationships. Many social reformers, whether from middle- or working-class background, dichotomized their public activity and private lives, fighting for equity, independence, and compassion in the marketplace but often ignoring their contradictory behavior in domestic relationships and in personal friendships. The effort by interwar pacifists to combat aggressive and domineering behavior in the interpersonal sphere often required a radical transformation of personality and consciousness, a process generally associated with evangelical rebirth.

The combination, then, of pacifism's "religious" appeal and its potential to offer a possible path to peace forms the context for interwar pacifist advocacy. The many new developments in pacifist reasoning reflect this context and also serve to highlight the diverse ways interwar intellectuals struggled for new sources of validation for their moral tenets.

The secular justifications for pacifism constituted not only the principal underpinnings of the religious skeptic's pacifism but were commonly invoked as well by religious pacifists either for the purpose of convincing others or because they genuinely served to bolster their own commitment. The object of secular reasoning was to establish both the irrationality and immorality of waging war. If not in an absolute sense, then at least in a comparative sense, it was necessary to prove that engaging in war was more absurd and immoral than refusing to fight. Secular pacifist rationale tended to assume three principal forms— utilitarian, ends and means, and liberal-democratic political theory.

In *Which Way to Peace*, Bertrand Russell began his pacifist apologia by affirming an utilitarian ethic: "What is right and what is wrong depends, as I believe, upon the consequences of actions so far as they can be foreseen. . . ."[3] Applying this ethic to the issue of war, he concluded:

> I cannot say simply "war is wicked" but only modern war is practically certain to have worse consequences than even the most unjust peace. . . . What I assert is that wars between civilized states, at the present time, are sure to do more harm than would be done by the peaceful submission of one side, and further, that the actual harm which a nation would suffer through unilateral disarmament is very much less than most people suppose.[4]

Insisting that he repudiated only modern war, Russell relied upon the information provided by military scientists on England's likely devastation in the event of aerial warfare. To their data he brought certain historical evidence and speculation. The type of annihilation he feared meant not only the destruction of life and property but also of democratic institutions and values. For England, to cope with the civil panic and anarchy accompanying aerial bombing, democracy would turn, he argued, into an "iron military despotism," England's civilized conventions would collapse, and, in the wake of such savagery and tyranny, Englishmen would never be able to construct, even if victorious, a meaningful peace.[5] In short, war was ironic. Its supposed objectives— peace, self-defense, or the preservation of democracy—would not be achieved at all.

Russell's statement of the utilitarian case for pacifism was foreshadowed in Lord Arthur Ponsonby's insistence that "by far the most tragic thing about war is not its immorality, nor its cruelty, but its manifest and colossal futility and imbecility."[6] The utilitarian evaluation of the relative consequences of waging or not waging war informed well-known writer Vera Brittain's assertion:

> I do not believe that any kind of peace has always been better than any kind of war; it is the wholesale massacres involved in modern warfare, and its penalization of those who are most helpless and least responsible, which causes me to regard war as the greatest calamity that can afflict a nation today.[7]

Oxford philosopher C. E. M. Joad likewise denied that either the long- or short-range effects of warfare could justify it. He shared Russell's belief that modern war undermined rather than defended the vital interests of the community.[8] Alex Wood, a prominent Cambridge scientist, spelled out the consequences of war,

> . . . an explicit denial of all the values which it sought to defend—of justice because it wreaks havoc on the innocent; of freedom because it invades very personal liberty; of truth because it can only be prosecuted in an atmosphere of misleading propaganda; of love because its every concrete act is a denial of love. It is essentially a Fascist method and its every victory is a Fascist victory.[9]

Clearly, several assumptions shape these theorists' calculations of the rationality of warfare: (1) England's physical vulnerability to massive destruction; (2) the necessity of engaging in the "wholesale massacre" of other nations; (3) the fragility of civilized conventions and democratic institutions in time of war. What does not enter their scales as detailedly are the consequences of *not* waging war. Very little thinking is directed toward the nature of enemy occupation. Nowhere in the writings of the 1930s can be found a picture of England ruled by a modern foreign dictatorship as vivid as H. G. Wells's description of modern warfare. We hunt in vain for a portrayal of England as one large Belsen or of Englishmen coerced to fight Americans or Frenchmen.

The failure of imagination is understandable. Prior to World War I such behavior as that of Hitler's government was not unusual for dictators who were attempting to consolidate power, stabilize government, and curry favor. The staggering atrocities of the Germans, although prefigured on a smaller scale in the 1930s, occurred primarily during wartime. The wholesale massacre of Jews and political dissenters, and the barbarities of concentration camps, were scarcely imaginable between the wars by most Germans or Britons. Hitler and his coterie, Britons would admit, were demonic, but the Germans, people they viewed not as wicked but confused, gullible, ignorant, without firm democratic values, would never knowingly permit large-scale atrocities. What was not anticipated by most pacifists, who failed to calculate the nature of modern propaganda and communications control, was the extent to which Hitler's regime could maintain secrecy and manipulate public opinion.

Brutality was expected from the conqueror. Aldous Huxley wrote:

> The regression from humanitarianism, characteristic of our age, will probably result in manifestations of non-violent resistance being treated with a severity more ruthless than that displayed by most governments of recent times.[10]

Nevertheless, Huxley was confident that:

> Confronted by huge masses determined not to use violence, even the most ruthless dictatorship needs the support of public opinion, and no government which mas-

sacres or imprisons large numbers of systematically non-violent individuals can
hope to retain such support.[11]

The author of *Brave New World* did not realize how near at hand were some of
his prophecies on thought control. Huxley's confidence in the inability of a
German army of occupation to rule England is echoed by most pacifists who
considered the prospects. In fact, the noted essayist and leading member of the
Peace Pledge Union, John Middleton Murry gave the German army of occupation no longer than a year before it would disintegrate.[12]

Since utilitarian logic so heavily relied upon judgments about future consequences, many pacifists considered it too speculative. For Max Plowman, secretary of the PPU, the future was too unpredictable, and, in any event, he
considered speculation irrelevant. He argued that if a person moved into the
country his practical problems were not how he would live if he were still in a
town. The pacifist, he declared, was unable to foresee the nature of problems
that would still exist if human beings acted pacifically and cooperatively. What
was imperative regardless of practical considerations, he maintained, was commitment to moral right.[13]

Utilitarian reasoning also suffered from its possible use for evil ends. If
acts possessed no intrinsic morality then the most monstrous behavior, e.g.,
torture, could be validated if it protected the welfare of the greatest number. For
John Middleton Murry, the utilitarian case was simply incapable of inspiring an
individual to risk her/his life as a pacifist. Murry insisted that the only depend-
able guide to pacifism was a "moral intuition" of war's evil, what Max Plowman
defined as appreciation of the incalculable evil of indiscriminate bombing.[14]

The insufficiency of utilitarian arguments led many pacifists to search for
other grounds of belief. The argument of ends and means appealed to many of
these pacifists. This theory of pacifism, epitomized in Aldous Huxley's book by
that title, purports that "to employ good means is of greater importance than to
pursue good ends. . . ." According to Huxley it is precisely at this point that
pacifists part company with Communists, Fascists, and all others "who believe
that the world can be bludgeoned into the likeness of Utopia."[15]

The ends-and-means premise was and is the familiar anti-Machiavellian
axiom that the means must justify the end. The employing of reprovable means,
it was argued, would endanger or preclude the desired end in either the long or
the short run. Since, according to this premise, the ends preexist in the means,
people are obliged to behave humanely if humane goals are to be achieved.
Working with the specific question of war, pacifists employed the ends-and-
means theory in one or both of two ways, the first of which *appears* nearly
identical with the utilitarian argument but can be clearly distinguished from it:
(1) War as a way to peace is futile; it merely engenders more war, for the evils
accompanying the conduct of war generally preclude peaceful sentiments and

judicious peace arrangements following the war. (2) Certain acts or means are absolutely immoral regardless of the consequences.

These two conclusions were reached by two distinct paths of reasoning. Pacifists claimed that the morality of the premise was verified by empirical and psychological observation, personal and historical experience, and rational deduction.[16] At the same time, they insisted that moral intuition was their ultimate authority. Empirical substantiation, while helpful, was not decisive; if intuition and reason conflict, the former would take priority.[17]

The ends-and-means rationale had twofold value for pacifists. It not only denied the effectiveness, rationality, or morality of modern war, it also explained the fundamental cause of war as previous war or violence. The only way to emerge from the vicious cycle of revenge was, as Huxley indicated, through nonresistance coupled with social reform.[18]

The converse premise—that pacifist means produced pacifist ends— likewise required justification. Most adherents to the premise, Huxley among the most vocal, based their reasoning on psychological observation. Richard Gregg and those Gregg saw as his sources—W. H. H. Rivers, C. Baudoin, E. A. Ross—were often cited.[19] Whereas Huxley acknowledged that a generous peace followed by mutual disarmament would counterbalance many of the evil effects of violence in war, his view of human nature led him to conclude such peaceful postwar behavior was improbable. Compassion and generosity were not characteristic of victors, viz., the Treaty of Versailles. On the other hand, the success of Gandhi in South Africa and India heartened such pacifists as Huxley.[20]

In *The Power of Non-Violence* (1935) and *Training for Peace* (1937) Richard Gregg set forth the psychological dynamic involved in disarming an aggressor. Through various specific examples, he demonstrated how a nonviolent reply to physical violence unnerved the aggressor. Confronted with brave endurance of pain, the attacker, Gregg contended, would plunge into a new reality and, in the confusion besetting his will, morale, and composure, become vulnerable to creative verbal and nonverbal acts of reconciliation. Requisite for such an unbalancing of the belligerent and such a grasping of initiative by the pacifist was the pacifist's full control, mental confidence, and impassioned love toward the attacker. Gregg acknowledged that, should the victim feel at all angry or fearful, then nonviolence, rather than startling the provoker, would lead to more harm than violence. Such perfection of character, he maintained, could be achieved through self-discipline taught in training sessions. He summoned the example of Gandhi and his followers.[21]

When not justifying pacifism on the general philosophical grounds of ends-and-means or utilitarian logic, pacifists built their case on the foundations of democratic political theory. Whether Liberal, Labour, or Conservative in party affiliation, whether socialist, anarchist or feminist values fundamentally shaped their political ethics, pacifists adhered to a set of liberal-democratic tenets that proclaimed: (1) the inherent dignity of each human being, (2) the priority of the individual conscience and its free expression over the group or state, (3) an ethic of mutual respect and sympathy and, (4) a belief in sufficient human rationality and potential goodness for the possibility to exist of self-government and social progress without violent revolution.

All of these tenets were subject, of course, to various interpretations or qualifications by each pacifist. Socialist and nonsocialists obviously disputed what political and economic conditions were required to maximize human dignity and freedom or to secure social progress. Socialists differed among themselves, as well, over the character of collective ownership of the means of production and over the means of bringing a socialist state into being. All socialists, however, felt capitalism spurred aggressive and violent individual and collective behavior, incompatible at its core with the ethical ideals of a peaceful, democratic community.

Comparably, an anarchist pacifist such as Herbert Read considered the political apparatus of a government automatically at odds with the conditions essential for the promotion of humane values. The presence of state machinery, Read maintained, abetted the natural "death instincts" of the human personality. In his view, all government is force; force is repression, repression leads to reaction, engendering in turn the psychosis of power and, eventually, war.[22] Holding a very similar view, the Dutch anarchist Bart de Ligt profoundly influenced many British secular pacifists. As early as October 1934 the No More War Movement (NMWM) adopted "The de Ligt Plan" at the organization's annual conference at Leeds. By the mid-1930s roughly eight hundred pacifist groups were engaged in intensive study of de Ligt's theories and strategies.[23] De Ligt called upon pacifists in peacetime to refuse all military service, including noncombatant military work, indeed any work—intellectual, moral, or manual—that served military objectives. Other tactics he espoused were refusal to pay taxes, dissemination of antimilitarist propaganda within the armed forces, the promotion of pacifism within schools and through local and national media. In the event of war, he summoned pacifists to render useless all transportation and communication used directly for war and to mount a general strike. Since a general strike as a pacifist threat would only be effective if the police and armed services could be rallied to sympathize, de Ligt placed key importance upon pacifist infiltration of these coercive bodies.

For Virginia Woolf, pacifism and féminism were interwoven in her critique of society, in her explanation for the origins of war, and in her vision of genuine democracy. In *Three Guineas* (1938) Woolf elucidated how male dominance foments aggression and combat in the domestic and public sphere alike. ("The tyrannies and servilities of the one are the tyrannies and servilities of the other.")[24] Since men in all facets of gender socialization are trained to be fighters, male organization of education and the professions is consequently rife with possessiveness, jealousy, pugnacity, and greed. According to Woolf, only a feminist Society of Outsiders committed to "the rights of all—all men and women—to the respect in their persons of the great principles of Justice and Equality and Liberty" could offer hope against war.[25] The Society of Outsiders would cultivate pacifist traits among its members, specifically detachment from cravings for wealth, recognition, power, and popularity and commitment to a critical, disciplined search for truth. Outsiders would dispense with "dictated, regimented, official pageantry . . . with personal distinctions—medals, ribbons, badges, bands, gown—not from any dislike of personal adornment, but because of the obvious effect of such distinctions to constrict, to stereotype, to destroy."[26] Woolf hoped that long-conditioned "female" traits—altruism, gentleness, concern for human relationships—would come to characterize behavior among both sexes.

Common to the ethical idealism of the various forms of liberal-democratic pacifism is a shared belief in human plasticity and radical variation. Huxley pointed out that in certain societies war has never existed. For the Eskimos and Hopi Indians, war was unknown and unthinkable. Russell and Joad were characteristic of those who believed that, through proper child-training and social legislation, the instinctive destructiveness of human beings could be controlled or redirected.[27] Bertrand Russell in *Why Men Fight* pointed out that:

> Blind impulse is the source of war but it is also the source of science, and art, and love. It is not the weakening of impulse that is to be desired, but the direction of impulse toward life and growth rather than towards death and decay . . .[28]

Joad, citing the elimination of witchcraft, cholera, slavery, and torture, remarked, "Each of the evils must, at the time of its prevalence, have seemed, as war seems to-day, to be irremediable . . . [but] human beings really are teachable."[29] Echoing these assertions, novelist Storm Jameson equated the abolition of warfare with the effective renunciation of witch-burning.[30] Similarly, A. A. Milne pointed to the eradication of dueling, elaborating at length on its parallel with warring.[31] Human potential for rational nonviolence, no matter the absence of proper training in childhood, was a fundamental assumption of the belief of Huxley, Gregg, and de Ligt that individuals could be trained even as adults to bridle their anger and transmit friendly messages whatever the enemy provocation. Clearly, though the harsh realities of World War I, the development of Freudian ideology, and the rise of fascism had cracked the buoyant optimism of the prewar years, these historic influences had not shattered it utterly.

On the surface it may seem that secular justifications for pacifism, sufficient grounds for commitment among agnostic and atheist-pacifists, may also have sufficed for religious pacifists. Such a judgment, however, is difficult to make. A brief biographical examination of the pacifist evolution of Wilfred Wellock, a principal founder and early leader of the British No More War Movement and the War Resisters International, will demonstrate the problems such a judgment poses. Wellock is generally associated with the militant socialist critique of war. Indeed, Wellock's writing for the periodicals of the British No More War Movement and other pacifist associations almost exclusively dwelt on the need to uproot capitalism and its values as a precondition for domestic and international peace. Nonetheless, the dynamic for both his pacifism and socialism was a profound devotion to Christianity.

Born in 1879 into a working-class home in Lancashire, where he was raised in "strict Puritan discipline," Wellock became in his adolescence an active leader in his local church.[32] At the same time he was stirred by the eloquent socialist speeches of Keir Hardie and by Ruskin's penetrating critique of industrial capitalism. Offended by the materialism, gross inequities in wealth and debasement of manual labor accompanying the evolution of British capitalism, he increasingly defined himself as a Christian socialist. With the outbreak of World War I he issued a series of broadsheets condemning warfare from both socialist and Christian perspectives and, as a conscientious objector, endured three successive two-year prison sentences. His pacifist writing, however, shifted during the interwar years. Intent upon rallying non-Christian socialists to the pacifist cause, he omitted or soft-pedaled his religious arguments. At that time his anticapitalism was probably sufficient for his pacifist commitment. In later years, struck in part perhaps by the unreliability of socialist pacifist idealism when faced with a serious challenge, e.g., the defection of many socialist pacifists triggered by the Spanish Civil War, Wellock again affirmed Christian as well as socialist sources of his pacifism, declaring that the way of justice and love is "the way of Christ" and "the straight way to the redemption of the individual and of society."[33]

Although, in any particular instance, a precise assessment of the strength of a pacifist's secular over religious theory is problematic, the mere presence of religious rationale in a time of mass secularization and widespread religious skepticism deserves analysis. How, after all, did religious pacifists frame their spiritual arguments in light of the erosion of Christian conviction? How, furthermore, could Christian pacifists convince their respective churches that warfare contradicted Christian doctrine when, except for the Society of Friends, Christian churches were at the forefront of the patriotic defense of England during World War I? (In fact, a distinctive trait of interwar Christian pacifism was its unsparing attack on the churches for their collaboration with the state in the prosecution of the war.) The necessary recasting of traditional Christian pacifism among both Protestants and Catholics, as well as the prevalence in pacifist writing of nontraditional and non-Christian religious arguments, testified both to the ingenuity of pacifists and to their immediate historical circumstances.

It was not uncommon for interwar intellectuals in search of a new basis of metaphysical belief to turn to Eastern religion. This pattern was already evident in the late nineteenth century and gathered momentum after World War I. In particular, Buddhist writing and teaching, with their pronounced emphasis on pacifist behavior, seemed to offer an attractive alternative to those who deemed Christianity intellectually and morally bankrupt.

The interconnection of pacifism and Buddhism appeared early in British pacifist exposition. Among her many social campaigns, Olive Schreiner's defense of conscientious objectors during World War I emerged from a personal deism profoundly shaped by Buddhist values. For Schreiner, the essence of Buddhism was its insistence upon the fundamental unity and sacredness of all creation. Christianity, she felt, was impoverished by its failure to incorporate reverence for animal creation. With regard to Jesus, she writes:

> I think among great religious teachers he does not quite draw me as Buddha and others, because his teaching stops short with the human world; it is to me doubtful whether he ever caught sight of that larger entity; whether he ever realized the divinity in plant and animal, as well as man.[34]

Schreiner's personal acquaintance with Gandhi during his vigorous nonviolent campaigns in South Africa heightened her regard for Indian philosophy.[35] For other British pacifists of the First World War, e.g., Max Plowman, it was the pacifist poet Rabindranath Tagore who served as a formative influence.[36] In the case of Eric Gill it was the influence of the Hindu Ananda Coomaraswamy that impelled him towards pacifism.[37]

During the 1920s eminent Indian scholars visited England, as part of the swelling stream of cultural exchanges between the two countries and, too, a crucial component of India's political quest for national autonomy. The distinguished Hindu scholar Sarvepalli Radhakrishnan, a disciple of Gandhi, became a particularly notable influence upon numerous prominent intellectuals. Indeed, so well regarded were Radhakrishnan's writings on Hindu philosophy that in 1936 he was appointed Spalding Professor of Eastern Religions and Ethics at Oxford University, becoming the first Asiatic to hold such a position at Oxford. Many British pacifists of the 1930s, e.g., C. E. M. Joad, relied on Radhakrishnan's elucidation of Eastern thought and Gandhian principles.[38] Fittingly, Radhakrishnan acted as editor of a remarkable collection of essays, published in 1939 in celebration of Gandhi's seventieth birthday. The list of writers contributing essays to this volume constitutes an imposing roster of eminent British pacifists. Their tributes to Gandhi consisted of explicit and at times lengthy reaffirmations of their pacifism.[39]

British anticolonialists and socialists affiliated with the No More War

Movement and the War Resisters International supported India's efforts for liberation and found Gandhi's nonviolent approach inspiring, particularly his Civil Disobedience Campaign in 1930. In the early 1920s Wilfred Wellock issued a series of lectures on Indian liberation and on Gandhi, eventuating in his publication *India's Awakening* (1922). Despite the decidedly secular approach of the NMWM periodicals, the religious basis of Gandhi's pacifism was not concealed. It was one of Gandhi's cardinal *Six Points for Pacifists* that essential for effective pacifism was faith in a God of love.

Within pacifist circles, however, it was the writings of two widely published, well-known American pacifists, Devere Allen and Richard Gregg, that were decisive to the adoption of Gandhi's nonviolent creed and techniques. The various American and British contributors to Devere Allen's collected essays, *Pacifism and the Modern World* (1929), introduced the English public to Gandhi's successes in South Africa and India as well as to the positive and practical dimensions of the "new" Gandhi-influenced pacifism.[10] Of even wider impact, Gregg's *Power of Non-Violence* and *Training for Peace* became "texts" for the PPU.

Apart from Allen and Gregg the foremost English pacifist advocate of Oriental philosophy was Aldous Huxley. The Buddhist notion of *ahimsa* (a vision of ultimate peace involving harmlessness, unity, and love with all beings) suffuses Huxley's pacifist and philosophical writing. Inspired by the nineteenth-century Hindu sage Sri Ramakrishnan, Huxley clarified that the spiritual reality, which ahimsa represents, resides within and unifies all creatures. For Huxley "such a belief is the best metaphysical environment for pacifism."[11] Huxley maintained that this spiritual reality was fundamentally harmonic and moral while evil was cosmically disruptive. Violence, one form of evil, promoted fragmentation, separation and was intrinsically destructive. By contrast good (nonviolence) made for integration and peace.

Violence, Huxley argued, was a consequence of individual attachment to egoistic goals. Nonattachment to such cravings represented the path to ahimsa. Nonattachment, according to Huxley, consisted neither of Christian asceticism nor secular altruism; rather, it involved the intense cultivation of self-awareness, a full consciousness of the possible consequences of any behavior, and a perception of the self as a participant within a system of social and cosmic relations. The cultivation of nonattachment demanded far more than faith and good works. It required a strenuous exertion of intellect. It was this emphasis upon cognition that led Huxley to assert, "In this respect, it seems to me, Buddhism shows itself decidedly superior to Christianity. In Buddhist ethic stupidity, or unawareness, ranks as one of the principal sins."[12]

Huxley was confident that nonattachment, hence nonviolence, was, with proper training, possible for all individuals. He observed that Buddhism "is the only great world religion which has made its way without bloodshed or persecution, without censorship or inquisition . . ."[43] He concluded that if Buddhists could fulfill his ideal of national idealism so could all people.

The same themes appear in the writing of Gerald Heard, another notable interwar pacifist and transmitter of Eastern philosophy, and a close friend of Huxley's. In Heard's general writing and speeches in support of the Peace Pledge Union he proclaimed that nonviolence was a cosmically sanctioned natural law. In *The Source of Civilization* (1945) Heard posited a new strain of individuals, Brahmin saints, who would spearhead the next stage of racial evolution. In place of violence, these people would cultivate nonattachment and love.[44]

Far more characteristic of interwar religious pacifism than that based upon Buddhist convictions was the variety of Christian pacifist commitments. The unprecedented blossoming during the 1930s of pacifist associations in every Christian denomination was associated with considerable rethinking of traditional Christian pacifism and the appearance of new religious arguments to diversify and enlarge the prewar Christian peace testimony. This activity was part and parcel of wider efforts to revivify Christianity and to ally it to interwar struggles to salvage human values and promote social justice.

The emergence of PAX, a Roman Catholic pacifist affiliate of the Council of Christian Pacifist Groups (the umbrella organization in the 1930s for all Christian pacifist groups) ably illustrates the new breadth and fresh thinking of interwar Christian pacifism. Prior to the appearance of PAX in 1936, no Catholic pacifist organization existed in England. However, we can trace the origins of PAX through the appearance in the 1920s of Catholic pacifist groups in Europe, most pertinently a number of German Catholic pacifist groups belonging to the War Resisters International. German Catholic pacifism had its impact in England in 1929 with the British publication of *The Church and War* by a German Dominican pacifist priest, Fr. Strattmann. This work marked the first attempt to bring together statements on war by recent popes. Fr. Strattmann found confirmation for his pacifism in the words of various popes, particularly Pope Pius XI's condemnation of any future war as "mass murder," "national suicide," and "a monstrous crime."[45]

By the early 1930s Catholic pacifist sentiment had surfaced in England. No less than the highest Catholic ecclesiastical authority in the British Isles, Cardinal McRory, declared himself opposed absolutely to modern war.[46] The principal exponent of Catholic pacifism in England, however, was Eric Gill, a Dominican lay preacher, widely esteemed for his accomplishments as a sculptor, fine-letterer, and architect, who at the height of his career founded PAX.

Gill's pacifism, like that of all interwar Catholic pacifists, had its philosophical basis in traditional Catholic criteria of a Just War as enunciated by Saint Thomas Aquinas. According to Gill, all modern wars, if judged by Thomistic standards, violate Christian morality. Thomistic requirements, such as the protection of noncombatants among the enemy population, could not possibly be satisfied given indiscriminate aerial bombardment.[47]

While Thomistic criteria formed the core of Gill's pacifism, he viewed natural reason without the aid of faith capable of reaching comparable conclusions. In creating PAX, Gill emphasized that PAX was providing community and moral support to those Christian pacifists who would not join pacifist organizations that professed the doctrine of the intrinsic unlawfulness of all war. PAX was distinct among Christian pacifists groups in limiting its absolute condemnation to *modern* warfare; in that sense PAX members shared certain affinities with those secular pacifists who adhered to utilitarian pacifist arguments.[48]

The process of Gill's conversion to pacifism exemplifies the impact of contemporary religious skepticism. Bred as a non-Catholic, Gill experienced an agonizing period of agnosticism and a passionate yearning for a life that would integrate and subject to strict discipline his artistic, political, psychological, and metaphysical concerns.[49] This led him to monasticism and Christian Guild Socialism. A trip to Palestine in 1934 kindled in him a combined aversion to capitalism and war. In the Holy Land Gill beheld "dirty materialism which inspired all modern militarism . . . the impossible ungodliness of modern mechanical warmaking."[50] He concluded, "I believe that capitalism is robbery, industrialism is blasphemy and war is murder."[51] War as a concomitant of industrial capitalism figures as a prominent theme in his pacifism just as it had in Wellock's, though the socialism they upheld was of a very different order. Conceivably, in fact, Thomistic arguments serve primarily as a rationale with Gill, for a more deep-seated hostility to capitalism, the flip side of my hypothesis with regard to Wellock whose anticapitalism may simply enhance a Christian aversion to war.

While Catholic pacifism represented one of the most innovative developments of interwar Christian pacifism, the struggle of many Protestants, spurred initially by Quakers, to forge a compelling case for pacifism equally involved the refurbishing of traditional Christian arguments and the fashioning of new ones. Whether espoused by Quakers before 1914 or by Christians of those denominations that arrived at pacifist positions after 1914, Christian pacifism relied for its validation primarily upon various scriptural texts, the writings of early church fathers and, above all, on the example of Jesus' life and death.

A cardinal scriptural source was Saint Paul's Second Epistle to the Corinthian Church, in which he asserted:

If any man be in Christ, he is a new creature; old things are passed away; behold all thing are become new. And all things are of God who hath reconciled us to Himself by Jesus Christ, and has given to us the ministry of reconciliation: to wit, that God was in Christ reconciling the world unto Himself, not imputing their trespasses unto them and hath committed unto us the word of reconciliation (2 Cor. 5:17–19).

This passage become the cornerstone of the British Fellowship of Reconciliation, which formed in 1914 and constituted the first national interdenominational Christian pacifist organization. The heart of Paul's message is Jesus' command to love and reconcile one's enemies. Other biblical passages with this same import were frequently adduced, most commonly the Sermon on the Mount. Even nonpacifist biblical scholars such as Adolf von Harnack and Hans Windisch admitted that the teaching of Jesus forbade all bloodshed.[32]

Many interwar Protestant pacifists, like their Catholic counterparts, were responding with particular intensity to the dramatically widening chasm between Jesus' message of love and the nature of modern technological warfare. For them, the Just War tradition, whatever its validity at one time, was no longer applicable. Cecil John Cadoux underscored the novel circumstances facing contemporary Christians when he stated that what needed moral justification was not Christians' defiance of the state or personal endurance of the horrors of war but, rather, their willful infliction or support of indiscriminate bombing and tolerance of the inevitable "orgy of hate, fear and lying" accompanying modern combat.[33]

Reliance wholly upon scriptural text posed, nevertheless, certain problems. While pacifist church historians refuted nonpacifist interpretations of those biblical passages appearing to support violence, some acknowleged that Jesus' words were not absolutely explicit with regard to warfare. Furthermore, liberal Protestants were no longer basing their general religious belief on specific textual documentation; many of them regarded this form of evidence a dangerous literalism and turned instead to arguments derived from the "spirit" of the Scriptures. Additional evidence for Christian pacifism was, therefore, necessary.

Christian pacifists lent added authority to their position by citing the early church fathers. Until the fourth century these classic Christian writers adamantly opposed soldiering. The writings of Justin Martyr, Marcion, Origen, Tertullian, Cyprian, Lactantius, and Eusebius were rallied as further verification of what was regarded as the authentic Christian stance on war and peace.

Of greater weight in Christian pacifist advocacy was the example of Jesus' life and death, in particular his compassionate self-sacrifice and his resurrection. The example of Jesus' life was clearly decisive in the conversion to pacifism in the late 1920s of H. R. L. Sheppard, the popular Anglican minister who more than any other Christian leader in the 1930s mobilized pacifist sentiment in England. On February 12, 1927, Dean Sheppard wrote:

> I, myself, am now a pacifist and do not think a Christian can take part in any work of telling or propagating lies, or stirring up passion to kill; or doing anything that he cannot believe that Christ would have done; or for which he cannot ask a blessing 'for Jesus Christ's sake.'[54]

Another eminent Anglican, Canon Raven, focused upon the cross as a symbol of God's way of grappling with evil. Jesus, in explicitly urging his followers to love and forgive his and their enemies, argued Raven, posited not only a new way of individual salvation but, as well, communal salvation. In Raven's view: agape, Christian love, came to surpass Hebraic and Greek attitudes on mercy and justice. While mercy was the condescending gift of a judge, Christian love repudiated judges and did not distinguish judge from judged, embracing in like compassion the innocent and evildoer.[55] Restated by Sheppard, one simply could not massacre those whom Christ loved.[56]

For pacifists, Jesus' death and resurrection were as significant as his life. Cadoux saw the fundamental feature of the cross as the paradox of success through failure. The cross, he elaborated, stood for the voluntary submission unto death at the hands of the enemy, in order that the enemy might be changed into a friend; whereas the sword stood for the infliction of death on the enemy, in order that he might be overpowered and destroyed. What Cadoux sought to expose was the illusory victory of violence. The Crucifixion was followed, after all, by the Resurrection. The lesson for pacifists that Cadoux felt implicit in this sequence was the ultimate triumph of a small determined band of believers.[57] The Christian optimism of the Resurrection pervaded both the historic personal witness of the Quakers as well as the interwar pacifist conviction that a nucleus of dedicated and disciplined pacifists would, like Christianity itself, ultimately triumph.

Occasionally, even non-Christian pacifists found it useful to summon Christian symbolism to their cause. Max Plowman, a non-Christian mystic, frequently alluded to divine incarnation and the Crucifixion as metaphors for each person's moral responsibility.[58]

Protestant pacifists denied that Jesus' life served as a model only for missionaries and ministers. They insisted that Jesus' example was intended for all, the essence of the Christian vocation. Furthermore, they deemed no less tenable the notion that the Sermon on the Mount constituted rules to be followed only upon the Second Coming and its anticipated Utopia, for in a perfect world one would not have enemies, and hence, no need for counsels to love one's enemies. Cadoux concludes, "The one thing about these teachings concerning which there can be no mistake is that they have reference to life, not in a perfect, but in a very imperfect world."[59]

The prime pitfall in much Christian pacifist reasoning was the failure to come to terms with ethical issues connected with protection of victims. This shortcoming derived in part from the fact that nowhere did Jesus confront the issue of defense of others than oneself in the face of physical aggression.[60] Canon Raven and Cecil Cadoux were among the few church leaders who rose to the challenge.[61] They recognized that feelings and moral intuition fueled two contradictory reactions—compassion for the suffering friend and compassion for the injured enemy, or, on another level, rage against atrocities committed by the aggressor and rage against atrocities committed by the attacked. This ambivalence has its moral articulation in judging the effects of acts of commission (slaughter of enemy combatants and noncombatants) as against acts of omission (failure to defend victimized allies). Whatever the Christian chose to do in wartime, there was no escaping guilt within this tragic vise. The religious pacifist might claim the character of the sin of commission to be more horrendous and culpable, for he anticipated the evil effects of submitting to enemy occupation as less lasting or less profound than those entailed in actively inflicting death. Clearly, in making such a claim, the religious pacifist no longer remained in the realm of religion, but entered the realm of speculation and pragmatics. This was the same realm inhabited by secular pacifists in their calculation of the relative consequences of waging and not waging war.

Cadoux, fully aware of this logical progression, explicitly enumerated as one criterion of a moral Christian act "the test of expediency," by which he meant practical consequences. While doubting whether national retaliation through modern warfare actually defended the aggrieved country, he admitted:

> There are undoubtedly cases in which successful defense does involve the infliction of serious injury on the aggressor. The Christian, therefore, whatever his final answer, must be prepared to find himself faced with the need of choosing between alternatives, both of which seem at first sight to be equally repugnant and insufferable.[62]

At the same time Cadoux regarded crystal-ball-gazing as difficult. If, after rigorous, rational, utilitarian analysis, the Christian is still uncertain, then, Cadoux maintained, an overriding priority must be placed on Christian principles, specifically compassion toward one's foes. Basically, Cadoux invoked the argument that consequences are irrelevant when crucial Christian commands are at stake. Cadoux placed his trust in the eventual victory of the martyr. "A man may assure himself that, whatever may supervene, the results cannot be *ultimately* disastrous . . ."[63]

Cadoux's marriage of secular and religious reasoning is indicative of a pivotal shift in Christian pacifism during the interwar years. The Christian pacifist readiness to collaborate with non-Christian pacifists, to rely on secular arguments, and to join in common campaigns is distinctive of the interwar period and a mark of the increasing social and political involvement of interwar Christian pacifists. Stung by World War I, swelling numbers of Protestant pacifists were convinced that war was rooted in outmoded national economic and social practices. Socialist critiques of capitalism, imperialism, and war increasingly figured in Christian pacifist propaganda and even nonsocialist pacifist Christians were calling for sweeping social reforms.

Certainly, for many Christian pacifists, complex issues of morality were overshadowed by the persuasiveness of simple, arresting images, such as the one marshaled by Brigadier-General Crozier, who underscored war's immorality when he asked if Christ would don a pilot's suit and drop bombs on innocent children.[64] The intricate reflections of Raven and Cadoux were not those of most new pacifist recruits. This prevalent moral shallowness led Canon Raven, with reason, to question the depth of the conviction of many of the new pacifist adherents:

> Few who study the change of outlook, whatever their personal attitude towards it, will deny that it was largely due to motives of which the Christian can only disapprove . . . *Disgust* and *fear*, the accumulated effects of nervous exhaustion and disappointment, were responsible for many of the converts to pacifism . . .[65]

No less ominous for the fate of interwar pacifism than its superficial and sentimental qualities was pacifist division over strategies. These conflicts over methods cut across philosophical and religious ideologies. They intensified during the late 1930s when the pacifist movement, while still gaining in numbers, suffered a loss of momentum. Under the increasing threat of Hitlerian Germany, British public opinion shifted from antimilitarism to hearty endorsement of military sanctions. By 1938 the leaders of the Labour, Liberal, and Conservative parties enunciated a program of national rearmament. If the several hundred thousand pacifists in a country of over forty-four million cherished any hope of dissuading the government from rearming, the final years of the 1930s proved such aspirations futile.

This shift in national consciousness and politics, coupled with the appearance of vigorous antipacifist writing, coincided with the death of H. R. L. Sheppard (October 31, 1937). As founder and leader of the Peace Pledge Union, he had reconciled, through dint of his magnetic personality and persistent efforts, divergent groups of pacifists. In the months following Sheppard's death, articles criticizing and defending modes of pacifist organization and strategy increasingly filled the pages of the PPU weekly, *Peace News*. If pacifists were unable to quell violent feelings among one another, some wondered how they were ever to persuade Britons that a more loving society could in general emerge.[66]

The Peace Pledge Union was divided into two broad camps. On one side were many who continued to believe that fresh government initiatives for peace, along the lines of the recently publicized Van Zeeland report, might still avert war.[67] They advocated the continued bombarding of the public with information about the nature of modern warfare and proposals for international arbitration. Their foremost concern was the practical prevention of England's entrance into war.[68] Belonging to this camp, too, were more radical political activists who, following de Ligt's precepts, felt it possible to mobilize a cohesive and trained minority of citizens sufficiently large to deter the government from war. This critical mass of individuals, through the threat of a general strike, would make waging war impossible.[69]

Opposed to these radical and moderate "political" pacifists were those members of the PPU who no longer believed war could be averted and who, in any case, placed little faith in government policies and burgeoning rosters of pacifists' names. Some of the PPU pacifists even claimed that an immediate and total disarmament would involve so momentous a risk as to be imprudent and immoral.[70] For Cadoux, the state should represent the highest ethical level that its citizens en masse could support as reasonable. The demand that the state act as though it shared the exacting ethical ideal of a fraction of the population was unreasonable and undemocratic.[71] For these pacifists what chiefly mattered, especially in the event of war, were groups of individuals who were thoroughly trained, deeply dedicated pacifists. They contended that a psychic conditioning, comparable to that which shapes a soldier's patriotic reflexes, combined with a solid grasp of pacifist and antipacifist reasoning, were indispensable if pacifism was to endure in the face of popular ostracism.[72] Perceived by the opposing camp as elitist, and without a positive program, these pacifists simply reiterated their conviction that pacifist consciousness without adequate psychic conditioning would prove, in practical terms, self-defeating: they envisioned a mass of intellectually and psychologically rickety pacifists toppling at the first violent challenge to their nonresistance and thereby seriously damaging the credibility of pacifism to the public at large.[73]

Secondary controversies mingled with this primary rift. There were those who felt the PPU hampered by its organizational structure.[74] Others charged that certain leading pacifist writers were too "fluffy" in their speculations and naive in their psychology. To these accusations, of course, came a legion of refuters.[75]

The positions of Huxley and Plowman are illustrative of these controversies. Huxley and Plowman, both nontraditional religious pacifists, both liberal-democrats and socialists, nevertheless inhabited opposing camps with regard to pacifist strategy. Huxley demanded concentration upon in-depth pacifist training of small groups; whereas Plowman, though endorsing the idea of a dedicated vanguard, emphasized legislative action and appealed for mass support. In most instances, the heated dispute over methods stemmed primarily from differences in personality and over attitudes about the viability of large-scale planning. Huxley's socialism, for example, stressed decentralized socioeconomic organization while Plowman was comfortable with state initiative and centralized planning in a socialist society.

The variety of philosophical and strategic pacifist positions, though a source of disaffection among pacifists, was in another sense a source of vitality to the movement. It reflected how readily pacifism could serve the needs of a highly diverse range of interwar individuals concerned with moral and social issues. The fervent devotion of pacifists to humane and democratic values contrasted markedly with triumphant fascism throughout Europe and the routine patriotism and anemic democratic convictions of countless English antipacifists. John Lewis, among the more penetrating interwar critics of pacifism, acknowledged:

> Pacifism, which was the belief of a very small minority during the Great War, . . . now upheld by a large and influential body of public opinion . . . cannot lightly be dismissed, indeed even those who cannot accept the pacifist position must bear witness to truths which today are too frequently and too easily forgotten, but which must at all costs be maintained if civilization is to endure. [76]

The heterogeneity of the pacifist movement helped to assure continued protection of democratic values.

A quintessential expression of the simultaneous strength and instability of pacifist diversity was the pacifist odyssey of John Middleton Murry. Murry's meandering interwar intellectual development also illustrated how pacifism constituted a means to recover fundamental human values shaken by the war and the erosion of traditional religious belief.

In 1938, Murry, attempting an explanation of his pacifism, honestly admitted:

> My evolution has been a painfully spiral affair; and because of that I could not say, with entire truthfulness, that I became a Christian because I had become a pacifist: but there would be vastly more truth in saying that I became a Christian because I had become a pacifist than in saying that I became a pacifist because I was a Christian. And to add to complications, I became a pacifist largely because I had become a socialist. [77]

Unlike Gill and Wellock, for whom pacifism was a natural manifestation of their religious and socialist convictions, Murry's pacifism challenged his religious and political beliefs and worked upon them as an agent of change.

The underlying motif of Murry's myriad spiritual and political adventures was a concern for both personal and social redemption. This concern acquired urgency with the death of his wife, the writer Katherine Mansfield, late in World War I. He fused Mansfield's death with that of countless other young people to heighten his hatred of war and, given the Versailles treaty, which he regarded as a destructive, immoral, and vengeful document, his sense of war's futility.[78] Throughout the interwar years, he was convinced that a moral renaissance was Europe's only hope for civilization's survival. In particular, he longed for a psychology and ethic that would deliver people from mass conformity and blind obedience to social authority. An agnostic, he could not turn to traditional religion for that psychology and ethic.[79] And so the search began.

During the 1920s Murry shed his prewar agnosticism for various forms of mystic deism.[80] During these same years he professed a vague, self-styled Marxism and pacifism. With the confluence of the Depression, the exacerbation of international tensions, and the death of his third wife, Violet de Maistre, Murry's ramshackle belief structure collapsed. Looking to redemptive political and historical theories, he temporarily discarded his pacifism and adopted revolutionary Marxism, composing in 1932 *The Necessity of Communism*. Abjuring Russian communism, he affirmed a class struggle alive to Marx's historical vision and also in accord with the traditions of English democratic and liberal individualism. Soon, though, he found the Independent Labour party, (ILP) which he had joined, too militant and too indifferent to individualism and spiritual values. In 1934, abandoning the ILP, he launched his own model of socialism, the Adelphi Summer School and, later, the Adelphi Center. Both of these endeavors were outgrowths of his role as founder and editor of the *Adelphi*, an interwar periodical devoted to literary, philosophical, and political criticism. The Adelphi Summer School was to serve as an experiment in the creation of a "genuine community," built on love and the quest for truth. Promoting the strategy of a dedicated socialist vanguard, he wrote:

> Today one can easily conceive a condition so chaotic and so barbarous that a socialist movement which had educated itself into community and frugality would be the sole indigenous vehicle for the continuity of civilization.[81]

The experience of the first Adelphi Summer School (1934) convinced him of the possibility of realizing his ideal of a nucleus of imaginative socialists bent on fostering a model community.

At the same time that Murry was experimenting with socialism, he became susceptible to the pacifist crusading of his Adelphi friends. At the 1934 Summer School, Max Plowman, then in the throes of writing *The Faith Called Pacifism*, addressed his comrades on the urgency of pacifism. Another Adelphi pacifist, Rayner Heppenstall, appealed likewise to Murry to convert to pacifism.

Their efforts were successful. By late 1937 Murry had established a close rapport with H. R. L. Sheppard, had presented a forceful pacifist address to the PPU camp at Swanwick, had helped draft the PPU Manifesto and had published his first major pacifist book, *The Necessity of Pacifism*.

During those same years his spiritual restlessness resumed; he was again entering into mystic states and yearning for some structure of spiritual belief. Sheppard's influence on him, coupled with his reading of Bernanos's *Diary of a Country Priest*, sparked his decision to convert to Anglicanism.[82] The conversion was short-lived. He soon withdrew from the church and in 1938 identified himself as a nondenominational Christian deist. Nevertheless, by that year he became convinced that a religious basis was necessary to anchor his pacifism and argued that, without such an anchor, pacifism was not stable. This claim marks the central difference between *The Necessity of Pacifism* and his later published collection of essays, *The Pledge of Peace* (1938). Through 1938 and 1939 Murry wrote extensively for *Peace News* and, together with Max Plowman, became a major arbiter of Peace Pledge Union philosophy and policies after Sheppard's death. In 1940 he contributed one of the four pamphlets in *The Bond of Peace*, his pamphlet summarizing his basic pacifist philosophy, a blend of ends-and-means, socialist, liberal-democrat, and Christian tenets. Tellingly, Murry's pacifism was not to weather World War II. Late in the war, he recanted. Given his enormous prestige in the Peace Pledge Union—according to Sybil Morrison, Murry's "opinions were almost sacrosanct"[83]—immeasurable harm was done to the union by his defection.

Only for a time, then, pacifism, with its uncompromising insistence on the dignity of the individual and on mutual love, provided an attractive faith to someone like Murry intent on rooting and propagating traditional liberal-democratic values. Through pacifism, Murry found a way to integrate his moral and metaphysical concerns as well as his political values. And, yet, in the final analysis, his pacifism withered.

Whether a religious framework is necessary for pacifist belief and action remains, therefore, an open issue. Religious as well as secular pacifists often lacked the moral fortitude required of pacifism. Nonpacifists might well argue that such absolute conviction is arrogant and wrong-headed, and applaud a degree of moral insecurity and relativism as a healthy, realistic attitude in the face of complex political and moral issues. Were these nonpacifists also religious skeptics, they might charge that a religious foundation for moral action precluded creative open investigation of social experience, citing pacifism as an example of how religion can simplify and distort moral perception. To be sure, there are occasions in any age when an individual, or small group of individuals, may come to be at odds with the multitude, convinced too that they must maintain their beliefs against massive opposition. At such times some kind of faith, secular or religious or both, is essential. For a number of Britons, interwar pacifism was such a faith; for many other interwar pacifist Britons, a still deeper faith was required.

Notes

1. John S. Hoyland, *The Friend*, vol. 66, no. 14 (Apr. 2, 1926), p. 275. Unfortunately, standard dictionary and scholarly definitions of pacifism are either too broad, encompassing all proponents of peace, or too narrow, excluding situational, relative, or conditional pacifists. For the purpose of this essay I will employ the following definition: absolute opposition to one's government's and one's own participation in modern international warfare. By modern warfare these pacifists had principally in mind aerial warfare, involving indiscriminate bombing of the enemy population, inflicting inevitably heavy injury upon noncombatants. *Excluded* by this definition are those advocates of peace who, in the last resort, were willing to use national armaments (either unilaterally or under some collective aegis) in the defense of a nation's interests. *Included* by this definition are not only traditional objectors to all forms of civil and international military combat but as well those peace advocates who opposed *only* modern, international warfare. They might justify civil warfare, premodern warfare, or even an international army of an authentic international government. My proposed definition corresponds to the distinctions pacifists by mid-1930s articulated themselves though the public at large continued to blur the lines between ardent peace crusaders and pacifists.

2. The following historical account of the evolution of interwar pacifism stems in large measure from sections of my doctoral dissertation, "Pacifism in England: 1914–1939" (Yale University, 1967), which have been modified by subsequent research and more mature reflection, and recast to suit the particular focus of this essay. To date, no comparable study has been published. While the twentieth-century American pacifist movement has enjoyed considerable scholarly attention during the past decade, the British pacifism movement after 1918 remains generally neglected. During the 1970s my research and writing shifted away from British pacifism onto other concerns, principally the life and writing of the remarkable turn-of-the-century feminist Olive Schreiner. I am grateful for the opportunity to return to the topic that so gripped me in the 1960s and which again in 1980 is regaining its freshness in the light of current international tensions.

3. Bertrand Russell, *Which Way to Peace* (London, 1936) p. 211; see also pp. 15, 51, 134.

4. Ibid., p. 212.

5. Ibid., pp. 45–49.

6. Arthur Ponsonby, *Now Is the Time* (London, 1925) p. 102.

7. Vera Brittain, *Thrice a Stranger* (London, 1939) p. 21.

8. C. E. M. Joad, *Guide to Modern Wickedness* (London, 1939) p. 166; see also his *Why War* (London, 1939) pp. 60, 82–83.

9. Alex Wood, *Christian Pacifism and Rearmament* (London, 1939) p. 5.

10. Aldous Huxley, *Ends and Means* (London, 1937) pp. 7–8.

11. Ibid., p. 156; see also his *What Are You Going to Do About It?* (London, 1936) p. 8, and Robert Duncan, *The Complete Pacifist* (London, 1937) p. 14.

12. John Middleton Murry, *The Necessity of Pacifism* (London, 1937).

13. Max Plowman, *The Faith Called Pacifism* (London, 1936) pp. 10–11, 51, 61, 114.

14. John Middleton Murry, *The Pledge of Peace* (London, 1938) p. 9; see also pp. 11–12, 19, 102–103.

15. Aldous Huxley, *The Encyclopaedia of Pacifism* (London, 1937) p. 40; see also his *Ends and Means*, p. 10.

16. Plowman, *Faith Called Pacifism*, pp. 12–14; see also, Richard Gregg, *The Power of Non-Violence* (London and Philadelphia, 1935) pp. 69, 301–302, and Huxley, *What Are You Going to Do About It?*, p. 26.

17. Murry, *The Pledge of Peace*, pp. 103, 124, and his *The Necessity of Pacifism*, pp. 116, 118.

18. Huxley, *Ends and Means*, pp. 106, 32; Joad, *Why War*, pp. 86, 110; Murry, *The Pledge of Peace*, pp. 38, 91–93, 169–170; Murry, *The Necessity of Pacifism*, p. 118; Gregg, *The Power of Non-Violence*, p. 89.

19. Gregg, *Power of Non-Violence*, pp. 56, 69, 301.

20. Huxley, *What Are You Going to Do About It?*, p. 14; Huxley, *Ends and Means*, p. 158; Huxley, *Encyclopaedia of Pacifism*, pp. 80–82.

21. Gregg, *Power of Non-Violence*, pp. 41–47, 50–64, 233, 260, and his *Training for Peace* (Philadelphia, 1939) pp. 5–20, 23, 35, 294.

22. Herbert Read, *Poetry and Anarchism* (London, 1938) pp. 46–47, 109, 116–119, and his *The Philosophy of Anarchism* (London, 1940) p. 53.

23. Sybil Morrison, *I Renounce War: The Story of the Peace Pledge Union* (London, 1962), pp. 18–19; see also Bart de Ligt, *Plan of Campaign against All War and All Preparation for War* (London, 1939).

24. Virginia Woolf, *Three Guineas* (New York, 1966) p. 142.

25. Ibid., pp. 143–144.

26. Ibid., p. 114.

27. Huxley, *Ends and Means*, p. 101; Huxley, *What Are You Going to Do About It?*, p. 8; Russell, *Which Way to Peace*, pp. 73, 198.

28. Russell, *Why Men Fight* (New York, 1917) pp. 31–32.

29. Joad, *Guide to Modern Wickedness*, pp. 183–185.

30. Storm Jameson, *No Time Like the Present* (London, 1933) pp. 278–279.

31. A. A. Milne, *Autobiography* (New York, 1939) pp. 14, 23–29, 35–37, 41–45.

32. The following biographical remarks rely upon Wilfred Wellock's autobiography, *Off the Beaten Track: Adventures in the Art of Living* (Varanasi, 1962).

33. Ibid., pp. 90–91.

34. Olive Schreiner, letter to Rev. John T. Lloyd, October, 1892, quoted in Samuel Cronwright-Schreiner, *The Life of Olive Schreiner* (Boston, 1924) p. 220.

35. M. K. Gandhi, *Satyagraha in South Africa*, trans. by V. G. Desai (Madras, 1928).

36. Plowman, *The Faith Called Pacifism*, pp. 2–4, 45–47; see also, D. L. P. [Dorothy Lloyd Plowman], ed., *Bridge Into the Future: The Selected Correspondence of Max Plowman* (London, 1944) pp. 307, 312, 322–323.

37. Eric Gill, *Autobiography* (London, 1940) p. 174.

38. C. E. M. Joad, *Counter Attack From the East* (London, 1933) pp. 35, 44, 53, 121, 265; see also, Paul A. Schilpp, ed., *The Philosophy of Sarvepalli Radhakrishnan* (New York, 1952), and H. V. Routh, *British Literature and Ideas in the Twentieth Century* (London, 1948), pp. 141–142.

39. S. Radhakrishnan, ed., *Mahatma Gandhi* (London, 1939); among the prominent British pacifist contributors to the volume of essays were: Gerald Heard, Carl Heath, Stephen Hobhouse, Laurence Housman, C. E. M. Joad, George Lansbury, Maude Royden, Vera Brittain, John Middle-

ton Murry, John S. Hoyland, Dame Sybil Thorndike, Aldous Huxley, Horace Alexander, Roy Walker, Reginald Reynolds.

40. Devere Allen, ed., *Pacifism in the Modern World* (New York, 1929); see especially A. Fenner Brockway, "Does Non-Cooperation Work?" During the 1930s Brockway emerged as a leading pacifist within Parliament and the Independent Labour Party. Born in Calcutta, he developed there a profound regard for Indian thought.

41. Aldous Huxley, "Philosophy and Pacifism," *The Friend* (London) vol. 93, no. 49, Dec. 6, 1935, p. 1114; for Huxley's metaphysical outlook in the 1930s see his *Ends and Means* and *Encyclopaedia of Pacifism* as well as his novel *Eyeless in Gaza*.

42. Huxley, *Ends and Means*, p. 208.

43. Huxley, *Encyclopaedia of Pacifism*.

44. Gerald Heard, *The Source of Civilization* (London, 1935) pp. 29, 31, 36, 45–47, 70–71, 96; see too his *The Third Morality* (London, 1937) pp. 26–27, 53–54, 216–217 and his essay, "Constructive Pacifism" in *New Statesman and Nation*, May 20, 1936, p. 856.

45. Quoted by J. M. Walsh in "Catholic and Pacifist," *Christian Pacifist*, May 1943, p. 152; see also H. Runham Brown, *Cutting Ice* (London, 1930), p. 45 and his remarks in the *War Resister*, Winter 1929/1930, pp. 18–19.

46. Ibid.

47. Donald Attwater, "Eric Gill," *Modern Christian Revolutionaries*, ed. by Donald Attwater (New York, 1947) p. 197.

48. National Peace Council, *Peace Year Book*, 1936, p. 134.

49. The following biographical discussion relies upon Gill's autobiography cited above.

50. Ibid., pp. 256–257.

51. Ibid.

52. Cecil John Cadoux, *Christian Pacifism Re-Examined* (Oxford, 1940) p. 3.

53. Ibid., pp. 2–3, 30–33, 35–56, 39.

54. Laurence Housman, *What Can We Believe?* (London, 1939) p. 87, letter from H. R. L. Sheppard to L. Housman, Feb. 12, 1927.

55. Charles E. Raven, *War and the Christian* (London, 1935) pp. 68, 125–127.

56. H. R. L. Sheppard, *100,000 Say No!* (London, 1936) pp. 4, 61, 70–74.

57. Cadoux, *Christian Pacifism*, p. 111; see also Alfred Salter's similar view in A. Fenner Brockway, *The Bermondsey Story* (London, 1949) p. 19.

58. Plowman, *The Faith Called Pacifism*, p. 40.

59. Cadoux, *Christian Pacifism*, p. 85.

60. Roland Bainton, *Christian Attitudes toward Peace and War* (New York, 1960) pp. 63–64.

61. Cadoux, *Christian Pacifism*, pp. 26, 32, 73–74, 99, 101–103, 120–121; Raven, *War and the Christian*, p. 84.

62. Cadoux, *Christian Pacifism*, pp. 123–124.

63. Ibid., p. 97.

64. Brigadier-General Frank Percy Crozier, *The Men I Killed* (New York, 1938) pp. 161, 184.

65. Raven, *War and the Christian*, p. 21.

66. John Lewis, *The Case Against Pacifism* (London, 1940) p. 8; see also C. E. M. Joad's remarks in *Peace News*, Apr. 21, 1939.

67. In 1938 Paul Van Zeeland, premier of Belgium from 1935 to 1937, urged a conference of the great powers to restore international economic cooperation.

68. George Lansbury, *My Quest for Peace* (London, 1938), pp. 10, 14, 20–23, 29, 32–33; Crozier, *The Men I Killed*, p. 165; Brockway, *Bermondsey Story*, p. 208; see also Max Plowman's comments in *Peace News*, Mar. 17, 1939, pp. 5, 9 and Jan. 23, 1937, p. 10; and Arthur Ponsonby's remarks in *Peace News*, May 1, 1937.

69. Bart de Ligt, *Plan of Campaign*, p. 3. The de Ligt Plan's endorsement by the No More War Movement is recorded in the *War Resister*, Sept. 1934, pp. 27–35; see also *Peace News*, Jan. 30, 1937.

70. Cadoux, *Christian Pacifism*, pp. 131, 166–167, 216.

71. Philip Mumford's comments in *Peace News*, Oct. 15, 1938, p. 7.

72. Max Plowman, *The Meaning of Rearmament* (London, 1937) p. 8; Gerald Heard, *Pain, Sex and Time* (London and New York, 1939) pp. 280, 290; Huxley, *What Are You Going to Do about It?*, p. 31; Huxley, *Ends and Means*, pp. 146–155, 174–175; Gregg, *Training for Peace*, p. 8; Richard Gregg's comments in *Peace News*, Apr. 24, 1937.

73. Andrew Stewart's remarks in *Peace News*, May 17, 1938; C. E. M. Joad, *Guide to Modern Wickedness* (London, 1939) pp. 34–35.

74. Patrick Richards' remarks in *Peace News*, Oct. 29, 1938; E. M. Thompson's remarks, *Peace News*, Sept. 24, 1938; Max Plowman's remarks, *Peace News*, Mar. 17, 1939, p. 5.

75. F. A. Lea, *The Life of John Middleton Murry* (London, 1959) p. 273.

76. Lewis, *Case against Pacifism*, p. 13.

77. Murry, *The Pledge of Peace*, p. 97.

78. Lea, *Life of Murry*, pp. 150–154, 273; John Middleton Murry, *The Evolution of An Intellectual* (London, 1920) pp. 1, 168–172.

79. John Middleton Murry, *Things to Come* (London, 1928) pp. 14–15.

80. The following biographical remarks rely upon Lea's biography of Murry cited above as well as Murry's autobiography, *Between Two Worlds* (London, 1935).

81. Murry, *The Necessity of Pacifism*, pp. 67–68.

82. In addition to Lea's biography of Murry, consult R. Ellis Roberts, *H. R. L. Sheppard, Life and Letters* (London, 1942) p. 298.

83. Morrison, *I Renounce War*, p. 22.

IX

"Who Dies if England Live?": Christianity and the Moral Vision of George Orwell

JAMES CONNORS

For a year before he died in January 1950, George Orwell kept a notebook in which he recorded odd bits of information and outlined future writing projects. Two entries offer revealing insights into his attitude toward "orthodox" Christianity.[1] One contains a grotesque detail from an account he had read of an Italian curio dealer's efforts to peddle a seventeenth-century crucifix to the American financier J. P. Morgan: the crucifix was apparently undistinguished, save for the fact that its hollow interior contained a stiletto. Orwell's gloss on the story is venomous: "What a perfect symbol of the Christian religion." The other entry consists of key arguments for a projected essay on the Catholic novelist Evelyn Waugh. The conclusion Orwell planned reads: "One cannot really be Catholic & grown-up. . . . Waugh is abt as good a novelist as one can be (i.e. as novelists go today) while holding untenable opinions."[2]

Some thirty years earlier while a student at Eton (1917–1921), Orwell abandoned faith in Anglican Christianity. Unlike others of his generation who had lost their faith in their youth, Orwell never regained his. He thought often about what he called "the movement"—i.e., prominent intellectuals who had experienced an adult, often highly publicized conversion to Christianity—but his reflections were invariably severe, frequently Voltairian in their ferocity.

The entry concerning the symbolic significance of the crucifix-stiletto captures the core of Orwell's belief that Christianity, particularly since the Industrial Revolution, had been a sinister, reactionary force in human history. It had been deeply implicated in the labor swindle. The Christian clergy, like the parasitic raven Moses in *Animal Farm*, with his cruel lies about "everlasting fields of clover" on Sugarcandy Mountain awaiting the exploited animal workers, had preached the doctrine of eternal bliss and urged resignation in the face of gross social and economic inequalities. Within the dark, ominous context of twentieth-century European politics, Orwell regarded the Catholic church and most Catholic intellectuals as part of the larger totalitarian menace threatening those fragile values—freedom, equality, honesty—cherished by all "decent" people and "true" socialists.

Orwell's condescending judgment on Evelyn Waugh is related to a second major line of attack that he developed against Christianity and Christian intellectuals. He believed that the campaign launched during the Enlightenment to de-Christianize European civilization had largely succeeded: most men, he thought, no longer believed they possessed immortal souls, no longer believed in or feared God, no longer took seriously Christian ethical imperatives. He approved of this trend. In his view, the central doctrines of Christianity—the belief in a personal God, the belief in the divinity of Jesus, the belief in personal immortality, the belief in the superiority of Christianity over other world religions—were colossal affronts to the modern secular mind. It was precisely for this reason that Orwell viewed the efforts of those who sought to articulate a Christian commitment either as transparently clumsy or as verging perilously close to (and often spilling over into) willful dishonesty.

Although Orwell welcomed the apparently imminent demise of Christianity, he realized that its actual decline—particularly the disappearance of the belief in personal immortality—had created an unprecedented moral crisis. "For two hundred years," he wrote in 1940, "we sawed and sawed and sawed at the branch [i.e., Christianity] we were sitting on. And in the end, much more suddenly than anyone had foreseen, our efforts were rewarded, and down we came. But unfortunately there had been a little mistake. The thing at the bottom was not a bed of roses after all, it was a cesspool full of barbed wire. It is as though in the space of ten years we had slid back into the stone age."[3] What to do? Christianity, he was certain, was devoid of solutions: indeed, much of the anger that he directed against Christian apologists and converts to Christianity stemmed from his belief that their writings helped to prevent an accurate assessment of Europe's moral crisis.

Orwell's response to the moral anarchy spreading throughout Europe was basically twofold. First of all, he tried to be a faithful recorder of the sordid details of life in a civilization where too many people no longer recognized moral constraints. Prior to 1936, before he became obsessed with totalitarianism, he tended to focus on the commerical vulgarity, the naked self-interest prevading English society. The epigraph for his third novel, *Keep the Aspidistra Flying* (1936), was a cynical adaptation of I Corinthians xiii: "And now abideth faith, hope, and money, these three; but the greatest of these is money." The hero of the novel, Gordon Comstock, believes that

> money-worship has been elevated into a religion. Perhaps it is the only real religion—the only really *felt* religion—that is left to us. Money is what God used

to be. Good and evil have no meaning any longer except failure and success. . . .
The decalogue has been reduced to two commandments. . . . "Thou shalt make
money" and . . . "Thou shalt not lose thy job". . . .[4]

From 1936 until his death he riveted his attention on the obscene realities of
European power politics. Here, Orwell believed, the waning influence of Christianity had had appalling consequences. Ruthless political rulers, abetted by a
sizeable segment of the European intellectual community, were engaged in
forging a new immorality based on systematic lying, calculated cruelty, and a
contemptuous disregard for every generous human impulse and aspiration.

The second aspect of Orwell's response was his espousal of a secular faith,
an alternative to both Christianity and the fashionable immorality of the political
and intellectual "realists." At the heart of his faith was the word "decency."
From the mid-1930s until his death the word recurred with strategic regularity
in his prose, and it was almost always linked, either tacitly or explicitly, with
values or forms of political, social, and private behavior—freedom, equality,
tolerance, honesty, compassion, respect for human life—of which he approved
and that he sought (not always with success) to embody in his own life and
writings. Decency constituted the core of what he called "true socialism," and
his lifelong idealization of the English common man was based on the conviction
that the latter was its concrete embodiment.

The ultimate secular sanction for decency and the only viable solution to
man's desire for immortality, he believed, lay in a sense of universal brotherhood, a sense that one is a part of a larger, immortal organism. Reflecting on
one of Kipling's lines—"Who dies if England live?"—during the perilous times
of 1940, Orwell said:

> Man is not an individual, he is a cell in an everlasting body, and he is dimly aware
> of it. . . . [Men] are aware of some organism greater than themselves, stretching
> into the future and the past, within which they feel themselves to be immortal.
> "Who dies if England live?" sounds like a piece of bombast, but if you alter
> "England" to whatever you prefer, you can see that it expresses one of the main
> motives of human conduct. People sacrifice themselves for the sake of fragmentary
> communities. . . . A very slight increase in consciousness, and their sense of
> loyalty could be transferred to humanity itself, which is not an abstraction.[5]

During the last ten years of his life Orwell grew increasingly pessimistic over the
possibility of ever seeing such a faith established. The likelihood of creating
even a partial basis for it—i.e., a federation of democratic socialist states in
Western Europe—was, he came to believe, exceedingly slim. Yet he never
despaired. Until his death he fought relentlessly against a host of "indecent"
isms that were seeking to divide humanity into warring factions, and he continued to proclaim the worth of the English common man.

Orwell acknowledged, sporadically and very reluctantly, that the decency of the English common man had historic links with Christianity. But the main drift of his thinking is unmistakable—to put as much distance as possible between decency and Christianity. "The real problem of our time," he wrote in 1944, "is to establish the sense of absolute right and wrong when the belief that it used to rest on—that is, the belief in personal immortality—has been destroyed. This demands faith, which is a different thing from credulity."[6] Unable to envision the creation of a religion of humanity in the immediate future, he pinned his own faith on the fidelity of the English common man to his code of decency. Winston Smith's final observation on the proles in Orwell's last novel, *Nineteen Eighty-Four*, was an affirmation of that faith.

> The proles were immortal; you could not doubt it when you looked at the valiant figure [a prole woman] in the yard. In the end their awakening would come. And until that happened, though it might be a thousand years, they would stay alive against all odds, like birds, passing on from body to body the vitality which the Party did not share and could not kill.[7]

Eton: The Origins of Orwell's Atheism

By his own testimony Orwell still believed in God, still considered himself a Christian, up until the time he entered Eton in 1917. His first formal educational experience was furnished by Anglican nuns, and he continued to receive religious instruction during the five years (1911–1916) he spent at Saint Cyprian's. On the eve of his departure from Saint Cyprian's, however, he was in a troubled state over the seeming contradictions he perceived in the Christian faith. He wrote:

> You were supposed to love God, and I did not question this. Till the age of about fourteen I believed in God, and believed that the accounts given of him were true. But I was well aware that I did not love him. On the contrary, I hated him, just as I hated Jesus and the Hebrew patriarchs. . . . The whole business of religion seemed to be strewn with psychological impossibilities. The Prayer Book told you, for example to love God and fear him: but how could you love someone whom you feared.[8]

During the next four years at Eton his distress became more acute and he finally rejected Christianity completely.

Evidence supplied by former Eton classmates, and collected by Stansky and Abrahams in *The Unknown Orwell*, indicates that the "atheist"—a label he sported—was not remiss in exploiting opportunities to display his irreverence.[9] While undergoing preparation for confirmation in the Church of England, for example, he apparently derived pleasure from baiting one of his instructors by mocking the third member of the Holy Trinity—"Old Man Ghost"—and dismissing him as a joke.[10] On another occasion with a different instructor, he produced an essay on the Gospels that was considered sufficiently blasphemous to merit the standard maximum punishment—"Take a Georgic."[11]

Former classmates and Orwell himself have identified some of the major literary influences that shaped his youthful atheism. George Bernard Shaw was one of his favorite authors during the Eton years: indeed, it was Shaw's preface to *Androcles and the Lion* that served as the model for the intemperate essay that resulted in Orwell having to "Take a Georgic." Another important force was A. E. Housman's *A Shropshire Lad,* the whole of which Orwell knew by heart by his seventeenth year. In his essay "Inside the Whale" (1940), Orwell analyzed at length the basis for Housman's enormous appeal to him and others who were adolescents in the immediate postwar years. Apart from being a country poet at a time when Georgian nature poetry was fashionable, and apart from possessing a superb talent for tapping the springs of youthful self-pity, Housman, said Orwell, was cynical and "satisfyingly anti-Christian."

> Housman would not have appealed so deeply to the people who were young in 1920 if it had not been for another strain in him, and that was his blasphemous, antinomian, "cynical" strain. . . . He was satisfyingly anti-Christian—he stood for a kind of bitter, defiant paganism, a conviction that life is short and the gods are against you. . . .[12]

The term "antinomian" in the above quotation was apparently in vogue at Eton during the immediate postwar years. It signified a repudiation of traditional institutions and beliefs, and Orwell was viewed by some of his classmates as "a strong supporter of the antinomian faction. . . ."[13]

However, the book that may well have been decisive in molding Orwell's youthful atheism was "that queer, unhonoured masterpiece," Winwood Reade's *The Martyrdom of Man*. The book was first published in 1872 and, when a new edition appeared in 1946, Orwell reviewed it. While lamenting Reade's endorsement of imperialism and his open rejection of socialism, Orwell maintained that Reade "is a sort of irregular ally of the Socialist movement, fighting chiefly on the religious front." Reaching back to his Eton days, Orwell said:

> I well remember its effect on me when I first read it at the age of seventeen. When I came upon Reade's description of the typical Hebrew prophet, and saw the words "As soon as he received his mission he ceased to wash", I felt profoundly "This man is on my side." Then I went on and read Reade's examination of the character of Jesus. It was a curiously liberating experience. Here was somebody who neither accepted Jesus as the Son of God, nor, as was the fashion at that time, as a Great Moral Teacher, but simply presented him as a fallible human being like

any other—a noble character on the whole, but with serious faults, and, in any case, only one of a long line of very similar Jewish fanatics.

For Orwell, the antinomian in revolt, "Reade was an emancipating writer because he seemed to speak man to man, to resolve history into an intelligible pattern in which there was no need for miracles."[14]

A more detailed examination of *The Martyrdom of Man* is required, for the book had a profound impact on Orwell—more than he himself may have realized. Reade was absolutely certain that Christianity was false and that it was hostile to the well-being of humanity. He declared categorically: "Supernatural Christianity is false. God worship is idolatry. Prayer is useless. The soul is not immortal. There are no rewards and there are no punishments in the future state."[15] Such convictions led Reade to conclude that "the destruction of Christianity is essential to the interests of civilization. . . . [Man] will never attain his full powers as a moral being until he has ceased to believe in a personal God and in the immortality of the soul."[16] These statements appear in the fourth and final section of the book. Titled "Intellect," the section is buttressed throughout with the iron conviction that truth and morality are inseparable. "I am firmly persuaded that whatever is injurious to the intellect is also injurious to the moral life, and on this conviction I base my conduct with respect to Christianity. That religion is pernicious to the intellect."[17] For Reade, there must be no uncertainty, no hedging in this matter. "There should be no deceit in matters of religion. In my future assaults on Christianity I shall use the clearest language that I am able to command."[18]

Though convinced that Christianity was bankrupt, Reade believed that men had legitimate religious needs. These needs, including man's desire for immortality, he thought, could be met through a religion of humanity.

> We teach that the soul is immortal; we teach that there is a future life; we teach that there is a heaven in the ages far away—not for us single corpuscles, not for us dots of animated jelly, but for the One of whom we are the elements, and who, though we perish, never dies, but grows from period to period, and who by the united efforts of single molecules called men, or of those cell-groups called nations, is raised towards the divine power which he will finally attain. Our religion, therefore, is virtue; our hope is placed in the happiness of our posterity; our faith is the perfectibility of man.[19]

Suffering, torment, and pain, Reade allowed, had been and would continue to be the price that had to be paid for human progress. It was precisely this insight into the course of human history that had prompted him to title his book *The Martyrdom of Man*. Yet Reade was extremely hopeful. War and violence, he believed, were no longer necessary for human progress. With enlightenment spreading throughout the world, the struggle and sorrow upon which progress had been contingent could henceforth be confined to the arena of ideas. "A season of mental anguish is at hand," he concluded, "and through this we must pass in order that our posterity may rise."[20]

Roughly sixty years separated Orwell from Reade and there are notable differences between the two men. Orwell certainly was far, far less sanguine than Reade regarding the prospects of human progress, and as a socialist he explicitly repudiated—though partly for strategic reasons—the goal of human perfectibility. These differences granted, however, the similarities are numerous and quite striking. The sharp dichotomy between man and God, between heavenly and earthly happiness; the conviction that Christianity had been demolished by modern science; the manner of presenting humanity as the answer to man's craving for immortality and as the ultimate sanction for ethical behavior; the belief that honesty is the cardinal virtue in all intellectual discourse, especially in matters relating to religion; the commitment to simplicity and lucidity in the use of language; the belief that struggle in the face of adversity ennobles man—these common characteristics link the two men closely together, and they underscore Reade's enduring influence on Orwell.

There is an additional argument to be made in behalf of Reade's lingering impact on Orwell. Orwell was not a "brilliant" student at Eton: he finished 117th in a class of 140.[21] Upon graduation he did not go up to Oxford or Cambridge, but instead enlisted in the Burmese Imperial Police. More precisely, during his Eton years Orwell was not a member of the "modernist" circle that was then receiving national attention in the press. It was this group, led chiefly by Harold Acton and Brian Howard, that championed the work of avantgarde writers and artists such as T. S. Eliot, Cocteau, the Sitwells, Gertrude Stein, Augustus John, among others. Orwell, on the other hand, moved in circles that were much more conventionally schoolboyish and traditional. His reading tastes ranged from detective stories and westerns to such established stars as Wells, Shaw, Kipling, and Maugham. Former classmates recall that the bit of creative writing that he did was quite undistinguished, indeed, often a chore to read because of his fondness for edifying moral themes such as honesty is the best policy.[22] In later years, of course, he read, often with delight and envy, many of the giants of modernist culture.[23] But at the same time he remained deeply suspicious and ignorant of large areas of that culture. A compliment that Orwell paid to Bertrand Russell in 1939 contains a pertinent line that is worth pondering. Russell, said Orwell, had an "essentially decent intellect" because, among other things, he had remained during the previous thirty years "consistently impervious to the fashionable bunk of the moment."[21] When one recognizes that Orwell's definition of "fashionable bunk" included all modernist theology and Christian apologetics that he knew of, one gets a clearer perception of the full significance of his break with Christianity during the Eton years. Sometime around the year 1920, Orwell became convinced that Christianity was reprehensible, and he held resolutely to this conviction for the remainder of his life.

The Case against Orthodox Christianity

In 1932 after reviewing Karl Adam's *The Spirit of Catholicism*, Orwell wrote to a friend and noted "the great pleasure" he derived from being able "to lay the bastinado on a professional RC. . . ."[25] A year and a half before he died he wrote to another friend and, after describing the irritation he had recently experienced in reading works by Graham Greene and Evelyn Waugh, he said: "I think it's about time to do a new counter-attack against these Catholic writers."[26] Actually, Orwell had already launched the offensive. Within seven days of writing the letter, his devastating review of Greene's *The Heart of the Matter* appeared in the pages of the *New Yorker* magazine.

The criticisms that flowed from his lifelong antipathy to Catholicism fall into three rather loose and overlapping categories—the church as an institution, the content of Catholic thought, and the style of Catholic intellectuals.

Throughout his career Orwell depicted the Catholic church as a reactionary, semi-Fascist institution, a major threat to human progress. At the outset of World War II, at a time when England appeared weak and vulnerable, he warned that the Catholic hierarchy, along with the majority of Catholic intellectuals, had pronounced Fascist leanings, that if a Pétain-type government were ever to be established in England it would draw its main support from the Catholic church.[27] He believed that England's survival required the introduction of a number of sweeping economic reforms that would, in effect, transform the country into a socialist state. Should such a state come into being, he was certain that "the Catholic Church will war against it."[28] In his postwar writings the church appears again as an implacable foe of progress. In a 1947 essay in which he considered the prospects of democratic socialism and unity in Western Europe, he maintained that if the Catholic church "is allowed to survive as a powerful organization, it will make the establishment of true socialism impossible, because its influence is and always must be against freedom of thought and speech, against human equality, and against any form of society tending to promote earthly happiness."[29]

In his examinations of the content of Catholic thought, Orwell discerned the same reactionary tendencies. Midway through World War II, he considered the journalistic careers of two very popular English Catholic columnists, "Beachcomber" and "Timothy Shy," and said:

> Looking back over the twenty years or so that these two have been on the job, it would be difficult to find a reactionary cause that they have not championed—

Pilsudski, Mussolini, appeasement, flogging, Franco, literary censorship, between them they have found good words for everything that any decent person instinctively objects to. They have conducted endless propaganda against socialism, the League of Nations and scientific research. They have kept up a campaign of abuse against every writer worth reading.[30]

The comic style of the two writers, Orwell continued, should not be allowed to cloud the fact that "every word they write is intended as Catholic propaganda" and that they constituted a fairly influential force within English Catholic society. Far more dangerous, in his view, were those skilled Catholic writers associated with a larger, unorganized faction that he labeled "The New Pessimists."[31] Within this faction, which included T. S. Eliot, Evelyn Waugh, and Graham Greene, were found Catholics, Fascists, pacifists, and anarchists. What linked such men together, Orwell believed, was "their refusal to believe that human society can be fundamentally improved." With varying degrees of sophistication they pounded away at three themes: "man is non-perfectible, merely political changes can effect nothing, progress is an illusion." The effectiveness of "New Pessimist" literature, Orwell insisted, demanded the immediate attention of socialists for its exponents "have more influence and make more converts among the young than we sometimes care to admit." The key to a successful socialist response lay in conceding that, up to a point, the "New Pessimists" were correct. By abandoning the dream of human perfectibility, particularly the naive mechanistic version that promised the arrival of the millennium once socialism was established, part of the power and cogency of "New Pessimist" arguments could be blunted. Orwell also urged socialists to openly acknowledge that, even after the worst abuses of the capitalist system have been eliminated, "the fundamental problem of man's place in the universe will still remain."

In addition to its reactionary tendencies, the content of Catholic thought also offended Orwell because of the manner in which doctrines central to the Christian faith were handled. He was convinced that virtually no one living in twentieth-century Europe, least of all an educated intellectual, could honestly subscribe to the Apostle's Creed, could actually believe in doctrines such as the divinity of Jesus or the immortality of the soul. Yet this was precisely what Christian churches required of their members. The consequences of this impossible situation, Orwell believed, were evident in Christian and especially Catholic thought: wherever one looked one found tortured rationalizations, self-delusion verging on dishonesty, and always the absence of *felt* religious conviction.

If you talk to a thoughtful Christian, Anglican or Catholic, you often find yourself laughed at for being so ignorant as to suppose that anyone ever took the doctrines

of the Church literally. . . . . Catholic intellectuals . . . who snigger at anyone
simple enough to suppose that the Fathers of the Church meant what they said, are
simply raising smoke-screens to conceal their own disbelief from themselves.[32]

Variations of this charge can be found in Orwell's critical assaults on
specific Christian thinkers. In his review of T. S. Eliot's *Burnt Norton*, he
maintained that, no matter how clever the arguments devised by Christian
apologists in behalf of personal immortality might be, the simple fact remained
"that hardly anyone nowadays *feels* himself to be immortal." The declining
power of Eliot's mature work, Orwell held, traced to the fact that he "does not
feel his faith, but merely assents to it for complex reasons."[33] Orwell made the
same charge much more abrasively in his review of Graham Greene's *The Heart
of the Matter*. Greene's "cult of the sanctified sinner," he said, was not only an
insult to "ordinary human decency," it was symptomatic of a serious "weaken-
ing of belief, for when people really believed In Hell, they were not so fond of
striking graceful attitudes on its brink." This lack of genuine religious belief, he
insisted, was the root cause of the novel's many "psychological absurdities"
and, by extension, its total failure as a work of art.[34]

Orwell's criticisms of the style of Catholic thought were based almost
exclusively on the similarities he detected in the mind-sets of English converts
to Catholicism, on the one hand, and communism, on the other. During the
interwar years, he held, Catholicism and communism were the two most seduc-
tive creeds contending for converts on the English intellectual scene. "Between
1935 and 1939 the Communist Party had an almost irresistible fascination for
any writer under forty. It became as normal to hear that so-and-so had 'joined'
as it had been a few years earlier, when Roman Catholicism was fashionable, to
hear that so-and-so had 'been received.' "[35] Whether one embraced Catholicism
or communism, Orwell was convinced one gratified the same psychological
need. Converts to Catholicism, he held, desperately needed "something to
believe in": they selected "the Church with a world-wide organization, the one
with a rigid discipline, the one with power and prestige behind it." The same
was true of converts to communism.

Since communists and Catholics sought and embraced rigid orthodoxies for
similar reasons, it followed, for Orwell, that the consequences of conversion
would also be similar. To observe a Catholic or communist thinker at work, he
believed, was to witness virtually the same thing. He thought each totally
unable to handle criticism, totally unable to accord an adversary either dignity
or a portion of the truth.

The Catholic and Communist are alike in assuming that an opponent cannot be
both honest and intelligent. Each of them tacitly claims that "the truth" has

already been revealed, and that the heretic, if he is not simply a fool, is secretly aware of "the truth" and merely resists it out of selfish motives.[36]

When not contending directly with critics, Catholics and communists both displayed the major characteristic of what Orwell called "transferred nationalist thought," that is, an all-consuming, obsessive need to prove that a remote locus of loyalty (Moscow, Rome) and the orthodoxy identified with it was absolutely right.[37] More than mere narrow parochialism was involved in this sort of obsession. It led directly, Orwell believed, to major intellectual crimes—to the willful distortion and suppression of evidence, to the dishonest manipulation of reality in the interests of a polemical requirement. Orwell put it bluntly: "the Catholic gang, the Stalinist gang . . . . My case against all of them is that they write mentally dishonest propaganda."[38]

Underlying all of Orwell's criticism of Catholicism and Christianity in general was a simple assumption. He believed that in the final reckoning there were but two irreconcilable approaches to life, the religious and the humanistic. One must choose between them. "One must choose," he said in his defense of Shakespeare against the attacks of the saintly Tolstoy, "between this world and the next."[39] This choice, he believed, was momentous because it had far-reaching political, economic, social, and ethical consequences. Significantly, the one major difference that Orwell believed decisively distinguished communism from Catholicism was that the former, at least theoretically, was dedicated to improving the conditions of human existence. Catholicism, however, entailed acceptance of "exploitation, poverty, famine, war and disease as part of the natural order of things."[40]

Decency: Its Communal, Ideological, and Moral Meaning

Orwell rarely referred to Nietzsche in his published writings, but he shared in his own fashion that philosopher's appreciation of the enormous implications of the decline of Christianity. Although openly aligning himself with those who had contributed to this trend, Orwell realized that "a big hole" had been created in European civilization. In his view, the fading of the belief in personal immortality—the major prop of European morality for close to two thousand years—had had repercussions as important as "the rise of machine civilization."[41] Toward the end of World War II, he wrote:

Politics, internal or international, are probably no more immoral than they have always been, but what is new is the growing acquiescence of ordinary people in the doctrines of expediency, the callousness of public opinion in the face of the most atrocious crimes and sufferings, and the blackout memory which allows blood-stained murderers to turn into public benefactors overnight if "military necessity" demands it. Quite new, too, is the doubt cast by the various totalitarian systems on the very existence of objective truth, and the consequent large-scale falsification of history. [Nor should one] under-emphasize the harm done to ordinary common sense by the cult of "realism", with its inherent tendency to assume that the dishonest course is always the profitable one.[42]

This spreading moral anarchy, Orwell believed, posed a major challenge for the responsible socialist, for the latter is not "likely to salvage civilization unless he can evolve a system of good and evil which is independent of heaven and hell."[43]

The key to Orwell's own response is the word "decency," a word that occupies a central place in his moral vision. Whether praising or censuring, this term defines his frame of reference. It has a three-dimensional presence in his writings—a communal or social basis, an ideological affiliation, and a moral content.

In his early works the specific moral content of decency is often left vague and ambiguous, but the communal and ideological components emerge quite clearly. In *Keep the Aspidistra Flying* (1936), Gordon Comstock, aspiring poet, is completely alienated from English society. No matter where he looks, he sees signs of decadence—greed, vulgarity, emptiness, and despair. The cause of this terminal disease is money, the new English religion: "All human relationships must be purchased with money. If you have no money, men won't care for you, women won't love you." Gordon decides to rebel against the money-god. He quits his position at an ad agency, where he has been a successful copywriter, and becomes a bookseller's assistant. However, "the glow of renunciation" quickly disappears. Gordon discovers that life "on two-quid a week ceases to be an heroic gesture and becomes a dingy habit. . . . Mental deadness, spiritual squalor—they descend upon you inescapably when your income drops below a certain point." At this juncture, Gordon elects to withdraw completely to plunge into the "indecent" subculture of London's underworld. The futility of this gesture suddenly becomes clear to him when, strolling through a lower-middle-class neighborhood, he realizes that the common man, in the face of rampant vulgarity and greed, has managed to retain his decency.

> The lower-middle class people in there, behind their lace curtains, with their children and their scraps of furniture and their aspidistras—they lived by the money code, sure enough, and yet they contrived to keep their decency. The money-code as they interpreted it was not merely cynical and hoggish. They had their standards, their inviolable points of honor. They "kept themselves respectable"—kept the aspidistra flying. Besides they were *alive*. They were bound up in

the bundle of life. They begot children, which is what saints and soul-savers never do.[44]

The "epiphany" provides Gordon with a solution to his moral dilemma. At the close of the novel he is thoroughly integrated into the lower-middle class: he has his job back at the ad agency, his new wife is pregnant, and he owns an aspidistra, a plant he once despised.

The ideological component of decency appears for the first time, fully stated, in *Road to Wigan Pier*, the Left Book Club selection for March 1937. *Wigan Pier* is actually two books. The first half consists of a descriptive account of the terrible impact of the Depression on the "depressed areas" of the industrial north of England. In the second half Orwell plays devil's advocate. Declaring himself a socialist, he nevertheless devotes almost all his energy to a searching criticism of the socialist movement in England. He concentrates on three problems—the socialist approach to class prejudice, the kinds of people affiliated with the socialist movement, and the emphasis on ideological correctness in socialist propaganda.

Orwell's basic point of departure is that socialism, though the obvious solution to England's and the world's problems, is in deep trouble. "We have got to face the fact that Socialism is *not* establishing itself. Instead of going forward, the cause of socialism is visibly going back. At this moment Socialists almost everywhere are in retreat before the onslaught of Fascism. . . ."[45] Orwell places the blame for this squarely on the shoulders of socialists themselves. Their approach to the problem of class prejudice has been naive, needlessly partisan, and hypocritical. By not acknowledging the deeply entrenched nature of class prejudice (their own included), socialists have actually hindered, rather than facilitated, the creation of an effective mass movement of all exploited people. "To get rid of class-distinctions you have got to start by understanding how one class appears when seen through the eyes of another. It is useless to say that the middle-classes are 'snobbish' and leave it at that. . . ."[46] The creation of a powerful socialist movement had also been impeded by the fact that too many socialists have been viewed by both workers and middle-class people to be nothing but hypocritical cranks: vegetarians, nudists, feminists, fruit-juice drinkers, birth-control fanatics—the socialist movement was filled with them.[47] "The truth is that to many people, calling themselves Socialists, revolution does not mean a movement of the masses with which they hope to associate themselves; it means a set of reforms which 'we' the clever ones, are going to impose on 'them,' the Lower Orders."[48]

The main issue for Orwell was the manner in which socialism was presented to the common man. In their preoccupation with the philosophic side of Marxism—"the pea-and-thimble trick with those three mysterious entities, thesis, antithesis, and synthesis"[49]—too many socialist writers resembled converts to Catholicism and communism.

> One of the analogies between Communism and Roman Catholicism is that only the "educated" are complete orthodox. . . . [Converts to Catholicism] have worked out the supposed implications of orthodoxy until the tiniest details of life are involved. Even the liquids you drink, apparently, can be orthodox or heretical. . . . And, *mutatis mutandis*, it is the same with Communism. The creed is never found in its pure form in a genuine proletarian. . . . Queer that Comrade Mirsky's spiritual brother should be Father ——— ———! The Communist and Catholic are not saying the same thing, in a sense they are even saying opposite things, and each would gladly boil the other in oil if circumstances permitted; but from the point of view of an outsider they are very much alike.[50]

Just as the converted Catholic intellectual is completely out of touch with the Catholic working man, so too the socialist/communist intellectual is far removed from the world of the worker and the common man in general. "I have yet to meet a *working* miner, steelworker, cotton-weaver, docker, navvy or whatnot who was 'ideologically' sound."[51] Yet despite this indifference to ideology, Orwell contends that the working man, in his desire for freedom and equality, "is a truer Socialist than the orthodox Marxist, because he does remember, what the other so often forgets, that Socialism means justice and common decency."[52]

Orwell ends *Wigan Pier* on a constructive note by offering suggestions for major revisions in socialist literature. Bourgeois-hating should cease, a greater sensitivity should be shown to thoughtful persons' legitimate reservations about a highly mechanized society, and, above all, it should be made clear that socialism means decency. He wrote:

> All that is needed is to hammer two facts home into the public consciousness. One that the interests of all exploited people are the same; the other, that Socialism is compatible with common decency.[53]

In the final paragraph of the book, Orwell creates a vision. Through the common struggle to establish a socialist society, people who have been in the past divided from one another "may feel differently about one another. And then perhaps this misery of class-prejudice will fade away, and we of the sinking middle class . . . may sink without further struggles into the working class where we belong, and probably when we get there it will not be so dreadful as we feared, for, after all, we have nothing to lose but our aitches."[54]

The specific moral content of the word "decency," largely implied in *Aspidistra* and *Wigan Pier*, is more apparent in Orwell's subsequent writings. To be precise, it emerges somewhat haphazardly in his attacks against assorted totalitarian opponents of true socialism and in his many tributes to the English common man.

Orwell, like many nineteenth-century English liberals of the John Stuart Mill persuasion, placed heavy emphasis on the role of ideas and intellectuals in history. "Intellectual decency," he wrote, ". . . has been responsible for all true progress for centuries past, and without [it] the . . . very continuance of civilized life is by no means certain."[55] This being so, Orwell believed that intellectuals had a deep responsibility to defend the values of freedom and tolerance: only in a society where these values were cherished could the open discussion of problems relating to human progress take place. Surveying the English and the wider European scene, however, Orwell found abundant evidence in the writing of communists, Fascists, and Catholics that the opposite was the case. "What is sinister . . . is that the conscious enemies of liberty are those to whom liberty ought to mean most. . . . The direct, conscious attack on intellectual decency comes from intellectuals themselves."[56]

The third ingredient in Orwell's conception of intellectual decency was the value of honesty. It implied for him absolute fidelity to one's firsthand observation and experience, the possibility of objective truth, and the constant monitoring of the insidious effects of one's partisan loyalties on one's desire and ability to be truthful. From the outset of his career Orwell was preoccupied with the question of honesty, but, after his participation in the Spanish Civil War, it became an obsession. Having witnessed the street fighting in Barcelona that erupted in connection with the suppression of the POUM (Partido Obrero de Unificación Marxista) militia, he was utterly shocked by what he regarded as an invented, willful distortion of the event in the English left-wing press. In his memoir on the war, *Homage to Catalonia* (1938), he sought to put on record a factual basis for an alternate version. He prefaced his account of the fighting with a series of cautionary remarks about truth.

> I myself have little data beyond what I saw with my own eyes and what I have learned from other eye-witnesses whom I believe to be reliable. . . . I have tried to write objectively about the Barcelona fighting, though, obviously, no one can be completely objective on a question of this kind. One is practically obliged to take sides, and it must be clear enough which side I am on. . . . I warn everyone against my bias, and I warn everyone against my mistakes. Still, I have done my best to be honest.[57]

These standards, crystalized by his experience in the Spanish Civil War, helped to shape a critical insight into the malaise of modern intellectual life that he utilized for the remainder of his life—"orthodoxy," whether religious or political, leads invariably to dishonesty.

> In theory it is still possible to be an orthodox religious believer without being intellectually crippled in the process; but it is far from easy, and in practice books by orthodox believers usually show the same cramped, blinkered outlook as books by orthodox Stalinists or others who are mentally unfree.[58]

This suspicion of orthodoxy, even group loyalty, posed a problem for Orwell himself—how was he, a man with strong partisan political convictions, to participate in politics and to write about politics without destroying himself as an intellectual? In his essay "Writers and Leviathan" (1948), he formulated a strategy that he had, in fact, followed throughout his career. It amounted to a basic partition of the intellectual into two people, citizen and writer.

> When a writer engages in politics he should do so as a citizen, as a human being, but not *as a writer*. . . . He should make clear that his writing is a thing apart. And he should be able to act co-operatively while, if he chooses, completely rejecting the official ideology. He should never turn back from a train of thought because it may lead to heresy, and he should not mind very much if his unorthodoxy is smelt out, as it probably will be.

This partition, however, did not preclude an intellectual writing about politics, providing he did so "as an individual, an outsider, at the most an unwelcome guerrilla on the flank of the regular army." Orwell allowed that the courage, independence, and vigilance he asked of intellectuals constituted a near impossible demand, but he saw no other alternative. "To yield subjectively, not merely to a party machine, but to a group ideology, is to destroy yourself as a writer."[59]

The many accusations of dishonesty that Orwell made against intellectuals during his life underscore the important place honesty occupied in his conception of intellectual decency. At times, when contemplating dishonesty, he could barely contain his rage.

> First of all, a message to English left-wing journalists and intellectuals generally: "Do remember that dishonesty and cowardice have to be paid for. Don't imagine that for years on end you can make yourself the boot-licking propagandist of the Soviet regime, or any other regime, and then return to mental decency. Once a whore, always a whore."[60]

Winston Smith, the main character in Orwell's last novel, *Nineteen Eighty-Four*, is just such a whore. For years Winston has functioned as a propaganda expert in the Ministry of Truth, destroying and recreating history as the Party directs. He has destroyed a picture that would have proven that a "fact," absolutely central to the Party's case in a famous treason trial, was actually a pure fabrication. Orwell makes clear that Winston not only enjoys this work, he does it skillfully—even after joining the bogus Goldstein conspiracy against Big

Brother.[61] On the very day Winston acquires a copy of Goldstein's book, a major reversal in Oceania's relations with Eurasia and Eastasia occurs, requiring a massive alteration in the historical record. Orwell writes: "Insofar as he had time to remember it, he was not troubled by the fact that every word he murmured into the speakwrite, every stroke of his ink pencil, was a deliberate lie. He was as anxious as anyone else in the Department that the forgery should be perfect."[62]

The full significance of such dishonesty for Orwell can only be appreciated once one understands what it was, he believed, that was being lied about. The answer is the abuse of power, in a word, brutality. Far too many European intellectuals, he was convinced, had become infected with the cult of power, had transformed themselves into apologists for the vilest, criminal acts—large-scale political murder and the cruelest kind of exploitation. This willingness to condone brutality constituted the chief difference, for Orwell, between the modern intellectual and the common man. The latter, unlike the intellectual, had a deep reverence for life, a compassion for the sufferings of people, and abiding loyalties to people. For Orwell, these characteristics, along with a devotion to freedom and equality, comprised the core of the common man's decency.

These distinctions first appear full-blown in Orwell's essay "Charles Dickens" (1940). Orwell opens with the argument that Dickens's "whole 'message' . . . at first glance looks like an enormous platitude: If men would behave decently the world would be decent."[63] The English common man, Orwell maintains, still inhabited Dickens's moral world: indeed, the latter's enduring popularity among ordinary people stemmed from his skill in expressing in a "memorable form the native decency of the common man." This decency, Orwell believed, exhibited itself in a compassion for the underdog in any situation, in a deep longing for a society animated by the values of freedom and equality, and in a profound loathing for violence. In all three respects, Dickens and the common man differed sharply from nearly all modern intellectuals who, almost to a man, "have gone over to some form or other of totalitarianism."[64]

In subsequent writings Orwell repeatedly returned to these distinctions. In *Lion and the Unicorn* (1941), he said: "The power worship which is the new religion of Europe, and which has infected the English intelligentsia, has never touched the common people. They have never caught up with power politics."[65] Several years later when he was contemplating the future of Europe, he wrote that the greatest contribution that the English common people would make to the future of Europe was a political style based on respect for human life. "The outstanding and—by contemporary standards—highly original quality of the English is their habit of *not killing one another*. . . . England is the only European country where internal politics are conducted in a more or less humane and decent manner."[66]

Without doubt Orwell's most powerful statement contrasting the common man's compassion and respect for life and the intellectual's acceptance of brutality appears in *Nineteen Eighty-Four*. From the outset of the novel, it is apparent that Winston Smith, Party propagandist, has a large tolerance—even appetite—for the most repulsive acts of violence. In one of his early diary entries, he records his reactions to a war film featuring the bombing of a lifeboat filled with children.

> Last night to the flicks. All war films. One very good one of a ship full of refugees being bombed somewhere in the Mediterranean . . . then you saw a lifeboat full of children . . . then the helicopter planted a 20 kilo bomb in among them terrific flash and the boat went all to matchwood . . . then there was a wonderful shot of a child's arm going up up up right into the air. . . . [67]

Subsequently when Winston and Julia first join the Goldstein conspiracy, they are asked how far they will go in order to end the tyranny of Big Brother.

> "You are prepared to commit murder?"
> "Yes."
> "To commit acts of sabotage which may cause the death of hundreds of innocent people?"
> "Yes." . . .
> "If, for example, it would serve our interests to throw sulphuric acid in a child's face—are you prepared to do that?"
> "Yes."[68]

This willingness to perform the most dreadful acts in order to promote the Goldstein conspiracy is precisely what distinguishes Winston from the proles. To be sure, Winston in time comes to appreciate the compassion of the proles, their loyalty to one another, their humanity: it is this very insight that is responsible for the pact that he and Julia make not to betray each other if arrested. But the passage in which this insight occurs contains a crucial qualification—the inability to relate insight to action, the inability to feel compassion. Winston *understands* that what makes his own mother, a refugee woman whom he has seen in a film shielding her child from gunfire, and the proles admirable is the fact that they had "not become hardened inside," but he cannot establish a connection between this insight and his own recent callous actions.

> The proles, it suddenly occurred to him, had remained in this condition. They were not loyal to a party or a country or an idea, they were loyal to one another. For the first time in his life he did not despise the proles or think of them merely as an inert force which would one day spring to life and regenerate the world. The

proles had stayed human. They had not become hardened inside. They had held onto primitive emotions which he himself had to relearn by *conscious effort*. And thinking this, he remembered, *without apparent relevance*, how a few weeks ago he had seen a severed hand lying in the pavement and had kicked it into the gutter as though it had been a cabbage stalk.[69]

Winston's basic flaw, the absence of human feeling, looms large in later passages dealing with his state of mind following his arrest. "He hardly ever thought of Julia. He could not fix his mind on her. He loved her and would not betray her; but that was only a fact, known as he knew the rules of arithmetic. He felt no love for her, and he hardly ever wondered what was happening to her."[70] The foreshadowing here of Winston's scream of betrayal, "Do it to Julia," is obvious. And so too is Orwell's moral point. An intellectual who serves a brutal regime can never recover the sense of decency that defines the humanity of the common man.

Decency: Its Relationship to Christianity and Humanity

Though Orwell occasionally referred to the common man's decency as "innate," it is clear that he believed that this quality had been acquired in the course of history and therefore could conceivably vanish at some point in the future. In his most optimistic moods, Orwell envisioned the common man clinging tenaciously to his standards and his moral code—just as the aspidistra clings to life.

Gordon had a sort of secret feud with the aspidistra. Many a time he had furtively attempted to kill it—starving it of water, grinding hot cigarette-ends against its stem, even mixing salt water with its earth. But the beastly things are practically immortal. In almost any circumstances they can preserve a wilting, diseased existence.[71]

Yet at times he was apprehensive. In a letter written to a friend in 1944, he noted that although the common man in England, unlike the bulk of the English intelligentsia, had not yet converted to the new religion of power politics, there was no guarantee that he would not. "I hope they won't. I even trust they won't, but if so it will be at the cost of a struggle. If one proclaims that all is for the best and doesn't point to the sinister symptoms, one is merely helping to bring totalitarianism nearer."[72]

On several occasions Orwell admitted that the common man's decency owed something to Christianity. But such concessions were always hedged with qualifications designed to diminish the importance of the influence or contribution that he was acknowledging. His account of the sources of Dickens's moral vision betrays more than a little discomfort in having to confront the Christian factor.

> Roughly speaking, his morality is the Christian morality, but in spite of his Anglican upbringing he was essentially a Bible-Christian as he took care to make plain when writing his will. In any case he cannot properly be described as a religious man. He "believed," undoubtedly, but religion in a devotional sense does not seem to have entered much into his thoughts. Where he is Christian is in his quasi-instinctive siding with the oppressed against the oppressors.[73]

In his assessments of Christianity's influence on the common man's aversion to power politics, there is evident a strong inclination to explain it away. In *Lion and Unicorn* (1941), he wrote:

> The Common People are without definite religious belief, and have been so for centuries. The Anglican Church never had a real hold on them, it was simply a preserve of the landed gentry, and the Non-conformist sects only influenced minorities. And yet they have retained a deep tinge of Christian feeling, while almost forgetting the name of Christ. The power worship which is the new religion of Europe . . . had never touched the Common People.[74]

A few years later, in his pamphlet *The English People* (1944) he deals with the same question in an almost identical manner.

> For perhaps a hundred and fifty years organized religion, or conscious religious belief of any kind, have had very little hold on the mass of the English people. Only about ten percent of them ever go near a place of worship except to be married and buried. A vague theism and an intermittent belief in life after death are fairly widespread, but the main Christian doctrines have been largely forgotten. Asked what he meant by "Christianity" the average man would define it wholly in ethical terms ("unselfishness" or "loving your neighbour", would be the kind of definition he would give). . . . But there is one sense in which the English common people have remained more Christian than the upper classes, and probably more than any other European nation. This is their non-acceptance of the modern cult of power worship. While almost ignoring the spoken doctrines of the Church, they have held on to the one the Church never formulated, because taking it for granted: namely, that might is not right.[75]

The pattern of denial, concession, qualification in the three passages just cited, the tendency to separate the valuable part of Christianity from church doctrine and the church, the calculated use of quotation marks around the words "believed" and "Christianity" underscore the difficulties Orwell experienced in treating the relationship between Christianity and decency.

The question of Christianity's influence on decency was a troublesome one for Orwell because one of his basic assumptions was that decency, if it was to survive and thrive in the future, could not rely on support from Christianity. Indeed, he wrote a novel, *A Clergyman's Daughter* (1935), that was decidedly shaped by this assumption. Dorothy, as the novel opens, dutifully performs numerous kindly services for her selfish father and the members of his congregation. Suddenly she becomes an amnesia victim and is plunged into a life of hop-picking and vagrancy. When she eventually recovers her true identity, she discovers that she has lost her faith. "Prayer which had been the mainstay of her life had no meaning for her any longer."[76] On the road back to respectability, she gets a job as a schoolteacher and becomes so engrossed in her work that "she did not think very deeply about the loss of her faith and what it might mean to her in the future." It is only when she decides, toward the close of the novel, to return to her father's parish and to resume her former life of service that she confronts the full implications of loss of faith. She is especially distressed by the realization that death ends existence.

Life, if the grave really ends it, is monstrous and dreadful. No use trying to argue it away. Think of life as it really is, think of the *details* of life; and then think that there is no meaning in it, no purpose, no goal except the grave. Surely only fools or self-deceivers, or those whose lives are exceptionally fortunate, can face that thought without flinching? . . . It is all or nothing. Either life on earth is a preparation for something greater and more lasting, or it is meaningless, dark and dreadful.[77]

Moments after these grim thoughts, however, her mood changes dramatically: she puts her plight in a global context and is ashamed of her yearning for a faith that she knows to be false.

All over the world, thousands, millions of them; people who had lost their faith without losing their need of faith. . . . Perhaps even nuns in convents, scrubbing floors and singing Ave Marias, secretly unbelieving.
    And how cowardly, after all, to regret a superstition that you had got rid of—to want to believe something that you knew in your bones to be untrue![78]

Yet old habits die hard. Dorothy's new-found courage disappears, and she drops instinctively to her knees to pray, but the words bring no consolation. "It was useless, absolutely useless. Even as she spoke the words she was aware of their uselessness, and was half ashamed of her action."[79] At this point Dorothy ceases to reflect and becomes totally absorbed in a theater project she had been working on. Orwell enters as omniscient author and closes out the novel with a statement intended to resolve the problems arising from loss of faith.

The smell of glue was the answer to her prayer. She did not know this. She did not reflect, consciously, that the solution to her difficulty lay in accepting the fact that there was no solution; that if one gets on with the job that lies to hand, the ultimate purpose of the job fades into insignificance; that faith and no faith are very much the same thing provided that one is doing what is customary, useful and acceptable.[80]

From Orwell's later writings it seems clear that he came to view the solution advanced in the final pages of A Clergyman's Daughter—a decent person through unreflective immersion in useful activity can survive the loss of faith—to be inadequate. Put differently, from 1940 until his death, he displayed a greater awareness of, a deeper sympathy for, the human needs that had created religious systems in the first place. Commenting on the distortion of Marx by his modern disciples, Orwell said that too often the impression is conveyed that Marx viewed religion as merely a dope. The line "Religion is the opium of the people," said Orwell, needed to be placed in context with the previous line, "Religion is the sigh of the soul in a soulless world." The two lines together, Orwell argued, showed that Marx saw religion as "something the people create for themselves to supply a need that he recognized to be a real one."[81]

Orwell's own answer to man's religious needs and to the problem of establishing a secular basis for morality was the religion of humanity. A global concept was essential. One of the reasons Orwell opposed Christianity, quite apart from the fact that it was reactionary and untrue, was that, given the realities of the modern world, it was hopelessly parochial. "About a quarter of the population of the world," he wrote in 1944, "is nominally Christian and the proportion is constantly diminishing. The vast block of Asia is not Christian, and without some unforeseeable miracle it never will be. Are we to say that a decent society can never be established in Asia? If so, it cannot be established anywhere, and the whole attempt to regenerate society might as well be given up in advance."[82]

Yet, though Orwell recognized the need for a religion of humanity—in an ideal world, the spiritual complement to a global socialist order—he rarely discussed it. The most straightforward statement he made in its behalf occurs in his review of Malcolm Muggeridge's The Thirties. Orwell conceded Muggeridge's contention that the decline of Christianity had had horrifying consequences: "endless war and endless under-feeding for the sake of war, slave populations toiling behind barbed wire, women dragged shrieking to the block, cork-lined cellars where the executioner blows your brains out from behind."[83] But he refused to accept Muggeridge's solution, namely, a return to traditional Christianity. The key questions, said Orwell, were whether men could develop a sense of community without believing in God as a common father, and a viable secular morality without believing in an otherworldly form of personal immortality. Orwell answered yes to both questions. Men, he said, were already developing a sense of community in a secular sense on a partial basis, and they were merging their desire for immortality with the expectation that such communities would endure.

> Man is not an individual, he is only a cell in an everlasting body, and he is dimly aware of it. . . . [Men] are aware of some organism greater than themselves, stretching into the future and the past, within which they feel themselves to be immortal. "Who dies if England live?" sounds like a piece of bombast, but if you alter "England" to whatever you prefer, you can see that it expresses one of the main motives of human conduct.[84]

What was necessary was that men take the next step and transfer their loyalty from a fragment of humanity—nation, race, creed, class—to humanity itself. With "a very slight increase of consciousness," he thought, such a transfer could take place.

Such a statement, astonishingly optimistic given the frightening world Orwell saw as a future possibility at this time (1940), never appears again in his writings. But it was not because he had abandoned his belief that humanity was the appropriate secular religion for a worldwide socialist order, but because he acquired a more sober appreciation of the power of the formidable forces militating against it. Much of the anger that Orwell directed against the various isms flourishing in the modern world that encouraged men to revel in some narrow, sectarian loyalty drew nourishment from his commitment to humanity. In his essay "Notes on Nationalism" (1945), it is the concept of humanity that furnishes him with the springboard for a comprehensive indictment of those whose moral vision is limited to a particular group.

> By "nationalism" I mean first of all the habit of assuming that human beings can be classified like insects and that whole blocks of millions or tens of millions of people can be confidently labelled "good" or "bad." But secondly—and this is much more important—I mean the habit of identifying oneself with a single nation or other unit, placing it beyond good and evil and recognizing no other duty than that of advancing its interests.[85]

Equipped with this broad definition, he lashed out in all directions: communists, Catholics, pacificists, Tories, Zionists—all demanded that men deny their species identity. Even men of good will often display the insidious effects of "nationalist" thought. Yet Orwell ends on a note of cautious hope. To cope with "Nationalism" one must first acknowledge the extent of one's contamination and then make a moral effort to struggle against it.

As for the nationalistic loves and hatreds that I have spoken of, they are part of the make-up of most of us, whether we like it or not. Whether it is possible to get rid of them I do not know, but I believe that it is possible to struggle against them, and that this is essentially a *moral* effort.[86]

This determination to make the moral effort to transcend the narrowing categories of "nationalist" thought is also apparent in Orwell's later writings. His 1947 essay "Towards European Unity" is riddled with the bleakest pessimism. "If I were a bookmaker, simply calculating the probabilities and leaving my own wishes out of account, I would give odds against the survival of civilization within the next few hundred years."[87] Yet he does not despair, but offers an alternative to the nightmarish societies—quite similar to those he described in *Nineteen Eighty-Four*—that threatened the future of humanity.

The only way of avoiding them that I can imagine is to present somewhere or other, on a large scale, the spectacle of a community where people are relatively free and happy and where the main motive in life is not the pursuit of money or power. In other words, democratic socialism must be made to work in some large area.[88]

The area Orwell identified was Western Europe, where there were "large numbers of people to whom the word 'Socialism' has some appeal and for whom it is bound up with liberty, equality and internationalism."[89] Though he conceded that socialism, if it was to prevail, must ultimately be introduced throughout the world, he insisted that "the process must begin somewhere, and I cannot imagine it beginning except for the federation of western European states, transformed into Socialist republics without colonial dependencies." Russia, America, and the Catholic church would probably oppose the creation of such a state, but he refused to believe that the task was insurmountable. The bulk of the residents in Western Europe, he said, were prepared for such a union "in a passive way." What was required was imaginative and courageous political leadership, one that would demand sacrifices from the people. "The actual outlook," he concluded grimly, ". . . is very dark, and any serious thought should start out from that fact."[90]

In 1940 Orwell said: "All we have done is to advance to a point at which we *could* make a real improvement in human life, but we shan't do it without the recognition that common decency is necessary. My chief hope for the future is that the common people have never parted company from their moral code."[91] In the best of Orwellian worlds, the common man's decency would inform a new political system in Western Europe, and ultimately form the core of a religion of humanity in a global socialist order. In calculating the possibility of either of these goals being realized after the conclusion of the Second World War, he drew very gloomy conclusions. Yet the core of his faith, though perhaps shaken a bit, remained firm. Winston Smith's last thoughts about the proles prior to his arrest are shaped by a feeling of global solidarity among all exploited people: "It was curious to think that the sky was the same for everybody, in Eurasia or Eastasia as well as here. And the people under the sky were also very much the same—everywhere, all over the world, hundreds or thousands of millions of people just like this [prole woman] . . ." Party intellectuals with their lies and their messages of hate have kept the proles of the world ignorant of each other, isolated from each other. But Winston has hope:

> If there was hope it lay in the proles! . . . The future belonged to the proles. And could he be sure that when their time came, the world they constructed would not be just as alien to him, Winston Smith, as the world of the Party? Yes, because at least it would be a world of sanity. Sooner or later it would happen: strength would turn into consciousness. The proles were immortal: you could not doubt it when you looked at the valiant figure [a prole woman] in the yard. In the end their awakening would come. And until that happened, though it might be a thousand years, they would stay alive against all odds, like birds, passing on from body to body the vitality which the Party did not share and could not kill.[92]

Notes

1. The term "orthodox Christianity" is admittedly vague. But it is Orwell's term, and it does convey his belief that Roman Catholicism and Anglo-Catholicism were linked in significant ways to various secular orthodoxies such as communism and fascism. Richard Voorhees's remark in 1955 that Orwell's hostility "to religion seems to have gone largely unnoticed" continues to be true. See Voorhees's "Orwell's Secular Crusade," *Commonweal*, LXI, 17 (Jan. 28, 1955), 451. For the best treatments of Orwell's attitude toward Christianity, see Alan Sandison, *The Last Man in Europe* (New York, 1974).

2. George Orwell, "Extracts from a Manuscript Notebook," in *Collected Essays, Journalism and Letters of George Orwell*, Sonia Orwell and Ian Angus, eds. (New York, 1968), IV, 511. Hereafter cited as *CEJL*. All subsequent notes are to Orwell's writings unless otherwise indicated.

3. Review of Malcolm Muggeridge's *The Thirties* (April 1940) in *CEJL*, II, 16.

4. *Keep the Aspidistra Flying* (New York, 1936), 43–44.

5. Review of Muggeridge's *The Thirties*, *CEJL*, II, 18.

6. Review of Alfred Noyes's *The Edge of the Abyss* (February 1944), in *CEJL*, III, 100.

7. *Nineteen Eighty-Four* (New York, 1949), 221.

8. "Such, Such Were the Joys" (March 1947), in *CEJL*, IV, 360.

9. Peter Stansky and William Abrahams, *The Unknown Orwell* (New York, 1972), 100.

10. Ibid., 105.

11. Ibid., 106. An offender ordered to "Take a Georgic" had to write out several hundred lines of Latin verse.

12. "Inside the Whale" (1940), in *CEJL*, I, 505.

13. Stansky and Abrahams, *Unknown Orwell*, 122.

14. Review of Winwood Reade's *The Martyrdom of Man* (March 1946), in *CEJL*, IV, 117.

15. Winwood Reade, *The Martyrdom of Man* (London, 1948), 420.

16. Ibid.

17. Ibid., 422.

18. Ibid., 423.

19. Ibid., 432.

20. Ibid., 437.

21. Stansky and Abrahams, *Unknown Orwell*, 84ff. For some thoughtful observations on the significance of the term "brilliant" at Eton, see Martin Green, "Orwell as an Old Etonian," *Modern Fiction Studies*, XII, 1 (Spring 1975), 3–10.

22. Ibid., 190–211. Stansky and Abrahams reproduce a short story called "The Slack-Bob," which Orwell wrote in 1918, and it concludes with the homily, "Honesty is the Best Policy."

23. See Orwell's letters to Brenda Salkeld dealing with James Joyce. Sample: "I managed to get my copy of *Ulysses* through safely this time. I rather wish I had never read it. It gives me an inferiority complex. When I read a book like that and then come back to my own work, I feel like a eunuch who had taken a course in voice production and can pass himself off fairly well as a bass or a baritone, but if you listen closely you can hear the good old squeak just the same as ever." *CEJL*, I, 139.

24. Review of Bertrand Russell's *Power: A New Social Analysis* (January 1939), in *CEJL*, I, 376.

25. Letter to Eleanor Jaques, June 1932, in *CEJL*, I, 82.

26. Letter to Julian Symons, July 1948, in *CEJL*, IV, 438.

27. London Letter to *Partisan Review* (August 1941), in *CEJL*, II, 149.

28. *Lion and the Unicorn: Socialism and the English Genius* (February 1941), in *CEJL*, II, 102.

29. "Towards European Unity" (1947), in *CEJL*, IV, 374.

30. "As I Please" (June 1944), in *CEJL*, III, 174. "Beachcomber" was the pseudonym of J. B. Morton and "Timothy Shy" was the pseudonym of D. B. Wyndham Lewis.

31. "As I Please" (December 1943), in *CEJL*, III, 63–65.

32. "As I Please" (March 1944), in *CEJL*, III, 101–104.

33. Review of T. S. Eliot's *Burnt Norton* (October–November 1942), in *CEJL*, II, 236–242.

34. Review of Graham Greene's *The Heart of the Matter* (July 1948), in *CEJL*, IV, 439–443.

35. "Inside the Whale" (1940), in *CEJL*, I, 512ff.

36. "The Prevention of Literature" (January 1946), in *CEJL*, IV, 61ff.

37. "Notes on Nationalism" (May 1945), in *CEJL*, III, 365.

38. Letter to *Partisan Review*, (September–October 1942), in *CEJL*, II, 229. Orwell made this remark in a rejoinder to several critics who were unhappy with his treatment of pacificism in an earlier issue of the *Partisan Review*.

39. "Lear, Tolstoy and the Fool" (March 1947), in *CEJL*, IV, 299.

40. Review of F. J. Sheed's *Communism and Man* (January 1930), in *CEJL*, I, 385.

41. "As I Please" (March 1944), in *CEJL*, III, 103.

42. Review of Noyes's *The Edge of the Abyss*, in *CEJL*, III, 100.

43. "As I Please" (March 1944), in *CEJL*, III, 103.

44. *Keep the Aspidistra Flying*, 239.

45. *Road to Wigan Pier* (New York, 1937), 171.

46. Ibid., 131.

47. Ibid., 173ff.

48. Ibid., 179–180.

49. Ibid., 177.

50. Ibid., 177–182.

51. Ibid., 177.

52. Ibid., 176.

53. Ibid., 230.

54. Ibid., 231–232.

55. Editorial to *Polemic* (May 1946), in *CEJL*, IV, 160.

56. "The Prevention of Literature," in *CEJL*, IV, 70.

57. *Homage to Catalonia*, (New York, 1938), 150–160.

58. Review of T. S. Eliot's *Burnt Norton*, in *CEJL*, II, 241.

59. "Writers and Leviathan" (March 1948), in *CEJL*, IV, 412–413.

60. "As I Please" (September 1944), in *CEJL*, III, 227.

61. *Nineteen Eighty-Four*, 44. Orwell wrote: "Winston's greatest pleasure in life was his work. Most of it was a tedious routine, but included in it there were also jobs so difficult and intricate that you could lose yourself in them as in the depths of a mathematical problem—delicate pieces of forgery in which you had nothing to guide you except your knowledge of the principles of Ingsoc and your estimate of what the Party wanted to say. Winston was good at this kind of thing. On occasion he had even been entrusted with the rectification of the *Times* leading articles, which were written entirely in Newspeak."

62. Ibid., 183–184.

63. "Charles Dickens" (March 1940), in *CEJL*, I, 417.

64. Ibid., 459.

65. *Lion and the Unicorn*, in *CEJL*, II, 59.

66. *The English People*, in *CEJL*, III, 30.

67. *Nineteen Eighty-Four*, 9–10.

68. Ibid., 142.

69. Ibid., 166–167. Italics added.

70. Ibid., 232.

71. *Keep the Aspidistra Flying*, 28.

72. Letter to F. J. Willmett (May 1944), in *CEJL*, III, 150.

73. "Charles Dickens," in *CEJL*, I, 458.

74. *Lion and the Unicorn*, in *CEJL*, II, 59.

75. *The English People*, in *CEJL*, III, 7.

76. *A Clergyman's Daughter*, (New York, 1935), 152.

77. Ibid., 315.

78. Ibid., 317.

79. Ibid., 318.

80. Ibid., 318–319.

81. Review of Muggeridge's *The Thirties*, in *CEJL*, II, 18.

82. Review of Noyes's *The Edge of the Abyss*, in *CEJL*, III, 100.

83. Review of Muggeridge's *The Thirties*, in *CEJL*, II, 16.

84. Ibid., 17.

85. "Notes on Nationalism," in *CEJL*, III, 362.

86. Ibid., 371.

87. "Towards European Unity," in *CEJL*, IV, 370.

88. Ibid., 371.

89. Ibid.

90. Ibid., 375.

91. Letter to Humphrey House, April 1940, in *CEJL*, I, 532.

92. *Nineteen Eighty-Four*, 221–222.

X

The Twentieth-Century Revolt against Time: Belief and Becoming in the Thought of Berdyaev, Eliot, Huxley, and Jung

DOUGLAS K. WOOD

Time the leech; time the destroyer; time the bloody tyrant; portrayed in a thousand forms, hypostatized in a thousand metaphors, described in a thousand symbols. From the dawn of civilization to the present, the same lament continues: time is a devious slayer, a traitorous provider who gives only to take away; a patron of life who wears the black cowl of death beneath a disguise of light and laughter. As an Elizabethan poet has said:

> Even such is Time, which takes in trust
> Our Youth, and joys, and all we have;
> And pays us but with age and dust,
> Which, in the dark and silent grave,
> When we have wandered all our ways,
> Shuts up the story of our days. . . .

Mutability Tradition

In the twentieth century the lament against the eroding power of time endures and frequently appears to increase in its intensity. On occasion it clearly resembles the melancholy protest of the Elizabethans. Dylan Thomas, for example, bitterly describes the "Grief Thief of Time" who sets "its maggot" on our track and, in another poem, the destructive "force that through the green fuse drives the flower"—a force which he equates with "The lips of time," which "leech to the fountainheads" of youth. Or again, in "Variations on a Time Theme" the Scottish poet Edwin Muir registers his dismay with the apparently meaningless "sad stationary journey" of time which consumes each successive generation. Such expressions of hopelessness, of protest and impotent rage "against the dying of the light" inevitably wrought by time are not uncommon in any age: they are representative of the "mutability tradition" in literature. When Muir and Thomas recoil in horror or sadness at the spectacle of temporal decay, they are giving contemporary expression to a sentiment that can be traced in the primitivist poetry of antiquity, the verse of Lorenzo de Medici, or the stanzas of Lord Herbert of Cherbury. According to this tradition, time is synonymous with change, the process that exhausts life-forms and insures the eventual decomposition of every sentient and inanimate object in the universe. It is the principal enemy whose very omnipotence often inspires a spirit of resistance. Thus, for instance, Muir and Thomas, like Shakespeare or other twentieth-century writers (e.g., Edward Thomas, Walter de la Mare, Robert Graves, Rupert Brooke, James Joyce, Nikos Kazantzakis, and C. Day Lewis), admit that they would like to "Make war upon this bloody tyrant, Time." But—and here is the rub—they also realize that, in the last resort, "nothing 'gainst Time's scythe can make defence." A private mythology, an exaltation of love and life, an *amor fati* or a deliberate flaunting of death may enable the individual to reconcile himself to nothingness, but they are not not enough, in Edwin Muir's phrase, to "put all Time's display to rout."

The Revolt against Time

While the vitality of the "mutability tradition" is maintained in twentieth-century European literature, it does not represent the only protest against the destructive characteristics of the temporal process. For in fact this century has witnessed a far more dramatic and significant protest against mutability—an attack on time that not only laments the ravages of contingency, but demands and tries to achieve the transcendence and abolition of the temporal process. Whereas Thomas and Muir helplessly lament the passage of time, the major proponents of the twentieth-century revolt against time not only denounce the sad waste of the temporal process, but try to accomplish either a permanent or temporary destruction of time itself. Their rallying cry is that of the hero of Kazantzakis's novel *The Rock Garden:* "I declare war on time! I declare war on time!" Yet their protest—their desire, in the Greek author's words, to turn "the wheel back" and resuscitate the dead—is not simply a product of romantic sentimentalism—a spontaneous reaction of the heart. For while it may be exemplary of Everyman's objection to the inexorable cycle of life and death, it represents a confident and determined assault on the process of temporal corruption; a thoroughgoing and self-conscious attempt to eliminate the flux of events.

Varieties of Time

Four of the most outstanding protagonists of the twentieth-century revolt against time—namely, the Russian religious eschatologist Nicolas Berdyaev (1874–1948), the British poet T. S. Eliot (1888–1965), the British novelist Aldous Huxley (1894–1963), and the Swiss psychologist C. G. Jung (1875–1961)—aim their respective attacks on temporal process primarily against the time of human *experience*—against what Georges Poulet has called *le temps humain*, i.e., psychological, qualitative, or subjective time. This is not to say that they are not also at war with what they regard to be *scientific time;* they are. Indeed, they wish to eliminate or surmount the *ontological dimension of time* itself whether it be viewed from a "human" or "scientific" perspective. But, it is important to note at the outset, they approach the problem of time in a different way from the scientist. The latter—as opposed, say, to the poet or novelist—is principally interested in constructing an "objectively" valid system of measurement. The quartet I have selected for study, however, are also concerned with the problems of measuring time, especially *historical time,* another form of temporality they yearn to transcend or destroy. Yet their methods of periodizing historical time are decidedly different from those the scientist employs when he attempts to measure *cosmic time*. For while it is undeniable that scientific concepts of time contain subjective elements and that some scientists have rebelled against "objective" conceptions of temporal process, it is nevertheless true that most scientists try to remove their ideas of time from the subjective foundations of individual experience. Instead of being concrete their conception of time is *abstract;* it is quantitative rather than qualitative, public rather than private or personal. In other words, the scientist is generally preoccupied with the measurement of physical events, while the poet, novelist, or speculative philosopher of history—or again the philosopher of physics—is chiefly concerned with the *nature* of time. The scientist is intent upon discovering an empirically verifiable concept of time that will enable him to calculate cosmic events—to construct a universal metric from which "calendars" and "clocks" can be derived—while the individual who, like Berdyaev, Eliot, Huxley, and Jung, ultimately bases his notion of time upon personal or subjective experience, is concerned with the *meta*physical dimensions of temporality—with the ultimate meaning as well as the ontological and axiological nature of time.[1]

Spatialization

Now although it is true that Berdyaev, Eliot, Huxley, and Jung derive their concepts of time from personal experience—and, concomitantly, that they direct their attacks on temporality primarily against subjective time *(le temps humain* or *Ich-Zeit)* and secondarily against what they understand as scientific time—it is equally true that they believe in the objective validity of their own notions of time. When Berdyaev refers to the Beginning and End of historical time, when Eliot describes the cyclical revolutions of the temporal process, or again, when Huxley discusses the dance of Shiva, or Jung the cycle of aeons, each is referring to an objective structure or pattern of events that he considers to be a universal aspect or condition of human existence. Such claims of objectivity are not uncommon. Individuals who shape their time-concepts on the foundations of personal experience usually extend their immediate perceptions of time (i.e., of succession, change, motion, supercession, simultaneity, and/ or transitional intervals)[2] by either interpreting time as a linear progression or as a cyclical repetition. Linear time-concepts no doubt arise from the ability to anticipate or remember events—circular (or spiral) concepts of temporal process, from the observance of enduring and repetitive aspects of human experience. Yet in both cases, the ability to extend the "blooming, buzzing confusion" of time as an immediate datum of consciousness through the use of a symbolic form (circle, spiral, line) provides the individual at once with an "objective" model with which to interpret, order, and control events, as well as a spatial diagram of time that may eventually enable him to destroy the temporal process itself.

The interrelation between the desire to abolish or transcend time and the transformation of experiential time into an objective (yet unscientific) dimension of human experience through the use of spatial symbols is a typical feature of Berdyaev's, Eliot's, Huxley's, and Jung's approach to the time-problem. Not only do they share a common and aggressively antipathetical *attitude* toward time; not only, that is to say, do they regard time as an enemy who must be surmounted or destroyed; but they also employ (spatial) *concepts* of time to annihilate the temporal process. They transform their subjective feelings about time into a personal concept of time (which purportedly has universal validity), and use their spatialized or pictorial representations of temporal process to eliminate time. As Milic Capek has observed, "The elimination of time and its spatialization are closely related." For in imposing a graphic symbol upon time or "in contemplating a spatial diagram of temporal process it is easy and psychologically natural to forget its underlying dynamic meaning."[3] Spatialization of time transforms succession into juxtaposition, and presents uncompleted moments of time as a completed or simultaneous whole. It represents time statically and deprives it of its inherent momentum. In Capek's view, this

"Eleatic" tendency can be discovered in early interpretations of Einstein's theory of relativity as well as idealistic trends in contemporary metaphysics. Yet (as Capek himself realizes) the use of spatial symbols to order, control, and destroy the temporal process is an extremely ancient practice—a practice that can be found in archaic as well as modern societies, in the presuppositions of the *Enuma Elish* or in the writings of Berdyaev, Eliot, Huxley, and Jung.

When Berdyaev, Eliot, Huxley, and Jung use the verbal equivalents of spatial images to describe the time-process, they not only retrace the path of a venerable tradition—a tradition, by the by, that was not seriously challenged until the end of the nineteenth century[4]—but they also achieve the same "epistemological" result as, for instance, "archaic man," the medieval eschatologist, the advocate of the idea of progress, or the champion of dialectical materialism. By imposing, in other words, a graphic symbol upon their immediate experience of time, they delimit the temporal process and establish its boundaries. This epistemological act (which orders and, in some cases, establishes direct control over the temporal process) in turn permits them to invest time with a teleological meaning, or to formulate a sharp distinction between the time-process and eternity that may eventually precede and ultimately facilitate the transfiguration of time into timelessness. Expressed concretely, when Berdyaev imposes a circle on cosmic time, a line on the historical process, and a point on existential time (i.e., that period of timeless time that precedes the destruction of the phenomenon of time itself and the return to eternity); or, analogously, when Eliot describes "The time of the seasons and the constellations/The time of milking and the time of harvest" as well as the time "of Heaven" that, in the last twenty centuries, has brought "us farther from God and nearer to the Dust" as a series of cycles,[5] each is using a spatial image to clarify and focus the realities of the time-process. Yet their use of time-symbols does not end here. For once they have interpreted time in terms of spatial images, they are prepared to destroy or transfigure the temporal process. Berdyaev, for example, gives the linear structure of historical time a "Beginning" and an "End," and, by making history finite and cosmic time subordinate to history (i.e., the unfolding of the divine-human drama) achieves the inevitable and irreversible abolition of every kind of time (cosmic, historical, and existential).[6] On the other hand Eliot— who, unlike Berdyaev, rarely appears to examine the nature of time under the aspect of eschatology, especially apocalyptic eschatology—uses the circular structure that he imparts to astronomical, biological, and "moral" time to formulate a relationship between timelessness and time. This relationship (that is, the relationship between the "still point" and the "turning world") is then employed to reconcile the temporal process and eternity. By introducing a third term, namely, his notion of the "dance" (which is a poetic transcription of Bradley's concept of the Absolute), Eliot not only reconciles time and eternity but transforms the temporal process into a "pattern/Of timeless moments."[7]

Eternity Images

Eliot's use of the circle demonstrates the way in which time-symbols are frequently transformed into eternity-images or symbols of timelessness. It is not only, as Capek observes, psychologically natural to eliminate time by portraying it as a spatial pattern; it is equally natural to suppose that the symbolic structure that makes time static and deprives it of its dynamic meaning must be related to, if not synonymous with, timelessness. The oldest symbol that has been employed to portray *both* time and eternity has been the circle. This popularity is no doubt ascribable to the basic and traditional function of the circle as an "ordering symbol." It must be remembered that the perfect geometrical structure of the circle (all points equidistant from the center) has not only been used to clarify and order the temporal process. Indeed, it can also be found demarcating the sacred precincts of a temple *(temenoi)*, delimiting the world-order (frequently in combination with a square representing the cardinal points of the compass), describing the movement of the planets (for instance, in Aristotle's "celestial world"), protecting man from inimical forces (as, for example, in the case of the magic circle), harmoniously rationalizing man's position in the universe (i.e., establishing the microcosm-macrocosm relationship), giving concrete expression to the emotions of a mental patient, or again, objectifying an individual's concept of eternity. Yet while the evidence suggests the ubiquity and preeminence of the circle as an ordering symbol (and here we are primarily interested in its capacity as a time-symbol and eternity-image), it is obviously but one of many symbols (and, in fact, types of symbols) that are used by human beings to order their realities.

Nondiscursive Symbols and Time

As a time-symbol the circle, like the straight line and its variants (e.g., what Berdyaev occasionally refers to as the "undulating line" of history), is what Ernst Cassirer and Susanne Langer would call a nonlinguistic or nondiscursive symbolic form. Nondiscursive forms of symbolism (viz., ritual, myth, religion, and art) articulate or objectify feelings or emotional concepts, rather than rational or discursive thoughts (such as the concepts of mathematics). Their meaning or import is essentially connotative (as opposed to denotative) because they lack the syntax or grammatical structure of linguistic symbolisms. But it is not just the circle or line—the graphic symbol or its verbal equivalents—that is nondiscursive, for often the prose used to elucidate a philosophy of history or idea of time is itself nondiscursive. In other words, although a description of the temporal process may be expressed in verbal symbols, in words that constitute a "language," their significance or import may be nondiscursive because the meaning conveyed by their language is metaphorical. It is undeniable that many linguistic treatises dealing with the problem of time often revert to a nondiscursive level, either to use the verbal equivalent of a pictorial symbol to express their philosophy (or, perhaps more accurately, their myth) of time, or to employ metaphorical or poetic symbols (poetry is defined as a nondiscursive form of symbolism) to articulate feelings they have about time that cannot be expressed with the verbal precision or grammatical rigidity of analytical thought. A dramatic example of the use of nondiscursive prose to describe the time-process is provided by Berdyaev's numerous works on the philosophy of history. For not only does he use spatial images to describe the time-process, but again and again, under the ecstasy of an overwhelming vision of man's destiny, he reverts to a metaphorical level of expression to convey the meaning of his apocalyptic interpretation of history. Underneath his discourses on Kantian epistemology, below the rational threshold of his examination of the problem of objectification lies the eschatological vision that permeates and unifies every strand of his thought. And his eschatology, like all eschatology, is created out of nondiscursive symbols—images that belong to the world of myth, rather than to the realm of logic and science. The linear pattern of Western eschatology probably rests upon an extremely ancient structure of feeling—a structure of feeling that, like the emotions associated with the circular notion of temporal process, may ultimately be derived from the birth-death-rebirth pattern of primitive initiations, from what the Dutch anthropologist Van Gennep has called "the rites of passage." At any rate, Berdyaev's language is shot through with an emotional terminology (a vocabulary that is strikingly reminiscent of primitive initiation rites), and, like Eliot, he relies on graphic symbols to order, control and eliminate time.

The same can be said of Huxley and Jung. They too appreciate the epistemological function of time-symbols, and, like Berdyaev and Eliot, use nondiscursive images of temporal process to express a group of interrelated ideas that they associate with the meaning of man's existence in time. According to Huxley and Jung, time is equivalent to physical change, to perpetual perishing and becoming—a process of growth and decay that conforms to the symbolic structure of a circular form. Thus while, like Eliot, they recognize the existence of different historical ages, they tend to de-emphasize or ignore the linear pattern of historical time. Their reason for not stressing the past-present-future structure of historical time lies partially in their conception of a homogeneous human nature. Like Thucydides (and T. S. Eliot) Huxley and Jung infer a cyclical movement of the temporal process from the constancy of human nature. If man is the same *in esse* (as he is assumed to be), he will act essentially the same throughout time. Therefore, human time, like cosmic and biological time—or again, the changes experienced by societies or civilizations— necessarily repeats the same fundamental pattern. *Corso i ricorso:* or almost, since Huxley, Jung, and Eliot recognize that although the formal pattern of the temporal process (what W. H. Auden calls the "general average way" of time) is constant, particular events—say, an individual's life history—may not be identical in detail. An individual possesses the potential of imposing his own signature upon the repetitive rhythm of the cyclical process. Yet on occasion Eliot, for example, even appears to deny this limited definition of (individual) novelty. And it is not impossible to find him describing human activity as a result of divine predestination. This deterministic streak runs throughout his later poetry and all of his plays, and it helps to elucidate his conception of what may be termed "moral time." Because of Original Sin, Eliot assumes, man—natural man, man living in the fallen time of creation—remains essentially the same throughout history. The repudiation of the concept of a plastic human nature (coupled with the notion of primordial sin) implies that all historical periods are essentially identical. Yet identical only in the sense that they are equally corrupt or morally inadequate. Thus antiquity, the era of the metaphysical poets, and the twentieth century are fundamentally the same because, in Eliot's view, Original Sin precludes moral progress *sub specie temporis*. But again this does not mean that every temporal situation repeats itself in exactly the same manner ad infinitum. For there *is* a difference between, for instance, the Middle Ages and our own age. Indeed Eliot (like Berdyaev and Jung) believes that modern civilization has declined since the Middle Ages (particularly the Age of Dante, or what Berdyaev and Jung refer to as the Age of Mystic Italy or the Age of Joachim of Flora), and that contemporary Western culture represents a tragic departure from the integrated society of medieval Europe. Even the grandson of "Darwin's bulldog," Aldous Huxley, can be caught looking back nostalgically to an age of mystics that, he poignantly regrets, disappeared in the cannon smoke of seventeenth-century power politics. Yet in spite of their recognition of historical or contingent differences between cultures past and cultures present, in spite of their belief that we are, as a waggish Huxleyean mouthpiece says in *Eyeless in Gaza*, well on in the third volume of Gibbon, they tend to ignore particular differences and insist that, since human nature is constant, time is cyclical (or spiral).

Initially puzzling as it may seem, Berdyaev—the linear eschatologist par excellence—also examines the rise and fall of civilizations under the aspect of circular time. Yet his concept of cyclical process (which he, like Hegel, also employs to interpret cosmic time) cannot be used to describe the general pattern of history. For, in Berdyaev's view, history is essentially a divine-human drama—a soteriological mystery play—that unfolds in a linear progression. But the pattern of cultural events—the history of individual civilizations—follows a spiral course.

Approaching the problem from the standpoint of analytical psychology, C. G. Jung arrives at a concept of cultural (or historical) transformation that bears a family resemblance to Berdyaev's. According to the Swiss psychologist, all time (biological, astronomical, and historical) is cyclical. The lives of individual men, the processes of nature, and the rise and fall of civilizations all follow a circular course. Yet whereas astronomical and biological time perennially recapitulate the same pattern, historical time allows for minor variations: its cycles never repeat themselves exactly, and therefore history develops as a series of spirals.

Although the implications of his theory of history are never fully developed, the end result of Jung's psychological interpretation of history—his law of *enantiodromia* or compensation that controls (without actually causing) the succession of historical aeons—is quite similar to Berdyaev's apocalyptic vision. Like Berdyaev, Jung gives the apparently meaningless process of growth and disintegration a meaning by assimilating the cyclical course of cultural history (or the history of civilizations) into an inclusive pattern of universal history. Civilizations, like human beings, may inevitably be born only to die; but (by imposing nondiscursive symbols upon the phenomenon of temporal flux) it is possible to see that they perish for a purpose. In Jung's schema the helix of historical time is transformed into the circle of timeless perfection—into a psychological condition (symbolized by the *mandala* [Sanskrit: circle] or the astrological symbol of Aquarius) that is homologous with what Teilhard de Chardin would call "point Omega." In Berdyaev's system, on the other hand, the jagged line of history eventually smashes the cycle of cultural and cosmic time by reaching its appointed End. It resolves the antinomies of the historical process, and accomplishes the return to timelessness—to eternity, which Berdyaev (like Jung, Eliot, and Huxley) describes as a timeless and spaceless circle.

If Jung had been asked to interpret Aldous Huxley's concept of time, he would undoubtedly begin by observing the similarity between his own notion of temporal process and that of the Englishman. For, like Jung, Huxley also imagines time and eternity as a circle. The Swiss psychologist may even (especially in later life) have agreed with Huxley's view—which he derived from Hindu and Buddhist sources—that the phenomenon of time is actually an illusion *(maya)* perceived by minds alienated from reality. In any case, Jung would probably have concluded his remarks about Huxley's concept of time with a discourse on the nature of mandala symbolism because Huxley's cones and circles (like Yeats's gyres or Eliot's still point and turning world, or again, Berdyaev's spaceless and timeless circle of eternity) perform all of the major functions that Jung ascribes to the mandala. That is, they impose order on the chaotic flux of experience, clarify the psychological relationship between the individual and (in this instance) the time-process, and (most significantly from Jung's point of view) represent the final achievement of man under the aspect of time—namely, the establishment of a permanent or at least temporary relationship between the individual and eternity. It is impossible to say whether Huxley, who was familiar with Jung's theories, ever recognized that his time-symbols and eternity-images could be interpreted as mandalas. Nevertheless his occasional (nondiscursive) descriptions of the relationship between the temporal process and timeless Reality appear to correspond to Jung's definition of the mandala or image of psychic wholeness. (Actually, it should be observed parenthetically, Jung and his followers would regard most time-symbols and all eternity-images as mandalas or, what one disciple has called, circles of the psyche—i.e., symbols that are analogous to but one step removed from genuine mandalas.) Sidestepping the issue, however, of whether Huxley's pictorial descriptions of time and eternity are really mandalas or not, it is important to point out that his use of graphic symbols to portray the temporal process offers a dramatic example of the intimate connection between the spatialization and destruction of time, on the one hand, and the transformation of time into eternity, on the other.

In his first full-blown mystical novel, *Eyeless in Gaza*, for example, Huxley describes time and eternity as two cones that share a common apex. The temporal world (represented by the first cone) culminates in a point—a point that, like Berdyaev's point of existential time, Eliot's still point, or Jung's point or center of the mandala, marks the end of time and the commencement of eternity. As the world of time (or the first cone) converges on its apex, it is gradually transfigured into timelessness. The second cone in its turn expands toward a base whose circle is equated with the ground of all being, eternal Reality, or timelessness. This intricate image, which is reminiscent of Yeats's famous description of time and eternity in *A Vision*, is directly related to another symbol that Huxley uses to describe the temporal process: viz., the dance. For like Eliot (whose concept of the dance reconciles the still point with the turning world by transforming time into "a pattern/Of timeless moments") Huxley uses the dance of Shiva Nataraja[8] to explain the mysterious connection between perpetual perishing and eternal stillness. Shiva represents becoming and timelessness: he is at once the spinner of the cosmic illusion and the pattern of unmoving movement or eternity. Unfortunately, however, the vast majority of human beings do not realize that the annihilating force of time is merely a product of their egocentric visions of reality. If only mankind could cast off the straitjacket of its collective ego, if only it could gain the experience of the mystic, it could see that time and eternity, *samsara* and *nirvana*, are one and the same—that Shiva or Reality is an eternal dance or process of timelessness.

Mysticism

Huxley's concept of "scientific religion"—his emphasis upon mysticism and empirical theology—is also found in the works of Berdyaev, Eliot, and Jung. In fact *mysticism is as important to the twentieth-century revolt against time as spatialization.* Together they form the principal prongs of the offensive: they provide the essential method or epistemological procedure by which Berdyaev, Eliot, Huxley, and Jung (as well as other twentieth-century anti-temporalists, e.g., Charles Williams, W. B. Yeats, and Hermann Hesse) achieve their victory over the temporal process. But, the question naturally arises, what is mysticism? Is it universally identical? And does it assume the same *degree* of importance, say, in Berdyaev's thought as it does in Huxley's, in Eliot's work as it does in Jung's?

According to William James (who realized that the words "mysticism" and "mystical" have a bewildering variety of connotations in common parlance), there are "four marks" that characterize an experience as mystical: viz., ineffability, noetic quality, transiency, and passivity.[9] That is, a mystical experience defies expression, exemplifies a nondiscursive form of knowledge, lasts for a short while, and occurs only in passive states of mind—i.e., when the subject (or individual mystic) "feels as if his own will were in abeyance," or "as if he were grasped and held by a superior power."[10] Now while it is undeniable that these "four marks" characterize all forms of mystical phenomenology (including the mysticism of Berdyaev, Eliot, Huxley, and Jung), James's definition of mysticism remains incomplete. For he leaves unmentioned the most typical, fundamental, and pervasive element or constituent of mystical experience: namely, the transcendence of time—the feeling of rising above or being liberated from the powers of temporality. And it is this archetypal characteristic of mysticism—more than any other single feature of preternatural experience—that receives by far the greatest emphasis in the writings of Berdyaev, Eliot, Huxley, and Jung. Eliot, for example, recognizes that the purest and most direct apprehension of Reality can be achieved only during a timeless state of mystical consciousness. For "Time past and time future/Allow but a little consciousness./To be conscious is not to be in time."[11] Aldous Huxley also believes that "Deliverance is out of time into eternity," and that "Men achieve their Final End in a timeless moment of conscious experience."[12] Again, Berdyaev, while insisting upon an eschatological interpretation of human destiny, feels that in "creative" ecstasy man discovers "a way out from the time of this world, historical time and cosmic time."[13] And finally, Jung, who believes that man's end is self-awareness—a state of psychic wholeness attained only after the arduous integration of the "temporal" conscious and the "eternal" unconscious—confides that the richest moments of his life were nontemporal states of consciousness.[14]

Given this amendment of James's definition, however, is it possible to say that this mysticism is universally the same? For even though reports of mystical experiences appear to be unanimous in stressing James's "four marks," temporal transcendence, and (to amend James's definition once again) the achievement of unity or communion with a supernatural Reality, is it accurate to say that mysticism is always identical in form and content? The answer is no, for while all mystics may, for example, wish to transcend time, their methods of attaining liberation—as well as their concepts of Reality—often differ. In a provocative book written in response to Aldous Huxley's *Doors of Perception*, R. C. Zaehner maintains that there are three fundamental types of mystical experience, viz., pan-en-henic, monistic, and theistic.[15] Ignoring for the moment both the Oxford don's axe-grinding and the probability that there may be other varieties of preternatural experience, it is possible to use two of Zaehner's categories to contrast the mysticism of Eliot, Berdyaev, and Jung, on the one hand, and that of Huxley, on the other. Eliot and Berdyaev, for instance, are definitely theistic mystics. Their goal—the final cause of their spiritual quests—is to achieve personal communion with God in a timeless moment of consciousness or "creative" ecstasy. While Berdyaev is a fairly consistent dualist and Eliot—especially in later life—a convinced monist, both agree that the personality is not destroyed during mystical experience. As they see it, the mystic (and it should be recalled that both of these men believed to the marrow that they had actually transcended time during moments of mystical contemplation) establishes, in Martin Buber's phrase, an "I-Thou" relationship with God. God and man are joined together—united—but *ex hypothesi;* their communion precludes the elimination of their respective identities. They are one yet separate, united yet distinct. Aldous Huxley, on the other hand, denounces the "personalist" emphasis of Western theology, for he believes that it represents a disguised form of egotism. Behind the admonitions to worship the personality of Christ—behind the eloquent orations on the dignity of the human personality lies the narcissistic self-image of Western man. In opposition to the theist's concept of communion Huxley proposes the perennial philosophy's notion of nonpersonal union with the divine Ground. When, according to Huxley, the genuinely "theocentric" mystic establishes direct contact with eternity, his ego (as well as his "personality") is dissolved in the timeless and all-consuming depths of the Absolute (Brahman). He realizes that his individuality—his self— is an indissoluble and indistinguishable part of a larger and all-encompassing Self (Atman) and that, like time, the personality is an illusion that separates man from the divine Ground of all being. Huxley's mysticism is obviously monistic: he ultimately reduces every thing and every soul in the universe to One spiritual principle, Reality, the divine Ground, or eternity.

In contrast, C. G. Jung, while appreciating and recognizing the similarities between his own analytical psychology and Eastern religious thought, repudiates the notion of annihilating the personality. The psyche must be transformed but not eliminated. A balance, a dynamic equilibrium, should be established between consciousness and unconsciousness—an equilibrium that Jung calls the self, i.e., that condition of psychic wholeness symbolized by the mandala. During his middle years, and especially in later life, Jung regarded individuation (or the attainment of psychic integration) as an experience of timelessness. According to the Swiss psychologist, the collective unconscious and its contents (i.e., the archetypes) represent a spaceless and timeless mode of being. This statement is more than a hypothesis, for, in Jung's view, the intrinsic space-timelessness of the objective psyche has been proved by J. B. Rhine's ESP experiments.[16] The existence of telepathic phenomena, however, not only establishes the space-timelessness of the lower depths of the psyche, but indicates that there is another form of being behind the veil of the archetypes. Thus when a person becomes individuated, he not only participates in the timeless dimension of the collective unconscious but is provided with evidence of an "absolute object" upon which everything depends for its existence.

While Jung's mysticism may stand in complicated yet necessary relation to his general approach to the time-problem—i.e., to his concepts of archetypal configuration and synchronicity—his peculiar variety of mysticism appears to be closer to the theistic category of preternatural experience than either to the pan-en-henic or the monistic. Like the theist, for example, Jung not only defends the integrity of the personality but stresses the notion of conscious communion or participation in a timeless reality. In spite of these similarities, however, there remain two significant differences that preclude Jung's complete entrance into the theistic ranks: namely, his belief that Christ is a symbol of the self and his opinion that individuation is a psychological experience. And yet, it cannot be forgotten that Jung never denied the validity of Christianity, and that he not only believed that he had transcended time in a state of "completed individuation"[17] but that the unconscious impinges upon a form of existence outside space and time. Professor Zaehner tries to explain monistic and pan-en-henic mysticism (i.e., nature mysticism) in terms of Jungian psychology (thus, by implication, equating monistic and nature mysticism with genuine or incompleted individuation and, by explication, emancipating theistic mysticism from psychology). But it is obvious that Jung's kind of mysticism defies exact classification, and that, if it were to be categorized at all, it would be more accurate to place it on the fringes of the theistic variety of preternatural experience.

Although it is obvious that mysticism plays a cardinal role in Jung's relentless attack on the temporal process—a role that exceeds either synchronicity or myth in its importance—what priority does mysticism assume in the thought of Eliot, Huxley, and Berdyaev? For Eliot and Huxley, mysticism—the direct experience of eternity here and now—represents the most significant method of overcoming time. While (as both authors state explicitly in several of their essays on aesthetics) creativity may afford the individual a way of destroying time, mystical consciousness (even if it is only what Catholic theologians call "gratuitous graces" as opposed to full-blown mystical experiences) is by far the most exalted mode of liberation from the flux of events. Time the destroyer can be eliminated by the artist—or again by the mythologist who, for instance, may, like Eliot in "The Waste Land," transform the chaos of temporal existence into an ordered pattern by using the timeless themes of myth and legend. But it remains for the mystic to achieve the highest and most comprehensive triumph over the temporal process. It is true that it is occasionally possible to detect an undercurrent of what appears to be eschatological expectation in the works of Huxley and Eliot. And yet neither author relies on eschatology to destroy time. Indeed, both Eliot and Huxley spurn eschatological visions of man's destiny, and, if they seem to refer to the future in apocalyptic terms, it is not in a spirit of exultation but of despair. Berdyaev, on the other hand, does not interpret the apocalypse pessimistically. He regards it as the noblest creation of the divine-human partnership—the consummation of the story of man's estrangement from eternity. Mystical communion with God may allow the individual to escape the power of time for an ephemeral moment in eternity (or to anticipate the eventual resolution of the conflicts of history in the Age of the Spirit), but mysticism cannot destroy the phenomenon of time itself. It enables the individual to *transcend* time, but it does not, it cannot, assure mankind of a final victory over the temporal process. The only way, Berdyaev insists, to *abolish* time irrevocably is to create a metaphysic of history—to accept the apocalyptic hope, the fervent belief, of an approaching End to the historical process that will destroy every kind of time and restore man to his former "theandric" status (or Godman-hood). The difference between the thrust of Berdyaev's argument, however, and that of Eliot, Huxley, and Jung should not obscure the fundamental importance of their mutual agreement on the necessity of overcoming time. Not only do they use spatial symbols to order, control, and destroy time, not only do they base their belief that time can be eliminated on personal mystical experience but they insist unanimously that man can only achieve redemption and save the world from suicide by grounding his life in eternity.

The Historical Importance of Twentieth-century Antitemporalism

"Spatialization" and "mysticism," "time-symbols" and "eternity-images," "apocalyptic eschatology," "creativity," and "the direct experience of eternity"—each of these terms, each of these phrases, is representative of ancient and yet enduring responses to the problem of transcending or abolishing time. And yet, if these patterns of reaction—if these epistemological procedures and methods—are merely symptomatic or exemplary of traditional responses to the problem of mastering and overcoming the time of human experience, is there anything unusual about the twentieth-century revolt against time? In other words, what is the historical and sociological importance of twentieth-century hostility toward time? In the first place (and this should be stressed), this study is not simply concerned with four exceptional individuals (rare birds or intellectual freaks) who yearn to transcend or abolish time: such individuals—and this should be obvious by now—can be found in almost any age. And while it is important to note the antiquity and pervasive continuity of the desire to transcend time, it is equally important to recognize the unusual configurations this desire has assumed in the twentieth century. Berdyaev, Eliot, Huxley, and Jung, for example, were all at one time agnostics, atheists, or sceptics who believed in the intrinsic value of temporal civilization and endorsed some form of "time-philosophy", that is, a philosophy in which time—real duration or historical time—is substituted for eternity and in which reality is equated with time or becoming, such as Bergsonism (Eliot), the liberal idea of Progress (Huxley and Jung), and Marxism (Berdyaev). Yet shortly before or after the First World War and the Russian Revolution, these (and many other) intellectuals began to reconsider their metaphysical presuppositions, and, as a consequence, they eventually repudiated their secular world views. This reappraisal (to draw a succinct and systematic summary) ultimately took the form of: (1) a strong reaction or revulsion from the time of human experience, expressing itself in (a) a revolt against time-philosophy in all its protean shapes, and (b) a refusal to accept the identification of time with Reality; and (2) a denial of a previously held agnosticism, atheism, or scepticism, as well as a "conversion" to a traditional form of religious phenomenology, namely, mysticism (the entire quartet), and/or an acceptance of the dogma of an institutional religion (Eliot and, to some extent, Berdyaev).

This comprehensive reversal of attitudes (which in itself is an extraordinary phenomenon) exemplifies the experience, not only of my quartet, but of religious antitemporalists in general. For the majority of the thinking men and women who revolted against time in the early decades of this century did so by attacking time-philosophies and by discovering (or returning to) religion. They rebelled against the secularization of modern consciousness by challenging the hegemony of the idea of (temporal) change in contemporary thought. Thus their "conversions-in-reverse" were a direct reaction against the "Great Substitution" of the previous century; they rejected out of hand the *Ersatzreligionen* that had substituted time for eternity, history or becoming for timelessness. It is worth recalling here that "the word *secularization* came to mean what we now mean when we use it"—namely, "a growing tendency in mankind to do without religion, or to try to do without religion"[18]—in the forty or more years following the publication of the *Origin of Species* (1859). This was the period, rather than the late seventeenth century or the Enlightenment, that witnessed the *secularization of the European mind*[19]—a fact that underscores the revolutionary nature of the antitemporalists' dramatic change in outlook. They stood the secular movement on its head and proceeded to build a *Weltanschauung* that had its roots in a prescientific age. And while it is not unusual to find intellectuals in various historical periods who criticize their societies for lacking spiritual values, it is striking to discover so many who, at the close of an era recognized for its optimistic appraisal of human affairs, abandon their secular world views to adopt a hostile attitude toward time, history, and culture. Yet it is on this last point, more than any other, that the twentieth-century revolt against time distinguishes itself from other efforts to transcend temporality in the modern era. Not only, in other words, do the religious antitemporalists attack the ontological limitations of time and condemn all varieties of time-philosophy; they also single out "time" as a symptom of the "disease" afflicting Western civilization. Or, to put it another way, they couple their personal desire to transcend or abolish time with an attack on the (secular or time-obsessed) values of Western culture.[20] In particular, they frequently criticize the preeminent value placed in an advanced industrial civilization on "clock time" and its economic correlative, expressed in Benjamin Franklin's aphorism "Time is money." Their cultural criticism is thus indicative of the broad-scale protests against the increasing complexity and materialization of modern life.

The Late Nineteenth-Century Background

Protests against the dehumanization of life are obviously not unique to the twentieth century, and in fact, recent denunciations of the mechanization of human existence have their origin in different (yet related) currents of nineteenth-century thought. It is important to be aware of this background to the twentieth-century revolt against time. For although, in most cases, nineteenth-century protests against the materialization of life do not involve a concomitant attack on temporal process, they nevertheless exemplify a significant change in attitude toward Western culture that (especially in the years following World War I) eventually culminated in a repudiation of the overwhelming value placed on time by the optimists of *la belle époque*.

A Change in the Spirit of Europe

By a striking coincidence, the period of the nineteenth century (1871–1900) that demonstrated the greatest confidence in "materialism"—i.e., in an attitude toward life characterized by a pride in material accomplishments, a this-worldly pragmatism, and a "philosophy" dominated by material and mechanistic conceptions[21]—was also a period of growing dissatisfaction with the development of Western culture in general, and the quality of nineteenth-century life in particular. Yet the chorus of criticism—which gradually increases in volume from the depression years of the 1870s onward—had already announced itself prior to the commencement of what Carlton J. H. Hayes has called *A Generation of Materialism*. Karl Marx and Charles Kingsley, for instance, excoriated the established classes for exploiting the poor laborer, Honoré de Balzac satirized the crass materialism of the bourgeoisie, John Henry Newman attacked the religious and political "liberalism" of his contemporaries, and Matthew Arnold noted the deracination and anarchy, the confusing whirligig of new and ever-swarming ideas, in nineteenth-century culture—all before 1870. Still, as Benedetto Croce once observed, there is an important "change in the public spirit of Europe" after 1870—a change that represents an acceleration of the critique of nineteenth-century life already inaugurated by such men as Newman, Marx, and Arnold.

The "change" described by Croce represents an intellectual and political response to the long-range effects (to use E. J. Hobsbawm's terminology) of the "dual revolution"—the Democratic Revolution and the Industrial Revolution—as well as the dramatic growth of Europe's population, the subsequent birth of the "masses," and the increase in the rivalries among "nations" and "classes." The growing standardization of life coupled with the rapid materialization of middle-class values, the depreciation of the "inner world" of the spirit and the glorification of the machine, the burgeoning discontinuity and dissociation of European culture as well as the dangerously naive equation of technological advancement with human "progress"—all features of nineteenth-century life criticized by such men as Baudelaire, Carlyle, Dostoievski, Nietzsche, Burckhardt, Samuel Butler, and Alfred de Vigny—intensified the perplexities and dissatisfactions of intellectuals living during the three decades after the Franco-Prussian War.

Revolt against Positivism

The growing antagonism toward nineteenth-century culture reached its apogee during the 1890s. This is not to say that by the last decade of the century the majority of educated Europeans had renounced their "materialism" or their confidence in the future.[22] On the contrary, most Europeans seem to have remained steadfastly loyal to their faith in the inventiveness and productivity of Western civilization until 1916. Some, such as Walter Mehring's father, even thought that the turn of the century would bring the millennium. Nevertheless, the decade of the 1890s inaugurated an intensive reevaluation of the direction and purpose of European civilization—a reappraisal that was marked not only, as H. Stuart Hughes has pointed out, by a "revolt against positivism," but by a new preoccupation with "spiritism" or the "occult."[23]

In Germany, France, Italy, and England the renunciation of positivism took the form of "a growing awareness of the things of the spirit." The protest was registered in the works of philosophers, sociologists, historians, and poets, in the writings of intellectuals such as Wilhelm Windelband (who issued a "declaration of war against positivism"),[24] Henri Bergson (who attacked the quantitative and ratiocinative "fallacies" of modern thought), Max Weber (who stressed the priority of ideas in shaping the origin and development of "material" events, for example, modern capitalism), Benedetto Croce (who tried to emancipate history from science), or again George Meredith (who championed the life of the senses and defended the achievements of the spirit at the expense of positivism).[25] Yet the desire to "escape from materialism"[26] (of which the revolt against positivism is representative) was not limited to a repudiation of nineteenth-century "scientism." For there is another current of thought in the 1890s—the "discovery" of spiritism—which also marks a change, although perhaps a minor change, in the spirit of *fin de siècle* Europe. As early as 1875, the world-traveling Russian occultist Madame (Helena) Blavatsky founded the Theosophical Society in New York City. She and her successor Annie Besant were able to create a religious organization that continued to influence European intellectuals (either directly or indirectly, positively or negatively) into the twentieth century (e.g., Nicolas Berdyaev, T. S. Eliot, Aldous Huxley, W. B. Yeats, and Charles Williams). This new concern for mysticism and the occult (which finds its counterpart in two currents of twentieth-century thought, the Anthroposophical movement of Rudolf Steiner and the vogue of Eastern and Western mysticism) was given further impetus by the "spiritual" interest of Sir Oliver Lodge and Alfred Russel Wallace, as well as the founding of the Society for Psychical Research in 1882—a society that, through its investigation and research activities, anticipated some of the results of J. B. Rhine's ESP experiments in the 1930s.

While there may have been attempts to "escape from materialism" during the generation of materialism, while there may have been protests against the state of nineteenth-century culture, against the increasing "multitudinousness," "sick hurry," complexity, and mechanization of life—the protests and attempted escapes were not indicative of a widespread dissatisfaction with the "bourgeois century."[27] On the contrary, they were generally made by a minority of exceptional, often hypersensitive, individuals. Yet not only were the limits of the protest circumscribed, but, most significantly, the protesters themselves failed to isolate "time" in their diagnoses as an essential ingredient of the "modern malady." This point is important, for it is not until shortly before or after the First World War and the Russian Revolution that the critique of modern life—conducted, particularly after 1916, by a dramatically expanding spectrum of intellectuals—singles out "time" as a symptom of the "disease" affecting Western civilization.

The Impact of World War I

Now the correlation between the outbreak of the revolt against time, on the one hand, and the waning years of the nineteenth century and the commencement of World War I, on the other, is not an accident. Europe, it should be recalled, had not known a war that could compare in magnitude with the wars of the Napoleonic period for nearly a century when the guns of August shattered the *pax Victoriana* in 1914. Of course, there had been the Franco-Prussian War in 1870 and the Crimean fiasco sixteen years earlier, but, as of summer 1914— four years after what became the real "Recessional" of Edward VII's funeral— Great Britain and the Continent had experienced a hundred years of relative peace. The absence of a major war, however, could not disguise the existence of serious social, economic, and political problems—of the wretched plight, for example, of most of the working classes, of political revolution, of many-faceted "Decadence," or of the violent growth of nationalism. And yet (and this is a striking point) while they were evidently aware of the gravity and complexity of these conditions, three members of my quartet (C. G. Jung, T. S. Eliot, and Aldous Huxley), for instance, did not begin to translate their dissatisfaction with Western culture into an attack on time until the First World War. Berdyaev, on the other hand, had become sufficiently unsettled before the war by what he considered the decadence of nineteenth-century culture to advocate an idealistic version of Marxist revolution. But even Berdyaev, who had joined the Russian Orthodox church in 1912, continued (like Jung, Eliot, and Huxley) to maintain a positive attitude toward historical time until the war and (although he is ambivalent on this issue) perhaps as late as the Bolshevik assumption of power.

The delay in the commencement of their revolt against time can perhaps be partially explained by the fact that Berdyaev, Eliot, Huxley, and Jung (like antitemporalists in general) all came from the established classes of society. That is to say: although they were dissatisfied with the state of Western society, they tended to view the future with confidence or indifference because of the secure positions their families occupied in the social hierarchy. Thus, if this hypothesis is correct, the experience of an enormous catastrophe (the war or, in Berdyaev's case, the failure of the Russian Revolution) was necessary before these men could renounce their allegiance to time-philosophy. There would, however, seem to be another reason for the delay, and that is, quite simply, the factor of age. Whereas Berdyaev and Jung were nearing middle age at the beginning of the War, Huxley and Eliot were respectively twenty and twenty-six. In other words, it might be supposed that what appears to be a common (if not coordinated) effort to revolt against time could not have taken place until the younger members of the quartet had reached a greater maturity. But, as an examination of their life-histories demonstrates, these discrepancies in age are not crucial. And in fact, only a few years (and in some instances perhaps no more than a few months) actually separate the independent development of their antagonistic attitudes toward time, and their identification of their attack on temporal process with an attack on Western culture.

The Engagement of a Quartet

The importance that Berdyaev, Eliot, Huxley, Jung, and other prominent religious antitemporalists ascribe to mysticism—perhaps even more than that which they accord to "spatialization" or the quest for timelessness in myth—has encouraged critics to regard the twentieth-century revolt against time as an example of sheer escapism—a manifestation of an invalid, if not cowardly, reluctance to confront the challenging complexities of modern life. Their attempt to transcend the ontological dimensions of time; their vigorous effort to move beyond history, time-philosophy, and the idea of Progress; and their equally forceful struggle to overcome religious scepticism by "re-creating" the concept of eternity from the images and metaphors of symbolic language have been too quickly interpreted as indications of a concerted endeavor to avoid the anxieties generated by a civilization in crisis. Yet it would be a mistake to view the protagonists of the twentieth-century revolt against time as escapists. For rather than experiencing a "failure of nerve," or withdrawing, like Koestler's yogi, from active participation in the affairs of the world, antitemporalists like Berdyaev, Eliot, Huxley, and Jung have responded energetically to the problems facing our time. It might be true that they have, to borrow Charles Frankel's phrase, "re-discovered sin," or the constancy of human imperfection, and they they have abandoned the optimistic anthropology of the nineteenth century. But their abandonment of the facile anthropocentric optimism of the previous century does not mean that they have abandoned humanity. For while they question the validity of Western culture, and while they are directly concerned with their own attempts to transcend or abolish time, they also suggest positive measures by which to improve the sad state of the West (and, by implication, the entire world). They refuse to accept the role of ivory-tower philosophers, for they are vitally concerned with man's fate in the modern world. This *engagement* should not be depreciated, for although they believe that man's greatest achievement is the transcendence of time in mystical intuition or the eschatological destruction of the temporal process, they would like every person to establish contact with reality. Thus they stressed the necessity of a massive reorientation of human values, a universal endorsement of the belief in spiritual reality, and a thorough-going denial of the ultimate importance of things in time. But they were not always confident that man would change the structure of his consciousness, effect a spiritual revolution, or transform the nightmare of history into sweetness and light. And yet, Berdyaev, Eliot, Huxley, and Jung persisted in diagnosing what they thought were the causes of twentieth-century ills; they continued to suggest remedies. For they never gave up trying to convince human beings of their higher calling and spiritual dignity—they never stopped insisting that man's final end lay outside the ontological limitations of the ephemeral universe in an eternal reality that could be apprehended by human beings in time.

Notes

1. See J. A. Gunn, *The Problem of Time* (London: George Allen & Unwin, 1929), p. 173f. and Hans Meyerhoff, *Time in Literature* (Berkeley: Univ. of California, 1960), pp. 1–26.

2. Cf. H. G. Alexander, *Time as Dimension and History* (Albuquerque: Univ. of New Mexico, 1945), pp. 13f.

3. Milic Capek, *The Philosophical Impact of Contemporary Physics* (New York: Van Nostrand, 1961), p. 162.

4. Henri Bergson appears to have been the first to criticize "the fallacy of spatialization" in his *Essai sur les données de la conscience*. The *Essai* (which was thought out and written during the period from 1883 to 1887) was originally published in 1889. An English edition *(Time and Free Will)* was brought out in 1910. Further works worth conferring (besides those of Bergson and Capek) on the problem of "spatialization" are: Ernst Cassirer's *The Philosophy of Symbolic Forms*, II, and *Essay on Man*, Susanne Langer's *Philosophy in a New Key*, John Gunnell's *Political Philosophy and Time*, and C. G. Jung's essays on mandala symbolism, e.g., in *The Archetypes and the Collective Unconscious*, Carl Hentze's *Mythes et symboles lunaires*, Alfonso Ortiz's *The Tewa World*, Mircea Eliade's *Cosmos and History*, F. M. Cornford's *From Religion to Philosophy*, Heinrich Zimmer's *Myths and Symbols in Indian Art*, *Man and Time* (Eranos) ed. J. Campbell, Erwin Panofsky's *Studies in Iconology*, Ananda Coomaraswamy's *The Dance of Shiva*, and M. H. Nicolson's *Breaking of the Circle*.

5. T. S. Eliot, *The Complete Poems and Plays, 1909–1950* (New York: Harcourt, Brace, 1962), pp. 124, 96.

6. For Berdyaev "cosmic time" represents the cyclical time of the physical universe. "Historical time," on the other hand, is synonymous with the divine-human drama which—as a finite series of unique events—unfolds as a linear (and dialectical) progression. Finally—to augment what has been said above—"existential time" designates the nontemporal time or period of world history (viz., the Age of the Spirit, which is symbolized by a point) that precedes the final destruction of the time-process.

7. Eliot, *Complete Poems and Plays*, p. 144.

8. Aldous Huxley, *Island* (New York: Bantam, 1965), pp. 170–173.

9. William James, *The Varieties of Religious Experience* (New York: Mentor, 1961), pp. 292–293.

10. Ibid., p. 293.

11. Eliot, *Complete Poems and Plays*, p. 119.

12. Aldous Huxley, *The Perennial Philosophy* (New York: Harper, 1944), p. 165. *Collected Essays* (New York: Bantam, 1960), p. 233.

13. Nicolas Berdyaev, *The Beginning and the End*, trans. R. M. French (London: Bles, 1952), p. 177.

14. C. G. Jung, *Memories, Dreams, Reflections*, trans. Richard and Clara Winston (New York: Pantheon, 1963). *Erinnerungen, Träume, Gedanken* (Zurich: Rascher Verlag, 1962), pp. 298–299.

15. R. C. Zaehner, *Mysticism: Sacred and Profane* (New York: Oxford University Press, 1961), p. 30f.

16. According to Professor Rhine, the existence of *extra*sensory modes of perception—which, he assures us, has been established by reliable experimentation—such as clairvoyance, precognition, telepathy, and intuition, proves unequivocally that part of man's nature is nonphysical. Man's ability to anticipate or predict events, to perceive distant states of affairs, and to know the thoughts of others intuitively, means—the conclusion is inescapable—that the human mind transcends "the organic functions of the material brain." Rhine goes further, however, and not only posits the existence of a "psychical oversoul," but the probability of immortality. The discovery that ESP can "function without limitation from time and space" is "taken to mean that the mind is capable of action independent to some degree of the space-time system of nature. Now" [and this is Rhine's conclusion] since "all that immortality means is freedom from the effects of space and time," it follows "as a logical derivation from the ESP research" that "there is at least some sort of technical survival" after death. J. B. Rhine, *The Reach of the Mind* (New York: William Sloane, 1962), pp. 206, 211, 213.

17. Jung, *Memories, Dreams, Reflections*, p. 296; *Erinnerungen, Träume, Gedanken*, p. 300.

18. Owen Chadwick, *The Secularization of the European Mind in the Nineteenth Century* (Cambridge: Cambridge Univ. Press, 1975), pp. 17–18.

19. Ibid., p. 11.

20. Examples of this attitude can be found in nineteenth-century thought (cf., for instance, the work of Schopenhauer). But the few nineteenth-century intellectuals who may qualify as "rebels against time" (in the sense that the term is used above) are not representative of a major pattern of nineteenth-century opinion. Indeed, they (as opposed to Berdyaev, Eliot, Huxley, and Jung, as well as the many other twentieth-century intellectuals who share their hostility to time) often appear to be isolated from the main currents of contemporary thought. Furthermore, it should be noted that even the ("non-Hegelian") Idealists, who flourished in the 1890s and early years of the twentieth century, did not aim their attack on time against nineteenth- (or twentieth-) century culture. Nor, for that matter, did the Theosophists or, apparently, the members of the Society for Psychical Research. For while they may have been interested in mysticism, in communing with supernatural powers, they did not interpret their desire to transcend time as a repudiation of the presuppositions of the "Bourgeois Century." On the contrary, as Carlton Hayes has pointed out, the program of the Theosophical Society represented but one of "many different ways of being enlightened and progressive." (*A Generation of Materialism*, p. 332.)

21. Carlton J. H. Hayes, *A Generation of Materialism* (New York: Harper Torchbook, 1963), p. 328.

22. W. W. Wagar, *Good Tidings, The Belief in Progress from Darwin to Marcuse* (Bloomington: Indiana Univ. Press, 1972), pp. 23–28.

23. "Positivism" refers to what Carlton Hayes would call the philosophical side of materialism, or, in other words, a form of thinking characterized by the use of analogies drawn from both Newtonian mechanics and Darwinian biology. One of the earliest discussions of the revolt against positivism is found in Alfred Fouillée's *Le mouvement idéaliste et la réaction contre la science positive* (Paris: Alcan, 1896). For further discussion of the revolt, see Franklin Baumer, *Modern European Thought* (New York: Macmillan, 1977), pp. 371–378, and Wagar, *Good Tidings*, p. 27, as well as Hughes's *Consciousness and Society*, cited below.

24. H. Stuart Hughes, *Consciousness and Society* (New York: Vintage, 1958), pp. 59, 47.

25. F. M. Cornford, "The Poems of George Meredith," *Supplement to the Working Men's College* (a lecture delivered Mar. 21, 1903), pp. 103–118.

26. Hayes, *A Generation of Materialism*, p. 332.

27. For a discussion of the growing uncertainty about the condition of Western civilization in late nineteenth-century thought, see Franklin Baumer, *Main Currents of Western Thought* (New York: Knopf, 1970), pp. 451–459 and *Modern European Thought*, pp. 389–400; and Richard Altick, *Victorian People and Ideas* (New York: W. W. Norton, 1973), pp. 107–113. I should note here my agreement with Warren Wagar that, although the number of critics increased after the 1870s, most thinking Europeans in *la belle époque* continued to believe in the vitality of their civilization until the First World War. Cf. Wagar, *Good Tidings*, pp. 23–28.

XI

In Complicity with Words: The Asymptotic Consciousness of E. M. Cioran

MICHAEL W. MESSMER

I

> What I know at sixty, I knew as well at twenty. Forty years of a long, a superfluous, labor of verification.
>
> E. M. Cioran, *The Trouble with Being Born*[1]

Cioran's dour dismissal of a lifetime of writing invites questions: if the labor was superfluous, why have bothered? if the initial insight remained unchanged, why the necessity of verification? Since one must age in order to have a younger self to serve as benchmark for rendering judgment on one's career, perhaps Cioran merely registers here a certain astonishment at (and honest acceptance of) the late realization that his life's work had been repetitive and redundant. The difficulty of such an admission would be matched only by its bitterness.

Like so many of Cioran's brief, aphoristic fragments, this one admits of another interpretation than that of retrospective recognition of excessive and unnecessary labor. Later in the same work he wrote: "For to repeat yourself is to prove that you still believe in yourself, and in what you have said."[2] Repetition, then, may not be superfluous at all; rather, it may be confirmatory, a way of securing both the self and what is said. Thus viewed, Cioran's work over several decades assumes the character of a continual elaboration upon and reworking of insights won early, a labor of necessity, hardly superfluous. And it is a labor executed with marked consistency as well. Cioran's mind does not change, his thought does not develop from one position to another, manifested in one book after another. Rather, he circles a perimeter, staking markers along it, in an attempt to keep constantly in view, albeit from different perspectives, that central vision which he claims he knew as well at twenty as at sixty. Or, changing the image, Cioran's is an asymptotic view, forever approaching but never attaining a point of direct contact with his subjects. He is a thinker who consistently seeks a position in the margins, away from the center.

This marginality is first of all that of the displaced intellectual. Cioran is one of that multitude of men and women dislodged from their native lands in post-World War I Europe who rooted themselves in other, unfamiliar countries and who then continued or began careers of significance and influence in their new environments. This diaspora of Europe's intellectuals is a major chapter in the history of the twentieth century, and the recent focus upon the transatlantic phase of the dispersion is only part of the story.

Cioran himself left his native Rumania for Paris in 1937 at the age of twenty-six and then remained there. An even more wrenching change came a decade later when he began writing in French, "the hardest experience I have ever undergone."[3] As in the case of Samuel Beckett, with whose career Cioran's has parallels and points of contact, the discipline required to effect this language switch was strenuous, but rewarding.[1] Just as Beckett's great burst of creative activity in the six years after 1945 began with his move into French, so too Cioran's first book in French, *Précis de décomposition*, published in 1949, brought him a modicum of attention and, more significantly, established concerns that would remain central for him. Unlike Beckett, however, Cioran's assimilation of French left him with a "feeling of uneasiness" that led him "to ponder the problem of style and the very *anomaly* of writing."[5] Caught in the web of language, cast into expatriate status, Cioran became (and has remained) acutely sensitive to the intricacies and depths of the human complicity with words.

In a short essay on the "Advantages of Exile" he contemplated the consequences of an expatriate's decision to adopt a new language: "Will he venture into another idiom? It will not be easy for him to renounce the words on which his past hinges. A man who repudiates his language for another changes his identity, even his disappointments. Heroic apostate, he breaks with his memories and, to a certain point, with himself."[6] Later in this short meditation Cioran provides a different but related perspective on his marginality from that which the consequences of a change of language provided. He suggests that exile begins as "an academy of intoxication," resembling "the extremity of the poetic state." Exile is natural for the poet, but extremely difficult to attain and maintain. Cioran employs two examples: "Think of Rilke, that expatriate *de luxe*, and of the number of solitudes he had to accumulate in order to liquidate his connections, in order to establish a foothold in the invisible. It is not easy to be *nowhere*, when no external condition obliges you to do so." Similarly, think of the "monstrous efforts" the mystic must mount to attain his or her *askesis*. "To

extricate oneself from the world—what a labor of abolition!" The exile, however, attains such abolition, at least in the beginning, "without turning a hair,
by the cooperation—i.e., the hostility—of history." Like disease in the case of
an invalid, so the "force of circumstance" in the case of the expatriate acts to
"strip him of everything" and to place him "without the detours of a discipline,
by no more than the benevolence of fatality" into that "limit-situation" of exile
which resembles the poetic state.

The danger, however, is that an exile may adapt to his fate, may *establish*
himself, even revel in the enforced state of detachment, and thereby erode "the
substance of his emotions, the resources of his misery as well as his dreams of
glory." When the wounds have healed and the cries become bitterness, he will
be "the epigone of his pains," his lyrical career will be over, and two choices
will remain: either faith, in the form of prayer or a "reassuring metaphysic," or
sarcasm and mockery.

The implication is that the exile, to avoid the choice of piety or sarcasm,
eventually must *will* the initial being-nowhere to which the impress of events
brought him. Such maintenance of marginality will require the effort of a Rilke
or of a mystic. Cioran consistently refused both piety and sarcasm although both
clearly tempted him, and instead sought to retain that "foothold in the invisible"
which exile initially bequeathed but which adoption of French threatened to
erode. Cioran's spiritual territory is bounded by Rilke's mastery of the word and
the mystics' mastery of wordlessness, "somewhere between the epigram and the
sigh."[7] This "fanatic of elliptical gloom," in seeking to be more detached and
more alien to everything than anyone else, eventually found that even indifference could become the basis of fanaticism.[8]

Despite the strenuous effort Cioran has expended to retain a position of
separateness, there are numerous points at which he seems to make direct
contact with his times, thus providing his reader with ample opportunity to
"place" him in the wider currents of twentieth-century intellectual life. Indeed,
when such an effort has been made, Cioran appears to share enough affinities
with the major concerns of contemporary European thinkers so that there is a
temptation to label him a "representative" or "symptomatic" figure, precisely
the opposite characterization from that "marginal" status which he sought. Such
a typing of Cioran serves to clarify the possible places that may be located for
him in the intellectual history of Europe in this century, but threatens at the
same time to diminish his singularity.

Susan Sontag offers one such placement by situating Cioran's writing in the
tradition of responses to the nineteenth-century collapse of philosophical sys-
tem-building. In the post-Hegelian European intellectual world, she argues,
two responses to the decay of philosophical systems were made: the rise of
ideologies, systems of thought that were "aggressively anti-philosophical,"
exemplified by Comte, Marx, Freud, and the early pioneers in the social sci-

ences and linguistics; and the rise of a new kind of philosophizing, antisystematic, lyrical, aphoristic, personal, of which Kierkegaard, Nietzsche, and Wittgenstein were the chief exemplars. She suggests that Cioran is the most distinguished exponent of this latter tradition writing at present, and does so with justification.[9]

In *A Short History of Decay* Cioran bade his "Farewell to Philosophy." "We begin to live authentically," he wrote, "only where philosophy ends, at its wreck, when we have understood its terrible nullity, when we have understood that it was futile to resort to it, that it is *no help*."[10] Philosophy was for him "the recourse of all who would elude the corrupting exuberance of life." In this typically short essay an opposition emerges between philosophers (Kant is Cioran's example) and the Old Testament, Bach, and Shakespeare. Have the thoughts of philosophers "materialized into a single page that is equivalent to one of Job's explanations, of Macbeth's terrors, or the altitude of one of Bach's cantatas?" The question is followed by an assertion that will remain Cioran's throughout his work: "We do not *argue* the universe; we *express* it. And philosophy does not express it." The great philosophical systems were no more than "brilliant tautologies," "mere proliferation of words," "subtle displacements of meaning." The originality of philosophers is merely the inventing of terms, and they have succeeded in engulfing us in a "pleonastic universe" surfeited with invented meanings.

Later in the same book Cioran rings a different, somewhat less strident note on this theme of the weakness of philosophy when he suggests that: "All means and methods of knowing are valid: reasoning, intuition, disgust, enthusiasm, lamentation. A vision of the world propped on concepts is no more legitimate than another which proceeds from tears, arguments, or sighs—modalities equally probing and vain. . . . The merest illiterate and Aristotle are equally irrefutable—and fragile."[11] Philosophy takes its place as one among many human ways—all incomplete—of experiencing the world. Twenty-four years later, in *The Trouble with Being Born*, the same ideas appear. "Each opinion, each view is necessarily partial, truncated, inadequate. In philosophy and in anything, originality comes down to incomplete definitions." Or: "Aristotle, Aquinas, Hegel—three enslavers of the mind. The worst form of despotism is the *system*, in philosophy and in everything."[12]

Cioran's deflation of the position of philosophy extends as well to philosophy's history. Writing in *The Temptation to Exist* he claimed that "the history of ideas is no more than a parade of labels converted into so many absolutes," just as seven years earlier he had argued that "it is time that philosophy, casting discredit upon Truth, freed itself from all capital letters."[13] Such a rejection of history is a leitmotif in Cioran's writing, a consequence of which is a vehement rejection of any and all "Truths." "What we call truth is an error insufficiently experienced, not yet drained, but which will soon age, a new error, and which waits to compromise its novelty."[11] "Truth" and "lie" are "mere words, one worth no more than the other, signifying nothing."[15]

Cioran's effort is, not to eliminate philosophy, but rather to *reduce* it, to *mere* philosophy. Such a circumscription of philosophy's tasks is congruent with Nietzsche's distrust of system and consistency and recalls Wittgenstein's enigmatic last sentence to the *Tractatus Logico-Philosophicus:* "What we cannot speak about we must pass over in silence."[16] Sontag's location of Cioran appears justifiable. And yet, as so often with this figure who counsels "Thinking Against Oneself," there is a doubt: is it not *too easy* to see him within the "tradition" of Kierkegaard, Nietzsche, and Wittgenstein, although clear affinities appear?[17]

The critic Edward Said finds a different niche for Cioran, even closer to *au courant* concerns than those invoked by Sontag, when he suggests that it is in the work of Roland Barthes and Jacques Derrida that Cioran's writing finds appropriate theoretical measure. Barthes's "writing at degree zero" and Derrida's critical scrutiny of writing as *mere* writing provide a perspective that can encompass Cioran's peculiar distrust of and complicity with the written word.[18] More evocative still is a further suggestion of Said's, that Cioran's relationship to the essay form is analogous to that of Jorge Luis Borges to the novel. He proposes that "when we read both writers we are constantly in the presence of the mask and of the apocryphal utterance, one undercutting the other, and so on until we are tired out by the unceasing game."[19] Images of masks and apocrypha ought to provide a cautionary warning to any and all attempts to see Cioran within one particular tradition or as typical of one current of thought or another.

And yet, two critics of great acumen have constructed plausible causes for him as a truly contemporary thinker, manifesting if not immersed in the crucial cultural concerns of the present. This contemporaneity is captured by Charles Newman, who fuses Sontag's and Said's perceptions:

> Cioran is clearly a self-styled straddler of the modern and post-modern eras. In his rigor, his erudition, his hatred of the dissolution of language, his formalism which constitutes its own morality, he is a legitimate heir to the great European modernists. But whereas the modernists never doubted their capacity to construct imaginary edifices against a world which revolted them, the post-modern era is characterized by a revulsion against our very means and materials, a hatred of our minds coextensive with our hatred for what passes for the world. Cioran stands for us, then, as that rarest of thinkers—a crucial transitional figure who occupies not a place so much as a synapse in the devolution of Western thought.[20]

Cioran himself might appreciate the synaptic position he is granted here, for, after all, a synapse *is* a place. It is a gap, nowhere, an empty space—precisely the location Cioran has with great consistency claimed for himself.

Still another of the many indices of Cioran's modernity is an extended diatribe that runs continuously through his work against the tyranny of history and the cancer of time.[21] "*Yesterday, today, tomorrow*—these are servants' categories. . . . I was, I am, or I shall be—a question of grammar and not of existence."[22] History is "a monster we have called up against ourselves, a fatality we cannot escape"; Hegel's heresy, the evolving absolute, "has become our dogma, our tragic orthodoxy, the philosophy of our *reflexes*"; our disease is "Centuries of attention to time, the idolatry of becoming."[23] "The burden of becoming," "the weight of history," "the terror of chronology"—all weigh upon modern consciousness, which has responded with the desire "to pulverize the *acquired*" that Cioran says is "the essential tendency of the modern mind."[24] History, that "inessential mode of being, the most effective form of our infidelity to ourselves, a metaphysical refusal" constitutes only an "indecent alloy of banality and apocalypse" and a "factory of ideals."[25] Seldom has more vituperation been poured upon the modern historicist consciousness, precipitant of "the fall into time."[26]

However, there is another side. In a characteristic selfward gesture, Cioran describes himself as having fallen *out* of time, having escaped the tyranny of Becoming. The escape, though, is of dubious benefit. To fall from time, to suspend Becoming is to "sink into the inert, into the absolute stagnation where the Word itself bogs down, unable to rise to blasphemy or prayer."[27] This posttemporal state Cioran describes with images of sterility, asphyxia, and of an abyss. Struggling to escape Time's clutches he has discovered only ennui and—paradox!—an "unslaked nostalgia for time." Cioran suggests that his own experience, where time is "sealed off, . . . out of reach," may very well be a prefiguration of the future experience of many. Crises such as his with time "are signs which we must get used to interpreting." The fate of humankind is to be subject to a double fall, the first into time out of eternity, the second out of time into—what? This "possible, even inevitable" second fall, after which humans will cease to be historical animals, Cioran suspects will precipitate a state of unremitting ennui, in which the "unslaked nostalgia for time" will condemn human beings to ruminate upon their double loss of both eternity *and* time.

There is an ambiguity embedded in this essay on "The Fall Out of Time." Cioran says that he has suffered the second fall, but there remains a lingering doubt based on the very fact that he *is writing about* that fall. Cioran has not yet reached that "absolute of stagnation" when the Word bogs down completely. Here, teetering on the brink of the fall from time and out of history, he takes his stand: against time, against history, but condemned to use the enemy's weapon, writing. For it is not the time of lived experience that has incurred Cioran's ire, but what he calls a "new time grafted onto the old one, . . . time elaborated and projected . . . objectivized. . . ." History, therefore, is "to go time one better, to add to its moments *our own*." It is the new time grafted onto the old with that most sophisticated instrument of projection and elaboration—writing—which has become virulent, monstrous; history is "a fatality we cannot escape, even by recourse to the formulas of passivity, the recipes of wisdom."[28] As Said has noted, writing is a moving image of time, proceeding by addition, with letters and words added to the past sum of writing, just as moments are added to a prior sum.[29] Cioran has repeatedly characterized Western civilization as exhausted, winded, sterile. Frequently he has recourse to a comparison that has become virtually a stereotype in twentieth-century cultural discourse: the present is comparable either to Alexandrian Greece or late Rome, times of decline and decadence, of barbarism and overcivilization. Cioran's response to the burden of history and the compulsion to write has been a stern commitment to a search for that mode of writing which would add the least to an already existing burden and at the same time prevent a fall out of time.

II

> . . . where I am, I don't know, I'll never know, in the silence you don't know, you must go on, I can't go on, I'll go on.
>
> Samuel Beckett, *The Unnamable*[30]

At about the time he was writing *The Unnamable*, Beckett engaged in a series of dialogues with Georges Duthuit in which he echoed the novel's closing lines: "The expression that there is nothing to express, nothing with which to express, no power to express, no desire to express, together with the obligation to express."[31] Beckett's submission to the "obligation to express" made him one of the twentieth century's greatest writers. As Cioran noted about him: "Words—will anyone love them as much as he has?"[32] Like Beckett, Cioran labored under the obligation to express and became a great lover of words. Like the protagonist in *The Unnamable*, he cannot stop writing; he must go on. In *The Temptation to Exist* he suggests the depths of his commitment to words: "Shards of instinct, nonetheless, compel me to cling to words. Silence is unbearable: what strength it takes to settle into the concision of the Inexpressible! It is easier to renounce bread than speech." He will continue even in the face of the fact that writing a book is "a repetition of our Fall" (i.e., the fall into time) and in the face as well of the ever-present danger that the verbal will turn to "verbiage, to literature."[33]

Cioran proceeds to an explicit connection between writing and thinking: both tend toward dilution and inflation. The "natural movement" of thought is expansive, "for the mind needs words *en masse*, without which, turned upon itself, it ruminates upon its impotence." Thinking becomes for Cioran an art of repeating. Just as the danger in writing is excess, the verbal become verbiage, so the tendency of thought is toward inflation: "Whence our systems, whence our philosophies."[34] The cumulative impact of these inflationary scriptive and mental processes is to squeeze the life out of words, to exhaust them, erode them, suffocate them under their own mounting weight. This is Cioran's depiction of the condition of modern consciousness and its transcribers, a situation in which: "There is nothing to say about anything. So there can be no limit to the number of books."[35] "Shall I tell you what I really think?" Cioran asks in a letter to a friend. "Every word is a word *de trop*. Yet the question is: to write. Let us write. . . , let us dupe each other."[36]

Under such conditions as these, however, to write as Cioran writes, in fragments, aphorisms, short essays, obsessed with brevity, vowing "never to sin against blessed concision," is to paralyze the mind, to throw a spanner in its networks, to prevent the cascade of words en masse that is the prerequisite of what in the modern world passes for intellectual progress.[37] This is a painful process, whose results are at times painful to read and apparently painful for Cioran to have written. The ideal remedy for this linguistic erosion, where words have become carrion, in need of burial, would appear to be absolute silence, *no* writing of any kind. This Cioran has always recognized: "To refresh language, humanity would have to stop talking: it would resort profitably to signs, or more effectively, to silence."[38] That way has been closed for him, however, for he is "still in complicity with words, and if I am seduced by silence I dare not enter it, I merely prowl on its peripheries."[39] Peripheral, marginal, Cioran seeks *askesis* through writing, "the least ascetic of all actions."[40] Total detachment would imply indifference to language and insensitivity to words, and Cioran could not go that far. To lose contact with words would be to lose contact with human beings completely; to withdraw confidence from them would be to put one foot into the abyss.[41] Hence he has remained "infected by Letters," "suspended between speech and silence," conjoined to words, dominated by them.[42]

The foci which that domination and suspension have taken—the fragment, the aphorism, the essay—thus become crucial in any assessment of Cioran. Several considerations arise. The first recalls the earlier discussion of marginality. Cioran is a writer of vast, if somewhat eccentric, erudition that ranges over the corpus of Western thought from the early Greeks onward. And it is not just the "major" figures who have captured his attention. For example, in his short essay "Dealing with the Mystics," the scope of allusion includes Meister Eckhart, Angelus Silesius, Luis of Léon, John of the Cross, Peter of Alcantara, Jakob Boehme, Margaret Ebner, Angela of Foligno—clearly Cioran finds this familiar spiritual territory.[43] Here, as everywhere in his writing, the erudition is worn lightly, unobtrusively, indeed, is marginal to Cioran's arguments. Many of his short fragments have the character of marginalia, brief comments on texts that are not present. In effect he places marginalia at the center of a page, displacing a central text to the periphery, even beyond the page itself. This procedure is especially clear in *Syllogismes de l'amertume* and *The Trouble with Being Born*. Such displacement accounts for the somewhat disconcerting feeling a reader of Cioran has that unseen presences from within the traditions of Western culture hover over his shoulder, as well as the equally disconcerting sense that something is being held back, retained, left unsaid by Cioran himself. But, if Cioran is to be believed, that is precisely the point: concision, verbal economy, scriptoral askesis are not only stylistic devices; they are the necessary means to reduce to a minimum the writer's complicity in the accumulating detritus of modern verbiage.

A related point emerges from a brief glance at the etymology of the word "aphorism." The original Greek root from which it derives had the sense of setting boundaries, as with markers.[44] An aphorism may be plausibly construed as a linguistic marker, and in Cioran's case that sense is peculiarly appropriate, for his fragments and aphorisms limn the boundary between writing and silence, that periphery he has continually prowled throughout his career.

In his recent book on La Rochefoucauld, a writer whom Cioran greatly admires, Philip Lewis makes some instructive comments concerning the *Maximes* that usefully illumine Cioran's work as well. Lewis raises several hypotheses to account for the apparent fragmentation of the great moralist's book or— by extension—any book so constructed, as Cioran's more aphoristic works are. His first suggestion is methodological, emphasizing the autonomy of each maxim. From this perspective, "Each maxim would be a blow administered by a demolition expert whose basic task is ex-posing or de-structuring. . . ." As a rhetorical instrument the maxim would reflect an unwillingness to accept either the logical or epistemological restraints of any discursive language or systematized position. "Set in the context of such linguistic reticence, the language of the maxim, as it suddenly erupts from the wisdom of silence, would resound with unprecedented force."[45] The desire to ex-pose, the hostility to system, and the linkage of wisdom and silence all manifest themselves in Cioran's work.

A second suggestion of Lewis's is also relevant here. He proposes that the discontinuity of the *Maximes* is itself a sign conveying their ultimate message. The accumulation of disjointed fragments militates against the continuous generation of meaning that a search for truth in a discursive mode would enjoin. The legitimacy of such a search would be directly challenged by the very disjointedness of the work's structure.[46] Again, the insight is appropriate to Cioran, whose distrust of rational discourse is an ever-present theme.

The fragmentariness of Cioran's writing does admit the possibility of (briefly) sustained argument, but the distrust of system remains paramount.[47] This raises yet a third point, namely, the demands that reading Cioran makes on his audience. Nietzsche was acutely aware of the problems involved. In the preface to *On The Genealogy of Morals*, he wrote: "people find difficulty with the aphoristic form: this arises from the fact that today this form is *not taken seriously enough.* An aphorism, properly stamped and molded, has not been 'deciphered' when it has simply been read; rather, one has then to begin its *exegesis,* for which is required an art of exegesis." He then goes on to point out that the third essay in his book, the famous "What Is the Meaning of Ascetic Ideals?" is itself a commentary upon its prefixed aphorism. His final remark is that the ingredient necessary to understanding his writing has been "unlearned" by "modern man"; the ingredient is rumination.[48] Two comments are in order. First, the prefixed aphorism to Nietzsche's third essay in the *Genealogy* is one of his own, taken from *Thus Spake Zarathustra.* That art of reading Nietzsche demands is thus an art of reading one's own work. Second, Cioran himself noted that an obsession with brevity paralyzes the mind's progress and prevents it from accumulating those words en masse that it requires and without which it turns in upon itself and "*ruminates* upon its own impotence." He then goes on to suggest that writers who favor "an approximate but piquant formula to an evident but insipid reasoning" amuse themselves at the expense of "truths."[49] The rejection of systematic discourse is as well a rejection of its "truths," both in Nietzsche and in Cioran.

This is not to suggest that each of Cioran's aphorisms (or any of them) required of him or his readers an exegesis such as Nietzsche provided in "What Is the Meaning of Ascetic Ideals?" But it does suggest another meaning to the fragment prefixed to the beginning of this essay. Cioran's long labor over his early insights is an exercise in self-interpretation, an exegesis of the nature and (for him) the inevitability of writing. It is why he can with justification say that all of his books are autobiographical.[50]

A further implication centers on the process of writing *about* Cioran. It is clear that to expound him, to explicate him, is to enter into complicity with the process of word accumulation that he himself rejects. It is to add further to the burden of history. This in turn suggests that anyone concerned with Cioran's writing will find himself slipping away from the ostensible subject and writing reflexively. That is to say, the historian or the critic will end up writing as much about themselves as about Cioran. This helps to explain the ease with which he may be placed within any number of the main currents of modern thought.

III

It would be far easier for me to live without a trace of belief than without a trace of doubt. Devastating doubt, nourishing doubt!
                    E. M. Cioran, *The Trouble with Being Born*[51]

Where, then, *is* Cioran? Mocker of all traditions, yet he seems to take a place within many of them. To cite a final example, the philosopher William

Gass has described *The Temptation to Exist* as "a philosophical romance on modern themes: alienation, absurdity, boredom, futility, decay, the tyranny of history, the vulgarities of change, awareness as agony, reason as disease."[52] This makes Cioran sound like the archetypal existentialist. Similarly, his interrogation of writing *does* link him with contemporary French critical activity as practiced by Barthes, Derrida, and others. This is especially the case when the "deconstructive" practice of such figures as Derrida is seen as "a commentary written in the margin of other philosophical and literary texts," a mode of criticism that is a "style of accusation."[53] Again, there appear to be affinities between Cioran and this currently fashionable French assault on Western intellectual history since Plato. Equally plausibly, Cioran may be seen as a connoisseur of civilizational decline and decadence in the Spenglerian mode, or as an apostle of unbelief in one of its modern variants, that one in which the thirst for lost religious traditions or unattainable ones (Eastern religions, for example) leads to the taste of nothing but the dryness and aridity of modern spiritual life after the disappearance and death of God. It is a taste so continually indulged that many have come to savor it.

Such categorization may proceed ad infinitum. Cioran knows it; indeed, his writing encourages it. Where, then, does *he* place himself? He conceives his era as the final arid stage of a "winded civilization," an Alexandrian time of desiccation, spiritual dryness, and sterility. Images of airlessness, of exhaustion, of the inability to *give vent* abound in Cioran's descriptions of the cultural climate of the modern European world, just as they do in his meditations on language. Similarly, images associated with death, decomposition, decay, bloodlessness, erosion, disease, and enervation appear over and over again as he relentlessly and remorselessly diagnoses the ills of his benighted time. "We are the great invalids, overwhelmed by old dreams. . . . In the Mind's graveyard lie the principles and the formulas: the Beautiful is defined, and interred there. And like it the True, the Good, Knowledge, and the Gods—they are all rotting there. (History: a context in which the capital letters decompose, and with them, the men who imagine and cherish them.)"[54] This is Cioran in 1949. In *Histoire et Utopie* eleven years later he described Western European culture as follows: "Imagine a society overpopulated with doubts; in which, with the exception of a few *strays*, no one adheres utterly to anything; in which, unscathed by superstitions and certainties, everyone pays lip-service to freedom and no one respects the form of government which defends and incarnates it. Ideals without content, or, to use a word quite as adulterated, myths without substance."[55]

Cioran repeatedly strikes variations on the theme of modern decadence to the point of triteness, if not boredom. This is not, or should not be, surprising. As Charles Newman has aptly put it: "Stop anyone over twelve on the street today and on a moment's notice he can provide a Spenglerian theory of our decline; any housewife can chart her loneliness in the grand tradition of Kafka and Kierkegaard. We have become proud of our pessimism, elevated our melancholy to the status of a metaphysic."[56] But, as always with him, there is another side to Cioran's abysmal pessimism. In *A Short History of Decay*, that early compendium of his hates and disillusions, he wrote: "The most fertile moments in history were at the same time the most airless; they prevailed like a fatality, a blessing for the naïve mind, mortal to an amateur of intellectual space. Freedom has scope only among the disabused and sterile epigones, among the intellects of belated epochs, epochs whose style is coming apart and is no longer inspired except by a certain ironic indulgence."[57] In his appreciation of Paul Valéry the same imagery is at work: "absolute lucidity [is] incompatible with existence, with breathing. And it must be recognized that the disabused mind, however complete its emancipation from the world, lives more or less in the unbreathable."[58] Thus, a final paradox: the modern world, "at a point symmetrical to the agony of the ancient world," an airless realm whose disabused intellects live in the unbreathable, is—in that very airlessness— likened to history's most fertile moments.[59]

In what sense might the modern world be a time of fertility as well as sterility? Is Cioran, archpessimist, holding out a ray of hope? Hardly. But more than a love of paradox is at work. In an airless time, a winded civilization, two possibilities present themselves: death from asphyxiation, hence infinite silence; or to catch one's breath, to find a means of inspiration. Where then will inspiration, the ability to breathe again, arise?[60] It will come, if it does, from the very decadence of the modern world itself, by encouraging it, rather than opposing it, and this because: "The mistake of those who apprehend decadence is to try to oppose it whereas it must be encouraged: by developing it exhausts itself and permits the advent of other forms. The true harbinger is not the man who offers a system when no one wants it, but rather the man who precipitates Chaos, its agent and incense-bearer."[61]

The agency in this precipitation of chaos is doubt, of a radical kind that Cioran distinguishes from negation or unbelief. The crucial discussion is the essay "Skeptic and Barbarian" in *The Fall into Time*, although the meditation on doubt is a continuous one throughout Cioran's work. The essay begins with his familiar comparison between the world of late antiquity and the modern era. "Imagine a reader of the *Pyrrhonian Hypotyposes* faced with the Gospels! What artifice could reconcile not two doctrines but two universes?"[62] He suggests that the works of Sextus Empiricus summed up all the doubts of the ancient world, thereby constituting "an exhaustive compilation of the Unbreathable, the most dizzying pages ever written and, it must be said, the most boring." Civilizations begin in myth and end in doubt and, Cioran asks, in the contemporary world, "when we too are about to change gods, will there be sufficient respite for us to cultivate it [i.e., Pyrrhonian scepticism]?" Can such radical doubt be genuinely cultivated in the present, confronted without succumbing to it? For Cioran there can be no definitive answer to that question, as his meditation on doubt demonstrates.

It is important to clarify precisely what Cioran means by what he terms "orthodox" or "rigorous" scepticism for it is *that* kind about which he raised the question whether or not it can be genuinely nurtured in the present. This rigorous doubt is to be distinguished from *negation*. The latter is "an aggressive, impure doubt, an inverted dogmatism, [which] rarely denies itself, rarely frees itself from its frenzies," while orthodox doubt "calls itself in question, prefers to abolish itself rather than see its perplexities degenerate into articles of faith." In a word, it is indeterminate. In order to shift from negation to doubt all truths must be questioned and discredited. Whereas negation is pursued in the name of something else external to it and is, therefore, a reverse affirmation (just as many variants of modern unbelief are themselves mirror images of rejected beliefs), doubt "attacks and overthrows its own foundations in order to escape the absurdity of having to deny or affirm anything at all." Such a rigorously pursued dubiety would—ideally—result in a situation analogous to that which Cioran depicts as thinking *"on the level of life itself"*: "anyone who is carried away by his reasoning *forgets* that he is using reason, and this forgetting is the condition of all creative thought, indeed of thought itself." Once, however, we have begun to think that we are thinking, then ideas oppose themselves, neutralize each other, and generate a sterile state "in which we neither advance nor retreat, this exceptional form of *marking time* [which] is precisely where doubt leads us, a state which in many respects is related to the *acidie* of the mystics." The ideal situation would apparently be to *forget* one's very doubting; it would be an almost *visceral* doubt, on the level of life itself. All mysteries, superstitions, certitudes, opinions wither in the face of such intractable scepticism. Such incurable honesty "discovers a lie wherever an opinion attacks indifference and triumphs over it." However, if living "is equivalent to the impossibility of abstaining," then rigorous doubt is incompatible with life. The consistent, persistent sceptic, doubting at a visceral level, is a "living dead man," who "crowns his career by a defeat unparalleled in any other intellectual adventure." He will have attained a "deliverance *without* salvation," leading to "the integral experience of vacuity," a "primordial vacancy," where "neither life nor death any longer excites his mind." This is the orthodox scepticism Cioran has ever sought, never quite attained.

In addition to the rigorous sceptic there exists another, one who suffers doubt, but only intermittently; who can suspend judgment and abolish sensations, but only temporarily. This type of sceptic will move from inertia to exultation, will seek to triumph over doubt, open himself to experiences of another order, thereby making of doubt a stage on life's way, " a provisional but indispensable hell." These are ultimately traitors to scepticism and, in Cioran's terminology, they are "barbarians," the contemporary analogue to Christians in the decaying Roman world. Barbarians are able, unlike the orthodox sceptic, to take sides, to affirm or deny. If there are new gods emerging, these heretical sceptics will be their followers. In declining periods, "today even more than at the beginning of the Christian era," barbarism will be celebrated; nostalgia for it will be a civilization's last word. "At the expiration of a cycle, what else can a disenchanted mind dream of but the impulse of brutes to count on the possible, to wallow in it?" And what of the "true" sceptic? "Indeed, we must not be surprised to find him, specialist in subtlety though he is, at the heart of the ultimate solitude to which he has come, turning himself into a friend and accomplice of the hordes."

Such are the choices: sceptic or barbarian. The insuperable difficulties of maintaining the former position pose the ever-present threat of succumbing to the latter. Cioran himself does not make explicit in this essay his own position and holds out, in a typically unresolved manner, the possibility of his own complicity—orthodox sceptic though he be, or try to be—with the coming barbarians and new gods. But earlier, in *A Short History of Decay*, he had claimed that: "A god is always threatening on the horizon. . . . Let us conduct ourselves so that the god does not settle in our thoughts, let us still keep our doubts, the appearances of equilibrium, and the temptation of immanent destiny, any arbitrary and fantastic aspiration being preferable to the inflexible truths."[63] And, a decade after "Skeptic and Barbarian," he repeatedly speaks of what is clearly an aspiration to continue to seek the "true" form of scepticism: "The certitude that there is no salvation is a form of salvation, in fact it *is* salvation. Starting from here, we might organize our own life as well as construct a philosophy of history: the insoluble as solution, as the only way out. . . ."[64]

Cioran emerges as the disciple of indeterminacy, the asymptotic aphorist. When the possibility of writing appears exhausted, he perseveres with his pen; when the rigors of orthodox scepticism appear unattainable, he embraces the insoluble as solution. His is a world of incertitude, bereft of capital letters, devoid of absolutes, deprived of salvation. These are the characteristics of the "modern" cultural condition and Cioran finds them—always—in himself. He finds (projects?) them as well in three exemplary moderns he admires—Valéry, Beckett, and Wittgenstein. His description of their concerns is as much auto-biographical as exegetical.

One side of Cioran thus surfaces when he pinpoints the key to Valéry's (Cioran's?) intellectual method, "the guiding principle, the rule and motto of his mind," as "the indefinite refusal to be *anything* whatsoever." Such a refusal has its price for it meant that "Valéry will never be *whole*, he will be *aside*, on the periphery of everything." Supremely aware, a consciousness infinitely subtle, Valéry's was "a boundary-line existence, semi-fictitious, devoid of all determinate content and totally unrelated to the psychological subject. [His was a] sterile self, a sum of rejections, the quintessence of nothing, an aware void. . . ."[65] So too Cioran.

Similarly, Cioran perceives Beckett as a *"separate* man," a man "of solitude and subterranean obstinacy, of being on the outside, implacably pursuing some endless task." This is the effort of every "true writer," Cioran suggests. Such a one "is a destroyer who *adds* to existence, who enriches it while undermining it."[66] Addition by destruction, without recourse to any Hegelian dialectical solution, implies infinite oscillation, as indeed Cioran suggested in 1949: *"Every step forward is followed by a step back:* this is the unfruitful oscillation of history—a stationary . . . becoming."[67] He goes on to stress the extremity of Beckett's position, and his courage in maintaining it. The passage is worth quotation in toto, for it describes, not only Cioran thinking about Beckett, but also about himself, and, in a further reflexive spiral he might appreciate, it describes the encounter of a reader with Cioran: "Right from our first meeting, I realized that he had reached the extreme limit, that perhaps he had started there, at the impossible, the extraordinary, at an impasse. And what is admirable is that he has *stood fast*. Having arrived at the outset up against a wall, he perseveres as gallantly as he always has: extremity *as a point of departure*, the end as advent! Hence the feeling that this world of his, this transfixed, dying world, could go on indefinitely, even if ours were to disappear."[68] The notion of an end as advent recalls Cioran's image of the fertility within sterility which he suggested as a characteristic of the modern world. The cyclic implication of the end as beginning is clear; but no sooner is it offered, than it is immediately balanced (in a characteristic Cioranesque gesture) by the opposite possibility of a world going on indefinitely.

What if—remote possiblity—the "true" sceptic were to triumph over the barbarian and his rigorous doubt extended indefinitely? What if the extremity of Beckett and the peripherality of Valéry became the generalized spiritual condition of "modernity"? Such indefinite prolongation into the future of the point of cyclic renewal is a possibility which Cioran appears to favor, at least part of the time, although he recognizes its virtual impossibility. Such a world of disabused consciousnesses would be one of long-term ennui, abulia, and acedia, to use Cioran's own idiosyncratic psychological lexicon. It is appropriate to recall here that, if one main branch of meanings of the word "secular" derives from a Latin root which in the Christian Middle Ages implied "of or pertaining to the world," there is a second branch whose sense is "of or belonging to an age or long period." The prolongation into the indefinite future of the disabused modern consciousness implies a twist on the meaning of "secular" which, again, Cioran might appreciate.[69]

A millennium and a half ago there was a viable alternative in the form of the monastery in the desert. Although he says he has never been particularly attracted to Wittgenstein's philosophy, Cioran confesses to "a passion for the man." He finds similarities between Wittgenstein and Beckett, notably his suggestion that both would have been drawn to the desert in another time because both manifest "the same distance from beings and things, the same inflexibility, the same temptation to silence, to a final repudiation of words, the same impulse to move up against boundaries never sensed before."[70] These remarks on Beckett and Wittgenstein, like those on Valéry, resonate with autobiographical tones.

Like the Irish dramatist and novelist and the Austrian philosopher, Cioran has not attained silence. He has remained a man apart, in precisely the manner Valéry did, despite his central position in modern French literature. The extravagance of Cioran's wish for silence rivals that of Valéry's mentor Mallarmé, though in reverse. Whereas Mallarmé dreamed of the one Great Work, the Book that would rival the world as it encompassed it, Cioran fantasized "a book whose syllables, attacking the paper, would suppress literature and readers alike, . . . a book that would be both carnival and apocalypse of Letters, an ultimatum to the pestilence of the Word." The fantasy remains just that, in Cioran's as well as Mallarmé's case.[71]

In *The Temptation to Exist* he wrote of those who have exceeded the truths of literature without embracing those of wisdom: "One is no longer a *littérateur;* yet one writes, even while despising *expression.*"[72] This is an equivocal, a tragic position, which preserves scraps of the vocation to write but lacks the courage to expunge those scraps forever. "Shards of instinct" compel him ever toward words, and he lacks that wisdom which is "the audacity to extirpate every vocation, literary or otherwise."[73] Cioran denies himself such a cenobitic silence, even as he desires it. The denial constitutes, however, an affirmation of language and the power of speech. Ultimately, this is the sole affirmation Cioran allows himself. The wisdom of silence is approachable only asymptotically, Cioran's work suggests, through subjecting writing, that least ascetic of actions, to the rigor of doubt and having it emerge, purified but in working order; or, more accurately, to emerge still able to *work order*. Lover of paradox, sceptic toward all certainties, refuser of positions, Cioran remains where he began, in complicity with words, rejecting any and all Words.

Notes

1. E. M. Cioran, *The Trouble with Being Born,* trans. Richard Howard (New York: Viking Press, 1976), p. 7. Originally published as *De l'inconvénient d'être né* (Paris: Gallimard, 1973). Hereafter abbreviated as TBB.

2. TBB, p. 133.

3. E. M. Cioran, *The Temptation to Exist,* trans. Richard Howard (New York: Quadrangle/New York Times Book Co., 1968), p. 233. Originally published as *La tentation d'exister* (Paris: Gallimard, 1956). Hereafter abbreviated as TE.

4. For a tracing of such parallels, see John Pilling, "Two versions of de-composition: Samuel Beckett and E. M. Cioran," *New Universities Quarterly* 31, 3 (Summer 1977), 305–315.

5. TE, p. 223.

6. See "Advantages of Exile," TE, pp. 74–78, for the series of quotations in this and the following paragraph.

7. TBB, p. 176.

8. TBB, p. 36. The full aphorism reads: "The fanatic of elliptical gloom is sure to excel in any career save that of being a writer."

9. See Sontag's introduction to TE, pp. 7–29; the quoted matter is on p. 11.

10. For this and the following quotations in this paragraph, see "Farewell to Philosophy," in E. M. Cioran, *A Short History of Decay*, trans. Richard Howard (New York: Viking Press, 1975), pp. 47–49. Originally published as *Précis de décomposition* (Paris: Gallimard, 1949). Hereafter cited as SHD.

11. SHD, p. 146.

12. TBB, pp. 33, 117. Cf. SHD, p. 145: "We lose ourselves in texts and terminologies: *meditation* is a datum unknown to modern philosophy. If we want to keep some intellectual decency, enthusiasm for civilization must be banished from our mind, as well as the superstition of History." Or: "We should philosophize as if 'philosophy' didn't exist, like some troglodyte dazed or daunted by the procession of scourges which pass before his eyes." See for this last quotation E. M. Cioran, *The New Gods*, trans. Richard Howard (New York: Quadrangle/New York Times Book Co., 1974), p. 119. Originally published as *Le mauvais demiurge* (Paris: Gallimard, 1969).

13. TE, p. 165; SHD, p. 167.

14. SHD, p. 147.

15. E. M. Cioran, *The Fall into Time*, trans. Richard Howard (New York: Quadrangle, 1970), p. 113. Originally published as *La chute dans le temps* (Paris: Gallimard, 1964). Hereafter abbreviated as FT. Cioran's repudiation of the "truth"/"lie" dichotomy recalls Nietzsche in an early essay (1873): "truths are illusions about which one has forgotten that this is what they are." See Friedrich Nietzsche, "On Truth and Lie in an Extra-Moral Sense," included in *The Portable Nietzsche*, trans. and ed. Walter Kaufmann (New York: Viking Press, 1954), p. 47.

16. Ludwig Wittgenstein, *Tractatus Logico-Philosophicus*, trans. D. F. Pears and B. F. McGuinness (London: Routledge & Kegan Paul, 1961), p. 151. Originally published in 1921.

17. See "Thinking against Oneself," TE, pp. 33–47.

18. Edward W. Said, "Amateur of the Insoluble," *Hudson Review*, XXI, 4 (Winter 1968–1969), 769–773. This is an extremely cogent appreciation of TE.

19. Ibid., 773.

20. See his introduction to FT, pp. 9–32; the quoted matter is on pp. 29–30.

21. Cf. Samuel Beckett's dissection of "the Time cancer" in his early book (1934) on Proust. For commentary, see A. Alvarez, *Samuel Beckett* (New York: Viking Press, 1973), pp. 11–24.

22. SHD, pp. 52–53.

23. TE, pp. 34, 37, 35–36. Modern European intellectual history over the last four centuries may be plausibly construed as manifesting a tension between "Being" and "Becoming," with the latter increasingly triumphant over the course of the past two centuries. The supremacy of the category "Becoming" has generated "two types of 'modern mind,'" one excited by change, filled with 'astonishment, presentiment, and expectation' at the prospect of it; the other weary from having constantly to adapt to it, and perplexed by the total lack of stability and certainty." Cioran speaks eloquently for the latter position. For this broader perspective, see Franklin L. Baumer, *Modern*

European Thought: Continuity and Change in Ideas, 1600–1950 (New York: Macmillan, 1977), passim; the quoted matter is on p. 22.

24. SHD, p. 117; TE, pp. 46, 133.

25. TE, p. 215; SHD, p. 4. Cf. also: "Vertige de l'histoire," in E. M. Cioran, *Syllogismes de l'amertume* (Paris: Gallimard, 1952), pp. 149–163.

26. For a brilliant evocation of this theme, see Hayden White, "The Burden of History," *History and Theory*, V, 2 (1966), 111–134, now reprinted in his *Tropics of Discourse: Essays in Cultural History* (Baltimore and London: Johns Hopkins Univ. Press, 1978).

27. This and the following quotations in this paragraph occur in "The Fall Out of Time," FT, pp. 173–183.

28. See TE, p. 34 for this and the preceding two quotations.

29. Said, "Amateur of the Insoluble," p. 772.

30. Samuel Beckett, *The Unnamable*, trans. the author, in *Three Novels* (New York: Grove Press, 1965), p. 414.

31. Quoted in A. Alvarez, *Samuel Beckett*, p. 137.

32. E. M. Cioran, "Encounters with Beckett," trans. Raymond Federman and Jean M. Sommermeyer, *Partisan Review*, 43, 2 (1976), 281. Hereafter abbreviated as EB.

33. See TE, p. 110, for these quotations.

34. Ibid., p. 111.

35. TBB, p. 79.

36. TE, p. 112. Cioran's ellipsis.

37. TBB, p. 205. Cf. SHD, pp. 19–20: "The qualifiers change: this change is called intellectual progress. Suppress them all and what would remain of civilization? The difference between intelligence and stupidity resides in the manipulation of the adjective, whose use without diversity constitutes banality. God Himself lives only by the adjectives we add to Him; whereby the *raison d'être* of theology. Hence man, by modulating the monotony of his misery ever variously, justifies himself to the mind only by the impassioned search for a new adjective." Or TBB, p. 134: "The idea of progress dishonors the intellect."

38. SHD, p. 161.

39. TBB, p. 205.

40. TBB, p. 89.

41. See TBB, p. 107, and TE, p. 190.

42. TE, p. 194.

43. "Dealing with the Mystics," TE, pp. 151–164.

44. *The Compact Edition of the Oxford English Dictionary* (New York: Oxford Univ. Press, 1971), I, 384. Cioran's opinion on the aphorism is in TBB, p. 153: "An aphorism? Fire without flames. Understandable that no one tries to warm himself at it."

45. Philip E. Lewis, *La Rochefoucauld: The Art of Abstraction* (Ithaca and London: Cornell Univ. Press, 1977), pp. 53–54.

46. Ibid.

47. For these examples of Cioran in his most discursively argued style, cf. "Beyond the Novel," in TE, pp. 136–150; "Skeptic and Barbarian," in FT, pp. 75–93; and "Sur deux types de société: Lettre à un ami lointain," in *Histoire et utopie* (Paris: Gallimard, 1960), pp. 7–37. The last essay has been translated by Richard Howard as "Letter to a Distant Friend," *TriQuarterly* 11 (Winter 1968), 21–23; hereafter abbreviated as LDF.

48. Friedrich Nietzsche, *On the Genealogy of Morals*, trans. Walter Kaufmann and R. J. Hollingdale (New York: Random House, 1967), pp. 22–23.

49. TE, p. 111. My italics.

50. TE, p. 223.

51. TBB, p. 90.

52. William H. Gass, "The Evil Demiurge," *New York Review of Books*, 22 August 1968, p. 19.

53. Denis Donoghue, "Deconstructing Deconstruction," *New York Review of Books*, 12 June 1980, p. 37.

54. SHD, p. 119. Cf. SHD, p. 114: *"From the Iliad to psychopathology*—there you have all of human history."

55. LDF, p. 27.

56. FT, pp. 9–10.

57. SHD, p. 80.

58. E. M. Cioran, "Valéry Before His Idols," trans. Frederick Brown, *Hudson Review*, XXII, 2 (Autumn 1969), 417. Hereafter abbreviated as VBI.

59. SHD, p. 35.

60. Beckett poses the same question in his play *Breath*. It is a drama with no actors, no words, lasting 35 seconds. Silence—a single breath—silence; that is the totality of the action. A. Alvarez comments: "The only Miserere Beckett has ever uttered is for those burdened with the compulsion to write, the only liberation he is interested in is from the oppression of language." A. Alvarez, *Samuel Beckett*, p. 132.

61. SHD, p. 117.

62. FT, p. 75. The following quotations in this and the subsequent two paragraphs occur in the same essay, FT, pp. 173–183. For a broader perspective on twentieth-century modes of doubting, see Franklin L. Baumer, *Religion and the Rise of Scepticism* (New York: Harcourt, Brace & World, 1960), pp. 187–292.

63. SHD, p. 36.

64. TBB, p. 195; Cioran's ellipsis. Cf., from the same book: "The final step toward indifference is the destruction of the very notion of indifference." (P. 183)

65. VBI, p. 423, for these quotations.

66. EB, p. 280, for these quotations.

67. SHD, p. 178; Cioran's ellipsis.

68. EB, p. 284.

69. *The Compact Edition of the Oxford English Dictionary* (New York: Oxford Univ. Press, 1971), II, 365. The phrase "secular trend" might then be appropriated from the economists and used to describe what—to Cioran, at least—appears highly likely: the long-term extension into the future of "modern consciousness."

70. EB, p. 284 for these quotations.

71. TE, p. 112. For Cioran's comments on Mallarmé, see VBI, 411–417.

72. TE, p. 194.

73. Ibid.

XII

World's End: Secular Eschatologies in Modern Fiction

W. WARREN WAGAR

The Persistence of Eschatology

A strategic insight of modern criticism is the discovery that much of the imaginative literature of the past one hundred years (and perhaps the past five hundred) translates into secular values the world view of the Book of Revelation and the other principal texts of Jewish and Christian apocalyptic. At its cutting edge, modern literature is nothing less than secular eschatology, posing and sometimes answering the same questions addressed by biblical prophecy, in terms credible to modern minds. For Frank Kermode, the "imminent" has become "immanent," and the naive apocalypticism of traditional images of the future has been internalized. Instead of doomsday, writers confront personal death or futility or meaninglessness. Tragic and, more recently, absurdist literature satisfies our human demand to know what can be known of our destiny. "What can be known"—in modern culture—is not much, perhaps no more than the knowledge that nothing can be known. But even this is knowledge.[1]

Kermode applies his thesis to a variety of appropriate writers of the cutting edge, from Yeats to Robbe-Grillet. John R. May, in a similar study of American literature, traces the secularization of apocalyptic themes from Melville to Pynchon. David Ketterer, analyzing science fiction, defines as apocalyptic "any work of fiction concerned with presenting a radically different world or version of reality that exists in a credible relationship with the world or reality verified by empiricism and common experience." All serious science fiction reveals "the apocalyptic imagination" at work in its purest form, credibly transforming old worlds, and offering new worlds in their stead.[2] Mainstream literature, he agrees, supplies the same product, but in a less radical form.

Eschatology itself has undergone a parallel secularization, both in the sense of the "secular" theology of Jürgen Moltmann and in the sense of the "demythologized" theology of Rudolf Bultmann. In such doctrines of last things, the endtime retains its validity only as a chance, a *kairos*, for acts of social or personal transformation: time itself is unscathed. In the decoding of the demythologizers, the Book of Revelation can have relevance to modern minds only if it is reconceived as a call to authentic living, like a treatise by Martin Heidegger or a novel by Albert Camus. Christians can no longer take it seriously as a prophecy of universal doom.

From all of this, it is difficult and even unnecessary to dissent. But what is to be done with works of modern literature that appear to preserve the "naive" consciousness of traditional eschatology, anticipating a literal end of the world? Do the thousands of world's-end novels, stories, and plays published since the beginning of the nineteenth century argue the persistence of a biblical sense of last things in modern consciousness? Even granting that most fictional scenarios of doomsday substitute natural or human agencies of world destruction for divine, are the men and women of letters who produce these scenarios closer in spirit to the fire-breathing Fundamentalist preacher than to the inward-turning Heideggerian novelist?

Probably not. All the same, these are questions worth asking and answering, as we shall try to do in this chapter. The existence of a literature of last things does strongly suggest that the traditional expectation of a Dies Irae continues in various ways to haunt the secular mind. For many unable to accept as credible a supernatural end of the world, belief lingers in an end caused by nature or made by man. It is also conceivable that if the literature of doomsday encodes fears of personal death or cultural fatigue, so the literature of death and fatigue dissected by Kermode may sometimes conceal a fear of doomsday.

Tales of the world's end, although extensive in themselves, account for only a small fraction of the total output of Western writers in the past two centuries. Too much should not be made of them. But the endtime is a stubbornly persistent theme in modern letters. It has attracted several major writers of the so-called mainstream, many writers of science fiction, and a growing number of popular novelists and filmmakers, for whom doomsday has become a lucrative industry. The first wave of literally eschatological fiction arrived early in the nineteenth century, in the form of stories and poems about "the last man," a melancholy romantic inversion of that ebullient hero of the Enlightenment, Robinson Crusoe. An important example is Mary Shelley's novel *The Last Man* (1826), whose protagonist became the final survivor of a world-destroying pestilence.[3] In the late nineteenth century, world's-end stories soon emerged as the stock in trade of the authors of "scientific romances," headed by H. G. Wells, but including as well Richard Jefferies, M. P. Shiel, William Hope Hodgson, and Arthur Conan Doyle in Great Britain; Camille Flammarion, Jules

Verne, and J. H. Rosny in France; and Jack London, George Allan England, and Garrett P. Serviss in the United States.

Since 1914 the roster of novelists and playwrights who have taken the end of the world as their subject has grown prodigiously. Almost every significant writer of speculative fiction, which is to say "science fiction," has tried his or her hand at it, sometimes in whole cycles of novels, such as the "Cities in Flight" novels of James Blish or the "Dancers at the End of Time" trilogy by Michael Moorcock. From time to time literati of the mainstream (the distinction is not really crucial in this context) have also succumbed to the apocalyptic temptation. One thinks of Aldous Huxley, Karel Čapek, R. C. Sherriff, Kurt Vonnegut, Jr., Robert Merle, Doris Lessing, and perhaps—in *Endgame,* for example—even the redoubtable Samuel Beckett. To go full circle, there is even a not undistinguished group of eschatological fictions written from the perspectives of Christian faith, secular in some of their trappings and details of plot, but essentially loyal to the New Testament kerygma. The master of the desecularized apocalyptic novel in our time is surely C. S. Lewis, in works such as *That Hideous Strength* (1945) and *The Last Battle* (1956). Walter M. Miller, Jr., author of the post-Holocaust classic *A Canticle for Leibowitz* (1959), belongs in this camp as well.

Of course the historian of modern thought is not limited to imaginative literature in his search for evidence of the persistence of the eschatological consciousness. As Franklin L. Baumer has shown, thoughts of the end of the world, or at least the end of Europe and of Western civilization, are ubiquitous in twentieth-century philosophy and, above all, philosophy of history.[4] In *Good Tidings,* I have devoted two chapters to major secular thinkers of both the nineteenth and the twentieth centuries who have labored to refute the belief in general progress and to foresee or at least to warn of the possibility of the end of Western civilization, or even of civilization itself.[5] From Burckhardt and Nietzsche to Spengler, Jaspers, and Sorokin, prophecies of disaster appear with regularity in modern Western thought. Although there has been a slackening in recent decades of grand theories of historical decline and fall, their place has been taken by political scientists anticipating a thermonuclear world war and ecologists warning of calamity through man's heedless manipulation of the environment for power and profit.[6]

But in this chapter, we shall be kept busy enough with fictional doomsdays. The essence of biblical eschatology is the ontological tension between everyday human existence and the promise of the end of existence itself: the end of time and history, the end of society and culture, the end of the stage on which the dramas of everyday human existence unfold. Although doom-crying modern philosophers and scholars draw freely on the symbols of biblical eschatology, and of pre-Christian thought as well, their work often lacks the full ontic menace of literary endtimes. It seldom provides for more than a temporary failure or gradual deterioration of the order of things. Above all, it cannot grip the imagination so viscerally. Despite neglect by intellectual historians, the richest and most abundant sources of radically eschatological thought in modern secular culture are no doubt fictions, of the sort discussed below.

Intentions and Meanings

Before we can proceed to the works themselves, it is important to consider in a preliminary way what eschatological fictions set out to accomplish, at both conscious and unconscious levels of intention. Why should so many otherwise unremarkable or at least thoroughly representative modern writers, above all those in whom God is dead, choose to set their stories in the endtime? What opportunities does the endtime supply to writers who view the Book of Revelation as a tangle of archaic myths?

Clearly, eschatological fictions attack fundamental concerns of the individual. They address, no less directly than the "classics" of modern imaginative literature analyzed by Kermode, such problems as the fear of death, the traumas of birth and separation from family, crises of identity and self-worth, resentment of parental authority, the struggles of Eros and Thanatos, the basic challenges faced in life by everyone, and identified in this century by Freud, Adler, Jung, Fromm, Erikson, and many others. In the endtime, as in the wastelands where Beckett sets his ontological puppet shows, man finds himself stripped to the bedrock of his existence. The elaborate machinery of civilization has been smashed. Nature has been ravaged or turned upside down. Death is everywhere. Survival is problematic. In such a drastically simplified situation, equivalent to that dreadful moment when the infant must draw his first breath, or the young adult must leave the nest, or the middle-aged man must come to terms with mortality and the relentless contraction of personal horizons, only the barest essentials matter.

Reference to two sample narratives may help to explain more fully the psychological dimensions of world's-end fiction. Our samples are chosen at random. They are not celebrated works, or works of unusual depth or artistry. But such is the power of terminal fictions that the setting in and of itself compels the author and his readers to deal with the fundamentals of human existence. Extraordinary gifts are not required, either literary or philosophical. The situation alone (even in comedic or satirical world's-end fiction) dictates a certain elementary seriousness about basic problems of life, including its meaning and purpose.

In the story "Adam and No Eve" by the American writer Alfred Bester, first published in 1941, the landscape is an earth roasted by a runaway nuclear chain reaction. The protagonist Steven Krane is the last man, dragging himself painfully across the cinders of the dead planet toward the sea. His own Promethean defiance of the good advice of an older scientist has caused earth's destruction. Now, despite a crushed leg, he feels an irresistible urge to reach the ocean. He is taunted by a hallucination of the scientist, who pours a goblet of cold water into the dust and ashes just out of his reach. He is consoled and urged on by another hallucination, of his fiancée, who reminds him of the cottage on the shore where they will live together as Adam and Eve. Her warnings help save him from the attack of the only other creature on the surface of the planet, his once faithful dog, now a hunger-maddened wild animal. Finally, he reaches the ocean and dies peacefully, secure in the knowledge that from his cells and from the microorganisms inhabiting his body will evolve a whole new cycle of life. His body is rocked gently by the sea, "the great mother of life," who had "called him back to her depths . . . and he was content."[7]

Our second sample narrative is a novel, one of several superbly realistic eschatological novels by the British writer of fantasy and science fiction John Christopher. In *A Wrinkle in the Skin* (1965), he tells the story of an earth devastated by a series of massive earthquakes. Christopher's scenario allows for a scattering of survivors here and there who form tentative communities that degenerate in a matter of weeks into tribes. The protagonist Matthew Cotter is a characteristic middle-aged Englishman, a quiet and decent man, divorced, with a beloved grown daughter away at college. In the aftermath of the disaster, he joins a small tribe headed by a bully, but abandons the fledgling community to look for his daughter. After various adventures, in which he is accompanied by a boy he has rescued, he gives up the search. Man and boy head back toward "home," and when nearly there, rediscover another, more congenial tribe encountered earlier in the odyssey. A handsome widow of the tribe who had at that time rejected Cotter, because of her bitterness against all men after having been raped by marauders, is now ready to take him into her bosom. The novel ends happily. Cotter will have a family and a community, and the world will replenish itself.[8]

No exceptional feats of psychoanalysis are required to see what both of these stories achieve. Like the greater part of world's-end fiction, they are curiously upbeat. The world comes to an end, in one case because of a man's defiance of a father figure, in the other case because of the inscrutable processes of nature. The day of wrath, however, is followed by a second chance. Krane is tortured by the father figure's scorn, but finds acceptance first from the memory of his chosen mate, and, finally, in a far more substantial and meaningful way, from reentry into the maternal body, to await rebirth in the next cycle. Cotter loses everything, including the person who meant the most to him before the holocaust, his daughter, but after wanderings emblematic of the young adult's search for self-knowledge and a distinctive identity and place in the social matrix, or the mid-life crisis of the older adult, he finds himself. Of equal

importance, he finds acceptance again by others, regaining fatherhood through
the boy and manhood (and sonship) through the widow.

Also noteworthy in both stories is the transformation in scale of the moral
content of biblical eschatology. In the biblical Last Days, not only is the world
battered by catastrophes and ultimately destroyed, but a grand culminating
struggle takes place between good and evil, with Christ and Satan in visible
captaincy of their respective forces. Most eschatological fiction reproduces this
terminal war, often giving it a central place in the narrative, but in a severely
secularized form. In the Bester story, it is fully internalized. Krane redeems his
satanic pride by obeying the instinctual urge to reach the sea. At a lower level,
the hero's dog is transformed from a loyal pet into a fiend by natural forces,
supplying a moment of apocalyptic terror when he springs at his former master.
For Christopher, the secular Armageddon is a battle between the "decent" folk
of the widow's tribe and a band of roving "yobbos," who specialize in rape,
pillage, and senseless violence.

Perhaps most telling of all is the way that world's-end literature brings the
predicaments of the self into the sharpest possible focus. All fiction has its
heroes, but the men and women of the endtime stand on the stage alone. In one
sense they are deprived, but in another sense they have enormous power,
wealth, and opportunity. They can go on wild rampages, feast on all the world's
surviving victuals, play emperor, regenerate the human race. Everything, literally, hangs on their whims and decisions. A classic case is the eschatological
career of Adam Jeffson, the last man of M. P. Shiel's *The Purple Cloud* (1901),
who alternately builds palaces and puts the torch to most of the world's cities,
before settling down to dull domesticity with his Eve. The point is that the
eschatological moment, in Bultmann's phrase, never presents itself more
fiercely than in world's-end fiction.[9] The choices of the protagnoist will determine the whole future of the human race. He chooses—as in the Kantian
categorical imperative—for all mankind. It would be difficult to imagine a more
effective way of symbolizing the high significance of personal decision.

Only in a secularized world view, it should be noted, can the individual's
choosing matter so critically. The psychologism that dominates so much of
modern thought and criticism is itself a striking example of secularization. In
biblical eschatology, merely human heroes and heroines do not appear: the
drama is universal, and the only significant actors are God, Christ, and Satan.
In secular eschatology, by contrast, not only does the supernatural vanish, but
the universal drama shrinks (at least under the lens of criticism) to the dimensions of a soap opera, a drama of individuals struggling with their individual
problems.

All the same, it is possible to carry psychologism too far, and to impose the
thesis of secularization too radically. The world of Beckett and of eschatological
fiction is a world not only of id, ego, and superego, but also of historic public

crises of identity and mortality comparable to those suffered by the Jewish nation in biblical times. That is to say, our civilization is not a changeless constant within which we play out our private troubles, but rather a society and culture in process of headlong change. Eschatological fiction addresses the perplexities of this public world, too. It does so sometimes quite deliberately, and at other times without conscious intent.

The sociocultural aspects of eschatological fiction are by no means obscure. The first secular visions of the world's end in literature go back to the era immediately following the French Revolution, when monarchical feudalism collapsed in Europe. The period 1789–1815 is a public eschatological moment in the history of the Western world, marking, if not the literal end of a system of relations of production, at least a turning point in its fortunes, after which its decay was more or less continuous. The colossal changes in politics, social relations, high and popular culture, economic life, and European and North American world power accompanying or roughly contemporary with the events of 1789–1815 produced public anxiety on a grand scale, which romantic art, literature, and thought attempted in a variety of ways, some backward-looking, others forward-looking, to relieve. One of those ways, patently, was to invent the genre of the eschatological tale, where the end of old Europe could be reenacted in imagination as the end of the world.

After the romantic generation, however, eschatological fictions became relatively scarce, not to reappear in force until the last decade or two of the nineteenth century. Since that time, Western civilization has entered into what must be termed, in defiance of proper etymology, a permanent crisis. This "crisis" involves, simultaneously, the culmination and decline of Western European and North American state power, the maturation and incipient decay of capitalism, the almost sudden foundering of Jewish and Christian belief after centuries of corrosive doubt and scepticism, and the development of technical means of war-making that permit human beings, for the first time in history, to annihilate civilization and perhaps life itself. The permanent crisis has been accompanied by a flowering of eschatological fictions that have destroyed the world in imagination thousands of times: great natural catastrophes, orgies of mass suicide, total wars, ecological disasters brought on by human abuse of the earth, alien invasions, and much more.

What do such fictions intend, and what do they achieve? In good part they furnish secular equivalents of biblical apocalyptic firmly grounded in modern secular natural science, philosophy, and social science, as the apocalyptic of the Bible (and other ancient texts, such as those of Stoicism) was well anchored in the kinds of knowledge available to ancient man. Physics, geology, and biology since the middle of the nineteenth century have produced many theories of how the world or even the cosmos may end.[10] The public appetite for such theories, and some of the concern felt by the theorists themselves, cannot be explained by reference to the internal history of science alone. Nevertheless, the theories exist. They lend credibility and, in a science-intoxicated age, respectability to the fictional scenarios that exploit them.

Thus, in our sample stories, the world is destroyed by runaway technology and by a major geological upheaval, respectively. Neither the Bester nor the Christopher tale could withstand close scientific analysis, but they prey on fears generated by the state of the art in nuclear physics and geological theory at the time each was written.

In other instances, the end is a function at least in part of the operation of presumed laws of history, sociology, or economics. One group of eschatological fictions has adapted the theories of Max Nordau, Oswald Spengler, Arnold J. Toynbee, and others to project visions of the decadence and fall of civilization through internal causes. One of the most thoroughly worked out is Olaf Staple-don's *Last and First Men* (1931), in which bourgeois materialism and class struggle bring the First Men—the civilization of Homo sapiens—to extinction. Fewer than three dozen human beings survive to breed a new species that also annihilates itself in a lunatic war of mutual assured destruction against Martian invaders. James Blish in *Cities in Flight* (1955–1962) presents a panorama of galactic history loosely based on the work of Spengler. Isaac Asimov's *Foundation* novels (1951–1953) recapitulate Gibbon, and Jack Williamson's short story "Breakdown" (1942) is directly inspired by the early volumes of Toynbee's *A Study of History*.

In a somewhat different vein are the many scenarios of a dying earth (or earthlike planet) in a far future characterized by loss of self-determination, moral decadence, and cults of suicide. Here the "scientific" basis is supplied by Max Nordau and other social psychologists who have inveighed against the alleged immoralism or psychic exhaustion of modern culture. Early examples from mainstream fiction are James Elroy Flecker's "The Last Generation" (1908) and E. M. Forster's "The Machine Stops" (1909). Representative efforts on the same lines among more recent fictions include Brian Aldiss's *Hothouse* (1962), John Brunner's *Total Eclipse* (1974), D. Keith Mano's *The Bridge* (1973), Michael Moorcock's *Legends from the End of Time* (1977), and *The Orchid Cage* (1961), by one of the few major writers of science fiction in the German-speaking world, Herbert W. Franke.

But what perhaps underlies all such fictions, to say nothing of scenarios of a terminal war and the innumerable predictions of man-made ecological dooms-days, is the sense of modern writers that they live in a moribund civilization. They may not understand the causes of its approaching demise, or of what the demise will consist. For although all civilized life or mankind itself might conceivably be wiped out by war or pestilence or blight or cosmic disaster or any of the other favored agencies of the end, the odds against universal devastation are high. The credible, in this instance, is not the probable. The most likely sociological explanation for the frequent use of literally eschatological plots in modern fiction is the same one that decodes eschatological prophecy in the first century A.D. or in the late Middle Ages. The prophets did expect a literal doomsday, but they were in the grip of a mass neurosis afflicting wounded and dying cultures. Modern writers may also expect a literal doomsday, but their fictions are one strategy among several for expressing the artist's intuition of imminent disaggregation for the particular order of society in which he lives. He may believe that he foresees the end of all life: in fact what he foresees is more likely the end of a stage in the history of his civilization, such as the stage of imperial monopoly capital and the armed national state. In the more vivid imagery of literal eschatology, he is conveying a message (after decoding) not unlike the apocalyptic philosophies of a Nietzsche or a Spengler referred to in the first section of this chapter, and not unlike the apocalyptic content of Marxian socialism.

Sometimes the writer of eschatological fiction gives signs of realizing that the Dies Irae is only a metaphor for the end of an age. A poignant example is the novel *Ice* (1967) by Anna Kavan, a surreal narrative strongly influenced by Kafka in which nothing is quite certain. The time and the place are left vague. The hero is engaged in a tortuous search for a pale thin woman whom he once loved, and the world is coming to an end. But no one knows just how it will end, whether by advancing glaciers, nuclear war, or growing worldwide anarchy. In the last analysis, it does not matter. "The race was dying, the collective death-wish, the fatal impulse to self-destruction." As the story draws to a close, the narrator finds his beloved, and they drive off together into a storm, feeling warm and unafraid although outside the world is freezing and "seemed to have come to an end already."[11] The vision of Kavan, whose own life was a long struggle with heroin addiction and suicidal depressions, gives voice both to a personal death-wish and to a presentiment of worldwide disaster in which the apparent causes and effects do not really signify. Yet the ease with which her fiction embraces the universe suggests that much more than private *Angst* is involved. Associating her fate with the world's, as Mary Shelley did in *The Last Man*, becomes an effective literary strategy only in a cultural milieu where the "death-wish," or the fear of a general breakdown, is indeed collective. In such a milieu, every hypothesis of science, every premise of military logic, every speculative philosophy of history is seized upon eagerly to confirm the gut feeling that the public order of things faces collapse.

Yet the frequency of somehow happy endings for these unhappy fictions of the world's end prompts the final observation that secular eschatologies are not merely minatory or cathartic. Like their biblical antecedents, they may also serve to nourish hope. After the End, comes the Beginning, whether a beginning again on the old or on a higher plane, or an entry into some sort of heavenly bliss. Here and there an eschatological fiction, such as Mordecai Roshwald's

Level 7 (1959), leaves no possibility of survival, much less of transcendence. But the majority of stories follow the model of "Adam and No Eve" or *A Wrinkle in the Skin*. The new world that emerges, or is prophesied to emerge, will renew and perhaps extend human life. In some futures, the hope is for a simpler, cleaner world, akin to an idealized Middle Ages; in others, it is for the consummation of progressive trends in our own society, as in H. G. Wells's forecasts of a scientifically managed world civilization arising from a catastrophic world war. [12] In still others, life merely repeats itself, in a cyclic pattern. But the End is seldom the end. Time and again the eschatological fiction turns out to be a device, like the utopia, the ideological program, the countercultural sect, or any number of other phenomena in our secular society, for declaring the bankruptcy of the Old Order and proclaiming a New World. In this, as in its symbology, it drinks deeply from the well of biblical tradition.

The First Endtimes: Grainville and Shelley

For students of the secularization of modern consciousness, the most engrossing period in the history of world's-end fictions is the earliest, when writers were making the difficult passage from the eschatological vision of biblical prophecy to the perspectives of secularism. The first world's-end novel, J.-B. Cousin de Grainville's *Le dernier homme* (1805), did not quite succeed in bridging the gap. [13] Set in the distant future on a barren and dying earth, *Le dernier homme* is simultaneously a realistic prose epic recording the efforts of mankind to stave off natural disaster and an eschatological morality play in which the principal actors (excluding the last man and his bride) are a resurrected Adam, sent to the end of time by God on a mission of mercy, and a supernatural being of almost pagan provenance, the "earth-spirit." The earth-spirit and Adam struggle throughout the tale. The spirit uses his magic to persuade the terminal spouses to reproduce, so that he himself and the planet with whose management he was entrusted at the Creation can go on living at all costs. Adam works for the opposite result, knowing with God's help that the offspring of the last fertile man and woman would be forced by the hunger of their terminal age to become ruthless killers.

As soon as Omégare, the last man, agrees to forsake his bride, rather than defy heaven (thereby undoing the original sin of Adam), the last days arrive promptly. Volcanoes erupt, comets shoot, the oceans turn livid, the sun cries tears of blood. The dead leave their tombs in preparation for judgment, and the narrative breaks off as the desperate earth-spirit is hunted down and killed by yet another mythological figure, Death. Grainville declines to describe the actual end of the world, but presumably it will hereafter follow the script provided in the closing pages of the Book of Revelation. God's wishes have been respected, and eternal life awaits the human race, spared from further suffering by the wisdom and piety of both the first man and the last.

Clearly, Grainville's narrative retains at least the essence of the biblical vision. Even if all the supernatural interventions are explained as a tissue of poetic metaphors, *Le dernier homme* is unmistakably closer in its world view to Milton, Bunyan, and Klopstock than to La Mettrie and Diderot. In fact Grainville was a believing Catholic, a priest, and an ardent polemicist against *les philosophes* and the vices of secular civilization. His end of the world was the end of time, a promise of resurrection, judgment, and eternity.

But as Henry F. Majewski observes, Grainville was also a typical member of the preromantic generation in France, afflicted with preromantic fears and anxieties about the decay of the *ancien régime* and the more disturbing implications of secular thought, which his faith was not strong enough to subdue. "The end of the world in Grainville," writes Majewski, "appears as an anguishing sense of metaphysical insecurity, a complacent projection of his personal conviction that the human condition is essentially and fatally *malheureuse*."[14] Although superficially loyal to Christianity, the author of *Le dernier homme*, in this reading, found the world of matter in motion disclosed by modern secular philosophy unbearable. His response was a *Weltschmerz* more negative than Beckett's, and a novel that takes grim pleasure in mankind's destruction.

Majewski goes too far. Christian pleasure in apocalyptic portents is an old story, having nothing to do with secularization. But certainly there is a measure of truth in Majewski's remarks, which owe much to the critical insights of Mario Praz in *The Romantic Agony*.[15] What we see is nothing stranger than a blending of early romantic alienation and melancholy, in the vein of Sénancour or Chateaubriand, with the fierce Christian apocalypticism of a Joseph de Maistre. The two can easily coexist in the same mind, even today.

It must also be noted that, at another level, *Le dernier homme* is a prototypical scientific romance. Whatever the importance or meaning of the supernatural actors in the drama, the purely human ones have a life of their own, largely untouched by outside forces until the very last of the last days. Of the two volumes into which the novel is divided, most of the first and part of the second offer a thoroughly secular history of the far future. Mankind inhabits a world exhausted by weather and human exploitation. Great wars, with scenes of aerial combat between winged balloons, had once ravaged civilization, although earth is now at peace. Scientific and technical progress bring various material blessings, which mean nothing any longer, since the dry soil supports few crops, the sun has cooled, and man himself has become sterile. Omégare, the last man to be born in Europe, and Syderie of Brazil, the only fertile woman still alive, are mankind's last hope. Grainville devotes some of his most convincing pages to the flight of Omégare to the New World in an airship, the wedding of the lovers, Syderie's imprisonment by her own people, and her rescue and flight

back to France with the brave Omégare. No sooner have the young couple set up
housekeeping than Adam appears to Omégare, with his unhappy message from
heaven. Adam persuades the last man of his duty, and the rest of the tale
unfolds as already sketched.

For all the biblical flavor of the events that follow, Grainville's story of an
earth worn out by time and humanity reduced to one fertile pair, together with
the adventures of Omégare and Syderie in Brazil, can readily be imagined
between the lurid covers of a science fiction magazine. Nothing in the biblical
version of the last days prepares us for such scenes. Grainville has taken the
Epicurean view of nature, reinforced by scraps of modern science and metaphysical anguish, and has painted a terminal landscape that is both original
and—within the limits indicated—secular.

Le dernier homme is also the ancestor of that important subgenre of
speculative literature, the history of the future. Looking at eschatological
fictions broadly, one is tempted to divide all of them into just two large categories—those that place the end in a relatively distant time, after a long history,
which may or may not involve cycles of rise and fall; and those that imagine a
proximate doomsday, usually the outcome of a single tremendous cataclysm.
The future histories sport big casts of characters and lend themselves especially
well to exercises in cosmological speculation. The proximate doomsdays hew
more faithfully to the canons of modern mainstream fiction, and ordinarily have
more to offer in the way of psychological, and sometimes sociological, insight.

Of the second category, the world's-end fictions that set doomsday in the
near future, the model is another romantic novel with the same title used by
Grainville. *The Last Man* by Mary Shelley appeared only twenty-one years after
Grainville's work, but now we are dealing with an author deeply ensconced in
the romantic movement and a half century younger than her French predecessor. Shelley's remarkable novel is the first major secular novel of the world's
end—despite a few ambiguities. In its pages we very nearly complete the
transition from biblical to secular doomsdays bravely begun by the French
priest who despised *les philosophes*.

At first glance, Shelley's *The Last Man* may seem to be a "history of the
future" after all. It is set late in the twenty-first century, two hundred and fifty
years after its publication, and alludes to technological and material progress,
planned or already achieved, reminiscent of the progress chronicled in Grainville's novel. But the differences between the England of the author's imagination and of 1826 are not great, and her attention focuses almost entirely on a
small cast of characters drawn from the people in her own life, including
obvious versions of her late husband Percy and her late friend Lord Byron. As
she wrote in her journal, work was begun on the novel in 1824, during the long
period of depression that followed Percy's death, and just after the news that
Byron had died in Greece, a time when she felt alone in the world.[16] She might

have been the woman whose lover has gone to war, in the poem by Gautier: "Il semble à mon coeur désolé/Qu'il ne reste que moi sur terre."

Even the disaster that overwhelms the world of *The Last Man* was suggested to Shelley by a contemporary misery, the epidemic of Asian cholera that had broken out in India in 1817 and was predicted eventually to reach England. In the novel, the Byron-figure (the dashing Lord Raymond) encounters a virulent strain of plague in Constantinople as he is fighting a war much like the struggle for Greek independence in which Byron himself had participated. The plague enters Europe through Thrace, and spreads to Africa and the Americas as well. In eight years, the human race is extinct, with the sole exception of Mary Shelley's own character Lionel Verney. Early in the year 2100, Verney decides to put to sea, sailing the coastlines of the world in search of other survivors. But he has little hope.

Hugh J. Luke, Jr., in his introduction to a recent edition of the novel, follows critical trends in viewing *The Last Man* as a tale of romantic alienation. Like Shelley's *Frankenstein*, it is "built on the theme of human isolation, of the ineluctable separateness of the individual being." Cast adrift in an unintelligible universe, romantic man feels estranged from all being.[17] If Luke is right, Lionel Verney is a metaphor for all of us. We are all last men, although it may take the jolt of personal tragedy such as Shelley experienced to make us fully aware of it.

Well and good. But let us add that *The Last Man* is also a secular eschatology. It expresses fears of the hostility of nature, the vulnerability of established social orders, and the uselessness of human effort against the tidal pull of history. On the one side, early in the novel, is the eloquent and lofty idealism of Shelley's Percy-figure Adrian, whose schemes for world betterment recall the Percy Shelley of real life and Mary's philosopher-father William Godwin. On the other side stands a growing sense of futility and doom. Lionel's sister Perdita, in a fit of melancholy, warns of the mortality of all things. "Nature grows old, and shakes in her decaying limbs—creation has become bankrupt!"[18] Later even the gallant Raymond has premonitions of the end of time, and a hitherto optimistic scientist, Merrival, goes mad, cursing God, and accusing nature of treachery. The end, when it does come, is complete. No hope remains of salvation.

Although the thoroughness of Shelley's disaster is unusual in world's-end fiction, it is typical of nearly all later specimens of the genre in its secularism. The cause of the disaster, the plague, is a wholly natural phenomenon, and not a punishment from God. Indeed, before it struck, the England of Shelley's sympathetic characters was happy and prosperous and well governed. When the Turks are defeated, the world is also at peace. The plague comes from nowhere, and for no man's fault. A secularized version of Antichrist, the Methodist preacher who leads a ragged band of English refugees in France, argues that his flock has survived because it is godlier, but in due course his false prophecies fail, and his followers succumb just like the allegedly godless. Shelley's detestation of his pious ranting could not be more plain. Finally, in the endtime, no Redeemer arrives, no last trump is sounded, no pearly gates or heavenly choirs beckon the righteous.

The only remnant of traditional eschatology is the assortment of miscellaneous apocalyptic calamities, unrelated by any natural cause to the plague, which also afflict and stun humankind in the last days. A. J. Sambrook contends that Shelley dispensed with "supernatural machinery, and even with comets, earthquakes, wandering planets and a fading sun," but this is not quite true.[19] As the plague begins to invade Europe, on June 21, 2093, a black orb the size of the sun rises in the west and sets in the east, intersecting with the sun at noon and eclipsing it for a brief period. A little later, Shelley provides a gratuitous outbreak of storms, floods, and earthquakes, and in the autumn of 2096, three sun-sized meteors greet the last English refugees on their arrival in Dover. It is not asserted that any of these events had a supernatural origin, but no scientific explanation is offered, either. None seems plausible except sheer coincidence, and even that will not work for the black orb of June 21. More likely, Shelley simply liked the dramatic effect and took a leaf from Saint John in spite of herself.

All the same, it is clear that in *The Last Man* we have a modern secular story of the world's end. God's name appears, but only to be cursed by a mad scientist and exploited by a false prophet. Nature is the sole source of our distress, the nature that sets limits on all her playthings, including mankind, and pounds them to dust whenever she pleases.

Doomsday at the Turn of the Century

During what may be called the era of positivist ascendancy in Western culture, roughly the period of 1830 to 1880, a time of restored faith in the powers of reason and science and technology, and of gathering confidence in capitalism, nationalism, and the whole fabric of Western civilization, eschatological themes were rare in imaginative literature. Yet almost suddenly, in the depressed and anxious 1880s, and still more in the 1890s and 1900s, they returned, and inspired far more fictions than in the heyday of romanticism.

As before, some were grand histories of the future, and others were tales of near-future world disasters and their few survivors. Four of the best eschatological novels in the tradition of Grainville appeared during la belle époque in France, beginning with *La fin du monde* (1893) by the popularizer of astronomy Camille Flammarion, and ending with J.-H. Rosny's somber *La mort de la terre* (1912). The others were posthumously published short novels by the sociologist

Gabriel de Tarde *(Fragment d'histoire future,* 1904) and by the greatest of French scientific romancers, Jules Verne *(L'éternal Adam,* 1910). All four works offered long and singularly impersonal vistas reaching into the distant future, with many opportunities, seldom missed, for reflections on human destiny. Comparable British works were H. G. Wells's Darwinian romance *The Time Machine* (1895), and *The House on the Borderland* (1908) and *The Night Land* (1912) by William Hope Hodgson.

But it was the nearer future that the writers of the generation before the Great War explored most often, in works that established all the major categories of world disaster familiar in contemporary science fiction. Richard Jefferies produced one of the first tales of a future return to medievalism after an ecological world breakdown in his novel *After London* (1885), skillfully imitated by the American writer Van Tassel Sutphen, who changed the locale to New York City, in *The Doomsman* (1906). From the prolific Wells came *The War of the Worlds* (1898), *The War in the Air* (1908), and *The World Set Free* (1914), stories of apocalyptic future warfare. The last-man theme was exploited by M. P. Shiel in *The Purple Cloud* (1901), a novel whose world-ending catastrophe was suggested by the explosion of Krakatoa in 1883. In *The Yellow Danger* (1898), Shiel also produced a vivid scenario of a planetary race war to the death between East and West, survived only by a victorious England. Arthur Conan Doyle contributed *The Poison Belt* (1913), and James Elroy Flecker, a minor poet and playwright of the mainstream, wrote one of the bitterest of world's end tales, "The Last Generation" (1908), in which the head of a proletarian army overthrows the unjust civilization he despises and eliminates hunger and poverty by the simple device of decreeing universal sterilization.

In American fiction of the period, the idea of the world's end furnished occasions for the triumph of science and engineering, as in *The Second Deluge* by Garrett P. Serviss (1912), and *Darkness and Dawn* by George Allan England (1914). In both melodramas, civilization was destroyed by natural disasters of apocalyptic proportions and renewed by American know-how. Less hopeful, and far superior in literary power, Jack London's story "The Scarlet Plague" (1912) reduced humankind through a worldwide pestilence to four hundred Neolithic savages clinging to life in the American Far West.

Despite the recurrent use of biblical imagery in all this work—such as the updated Noah's ark in *The Second Deluge* (an ark of science, rather than faith)—nearly all the eschatological fictions of the late nineteenth and early twentieth centuries are exhibits of secularization at high tide. Except for the occasional world war or revolution, the cause of doom is Nature herself, operating according to her own inexorable laws, which man survives if at all by taking advantage of his knowledge of still other laws. But of course Nature is no longer the sublime mechanism of Newton: she is now the savage mother of Darwin and anthropology, of Malthusian economics, of Pasteur, of entropy, of a scientific revolution that in the nineteenth century stripped Nature of her benevolence, or—in the Lamarckian paradigm—endowed Nature with powers of creative evolution but left her still fierce and dangerous, with little or none of the transcendence of the God of traditional faith.

The best known of fin-de-siècle terminal visions, Wells's *The Time Machine*, typifies the view of nature as a struggle for survival in an indifferent cosmos. An equally well-known novel in its own day, and perhaps a better choice to represent the many tendencies at work in the thought of the period, is *La fin du monde* by Camille Flammarion. Translated into every major European language, *La fin du monde* conveys both the stern fatalism of nineteenth-century science and the restless search for "higher" truth characteristic of the writer's generation. Flammarion was an odd mixture—like Wallace, Doyle, Bergson, and many others—of enthusiasm for scientific method and an ardent belief in spiritualism. In his vast apocalyptic novel of the 1890s, the competing claims of science and spirit are reconciled in a framework of thought that is thoroughly secular despite its rejection of dogmatic materialism.

Flammarion divides his narrative into two parts, the first set in the twenty-fifth century, and the second millions of years in the future, at the end of earth's history. In the first part, the threatened destruction of the world by a huge comet fails to take place. Despite widespread hysteria, and a false report—clearly relished by Flammarion—that a fireball had obliterated Saint Peter's in Rome, where the college of cardinals was celebrating the new dogma of papal divinity, the comet causes far less damage than expected. Only one-fortieth of the population of Europe is lost. "Earth continued to turn in the fruitful light of the sun, and humanity continued to rise toward higher destinies."[20]

In the second part, the author sketches those higher destinies, ten million years of steady progress, with the conversion of the planet into "the garden of humanity," a world united, at peace, and thoroughly tamed. Climatic engineering eliminated disasters of every kind. All religions were abandoned, having outlived their usefulness, as mankind devoted itself to science and art. But the glimpse of possible world destruction in the first part of the novel, which had included a long digression on the history of eschatological thought and prophecy, now regains its relevance. The time finally arrives when decline must succeed progress. Earth grows steadily cooler and drier, and the population begins to shrink. From ten billion, it dwindles to a few hundred million, and then to a handful of survivors, eking out their existence in the beds of evaporated oceans at the equator. Others, meanwhile, have reverted to the ape, following a "law of decadence" no less inescapable than the "law of progress" once had been. Flammarion closes with the story of the last man and woman, Omégar and Eva, united when the man flies to her distant home in his airship, a scene purloined from the rendezvous of Omégare and Syderie in Grainville's *Le dernier homme*.

But the terminal lovers have a quite different fate from Grainville's. Flammarion uses Omégar as his mouthpiece in a dialogue with Eva. The last woman wonders if the universe has a purpose, since the inhabitants of every planet must face extinction, sooner or later. Omégar assures her that life is not in vain. All is for love, and much has been achieved by every intelligent race, through the power of the spirit. The universe is not dead but a dynamic entity, ruled by energy rather than matter. After this edifying discourse, with its vitalist propaganda so typical of the late nineteenth-century rejection of positivism in France, the lovers embark on a search for what may remain of the planet's water supplies, find none, meet the immortal spirit of Cheops in Egypt, and learn from him that civilized life now flourishes on Jupiter. They die, but their own immortal spirits are wafted by Cheops to Jupiter, where the heritage of mankind will be blended with the young Jovian culture to produce new triumphs of intellect and love. Meanwhile, earth has become a cemetery. "An eternal silence enveloped the ruins of extinct humanity. All of human history had vanished like an empty dream."[21]

In a lengthy epilogue, Flammarion provides a still further view of the future, when the sun and all its planets have become cinders, and the Jovians have gone the way of their Terran brothers and sisters. No matter, says Flammarion. There is nothing special about earth, or human civilization. Our time is an instant lost in the infinite, "an imperceptible ripple on the immense ocean of the ages."[22] What happened in the solar system, had happened before, and will happen again, world without end, forever and ever. Space is infinite, time eternal, and the universe endlessly self-renewing.

The contrast with Grainville's story and its Christian message could not be more striking, all the more since the episodes of the last man and last woman are superficially so much alike. In Grainville's tale, the world's end facilitates the entrance of the resurrected dead into eternal life, as in the Book of Revelation. In Flammarion's, every end prefaces a new beginning, but always within time, in an infinite universe vested by secular science and philosophy with inexhaustibly creative powers. Even Flammarion's belief in the survival of the spirit after death lacks a biblical resonance: the spirits aid the living in the work of civilization, which acquires a self-validating significance alien to Christian thought.

But in one respect Flammarion's novel is in perfect harmony with the despised and embattled positivism of the 1890s: with his studies at the Paris Observatory behind him, Flammarion could not resist emphasizing the vastness of the cosmos revealed by nineteenth-century astronomy, and its obedience to natural laws. Whatever leading roles love and spirit and energy played in the scheme of things, all proceeded according to the deeply embedded design of the natural order. Mankind and mankind's earth were dwarfed by its immensity. As Flammarion's fellow spiritualist, Arthur Conan Doyle, explained in his own world's-end novel *The Poison Belt*, humanity was little more than an infestation of bacilli on a bunch of grapes, which a gardener might casually wipe out with a dusting of poison. The bacilli must realize that "their continued existence is not really one of the necessities of the Universe."[23]

The loss of the Christian sense of a special place and providence for mankind in a cozy little geocentric world order had not yet led in Flammarion's generation to the extremes of alienation from external reality felt by twentieth-century minds, but signs of approaching estrangement are not difficult to detect in a work such as *La fin du monde*. Spiritualism and vitalism, for all their hopefulness, could not make the universe what it had been in the world view of traditional faith. Nor could they endow visions of the end with the terror and grandeur of Saint John. The endtime lost all its supernatural import, and took its place alongside other natural events, as part of the burden of existence, no more meaningful in an ultimate sense than any other episode in the inexorable procession of natural history.

Eschatological Fiction since 1914

In the years since that first great historical doomsday of our century, the World War of 1914–1918, the geometric increase in fictions of the world's end makes ludicrous any attempt at comprehensive treatment in an essay such as this. From France, Britain, and the United States the literature of the endtime has spread to every Western country and to Japan. Hundreds of eschatological stories, novels, and plays make their appearance every year. Much of the increase is due simply to the rapid multiplication of futuristic or "science" fiction of all sorts, especially since the 1940s. But there are other reasons, explored above. The world wars, the tyrannies and genocides, the interminable political struggles of the post-1945 era, the doomsday weapons race, and the malaises of the world economy generate anxiety that finds both expression and catharsis in eschatological fiction.

It is noteworthy that at least half of the catastrophes conjured up in twentieth-century scenarios of the endtime continue to be the work of nature. Floods, earthquakes, comets, plagues, ice ages, alien or mutant monsters, entropy, and various other natural phenomena beyond human control do their worst. Usually, a remnant of mankind survives, to begin the round of existence again, or make a still better world. From the 1920s and 1930s representative novels in this vein include J. J. Connington's *Nordenholt's Million* (1923), S. Fowler Wright's *Deluge* (1928) and *Dawn* (1929), and R. C. Sherriff's *The Hopkins Manuscript* (1939). Of more recent titles, the classic American novel of worldwide natural calamity is George R. Stewart's *Earth Abides* (1949), but British authors continue to write more than their share of such fictions, from John Wyndham's *The Day of the Triffids* (1951) through the many disaster novels of John Christopher and J. G. Ballard to the eschatological comedies of Michael Moorcock, culminating in *The End of All Songs* (1976). The late 1970s witnessed a resurgence of tales of natural disaster in America, in the form of an epidemic of well-crafted drugstore novels midway between mainstream and genre fiction that called for earth's destruction through killer bees (Arthur Herzog's *The Swarm*, 1974), collision with a comet (Larry Niven and Jerry Pournelle's *Lucifer's Hammer*, 1977), bubonic plague (Gwyneth Cravens and John S. Marr's *The Black Death*, 1977), a new ice age (Arnold Federbush's *Ice!*, 1978), and the like.

The other half of twentieth-century eschatological fictions fix the responsibility for doomsday on mankind itself, usually because of global wars fought with nuclear, or other totally destructive, weapons. Ever since H. G. Wells's prescient novel of 1914, *The World Set Free*, the atomic war has been a nightmare of Western man well-grounded in the possibilities and now the fully realized powers of modern military engineering.

Significantly, most stories of thermonuclear Armageddon are the work of American writers. Ray Bradbury's *The Martian Chronicles* (1950), Leigh Brackett's *The Long Tomorrow* (1955), Pat Frank's *Alas, Babylon* (1959), Walter M. Miller's *A Canticle for Leibowitz* (1959), Mordecai Roshwald's *Level 7* (1959), and Philip Wylie's *Triumph* (1963) rank among the best. Now and then writers of other countries have equaled them. René Barjavel in *Le diable l'emporte* (1948) and Robert Merle in *Malevil* (1972) furnish worthy French competition, and a German example is Hans Helmut Kirst's *Keiner kommt davon* (1957). Australia has contributed Nevil Shute's *On the Beach* (1957). Major British entries are Aldous Huxley's *Ape and Essence* (1948) and Brian Aldiss's *Greybeard* (1964). Sometimes, in a variant scenario that holds man and his technology no less responsible for his own ruin, the cause of the calamity is an accident, as in Kurt Vonnegut's *Cat's Cradle* (1963), or the work of a madman, as in Gore Vidal's *Kalki* (1978). Mankind is just as dead, either way.

But to return to the issue explored at the beginning of this chapter, as the secular apocalypse becomes a stock literary device—just as the bearded man with a sign announcing the approach of Judgment Day is a stock figure of cartoonists—it also becomes a vehicle for the expression of ideas, beliefs, and anxieties that are not literally eschatological. Granted that various natural or man-made endtimes are quite possible, and that eschatological fiction cannot fail but derive some of its power and credibility from authentic secular fears of a secular doomsday, such fiction may have other uses. It obviously had other uses in certain nineteenth-century works, and in the period since 1914 the proportion of such works has increased. A number of recent novels, stories, and plays can be identified whose authors exhibit little or no interest in eschatology as such. Although they set their characters in literally eschatological scenes, their chief concern is the exploration of private consciousness or the testing (and usually the discrediting) of the values of the dominant culture.

We have already examined one of these works, Anna Kavan's *Ice*. The eschatological plays of Beckett *(Endgame)* and Ionesco *(Le piéton de l'air)* fit the same description. Doris Lessing's *The Memoirs of a Survivor* (1974), Samuel R. Delany's *Dhalgren* (1975), and Pamela Zoline's story "The Heat Death of the Universe" (1967), despite eschatological trappings, are studies of "inner space." Ray Bradbury's *The Martian Chronicles* and Kurt Vonnegut's *Cat's Cradle* are more significant for their critiques of American values than as eschatological fictions.

The contemporary master of what might be called the psychocultural apocalypse is the English writer J. G. Ballard. This chapter will close with a few pages about Ballard, and about one of his novels in particular, *The Drought* (1965), which is a fair sample of his remarkable art. No other writer of the 1960s and 1970s has worked the veins of eschatological romance so profitably. No other writer of science fiction has probed so deeply into the psychic underworld of modern industrial culture.

Ballard's fiction divides up to now into two halves, his "New Wave" science fiction, most of it written between 1956 and 1966, and his contributions to the literary mainstream since that time. But the distinction seems to matter less than it usually does, and Ballard has been received with a certain strain and reluctance in both worlds. Nearly all his work is, in any case, eschatological. At first, the endtimes were literal, if somewhat fuzzy at the edges. Since entering the mainstream, Ballard has supplied endtimes that are entirely private or local, but in fictions that reveal little change of atmosphere, cast of characters, structure, or message. The message, quite clearly, is the Nietzschean one that modern man—secularized, industrialized, and commercialized—by killing his gods has obliterated his knowledge of good and evil. Such a morally eviscerated culture can fall back only on the solipsistic pursuit of pleasure, pain, and death, and will soon perish altogether. What history offers beyond the self-destruction of industrial society, Ballard does not say. He retains his credibility as a truthteller by confining himself to the bare suggestion that when the paralysis of modernity is lifted, time will resume, and history will again become possible.

The reputation of J. G. Ballard was forged in the late 1950s and early 1960s when he was hailed as the champion of a new tendency in science fiction, the so-called New Wave, which sought to dissolve the boundaries between science fiction and the mainstream. Whatever mainstream writers did, whatever techniques, subject matters, or world views they embraced, writers of science fiction would also embrace. In practice this meant an abandonment of the positivism and naturalism of what by now was "traditional" science fiction, in favor of such obsessions of contemporary mainstream literature as sadomasochism, psychoanalysis, and mysticism, and of literary devices such as surrealism and stream of consciousness. Ballard's involvement in all this prepared him well for his exploration of the depths of modern unreason. He turned to the writing of eschatological romances that stand closer to the worlds of J.-K. Huysmans, Louis Ferdinand Céline, and William Burroughs than to such science-fiction forebears as H. G. Wells or John Wyndham.

The first phase of Ballard's career, from 1956 to 1966, was overtly eschatological. In several important short stories and a cycle of four novels, he brought the world to an end many times, using the tricks of the trade perfected by Wells and Wyndham, but always without his predecessors' easy confidence in the recuperative powers of modern culture, or their solid bourgeois decency.[24] In the later phase, he has shifted his attention from the future to the present, and from catastrophes in the macrocosm to catastrophes in the microcosm, in novels such as *Crash* (1973) and *High-Rise* (1975), where disaster overtakes only selected motorists and apartment dwellers. In both phases, although some of the details of the endtime are conveyed in a prose of devastating realism, the final effect is like that of a canvass by René Magritte. The details persuade, but the situation as a whole is clearly and deliberately impossible.

In the typical Ballard short story or novel, with the exception perhaps of the eschatological events themselves, the reader comes away with a sense that nothing has happened. The characters have not really interacted, despite spasmodic efforts to do so; they have produced nothing, felt nothing, learned nothing. They live in a world where time has congealed. Ballard's skill lies in conveying this state of universal apathy and disconnectedness without resorting to obvious literary tricks. His narrative is conventionally linear. He has a hero, or antihero, who is conventionally autobiographical. Intelligible conversations take place between characters who remain doggedly faithful to their roles. But in the final reckoning, nothing happens, except the joyless pursuit of obsessions, the consumption of dwindling stocks of material goods, and an inexorable winding down of the will to live, as the world itself wastes away.

In our sample narrative, *The Drought*, third in the cycle of four eschatological novels that Ballard wrote in the 1960s, the disaster is man-made. Ballard's explanation is limited to a few casual sentences, tossed at the reader almost contemptuously. In a lethal chain reaction, industrial pollutants have combined to cover the earth's waters with a resilient skin only one molecule deep, through which evaporation is impossible. The result is an end of rainfall, the drying up of all fresh water supplies, and the conversion of the planet into a desert that will soon be unable to support life in any form. Inexplicably, even the oceans are slowly shrinking.

At one level, *The Drought* offers a conventional scenario of human response to worldwide disaster. The scenes of survivors at the beach, wringing a bleak existence from seafood and rations of desalinated ocean water, are among the most horrible in recent literature. But overshadowing even the death of the planet is the disappearance of any sort of warmth or affection or feeling of solidarity among people. The characters of *The Drought*, as in most of Ballard's work, are lone wolves, each going his own way and needing others, if at all, only to use or abuse them. A representative incident occurs early in the story. The physician-hero Ransom and several traveling companions approach the southern coast where the army is setting up desalination facilities. An impatient swarm of refugees, hot and thirsty, make fitful attempts to storm the installation. Ransom chats with a couple camping at some distance from the beach. They advise Ransom and his party to sit tight, as they themselves are doing.

> The man gazed at Ransom with his calm eyes. "Sit here and wait." He gestured around at the camp. "This won't last for ever. Already most of these people have only a day's water left. Sooner or later they'll break out. My guess is that by the time they reach the water they'll be thinned out enough for Ethel and me to have all we want."
> His wife nodded in agreement, sipping her tea.[25]

The scene is flat, quiet, commonplace. An ordinary man and wife plan their survival, which will require the massacre of thousands of countrymen, with emotionless detachment. As Ballard writes in his introduction to the French edition of *Crash*, "the most terrifying casualty of the century [is] the death of affect."[26]

Many of the other characters in the story are anything but commonplace. Nevertheless, they are united in their almost total lack of feeling for one another. The wealthy architect Lomax, with his hoard of precious capital (a reservoir of fresh water) and his "bejewelled temple" constructed from abandoned cars and radio sets; Lomax's witchlike sister Miranda, a connoisseur of pain and fear, who symbolizes for Ransom "a world of infinite possibilities unrestrained by any moral considerations"[27]; and Quilter, a deformed young lunatic, who helps Lomax burn an empty city for sensual pleasure and eventually mates with Miranda, share little more than hatred.[28] Still worse is the mechanic Whitman, who talks of releasing the wild animals from their cages in the city zoo, his single eye gleaming "in his twisted face with a wild misanthropic hope." Later a pack of savage dogs under his command attacks a group of store window mannequins, helping Whitman vent his loathing of "even the residuum of human identity in [their] blurred features."[29]

But the central figure of the novel, Charles Ransom, transcends the hatreds and manias of his mad companions. In a world without love or hope or joy, the most appropriate response is withdrawal. By degrees Ransom manages to retreat into himself, like the protagonist of an earlier story, "The Overloaded Man" (1960) or the physician Sanders in *The Crystal World* (1966) or for that matter almost any Ballard hero. As the story progresses, Ransom feels "an increasing sense of vacuum." On the march to the sea, the four people with him become "more and more shadowy, residues of themselves" no more human than "the sand and dust, the eroding slopes and concealed shadows."[30] At the end of the novel, he cuts himself off from everyone, finally and completely, walking into the desert. When the sun disappears under a cloud, "he noticed that he no longer cast any shadow on to the sand, as if he had completed his journey across the margins of the inner landscape he had carried in his mind for so many years. . . . An immense pall of darkness lay over the dunes, as if the whole of the exterior world were losing its existence."[31]

Ransom's world is not only solitary: it is also timeless. He feels powerfully drawn to Yves Tanguy's "Jours de Lenteur," a reproduction of which hangs in the cabin of the houseboat where we find him vacationing alone at the beginning of the novel. The painting is of "smooth, pebble-like objects, drained of all associations, suspended on a washed tidal floor . . . eroded . . . of all sense of time."[32] At intervals throughout the novel, Ransom momentarily enters the trancelike world of the painting. The monotony of life at the beach and still more the motionless world of the desert, its dunes of sand like frozen waves, exert a hypnotic fascination. In the last chapter of the novel, entitled "Jours de Lenteur," Ransom's journey to nowhere transports him to an "inner landscape," as if he were walking into the painting itself. Time will have a stop.

Time stops quite literally in the African forest of Ballard's next eschatological novel, *The Crystal World*. Here, men and animals and plants turn to living crystal, a state of suspended animation caused by a spreading cosmic shortage of time. Characteristically, Ballard's hero cannot resist the lure of the timeless. After a narrow escape from crystallization, he returns of his own free will, heading up river to embrace a deathless death.

H. Bruce Franklin, in a class analysis of Ballard's fiction, identifies him as a shrewd symbolist of the moral disintegration of late capitalist culture and its growing obsession with the compulsory consumption of useless products. For Franklin, Ballard's alienated protagonists are modern versions of the tycoon-heroes of early capitalism. Drawn from the ranks of the professional classes, these transmogrified tycoons lack the will or the opportunity to amuse themselves with projects of conquest. Their only recourse is retreat into the self, since their class bias precludes any identification with the people's struggles. Their fear of time is nothing less than a fear of history, which will eventually sweep capitalism away and install the despised workers in power.[33]

For the most part, Franklin's reading of Ballard is cogent. But when he takes the further step, as he does, of arguing that Ballard shares the solipsistic alienation and amoralism of his heroes, he stumbles.[34] It is always dangerous to confuse a writer's professional integrity with his values and sympathies as a man. There can be no doubt that J. G. Ballard, the son of a doctor, a former medical student himself, a one-time journalist, and now a belletrist, writes from the class perspective that he understands best. Like Huysmans or Wilde before him, he is both repelled and morbidly fascinated by the decadence he catalogues. But his calling as a writer requires him also to speak the truth. He sees decadence for what it is: decadence. The madness, compulsiveness, and destructiveness of the world of his imagination, the world of late capitalism as to some degree it really is, give him no joy, and do not earn his approval. In his introduction to *Crash*, Ballard describes his work as "an extreme metaphor for an extreme situation," a series of progress reports from a safari or laboratory of the mind. *Crash* itself, he observes, is technological pornography, and as such "the most political form of fiction, dealing with how we use and exploit each other, in the most urgent and ruthless way." But he adds: "Needless to say, the ultimate role of *Crash* is cautionary, a warning against that brutal, erotic and overlit realm that beckons more and more persuasively to us from the margins of the technological landscape."[35] These are not—it is too obvious—the words of an amoralist. What Ballard discovers in himself and in his historical situation, he reports honestly, but not to proselytize on behalf of decadence and evil. Quite the opposite.

It remains only to repeat that often, and sometimes even in Ballard's doomsdays, the eschatological novelist traffics in hope. The secularizers of the biblical vision of the world's end have by and large held fast to the ultimate optimism of that vision. From *The Drought* we have literally saved the best until last. Immediately following the passage quoted above in which Ransom's shadow had disappeared as the sky above the desert darkened, the last sentence of the novel breaks the spell cast by despair. The last sentence reads, in full: "It was some time later that he failed to notice it had started to rain."[36]

Ransom, of course, does not notice the first rain to fall on the earth in more than ten years. But Ballard does. History, and with it the possibility of liberation from a dying culture, has resumed.

Notes

1. See Frank Kermode, *The Sense of an Ending: Studies in the Theory of Fiction* (New York: Oxford Univ. Press, 1967); and also David Ketterer, *New Worlds for Old: The Apocalyptic Imagination, Science Fiction, and American Literature* (Garden City, N.Y.: Doubleday, 1974); John R. May, *Toward a New Earth: Apocalypse in the American Novel* (Notre Dame: Univ. of Notre Dame Press, 1972); and Maurice Valency, *The End of the World: An Introduction to Contemporary Drama* (New York: Oxford Univ. Press, 1980).

2. Ketterer, *New Worlds for Old*, pp. 91 and 15.

3. A convenient modern edition is *The Last Man*, ed. Hugh J. Luke, Jr. (Lincoln: Univ. of

Nebraska Press, 1965). See also Jean de Palacio, "Mary Shelley and the 'Last Man': A Minor Romantic Theme," *Revue de littérature comparée* 42 (January–March 1968): 37–49.

4. Franklin L. Baumer, "Twentieth-Century Version of the Apocalypse," *Journal of World History* 1 (January 1954): 623–640.

5. W. Warren Wagar, *Good Tidings: The Belief in Progress from Darwin to Marcuse* (Bloomington: Indiana Univ. Press, 1972), chaps. 9 and 11.

6. Samples of such work are Paul R. Ehrlich, *The Population Bomb* (San Francisco: Ballantine, 1968); Richard A. Falk, *This Endangered Planet* (New York: Random House, 1971); Dennis L. Meadows et al., *The Limits to Growth* (New York: Universe Books, 1972); Gordon Rattray Taylor, *The Doomsday Book* (New York: World, 1970); William Irwin Thompson, *Darkness and Scattered Light* (Garden City, N.Y.: Doubleday, 1978); and Roberto Vacca, *The Coming Dark Age* (Garden City, N.Y.: Doubleday, 1973).

7. Alfred Bester, "Adam and No Eve," in Bester, *Starburst* (New York: Signet, 1958), p. 37.

8. John Christopher, *The Ragged Edge* (title in United Kingdom, *A Wrinkle in the Skin*; New York: Simon & Schuster, 1965).

9. "In every moment slumbers the possibility of being the eschatological moment. You must awaken it." Rudolf Bultmann, *History and Eschatology* (Edinburgh: The University Press, 1957), p. 155.

10. See Isaac Asimov, *A Choice of Catastrophes* (New York: Simon & Schuster, 1979) and Fred Warshofsky, *Doomsday: The Science of Catastrophe* (New York: Reader's Digest Press, 1977).

11. Anna Kavan, *Ice* (Garden City, N.Y.: Doubleday, 1970), pp. 136, 175.

12. See W. Warren Wagar, "H. G. Wells and the Radicalism of Despair," *Studies in the Literary Imagination* 6 (Fall 1973): 1–10.

13. The second French edition of 1811 has been reprinted. See J.-B. Cousin de Grainville, *Le dernier homme: Ouvrage posthume* (Geneva: Slatkine, 1976). There is also an English translation, *The Last Man: Or Omegarus and Syderia, A Romance in Futurity* (New York: Arno, 1978).

14. Henry F. Majewski, "Grainville's Le dernier homme," *Symposium* 17 (Summer 1963): 121–122.

15. Mario Praz, *The Romantic Agony* (London: Oxford Univ. Press, 1951).

16. Cited in A. J. Sambrook, "A Romantic Theme: The Last Man," *Forum for Modern Lanaguage Studies* 2 (January 1966): 31.

17. Hugh J. Luke Jr., in Mary Shelley, *The Last Man*, p. vii. Cf. p. xvii.

18. Shelley, *The Last Man*, p. 97.

19. Sambrook, "A Romantic Theme," p. 31.

20. Camille Flammarion, *La fin du monde* (Paris: E. Flammarion, 1917), p. 246.

21. Ibid., pp. 393–394.

22. Ibid., p. 402.

23. Arthur Conan Doyle, *The Poison Belt*, in Doyle, *The Professor Challenger Stories* (London: Murray, 1952), p. 240.

24. See J. G. Ballard, "The Overloaded Man" (1960), "Deep End" (1961), "The Garden of Time" (1962), "The Terminal Beach" (1964), "The Impossible Man" (1966), and other short stories, available in various collections; and his novels, *The Wind from Nowhere* (1962), *The Drowned World* (1962), *The Drought* (1965), and *The Crystal World* (1966).

25. *The Drought* (Harmondsworth, Middlesex: Penguin, 1968), p. 94.

26. Ballard, "Introduction to the French Edition of *Crash*," *Foundation: Review of Science Fiction* 9 (November 1975): 45.

27. *The Drought*, p. 49.

28. At several points, Ballard explicity identifies the three characters as latter-day versions of Prospero, Miranda, and Caliban, respectively, making *The Drought* perform extra service as a grim caricature of *The Tempest*. A later novel, *Concrete Island* (1974), hideously parodies *Robinson Crusoe*.

29. *The Drought*, pp. 47, 160.

30. Ibid., p. 87.

31. Ibid., p. 176.

32. Ibid., pp. 13, 113.

33. See H. Bruce Franklin, "What Are We to Make of J. G. Ballard's Apocalypse?" in Thomas D. Clareson, ed., *Voices for the Future: Essays on Major Science Fiction Writers*, vol. 2 (Bowling Green, Ohio: Bowling Green Univ. Popular Press, 1979), pp. 82–105.

34. Ibid., pp. 103–105.

35. "Introduction to the French Edition of *Crash*," p. 49.

36. *The Drought*, p. 176.

A Note on the Contributors

All the contributors to this volume except Mr. Pelikan took their Ph.D.'s at Yale University under the supervision of Franklin L. Baumer. In the sketches that follow, the year in parentheses after each name shows when the contributor earned his or her degree at Yale.

Joyce A. Berkman (1967). Ms. Berkman is Associate Professor of History at the University of Massachusetts, where she teaches modern English and women's history. The author of a monograph, *Olive Schreiner: Feminism on the Frontier* (Eden Press, 1979), she is also at work on a comprehensive critical study of Schreiner.

James Connors (1967). Mr. Connors has been a member of the Department of History at the University of Hawaii since 1965, and for several years directed its World Civilizations Program. He has published articles on George Orwell in *Modern Fiction Studies*.

John Frederick Logan (1971). A practicing New York attorney, Mr. Logan is the author of several articles on French and English intellectual history, including studies of the Abbé de Condillac and of Gilbert Burnet.

Michael W. Messmer (1972). Mr. Messmer teaches history at Virginia Commonwealth University. In 1977–1978, he was a Fellow of the National Humanities Institute at the University of Chicago. He is currently editing the volume *Interdisciplinary Studies* for the Garland Press Bibliographies in Criticism series.

John T. Miller, Jr. (1977). A staff member of the Defense Industrial Security Institute, Mr. Miller wrote his dissertation on the political and social thought of S. T. Coleridge.

David Pace (1973). Associate Professor of History and West European Studies at Indiana University, Mr. Pace has written extensively on Claude Lévi-Strauss and is now exploring the history of psychiatric theory, as well as the links of decadent literature to naturalism and positivism.

265

Jaroslav Pelikan.   Mr. Pelikan is Sterling Professor of History at Yale University. He took his Ph.D. at the University of Chicago, and has taught at Yale since 1962. His books include *Development of Christian Doctrine* (Yale University Press, 1969) and *The Christian Tradition* (3 vols., University of Chicago Press, 1971–1978). Mr. Pelikan holds honorary degrees from several universities, among them Yale and the Universities of Hamburg and Notre Dame.

David Spadafora (1981).   Mr. Spadafora taught at the University of Connecticut at Hartford while completing his dissertation on the idea of progress in eighteenth-century Britain. He is currently a collegiate dean and lecturer in history at Yale University.

Phyllis H. Stock (1965).   Professor of History at Seton Hall University, Ms. Stock is the author of *Better than Rubies: A History of Women's Education* (Putnam's, 1978), and has also completed a book on the development of a secular morality for education in nineteenth-century France.

Frank M. Turner (1971).   Mr. Turner is Associate Professor of History at Yale University, where he has taught since earning his doctorate. In 1974 Yale University Press published his first book, *Between Science and Religion: The Reaction to Scientific Naturalism in Late Victorian England*. He is the coauthor, with Donald Kagan and Steven Ozment, of *Western Civilization* (Macmillan, 1979), and most recently he has published *The Greek Heritage in Victorian Britain* (Yale University Press, 1981).

Jeffrey von Arx (1980).   Fr. von Arx is a member of the Society of Jesus. His dissertation studies historians of late nineteenth-century Britain and the relation between their scholarship and their religious and political opinions.

W. Warren Wagar (1959).   Mr. Wagar is Professor of History at the State University of New York at Binghamton. Among his books are *H. G. Wells and the World State* (Yale University Press, 1961), *Good Tidings: The Belief in Progress from Darwin to Marcuse* (Indiana University Press, 1972), and *World Views* (Dryden Press, 1977). His latest book, *Terminal Visions: The Literature of Last Things*, will be published by Indiana University Press.

Richard S. Westfall (1955).   Distinguished Professor of History and Philosophy of Science at Indiana University, Mr. Westfall has written several books, including *Science and Religion in Seventeenth Century England* (Yale University Press, 1958) and *Never at Rest: A Biography of Isaac Newton* (Cambridge University Press, 1981). He is the author of numerous articles on the thought of Newton and its place in the history of science.

Douglas K. Wood (1967).   Mr. Wood is currently working on an intellectual biography of F. M. Cornford. He has often written on the theme of hostility toward time in modern European thought. His most recent article, "Even Such Is Time," examines varieties of twentieth-century antitemporalism. The Regents Press of Kansas will publish his book *Men against Time* in 1982.

Books by Franklin L. Baumer

The Early Tudor Theory of Kingship: New Haven, Yale University Press, 1940.

Main Currents of Western Thought: Readings in Western European Intellectual History from the Middle Ages to the Present (ed.): First Edition, New York, Knopf, 1952; Fourth Edition, New Haven, Yale University Press, 1978.

Religion and the Rise of Scepticism: New York, Harcourt, Brace, 1960.

Intellectual Movements in Modern European History (ed.): New York, Macmillan, 1966.

Modern European Thought: Continuity and Change in Ideas, 1600–1950: New York, Macmillan, 1977.

Index

DATE DUE

DEMCO 38-297